SUMMER JOBS

BRITAIN

99

Incorporating

VACATION TRAINEESHIPS

EDITOR DAVID WOODWORTH

ASSISTED BY FIONA BENNETT

Distributed in the U.S.A. by Peterson's,
202 Carnegie Center, Princeton, N.J. 08543
Web site http://www.petersons.com

Published annually by
Vacation Work, 9 Park End Street, Oxford.
Web site http://www.vacationwork.co.uk

Thirtieth edition
THE DIRECTORY OF SUMMER JOBS IN BRITAIN
Copyright (c) Vacation Work 1999

ISBN 1-85458-204-6 (hardback)
ISBN 1-85458-203-8 (softback)
ISSN 0143 3490

Statement for the purposes of
The Employment Agencies Act 1973:
The price of *The Directory of Summer Jobs in Britain*
is £14.95 (hardback) or £8.99 (softback) and is for the book and
the information contained therein; it is not refundable.

Cover design by Miller Craig & Cocking
Design Partnership

Printed by Unwin Brothers Ltd., Old Woking, Surrey, England

Preface

It is gratifying that this, the thirtieth edition of **The Directory of Summer Jobs in Britain** contains its greatest ever number of employers offering an unprecented range of jobs. Whether you are looking for a job to occupy mind or body and whether you want to earn good wages or to help others, we hope that you will find what you are looking for in these pages.

The summer has always been a period when employers in Britain look for large numbers of additional staff. Even when the recent recession was at its worst people still, for example, ate fruit and vegetables and went on holiday, so agriculture and tourism continued to provide a reliable source of short-term work. **Summer Jobs in Britain** is designed to help you in your search for a job, whether you wish to work near home or further afield. And while many of the jobs are in the fields of tourism and agriculture, this book lists a wealth of other opportunities, ranging from putting up marquees to joining an archaeological excavation.

In the Directory we have collected details of job vacancies supplied to us by employers in England, Scotland, Wales and Northern Ireland. The jobs have been arranged in regional chapters under the following headings: Business & Industry, Children, Holiday Centres & Amusements, Hotels & Catering, Medical, Outdoor, Sport and Language Schools. The book also incorporates sections on Vacation Traineeships, which provide on-the-job work experience for students in business and industry.

Many employers in the book express a willingness to take on overseas applicants. While nationals of EU and EEA countries, young nationals of Commonwealth countries and American students can seek work in the UK without too much difficulty, it can be hard for most other foreign citizens. Nevertheless, there are a number of special schemes recognised by the Home Office which give non-EU nationals the opportunity to work for a limited period in this country. Detailed information is given about all such programmes in the introduction.

The companies and individuals listed in **Summer Jobs in Britain** are for job-seekers to apply to directly; the publishers cannot undertake to contact individual employers or to offer assistance in arranging specific jobs.

The Directory is an annual publication and is VALID FOR 1999 ONLY. A thoroughly revised edition will be published late in 1999.

David Woodworth

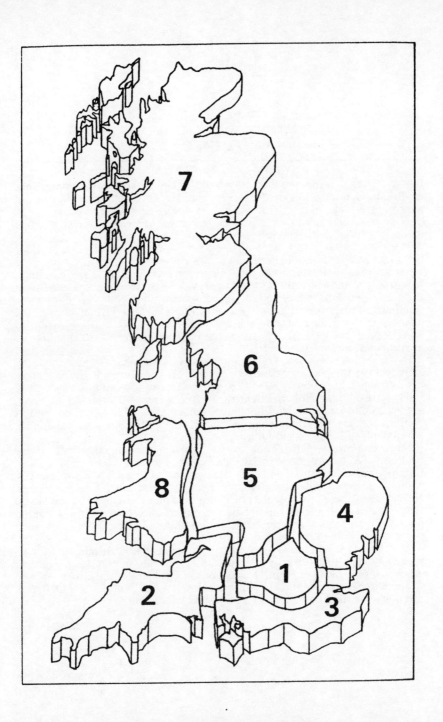

Contents

The Directory

Working this Summer

At the time of going to press, 5% of the workforce in Britain were unemployed, the lowest level of unemployment for eighteen years. Indeed, in some areas of Britain unemployment has fallen to such low levels that firms are having to seek workers from abroad. The problem is worst in parts of the the South East, where some employers are finding it almost impossible to recruit staff with the skills they need. But it is important to remember that figures for numbers of long-term unemployed people are not necessarily relevant to people looking only for temporary work; even when unemployment rates were at their peak several years ago the brief length of employment (and sometimes the low level of wages) offered by most summer jobs was not enough to attract people looking for permanent work near their home.

Now that student grants in Britain have again been cut drastically and the government is introducing university fees, increasing numbers of students are chasing what work is available. *The Independent* newspaper recently predicted that four out of five students now work in the summer holidays, and *The Daily Telegraph* newspaper estimates that two out of three students now leave university with a bank overdraft of £1,050 and with £3,000 in arranged loans to pay back. Furthermore, with the unemployment rate among recent graduates half as high again as the national rate many graduates are being forced to take menial jobs. Fortunately, as this book proves, there are jobs to be found.

The National Minimum Wage

Over the past 20 years there has been increased growth in inequality in earnings, as the gap between top earners and poorly paid employees continues to widen. For many workers, this inequality has led to in-work poverty, and an increased dependance on benefits. The Low Pay Commission has discovered that low pay is particularly prevalent among women and young people, especially among part-time workers, those working in small firms and in the hospitality/service industries, such as retail and catering. The implications, then, for those young people consulting this book to find seasonal work in these industries are far-reaching. It is estimated that 9% of all employees on average in the UK will benefit from the introduction of a National Minimum Wage, and it is expected that 20% of employees in the 18-20 year old age group will benefit.

The first report of the Low Pay Commission, which was published in June 1998, strongly recommends the introduction of a National Minimum Wage. The figure it proposes is £3.70 per hour to come into effect by June 2000. However, to make the change easier to bring about, it is expected that an initial Minimum Wage of £3.60 per will be introduced in April 1999. This rate will only apply to those over 20. The Commission recommends that a Minimum Development Rate should be introduced for 18-20 year olds at

£3.20 per hour in April 1999, rising to £3.30 per hour by June 2000. All those employees under 17 or on apprenticeships should be exempt from the National Minimum Wage.

It is thought that the National Minimum Wage will apply to the gross amount of an employee's earnings, i.e. will be calculated before tax, National Insurance, and other deductions. After tax and deductions, therefore, employees may find that they end up with less than the Minimum Wage. Incentive payments may also be included in the earnings that count towards the National Minimum Wage.

All agricultural pieceworkers must be paid no less than the National Minimum Wage on average for the period worked. The Wage should apply to the hours when the worker is required to be available and ready at the place of work, regardless of whether work is actually available. This is a definite improvement in conditions in an industry of unpredictable working hours, when rain and scarcity of crops have often meant poor wages.

Overtime pay, allowances and supplements may be excluded from the Minimum Wage. Employers that claim to provide free board and lodging should theoretically still be paying the National Minimum Wage or above. However, there may be a maximum of £20 per week deducted for accommodation. No employee living in accommodation provided by an employer should be earning less than £20 off the Minimum Wage per week if the bill comes into effect as anticipated.

Any service charge or centrally organised tips paid through a company's books looks likely to be included in the Minimum Wage, yet individually administered tips will not be. This is bad news for those in the catering industry, particularly waiting staff, who rely on tips to supplement wages. Many restaurants now offer customers who pay by credit card a pre-printed slip on which the customer writes the tip they wish to pay and signs for the total cost including tip to be charged to their card. This way of electronically tipping means that such tips are paid through a company's books, and will be included in the Minimum Wage, to the detriment of employees.

Although the introduction of the Minimum Wage seems superficially a good idea, no-one can quite predict the economic implications of it accurately. As a precautionary measure, the House of Lords have voted to reserve the right to exclude any region of the country, any age group or type of job from the Minimum Wage once the scheme has been tried and tested.

Business and Industry

Temping. Work as a 'temp' involves covering for staff away on holiday, on sick leave etc., and is usually arranged through an agency. These positions are primarily for those with secretarial skills, though some clerical jobs require no qualifications. Since the job prospects are better for those with word processing skills, you may consider doing an evening course before the summer starts.

One of the advantages of temping work is that it is available at any time of year and can be found at short notice. The availability of this sort of work has increased by 25% since 1992 and is likely to improve further, as temporary work is steadily becoming more widespread as employers realise the importance of a flexible workforce; taking on a temp to meet an increase in demand saves those nervous about the arrival of another recession from having to commit themselves to taking on permanent staff. A private employment agency recently estimated that temporary staff now make up nearly 8% of the workforce.

Another bonus is that it can be extremely lucrative, particularly if you have relevant qualifications. Good word-processing skills can earn around £8 an hour, with more for higher-level computer work. Unskilled clerical work may bring in about £5 an hour.

However, the advantages of temping work are not purely financial. It can also provide a valuable insight into different sectors of industry and the opportunity to develop computer and interpersonal skills, which according to graduate recruiters too many students lack.

In addition to the agencies listed in this book, most towns have a number of agencies specialising in temp work; to find them look under *Employment Agencies* in the Yellow Pages.

Shop Work. There is an extra demand for extra staff in the summer both to cover for regular staff who are away on holiday and to serve customers in tourist areas. The trend for late-night and Sunday shopping has created many extra jobs around the year. Most supermarkets now open until at least 8pm most nights of the week (and some do not close at all on weekday nights) and regularly require check-out staff and shelf fillers, especially those willing to work antisocial hours. The demand is primarily for part-time workers. But if a full-time vacancy comes up, anyone already working for the company has a good chance of being chosen as a replacement. Large homecare and DIY stores, such as Texas and Do It All, are another good source of this type of work.

For full-time jobs preference may be given to those showing an interest in staying permanently. This applies in particular to the more prestigious employers such as Marks and Spencer. Other department stores, including Littlewoods and C & A, tend to be less fussy.

Sales. Employment as a sales person conjures up outdated images of traipsing from house to house trying to sell dusters or encyclopedias. While this type of work still exists, telesales (which involves selling a product over the telephone) is a more popular method nowadays. At present, call centres employ more than 1% of the workforce, especially in Scotland and the North of England. *The Times* newspaper predicts that by the next century one out of every fifty employed people will be performing this type of work. Call centre staff tend to be young, according to a member of BIFU, the bank and insurance union. Apparently there is a burn-out problem, as staff may be continuously monitored to assess their performance. Pay is often fairly good. Salaries last year, according to Incomes Data Services, ranged between £9,500 to £11,500, with multi-lingual workers earning more.   A good telephone manner may be all you need to get a sales job with a holiday tour operator, though the ability to speak a European language will give you the edge over monolinguists; work with holiday companies needs to be arranged early, in the spring. Some companies may offer pay solely on a commission basis; make sure the terms of employment are clearly stated before signing a contract.

Cleaning. Office and industrial cleaning is another area that offers temporary vacancies. Most cleaning companies prefer to employ staff for long periods, but they will occasionally take people on temporarily for jobs such as cleaning newly-built or refurbished office blocks, or for the annual deep-clean of those factories which still shut down for a couple of weeks each summer.

Factory Work. Spending the summer on a production line may not be your idea of fun, but the potential for work in this field is good. The factories most likely to require extra staff are those that are preparing for the Christmas rush (they usually start increasing production in August) or those which specialise in the packaging and processing of seasonal food. Huge quantities of fruit and vegetables, harvested between late spring and early autumn, must be preserved by canning or freezing. Factories in this business have an urgent need for line workers, packers and delivery drivers.

Be prepared for early mornings, shift work and high levels of boredom. While pay for production line work is not outstanding, nor is it the worst in the country.

Removals and Marquee Work. While manual jobs with removal firms are available at any time of year, the summer is a real boom time for marquee erectors. During the sunny season there is a never-ending round of agricultural shows, wedding receptions and so on. And while a village dog show may require just one marquee, a music festival will require a whole range of tents plus large amounts of furniture and other equipment. All this has to be loaded and unloaded from lorries, as well as driven to and from a depot; for this and other driving work possession of an HGV driving licence will make you of more interest to employers. Overtime is often available, so marquee work can be lucrative. The disadvantage for women is that most employers take on only men for loading work.

Children

In response to the desperation of parents trying to occupy their children during the long summer holiday, over the last decade there has been a boom in the American style of holiday centres and playschemes designed to amuse the younger generation. Anyone looking for work in such a centre will frequently not usually require qualifications unless their job involves some hazardous sport or activity — most employers are looking for people with energy, enthusiasm and an outgoing personality. But anyone looking for work with children can expect to be carefully vetted, as the safety of the children is paramount. With parents increasingly worrying about political correctness amd safety, some centres are no longer offering more dangerous activities such as rifle-shooting.

Preference is likely to be given to those with experience of working with children. Trainee primary school teachers are particularly well suited.

Jobs on holiday camps can vary from teaching sports to organising discos. Since much of the work is similar to that in camps geared towards children and/or adults, more details are given below under *Holiday Centres* below.

Playschemes. Most local authorities organise playschemes for children during the summer holidays. Throughout the country dozens of playleaders and assistants are needed to run activities for children of all ages. Cash limits mean that some councils ask specifically for volunteers.

Domestic Work. Anyone preferring closer contact with children should consider working in a family as a mother's help or (for applicants from overseas) as an Au Pair. This work usually requires some experience and involves light housework and looking after children.

There are many agencies in the UK which specialise in placing home helps. Details of these and other au pair opportunities are listed in the *Au Pair, Home Help and Paying Guest* chapter towards the end of the book. If you prefer to find work independently, job advertisements appear in *The Lady* magazine and occasionally in *Horse and Hound*, both available from newsagents.

Tourism

Although most British families would now prefer a package holiday abroad to a fortnight at Blackpool, the British tourist industry remains huge. In 1997 tourists spent a record £11.7 billion, and spending was up by 9% on 1996, according to the English Tourist Board. The industry provides jobs for about 1.5 million people. Although many British people may go elsewhere for their main holiday they are taking more additional short breaks in the UK than ever, with the West Country officially the most popular area. In addition the recent hot British summers have encouraged more and more people to stay at home as there has been no need to go follow the sun abroad, although the the disappointing beginning to the summer of 1998 did drive many overseas. In turn, searing temperatures in excess of 40 degrees centigrade in some countries abroad in 1998 drove many home again to cool off in Britain.

Television and films provide a major force in marketing, as more and more tourists want to follow in the footsteps of their favourite stars and literary characters. For example, Glen Nevis in Scotland attracted 1.5 million visitors last year eager to experience the atmosphere of the film *Braveheart* which was filmed there. Testament to the lasting power of a kiss, Carnforth Railway Station in Lancashire, the setting for the embrace in *Brief Encounter* still draws more than 100,000 visitors a year.

Holiday Centres. One of the greatest recent trends in tourism in the UK has been the growth in the number of holiday camps, activity centres and theme parks. These centres are some of the largest seasonal employers in the country. Not only do they take on thousands of staff between them — the largest ones can employ hundreds of people each — but they also offer a wide range of jobs for both skilled and unskilled workers. Many chains of holiday centres are currently refurbishing and updating their images, such as Butlins whose revamped *Family Entertainment Resorts* at Bognor Regis, Minehead, and Skegness are due to reopen in Easter 1999. There may be vacancies for receptionists, lifeguards, bar and restaurant staff, car park attendants, shop assistants, cleaners, ride attendants, activities organisers, nurses, babysitters and so on. The work is often hard, with a high degree of participation in activities expected, but can also be very enjoyable.

Some holiday centre jobs do not require qualifications, though experience is an asset, and it depends which post you are applying for. As a result, this type of work is popular and competition for jobs is intense. It is essential to apply as soon as possible because many of the big employers start recruitment early in the year. Although extra people are hired later in the season, to cover bank holidays and particularly busy weeks, these are frequently selected from a reserve list compiled from the surplus of earlier applications.

If you fail to find a job with one of the centres listed in the book, try a speculative, personal approach. Your local tourist office will usually have a list of holiday parks in your area, and the British Tourist Authority (tel 0181-846 9000) can provide information about the major theme and leisure parks throughout the UK. The book *AA Days out in Britain and Ireland* (AA Publishing, £6.99) provides a comprehensive directory of attractions.

Sports. Sports holiday centres often specialise in sea, river or mountain activities and as such are often found in remote and beautiful places such as Scotland and the Lake District. They almost always need to recruit live-in workers. While there are opportunities for unskilled staff, most vacancies are for sports instructors, teachers and camp managers. Applicants will normally require governing-body qualifications and a reasonable amount of experience; growing concern about insufficent supervision and instruction at activity centres in the past has resulted in tougher new controls.

Sources of information for anyone choosing to approach an outdoor activity centre independently, on the off-chance of finding a vacancy, include the *RAC Activity Holiday Guide* and *Walking in Britain,* a BTA publication listing companies that offer guided walking holidays. Magazines specialising in sport activities, such as *Outdoor,* are another potential source of addresses.

Anyone with life-saving qualifications could consider working as a lifeguard at a leisure centre. Several local authorities advertise such vacancies in this book.

Riding: Riding schools and trekking centres (which are particularly common in Wales) take on experienced riders. Since a lot of the work is dealing with groups, the ability to get on well with people is also important.

There might be a riding school or holiday centre in your area where you could ask about the possibility of a temporary job. The British Horse Society (tel 01926-707700; fax 01926-707800; e-mail enquiry@bhs.org.uk; web site www.bhs.org.uk) publishes a register of approved riding centres called *Where to Ride,* price £6.50 including postage and packing. This is available by mail order from the BHS Bookshop, Building 65, BEC, Stoneleigh Park, Kenilworth, Warwickshire CV8 2RE (tel 01203-690676). The Association of British Riding Schools produces a directory of its 500 members, which is available for £5 including postage and packing from Queen's Chambers, Office No. 2, 38-40 Queen Street, Penzance, Cornwall TR18 4BH (tel 01736-369440; fax 01736-351390). You should also contact them for information about trekking holdays and centres. The British Tourist Association publishes its own booklet called *Riding Holidays.*

Also check the adverts in *Horse & Hound* magazine: stable staff and riders are sometimes needed to work on stud farms and in racing establishments.

Youth Hostels. Seasonal Assistant Wardens are employed to help in the running of the YHA's 240 Youth Hostels in England and Wales. Work is available, for varying periods, between February and October each year. For further information about working in a Youth Hostel see the entry in the nationwide chapter.

Hotels and Catering

Many of the temporary hotel and restaurant jobs during the summer are to be found in the country's main tourist resorts and beauty spots. If you are based in or near a big city, the best sources of work may well be be the big hotel chains, such as Forte or Hilton UK. Their hotels employ large numbers of staff, have a comparatively fast turnover and can have vacancies at any time of year. The disadvantage is that they are unlikely to provide accommodation and are more likely to want trained staff for particular duties.

Working in a big, impersonal hotel in the city is likely to be more regimented and therefore less fun than spending the summer in a family-run guest house in the South-West (unless you find yourself working for Basil Fawlty). If you choose a hotel in a remote area, such as the Scottish Highlands or the Welsh Mountains, you will also find it easier to save money. Many hotels begin advertising for summer staff before Easter, and in general applicants who can work for the entire summer season are preferred.

Hotel work can be hard and tiring, and you are usually expected to work shifts, sometimes at unsociable hours. Hotel and restaurant kitchens are particularly hot and frantic, with chefs notorious for their short tempers. On good days, however, hotel work is lively and can be exciting.

Always ask for precise details about your duties. Many of the job titles do not provide a clear definition of the work: a 'kitchen porter', for example, may spend most of his or her time washing up and being a general dogsbody. Small hotels tend to employ general assistants for a range of duties that can go from cleaning toilets to working in reception.

Fast food restaurants generally have a high turnover of staff at any time of year; the main chains, including McDonalds and PizzaLand, employ large numbers of people throughout the country. Motorway service stations and roadside restaurants, such as Little Chef, also take on extra workers in summer.

Unless you want to be a chef, you will seldom require qualifications to work in a hotel or restaurant; and while experience is often preferred, it is by no means always essential. A neat appearance and a resilient nature may be all you need, although increasingly a knowledge of more than one language can be an advantage.

The future looks bright for anyone seeking work in this sector, which was predictably very badly hit during the recession. Over recent years the tourist industry has recorded real growth and the English Tourist Board is lobbying for measures to promote this and to boost Britain's attractiveness as a tourist destination abroad.

Wages. While the majority of hotels do not indulge in exploitative practices nor do they pay through the nose for their staff; but some hotels will allow staff to use their sporting and leisure facilities.

Anyone with silver service or other specialist experience can expect to earn more than the average wage for this type of work, as can restaurant staff in London. Tips can be a bonus to those serving the public directly, but remember that centrally organised tips may be included in the National Minimum Wage.

Agriculture

While increased mechanisation has reduced the number of pickers required at harvest time, agriculture remains the second largest source of seasonal work after tourism. Soft fruit are still picked by hand; and since some other crops don't necessarily ripen at the same time machines can't always be used for them. Furthermore, fruit that goes to supermarkets must fit increasingly precise criteria in terms of size and shape, and extra staff are required to help in the selection process.

The increasing number of pick-your-own farms has dealt another blow to fruit and vegetable picking in some areas. But since food processing factories can't pick their own, pickers and packers will always be required. The summer of 1998 had a record 24 days of rain, which farmers claim put people off working as fruit pickers. Thousands of tonnes of mid-season strawberries were left to rot in fields. The bad weather also put people off buying strawberries, and not even Wimbledon could stimulate the demand. The rain also brought out armies of slugs and snails which devoured crops. Some farmers are preparing to cut back on production for next year.

The best areas for looking for fruit and vegetable picking work in the summer are: from the Vale of Evesham over to the River Wye (in the

Midlands); Kent; Lincolnshire; East Anglia (particularly the Fens); and north of the Tay in Scotland (especially Perthshire). Harvest times differ from region, so raspberries may ripen two weeks later in Scotland than in the South. Among the first fruits to ripen in southern Britain are strawberries and gooseberries, usually in June. Processing and packing work tends to be available in the vale of Evesham after the main harvest season. Work involving harvesting outdoor salad crops is also available in the Hampshire and West Sussex area.

Kent and Herefordshire are the centres of hop picking in the UK, with the harvest taking place in September. There is now a high degree of mechanisation employed, but people are still required to drive tractors, strip hop flowers from vines, etc. Women can get landed with the indoor jobs, so if this doesn't appeal ask about the availability of outdoor work.

The apple harvest, which runs from August until mid-October, is traditionally one of the longer-lasting and most lucrative crops to pick. The industry is currently however in a state of flux; due to an increasing number of cheap imports from hotter climates, the apple orchards of southern Britain are fast disappearing. Recently a number of apple farmers accepted offers of Common Market grants to destroy or 'grub up' their crop, while others are choosing to retire before the going gets too tough, a decision hastened for many by the disastrous 1997 harvest caused by a late frost.

The generous allowances for importing cheap wine from across the Channel and the easy accessibility of the French hypermarkets have similarly destabilised the young British wine industry. Despite falling farm-gate sales, some vineyards, found mainly along the South Coast, may still require local workers. Harvest times are difficult to predict as the sugar content of the grapes lies at the mercy of the sun. Out of the 400 vineyards in the UK, about 60 are commercial, and the rest are hobbies. For more information, contact the UK Vineyard Association (tel 01728-638080).

While fruit-picking work tends to be short term, it is possible to string several jobs together by following the ripening crops around the country. It is a line of work in which on-the-spot applications are often productive (but note that most farmers like the first approach to be made by phone). Harvests are unpredictable and may turn out better or later than anticipated: the number of pickers a farmer has hired in advance may prove to be inadequate, or some workers may be unable to wait around for apples to ripen if they have other commitments.

Picking fruit can be exhausting and back-breaking (try to learn the best techniques from more experienced pickers), and you can't always look forward to a comfortable bed to sleep in as the accommodation offered by farmers is often basic. While some provide comfortable bunkhouses and meals, others require you to take your own tent and to prepare your own meals. Some will provide cooking facilities and others will not. Where they are provided they can sometimes be in a poor state of cleanliness as they may be used by large numbers of people and yet it is no-one's reponsibility to keep them clean. The Food and Farming Information Service advises that workers take out insurance to cover their own personal belongings, and that where possible it is best to visit the farms in advance.

Farmers can recruit students from any part of the EEA. In addition, some farms take part in the Seasonal Agricultural Workers scheme which enables them to recruit student pickers from outside the EEA. This is done through two organisations, Concordia (YSV) Ltd (Heversham House, 2nd Floor, 20/22

Bound Road Hove, East Sussex BN3 4ET tel/fax 01273-422293) and HOPS(GB) (YFC Centre, NAC, Stoneleigh Park, Kenilworth, Warwickshire CV8 2LG tel 01203-696589; fax 01203-696559). The latter has an entry in the *Nationwide* chapter. Concordia also arranges voluntary work placements on farms for foreign students not in their graduation year. There is a registration fee of £70. For more details of such placements ring 01273-422218. Both organisations accept only overseas applicants, HOPS(GB) concentrating on students from Central and Eastern Europe, and all participants must pay a registration fee. In return HOPS(GB) and Concordia exercise control over participating farms and expect certain standards. The farms take from one up to as many as two hundred workers at one time, of many different nationalities, often largely from southern and eastern Europe. Further information about the Seasonal Agricultural Workers scheme is given under *Work Permits and Special Schemes.*

In addition to harvesting work, there are also opportunities for other types of farm work, as a general assistant on a family farm or as a groom, for example. Both these and picking jobs are listed in the *Outdoor* sections of the regional chapters in the book. Some organic farms take on volunteers: for details of one scheme see the entry for WWOOF in the *Voluntary Work* chapter.

Wages. Pay varies according to the fruit and the difficulty involved in the picking process. Many farmers pay piece work rates, which means that you are paid according to the quantity you pick. This method can be very satisfactory. The minimum wage for 8 hours casual work was almost £26 in 1998 but hard workers could earn more than this on a good day in peak season. But when fruit is scarce earning more than the minimum can be much more difficult. However, even if you are paid on a piece work basis the amount you earn for each hour worked must average the rates set out in the Aricultural Wages Order. Before starting work, you should obtain a copy of the current order from the Agricultural Wages Board. If you have any queries about the rate you are being paid the Agricultural Wages Board Regional Office staff should be able to advise you. Be prepared to cope with frustration when three days of rain means no picking and therefore no wages.

The Agricultural Wages Board (Nobel House, 17 Smith Square, London SW1P 3JR) sets minimum weekly and hourly rates for agricultural workers in England and Wales. For casual workers aged 19 and over the minimum rate in June 1998 was £3.21 an hour (50% more for overtime). The rate decreased steadily for younger workers, down to £1.61 an hour for those aged 15 and under. Many farmers calculate wages by a combination of piece work and hourly rates of pay. Remember that the farmer is legally obliged to pay you **at least** the minimum casual rate for your age. Ask exactly how much you will be paid before accepting a job: some people have been paid as little as 12p for picking a pound of strawberries. From April 1999 it is expected that the National Minimum Wage will come into effect. This will guarantee all adult workers (20 and over) at least £3.60 an hour.

Gangmasters. Gangmasters cen be involved in the recruitment of seasonal summer staff on farms. Whole most gangmasters treat their workers fairly, a significant minority could exploit their workers in some way. This exploitation can take different forms and might involve underpayment of wages, unsafe working conditions, use of illegal workers, and illegal deductions from pay for transport and accomodation. If you have any concerns or are unaware of your rights, you should ask for a copy of the leaflet *Pruning, Picking or Packing*

Agricultural Produce? Your Rights Explained from MAFF Publications (tel 0645-556000) or ring their Helpline on 0645-335577.

Useful Addresses. Many farmers have entries in this book, but you may find a farm near you which is too small to need to advertise nationally. Economic pressures have forced farmers to diversify, and an increasing number of farms are being opened to the public, sometimes generating a need for extra help. *The Harvest Times*, which lists almost 600 farms and farm shops, can be obtained by sending two first class stamps to PO Box 575, Southampton, SO15 7ZB.

Temporary jobs are sometimes advertised in *Farmers Weekly*, though prospective employers are likely to require some experience. Citybound job-hunters must be prepared to work as a volunteer since city farms are usually registered charities existing primarily for educational purposes. However, it must be noted that not all City Farms are able to take on workers. For a list of UK city farms send an A4 stamped addressed envelope to the National Federation of City Farms at The Greenhouse, Hereford Street, Bedminster BS3 4NA (tel 0117-923 1800).

Organic farms often rely on voluntary assistance too. Send a s.a.e. to WWOOF (Willing Workers on Organic Farms), PO Box 2675, Lewes, Sussex BN7 1RB for details of the opportunities available on organic farms in the UK and worldwide throughout the year. Membership is £10 per annum. In return for hard work, workers receive free meals, accomodation, the opportunity to learn and transport to and from the local station. The National Federation of City Farms arranges voluntary work in community gardens. A list of these gardens can be obtained by sending an A4 s.a.e to the above address.

Local Government

Local authorities advertise for temporary summer staff in the local press or in Jobcentres as well as in this book. Jobs as gardeners, litter collectors and ground staff may be available, usually through the city works department; and the leisure services and recreation departments take on lifeguards and recreational assistants. Other council departments may need people for clerical duties, cleaning or maintenance, though vacancies of this sort do not usually occur on a regular basis. See *Children*, above, for more information about local authority playschemes.

Language Schools

Ten years ago Teaching English as a foreign language (TEFL) was a major growth industry. The worldwide recession reduced demand slightly, but this is likely to be only a temporary blip in the industry's momentum. During the summer months people of all nationalities and ages come to spend time in Britain to learn or improve their English. The language schools that cater for them are found for the most part in London, Canterbury, Brighton, Hastings, Eastbourne, Bournemouth, Oxford and Cambridge.

Most British language schools require a TEFL qualification of their teachers, though some will take on either graduates with an English or modern language degree, or students doing PGCE and teacher training courses. Teachers are employed either for a complete holiday course for both classroom work and recreational activities (such courses are usually residential), or on an hourly basis for classroom teaching only.

Language schools that run residential courses may take on general staff to supervise day trips, visits and the more social side of the school's programme: qualifications are rarely required for this type of work, though experience is desirable. There are also opportunities for sports instructors as many of the schools offer a wide range of outdoor activities.

Voluntary Work

Many organisations throughout the UK need volunteers to help with a host of different types of work, from caring for people with disabilities or the elderly to taking part in conservation and archaeological projects. This type of job experience is strongly recommended if you are contemplating a career in any of these fields. Most of the voluntary organisations in this book do not require specific skills; willingness and enthusiasm are the most important attributes.

Working with people with special needs is demanding: you are expected to both work hard physically and to give a lot of time and commitment. However, many volunteers find the challenge to be both a rewarding and maturing experience. Most organisations provide free board and lodging, and sometimes a small amount of pocket money and help with travel expenses. Many social or community projects need volunteers all year round, but there is always a demand in the summer for extra staff to help with outings and holidays.

Conservation and archaeological projects are increasingly popular. The drawback is that such projects tend to be only short-term and most require volunteers to make a contribution towards their board and lodging.

Museums, stately homes and gardens frequently operate on a very tight budget and may be pleased to receive offers of voluntary help; some may even pay a small wage. Visits to museums and art galleries increased by 5% in 1998. *Historic Houses, Castles and Gardens* is published by Johansen's (tel 0171-490 3090) and *Museums and Galleries* is published by Hobsons (tel 01223-354551). Both books are crammed full of addresses. *The National Trust Handbook*, which lists all the UK properties open to the Public, is free with membership or available from all good bookshops for £4.50. The Trust also produces a variety of free leaflets about properties in certain areas.

Sources of Information. *The International Directory of Voluntary Work* (£10.99, published by Vacation Work, 9 Park End Street, Oxford OX1 1HJ) includes information on both short and long term opportunities. The National Council for Voluntary Organisations (Hamilton House Mailings, Earlstrees Court, Earlstrees Road, Corby NN17 4AX; tel 01536-399016; fax 01526-399012) publishes the *Voluntary Agencies Directory*, price £20.00, which lists over 2,500 organisations countrywide.

Signposts otherwise known as *The National Centre for Volunteering* (tel 0171-388 9888) is a national database of local volunteering opportunities that is updated annually, and is an excellent source of contact names and addresses of organisations requiring help in your area. It also provides details of Volunteer Bureaux which are found in most big towns and dispense information about, and do some of the recruiting for, local voluntary organisations.

On a regional level, the following organisations produce lists of voluntary opportunities in their area, or can put you in touch with your local volunteer bureau:

Wales Council for Voluntary Action: Llys Ifor, Crescent Road, Caerphilly

CF83 1XL (tel 01222-855100; fax 01222-855101). Offices also in Llandudno (tel 01492-862100) and Welshpool (tel 01938-552379).

In Northern Ireland volunteer placements are governed by local volunteer bureaux. There is also a publication titled *Residential Volunteering Opportunities in Northern Ireland* available from the *Northern Ireland Volunteer Development Agency* (Annsgate House, Ann Street, Belfast tel 01232-236100; fax 01232-237570).

Vacation Traineeships

Vacation traineeships are schemes which aim to provide young people with an opportunity to gain on-the-job training during their holidays. They have become increasingly important as competition for entry level jobs increases; indeed the Dearing Report recommends that this type of work experience should be integrated into Higher Education. These vocational positions may not appeal to those wanting a summer job simply to have fun or to earn enough money to finance a holiday or keep the bank manager at bay. Against this, in the long run they can prove to be a most valuable long-term investment of your time.

The jobs listed in the *Vacation Traineeships* section of each regional chapter in this book share a number of basic characteristics. They are short-term placements open to students from both schools and institutes of higher or further education. Jobs usually arise during the summer vacation, and last for two to eight weeks. Some short term positions are also available over the Easter and Christmas breaks.

The degree of actual training varies enormously from one firm to another, with the highest levels offered generally by companies involved in science, engineering and computing. Traineeships are also most numerous in these fields since students are increasingly reluctant to choose a career in Engineering or Science — and therefore have to be actively encouraged. The competition for placements is likely to be greater in other areas such as law and accountancy, both of which are now well established in the vacation training field. In recent years, the big retailers have also marked a new growth area in the field of on-the-job training schemes.

Some companies offer work shadowing schemes, which are ideal for students who are undecided about their future career. They usually involve the student observing a chosen person at work for a period of one to five days. Although these schemes are generally unpaid, students may receive free meals and travel expenses.

The Advantages of Vacation Training. Since students in higher education are no longer eligible for income support or housing benefit during the holiday periods, the financial rewards of doing a traineeship have become increasingly alluring: many trainees are paid a weekly wage of £150-£200. Even so, for many the value of the experience gained far outweighs that of the salary. Note that accommodation is rarely supplied with a traineeship, though assistance may be given in looking for a room.

The very principle of training is helpful even before the work starts, since it encourages you to consider your eventual career in good time before the end of your course. Then, once you have begun the traineeship, you can assess the working environment without having to make any commitments to a certain branch or employer. You also gain an insight into what will be expected of you later on, and can test your own capabilities.

The greatest benefits of taking part in a training scheme, however, come when you are applying for full-time work. Firstly, it gives you the chance to gain experience at interviews and to develop important skills; secondly, an employer is more likely to consider seriously an application from someone who spent their previous summer on a vacation traineeship than someone who worked in the local pub. And once at the interview, your experience as a trainee is likely to become a central subject of discussion, since it will be the main guide your prospective employer has for assessing your ability to do the job being advertised.

Another major advantage of vacation training is that a substantial number of companies treat traineeships as extended assessment periods and the best trainees either by-pass the preliminary interviews or are offered full-time positions after graduation. Even if the company doesn't give you a permanent job, by giving you a good reference they may indirectly help you find work elsewhere. In professions in the Media or the Arts where jobs are rarely advertised a work placement, whether paid or unpaid, is often the only way to find out about a vacancy or gain valuable contacts.

Experience and Qualifications. Many employers specify a preferred field of study relevant to the job. Not surprisingly, candidates reading English or Philosophy are unlikely to be employed on projects involving structural analysis calculations or computer programming.

Certain companies say they consider only university students, but these are an increasingly small minority. Others stipulate that candidates should be in their second undergraduate year. Where such information has been forthcoming, the entries specify which stage of their academic careers candidates should have reached.

More generally, employers are looking for self-motivated students with a positive attitude, the ability to work well in a team and an aptitude to analyse and solve problems quickly and effectively. If you give the impression that you really want just a holiday job, you are unlikely to be considered for a post.

Sources of Information

Jobcentres. These state employment agencies, run by the government's Employment Service, usually have at least one board devoted to temporary vacancies. Some, mainly in London, have a special Temporary Desk. Others run registration schemes, enabling you to put your name down on a list — but in order to do this you may be required to have a specific skill, and you will be advised to still check the boards regularly.

Big companies, such as Butlins, like to recruit early and advertise vacancies through their local Jobcentre in the spring. In the summer many jobs are available on the spot too. The organisers of big local events and farmers, for example, sometimes use Jobcentres to recruit staff.

Employment Agencies. While the number of agencies dealing with temporary work in London can be positively daunting, outside the capital the range is much more narrow. It is worth registering with as many agencies as possible in order to enhance your chances of finding work. The jobs offered are frequently office based, though some specialise in hotel and catering or manual work. Brook Street Bureau and Alfred Marks, which have branches all over the UK, both tend to concentrate on clerical work. Manpower, also with offices nationwide, has information on labouring and warehouse jobs. You can find their addresses in the Yellow Pages.

Under the Employment Agencies Act it is illegal for an agency to charge a fee for finding someone a job: agencies make their money by charging the employers.

National Institutes. One way of finding out more about Vacation Training opportunities within a specific field is to contact the relevant national professional body or institute. Institutes do not themselves offer traineeships, but may be able to offer general advice and/or give names and addresses of companies within their field.

Insurance and Related Financial Services N.T.O.: Careers Information Service, 20 Aldermanbury, London EC2V 7HL (tel 0171-417 4424; fax 0171-726 0131; e-mail http://www.cii.co.uk).

Hotel & Catering International Management Association: 191 Trinity Road, London SW17 7HN (tel 0181-672 4251, fax 0181-682 1707).

Institute of Chartered Accountants in England and Wales: Gloucester House, 399 Silbury Boulevard, Central Milton Keynes MK9 2HL (Student Recruitment Section: tel 0171-920 8677).

Institute of Chartered Accountants of Scotland: Head Office: 27 Queen Street, Edinburgh EH2 1LA (tel 0131-225 5673; fax 0131-225 3813; web site http://www.icas.org.uk).

Royal Town Planning Institute: 26 Portland Place, London W1N 4BE (tel 0171-636 9107; fax 0171-323 1582). This organisation runs a Vacation Employment Register which is designed to put prospective employers in touch with planning students on RTPI accredited courses who are looking for work over the summer vacation. It has nothing to do with formal vacation traineeships, although the work experience may be useful.

TAX AND NATIONAL INSURANCE

Income Tax. Single people are entitled to a personal tax allowance, which means that you don't pay income tax until your yearly earnings exceed £4,195. Few people are likely to earn this much over the vacation.

To avoid paying tax you need to fill out the right form; new employees will usually be taxed under an 'emergency code' until the Tax Office receives this form from your employer. Students in higher education should fill in form P38(S), and school and college leavers a P46. Ask your employer to send the form to the Tax Office as soon as possible after you start work. You should be put on the right code within a month or so, after which time you will get a rebate. If you have not been put on the right tax code by the time you leave your job, send a tax rebate claims form to the Tax Office together with your P45, which you will get when you finish work.

National Insurance. National Insurance contributions are compulsory for employees over 16 years of age if they earn over a certain limit. The rate you pay is calculated according to your wages. Currently, anyone who earns less than £64 a week pays nothing.

If you require information in addition to that given above, contact the Contributions Agency or the Tax Office (as relevant), or else your local Citizens Advice Bureau.

Creating Your Own Job

Some people may not want to spend time sending off speculative letters or phoning around potential employers asking for a job that may not exist. The alternative is to make a job for yourself, by creating a service which people in your local area might be willing to pay for. A company called LiveWire produces an information booklet on starting your own business. For a copy of this booklet call 0345-573 252 or write to LiveWire, FREEPOST NT805, Newcastle upon Tyne NE1 1BR. Window cleaning, car-washing, housework and babysitting are a few of the most obvious odd-jobs, and there are many more. Below are some questions to ask yourself before turning self-employed:

1. What do people want? You can find this out by (a) asking neighbours, (b) reading local papers and (c) looking at advertisements in local shops.

2. What can I offer? It is surprising how many different things most of us can turn our hands or minds to. It may well be that a hobby or spare-time activity can be turned into a moneyspinner. Some suggestions:
carpentry: simple woodwork, mending gates, making/putting up shelves.
cooking: lunch and dinner party catering or sandwich-making.
cycling: bicycle repairs (highly recommended), courier work (suitable for those with a mountain bike who live in a big city).
gardening: grass-cutting, weeding or pruning.
knitting: making jumpers, cardigans, etc. on commission.
music: busking, playing in pubs or being a disc jockey.
sewing: dressmaking, repairs and alterations, cushion-making.
walking: dog exercising, tourist guiding or shopping for the elderly.

3. Who wants me? After you have identified the job you can do and for which you think there will be a demand, you need to publicise your services. The best way to start is with advertisements in local shop windows (which are very cheap) and, if you can afford it, in your local newspaper. It will also be useful to run off a handbill and distribute it locally.

The principal feature of successfully creating a job for yourself is your reputation. If you impress someone with your hard work, promptness and efficiency, they will tell others.

Notes on Applying for a Job

1. Most employers like to make their staff arrangements in good time, so apply early (though never before the date mentioned in the job details).

2. Before applying for a position, check that you fulfil all the requirements, such as age and qualifications. In a time of high unemployment, employers are normally able to find someone who meets all their needs, so you are wasting your time (and the employer's) if you apply for a job for which you are clearly not suitable.

Period of work: employers generally prefer to take on one person for the whole season. If you are able to work for longer than the minimum period quoted, you are more likely to get the job.

Accommodation: it is particularly important to note whether or not lodging is provided, especially for those who are coming from abroad. In areas which attract a lot of tourists over the summer, temporary rented accommodation can be either difficult to find or prohibitively expensive. Some employers can recommend lodgings in the area or be of more positive help, but often they are reluctant to recruit those who have no pre-arranged accommodation.

3. Compose a short letter, preferably typed but if not at least legible. First impressions are very important: if an employer receives a lot of applications for a certain position, he or she may eliminate candidates whose presentation is less than perfect.

(a) explain which position interests you, why you are suitable for it and the maximum time you are available. If applying for a traineeship, it's worth going over the top in your praise both of the company and of yourself. Also mention whether or not you are available for interview.

(b) make it clear which area you would like to work in, if you have a preference, since some companies and organisations have branches in different parts of the country.

(c) Overseas applicants should ascertain whether or not they are eligible to work in the UK (see *Work Permits and Special Schemes*), and make this plain in the letter.

4. Enclose with your letter a *curriculum vitae* (c.v.), covering the following points and any others you consider relevant:

(a) Personal details (name, address, telephone number, nationality, age, marital status).

(b) Educational background and subjects you are currently studying if you are a student, otherwise your present occupation.

(c) Relevant qualifications, previous work experience, possession of driving licence, etc.

5. Address the letter to the person specified in the entry, whether this gives an actual name or merely the title, e.g. Personnel Manager, Student Training Officer, etc.

6. Always enclose a stamped addressed envelope (s.a.e.) or, if you are applying from abroad, an International Reply Coupon (IRC). It can be both expensive and inconvenient for employers to reply to a large number of applicants, especially once the positions have been filled. Some employers simply won't respond to applications without a s.a.e. or IRC.

7. Farmers rarely wish to interview prospective fruit pickers, but other employers or organisations often like to meet potential employees. This applies in particular to firms offering vacation traineeships: you should be able to show a basic knowledge of, and interest in, the activities of the company in question, as well as demonstrate that you are seriously considering a career in that particular field.

8. During the interview, but above all when you receive a job offer, check all the relevant information: the job details given in this Directory are supplied by the employer, but it is wise to obtain confirmation of them before accepting the position. Things to check include: wages, board and lodging, hours and the conditions of work. Some staff have ended up working unpaid overtime, others have been sacked without warning, so clarify **all** terms and conditions in advance.

Ask your employer to put the relevant details in writing (though for these to become legally binding, both parties must sign a contract).

9. If you are offered more than one job, decide quickly which you prefer and inform all employers of your decision as soon as possible.

10. Many young people regard their summer job as a holiday, but this is seldom the attitude taken by the employer. If the job details indicate that a hotel needs an assistant to serve three meals a day six days a week, or a hop farmer needs pickers to work seven days a week in all weathers, then you should be warned that there will be far more work than holiday.

11. Finally, ask for a reference when you leave your job, since this should enhance your chances of finding work in the future. In some fields, such as retail, the ability to produce a reference is considered important.

Work Permits and Special Schemes

Before writing letters to prospective employers, overseas applicants should clarify the terms under which they may visit and work in Britain. Anyone arriving at UK Immigration without the necessary visa, letter of invitation or other required documentation, could be sent back home on the next available flight. An outline of the regulations is given below. For further information, contact the nearest British Consulate or High Commission.

Visa Requirements

You may need a visa to enter the UK irrespective of the reason for your visit. Citizens of Western Europe, most Commonwealth countries and of the USA do not need a tourist visa to enter Britain. Since the fall of communism in the Eastern Bloc, many Eastern Europeans — including Poles, Czechs, Slovaks and Hungarians — no longer need visas either.

Nationals of the former Soviet Union and most Asian and African countries are required to obtain a visa. Exceptions include Israel, Japan, South Africa and Zimbabwe. It is advisable to check visa requirements at the nearest UK Diplomatic Post.

Work Permits

Wherever relevant, entries in this book specify if the company or organisation in question welcomes applications from overseas. Unfortunately, this does not mean that all foreigners can legally work for them in this country. It is an offence under the Immigration Act of 1971 to take employment in breach of conditions of stay, and a person found to be working illegally may be fined and may also be liable to deportation. An employer employing overseas nationals whom he or she knows to be working in breach of their landing conditions may also be liable to prosecution and a fine of up to £5000.

Having studied the section below carefully, if you believe you are eligible for some kind of permit, make enquiries with the consulate or relevant organisation as soon as possible: preparing the necessary documentation may take some months.

EEA Citizens Nationals of the European Economic Area are free to enter the United Kingdom to seek employment without a work permit. At present this applies to citizens of EU countries and Norway, Iceland and Liechtenstein. However EEA nationals still require a permit for the Channel Islands and the Isle of Man.

EEA nationals intending to stay longer than six months may apply for a residence permit, although there is no obligation on them to do so.

Non-EEA Citizens. The general position under the Immigration Rules is that overseas nationals (other than EEA nationals) coming to work in Britain must have work permits before setting out. The employer (**not** the employee) has to apply to the Department of Education and Employment, which administers the scheme. Permits are issued only for specific jobs requiring a high level of skill and experience for which resident or EEA labour is not available. In other words, a British employer cannot apply for a work permit for a non-EEA citizen unless it is for a job that no EEA National can do.

There are, however, a few exceptions to these rules:

Citizens of Commonwealth Countries: nationals of Commonwealth countries (including Australia, New Zealand, Canada and South Africa) between the ages of 17 and 27 are permitted to visit the UK as a 'Working Holiday Maker'. This allows them to take up casual employment which will be incidental to their holiday, but not to engage in business or to pursue a career. The total period which can be spent in the UK is two years. A six-month period may be granted initially, but this can then be extended.

Prior entry clearance is mandatory and must be obtained from the British High Commission in your home country.

Commonwealth citizens with at least one British-born grandparent may wish to apply for 'UK Ancestry employment entry clearance' from the British High Commission: this eliminates altogether the need for a work permit. Married couples must apply for separate entry clearance before travelling.

Students from North America: US students seeking temporary work in the UK can benefit from the 'Work in Britain Program'. This allows full-time college students and recent graduates over the age of 18 to look for work in Britain, finding jobs through programme listings or through personal contacts. Jobs may be pre-arranged, though most participants wait until arrival in Britain to job hunt. They must first obtain a 'British Universities North America Club (BUNAC) Card', which is recognised by the British Home Office as a valid substitute for a work permit ; this 'BUNAC Card' must be obtained before leaving the US for Britain, as it acts as an entry document. It allows the holder to work for a maximum of six months at any time of year: extensions are never granted. The BUNAC card is available for a fee of approx. $225 from the Council on International Educational Exchange (Council) at 205 East 42nd Street, New York, NY 10017, USA (toll free tel 1-888-268-6245).

A similar programme, called the Student Work Abroad Programme (SWAP), is organised for Canadian students aged 18-25. It is administered by the Canadian Universities Travel Service, which has over 40 offices in Canada.

Seasonal Agricultural Work Scheme: farm camps under this scheme are authorised by the Home Office and are the main hope for non-EEA and non-Commonwealth nationals wishing to work in this country. Special 'entrance authorisation cards' are issued to a certain number of non-EEA nationals each year, taking the place of otherwise impossible-to-obtain work permits.

Most of the recruitment for these farms is handled by two agencies, the Harvesting Opportunity Permit Scheme or HOPS (see the *Outdoor* section in the *Nationwide* chapter) and Concordia (for address see *Agriculture* above). Between them they recruit pickers for over 160 farms between April and

October. While you can contact the farmers directly, you are advised to apply through the above-mentioned agencies. Prospective participants should be aged 18 to 25 and should be full-time students in their own country.

Voluntary Work. Overseas nationals may be admitted for up to 12 months for the purpose of voluntary work without requiring a permit, providing he or she will be working for a registered charitable organisation and receiving no remuneration other than pocket money, board and accommodation. The work which they do must be closely related to the aims of the charity ie. working with people, and they must not be engaged in purely clerical, administrative or maintenance work (for which a work permit is required). Volunteers are expected to leave the United Kingdom at the end of their visit.

Traineeships. Permission can be given for overseas nationals with pre-arranged work placements to obtain permits for professional training or managerial level work experience for a limited ammount of time. The UK employer offering the placement has to apply for a permit to the Overseas Labour Service at the address below. For US citizens, the US/UK Career Development Programme can facilitate this process. This exchange programme is run by the Association for International Practical Training (AIPT), along with its UK co-operator, the Council on International Educational Exchange (Council). The US/UK Career Development Programme is a reciprocal exchange scheme and as such has special concessions under TWES guidelines. Interested applicants should contact AIPT at 104000 Little Patuxent Parkway, Suite 250, Columbia, MD 21044-3510, USA (tel 00 1 410 997 2200).

While many companies in the book are happy to employ overseas students as trainees, since most of them run their schemes in order to try out potential employees, they may not be keen to take on anyone who cannot return to them after their studies.

The Department for Education and Employment issues permits under its Training and Work Experience Scheme for limited periods of pre-arranged on-the-job training to gain a professional qualification, or for short periods of managerial level work experience. This can include students on recognised exchange placements through AIESEC, or the International Farm Experience Programme.

Non EEA Students Studying in the UK. Overseas students studying in Britain who wish to take up vacation work must fill in form OSS1, available from Jobcentres or Employment Service Offices in the UK.

Au Pairs. For details of regulations affecting au pairs see the chapter *Au Pair, Home Help and Paying Guest* at the end of the book.

Further Information

Once in the UK, general information about who needs work permits and other immigration matters can be obtained from the Home Office Immigration and Nationality Department, Lunar House, Wellesley Road, Croydon, CR9 2BY (tel 0181-686 0688): be prepared to wait in line for your call to be answered, it will be eventually. Guidance leaflets are also available from the Correspondence Unit of the Foreign and Commonwealth Office, Migration and Visa Department, 1 Palace Street, London SW1E 5HE (website http://www.fco. gov.uk). The Department for Education and Employment, Overseas Labour Service, W5, Moorfoot, Sheffield S1 4PQ (tel 0114-2594074) can advise employers on the rules of the work permit scheme.

N.B. The author and publishers have every reason to believe in the accuracy of the information given in this book and the authenticity and correct practices of all organisations, companies, agencies etc. mentioned; however, situations may change and telephone numbers can alter, and readers are strongly advised to check facts and credentials for themselves.

ABBREVIATIONS

approx.	approximately	max.	maximum
a.s.a.p.	as soon as possible	min.	minimum
B & L	board and lodging	p.a.	per annum
c.v.	curriculum vitae	s.a.e.	stamped addressed
IRC	International Reply		envelope
	Coupon	w.p.m.	words per minute

Glossary of Qualifications

The following list of qualifications (often the name of the institute or association which issues them) are listed in alphabetical order.

ACA/ACCA — (Chartered) Association of Certified Accountants
BASI — British Association of Ski Institutes
BCU — British Canoe Union
BHSIC — British Horse Society Instructor's Certificate
BTEC — Business and Technology Education Certificate
CIMA — Chartered Institute of Management Accountants
City and Guilds 706/1, 706/2 — catering qualifications
GCSE — General Certificate of Secondary Education
GNAS — Grand National Archery Society
HGV — Heavy Goods Vehicle driving licence
HND — Higher National Diploma
LGV — Light Goods Vehicle driving licence
LTA — Lawn Tennis Association
MLTB — Mountaineering Leadership Training Board
NAMCW — National Association for Maternal and Child Welfare
NNEB — National Nursery Examination Board
OND — Ordinary National Diploma
PCV — Passenger Carrying Vehicle
PLG — Pool Life Guard
RGN — Registered General Nurse
RLS (S) — Royal Life Saving (Society)
RSA — Royal Society of Arts (Examinations Board)
RYA — Royal Yachting Association
SEN — Senior Enrolled Nurse
TEFL/EFL — (Teaching) English as a Foreign Language

THE NATIONAL MINIMUM WAGE

Some of the wages quoted in this book may appear not to meet the requirements of the National Minimum Wage (see page 6) which is expected to be introduced in April 1999. This is partly because the details of the legislation had not been confirmed when the book was compiled and many employers had not yet set new wage rates as they were uncertain of their new legal requirements. There may also be certain circumstances in which the normal minimum rates do not apply, such as when food and accommodation are provided. Still to be settled at the time of writing is the question of whether or not minimum rates will apply in certain special circumstances such as in areas of high unemployment.

NATIONWIDE

Business and Industry

BETTERWARE: Headquarters, Stanley House, Park Lane, Castle Vale, Birmingham B35 6LJ (freephone 0800-0565646).
DISTRIBUTORS to deliver and collect Betterware's *Household Products* brochure to existing customers. Vacancies exist in all parts of the UK at all times of the year. Positions are full or part-time. Successful applicants can expect to earn £40-£200 dependent on the hours available, but must do a minimum of 8 hours per week. Full-time careeers opportunities in sales management also exist for the right candidates.
For more details apply in writing to Mr. P. Sykes, General Manager, at the above address.

MAJESTIC WINE WAREHOUSES: Odhams Trading Estate, St Albans Road, Watford WD2 5RE (tel 01923-816999; fax 01923-819105). Majestic retails beers, wines and spirits in wholesale quantities. It has 74 retail outlets in London, the South West, East Anglia, the Midlands and the North, and is expanding rapidly with plans for 10 new stores a year.
TEMPORARY DRIVERS to help with delivery driving, selling wine to customers, and merchandising. Wages £4.00-£4.20 per hour depending on the location. Vacancies available in all holiday periods, but mainly over Christmas and the summer. The only qualification needed is the ability to deal with the public and a full clean driving licence held for at least 1 year. No accommodation is provided. Applications to Nicola Blatch, Personnel and Training Manager, at the above address.

ODDBINS WINE MERCHANT: 31-33 Weir Road, Wimbledon, London SW19 8U9 (tel 0181-944 4400; fax 0181-944 4476). A national chain of 240 stores which pride themselves on their range of choice, advice, and service. Provides a good opportunity for employees to learn about wine. Wine merchant of the year 1997/8.
SALES ASSISTANTS (50) for positions across the UK. £3.95 per hour. To work variable hours from May to October including evenings and weekends. Retail, bar or catering experience is an advantage. Min. age 18; accommodation not available. Must speak fluent English. Apply from May onwards at your local branch to arrange an interview.

Children

ACTION HOLIDAYS LTD: Robinwood, Jumps Road, Todmorden, Lancashire OL14 8HJ (tel 01706-814554). Approx 200 staff needed to run multi-activity centres for children aged 5-15 in Greater London, Staffordshire, and Lancashire. Comprehensive training provided with the opportunity to gain national governing body qualifications at Robinwood Activity Centre in Lancashire.
ACTIVITY CENTRE DIRECTORS and DEPUTY MANAGERS (10). £200 per week. Considerable experience of working with children and managing teams of staff is necessary.
SENIOR SUPERVISORS (20). £110 per week. Responsible for co-ordinating and overseeing the care, welfare, and instruction, of children.
SUPERVISORS (70). £50-£80 a week. To look after general care, welfare, and instruction, of the children.
SPECIALIST INSTRUCTORS (70). £60 per week. To teach archery, arts & crafts, computing, go-karting, gymnastics, performing arts, swimming, tennis, trampolining, outdoor pursuits and watersports.
OFFICE MANAGERS (8). £100 per week. General administration and timetabling responsibilities.
EQUIPMENT SUPERVISORS (4). £100 per week. To maintain equipment and run tuck shop.
NURSES (8). £100 per week. Responsible for general and medical care, and welfare, of children.
GENERAL ASSISTANTS (4). £45 per week. Responsible for equipment, domestic and general supervisory duties.
GENERAL INSTRUCTORS (16). £60-£100 per week. For long season Jan-Nov in small permanent centre instructing outdoor activities.
   Staff get one full day and additional sessions off a week. B & L provided. Min. period of work 4 weeks during July and August. Enthusiasm and good sense of humour important. Min. age 19.
Preference given to those applicants with relevant qualifications and experience with children. For full details and application form contact the above address.

ARDMORE ADVENTURE LTD: Berkshire College, Burchetts Green, Maidenhead, Berkshire SL6 6QR (tel 01628-826699; fax 01628-829977; e-mail mailbox@ardmore.org.uk; website http//:www.ardmore.org.uk). Multi-activity and English Language centres for overseas children aged 8-17. Residential centres located throughout Britain.
GROUP LEADERS. £50 per week. Residential/non residential. Full B & L provided at residential centres. Experience with children essential, as is the ability to lead a broad range of sports, drama and art/craft activities. Pastoral care is also extremely important.
CENTRE DIRECTORS. Responsible for efficient management of centre, its staff, the activity and language programme, and the welfare and safety of the children. Salary negotiable according to age and experience.
   Staff aged 20 + preferred. Period of work 2-8 weeks during June, July and August.
Further details from Ardmore Adventure at the above address.

BARRACUDAS SUMMER ACTIVITY CAMPS: Graphic House, Ferrars Road, Huntingdon, Cambridgeshire PE18 6EE (tel 01480-435090). Recruits staff to work at children's multi activity day centres mainly in Greater London, Essex, Berkshire, Surrey and Cambridgeshire. Monday to Friday, 8.30am-5.00pm.
GROUP CO-ORDINATORS (200). To supervise groups of 20-30 children. Experience of working with children essential. £120-£150 per week subject to qualifications and experience. Min. age 19.
ACTIVITY INSTRUCTORS (100). To instruct in a variety of sports and activities. Enthusiasm and experience essential. Qualifications necessary wherever the appropriate governing body dictates, £120-£150 per week. Minimum age 18.
LIFEGUARDS (30). To supervise swimming pools. RLSS National Pool Lifeguards. £150-£180 per week.
NURSES (10). To help with administration, general assistance and occasional cuts and bruises. £150 per week. Should be aged at least 20 and hold RGN, SRN or equivalent.
  Full board and accommodation is available if required at some centres. The accommodation is available for the duration of the camps.   Training Courses leading to National Governing Body qualifications are organised prior to the camps. The cost of these courses and all accommodation during the course is met by Barracudas for staff who work a full season of between four and six weeks. All staff must speak fluent English. Barracudas is an equal opportunities employer.

EF LANGUAGE TRAVEL: EF House, 1-3 Farman Street, Hove, Sussex BN3 1AL. (tel 01273-723651; fax 01273-729561). Residential language courses held for European students in locations around Britain.
GROUP LEADERS AND TEACHERS (1,000 nationwide). Salary varies depending on region and experience. Min. age 21 years. Teaching or leadership experience preferred. Applicants must have a standard of English as high as that of a native speaker. Both residential and non-residential staff required, accommodation available for residential appointments only.
ACTIVITY ORGANISERS (60 nationwide) to plan an activity programme for all students in one particular town or residential centre. Salary varies depending on region and experience. Min. age 21 years. Previous organisational experience essential.
  All staff to work flexible hours, 7 days a week. No overtime payments. Min. period of work 3 weeks between late May and late August. All applicants must be available for interview. Applications as soon as possible to the Recruitment Officer at the above address.

HF HOLIDAYS LIMITED: Redhills, Penrith, Cumbria CA11 0DT (tel 01768-899525). A non-profitmaking organisation which owns 20 country houses in the UK, based in the National Parks. An excellent opportunity to demonstrate leadership skills while having fun.
CHILDREN'S ACTIVITY LEADERS are required by Britain's leading walking holiday company to organise games and activities and supervise children. Applicants should enjoy the countryside and short walks, and have empathy with children. Accommodation, travel expenses and approx. £15 per week equipment allowance will be provided. Students can be employed over the summer period at £60 per week. Leaders are required for 1 to 6 weeks in

July and August at numerous locations throughout the UK. Assessment and training courses are held during the winter (difficult for applicants living abroad) so early application is essential. For an information pack, contact Helen Sams, Walking Department, at the above address.

THE KINGSWOOD GROUP: Linton House, 164-180 Union Street, London SE1 0LH (tel 0171-922 1234; fax 0171 928 7733; e-mail jobs@kingswood-.co.uk). The Group operates educational activity centres and summer camps across the UK and France. It provides opportunities to work in a fun, young and enthusiastic environment. The company also runs Camp Beaumont and Freetime Summer Camps.

MANAGERS/ASSISTANT MANAGERS. Wages negotiable depending upon age and experience. Must be over 21.

ACTIVITY/IT & ENVIRONMENTAL STUDIES INSTRUCTORS. Wages £250+ per month depending on qualifications, experience and length of contract. Must be over 18. Training provided.

CHEFS. Wages £110 per week. Must be over 21 and have City and Guilds 706 I + II or equivalent.

COOKS. Wages £80 per week. Must be over 19. Training provided.

CATERING ASSISTANTS. Wages £250 per month. Must be over 19. Training provided.

DRIVERS. Wages £100 per week. Must be over 21 and have P.S.V./P.C.V. qualifications.

DOMESTIC ASSISTANTS. Wages £250 per month. Must be over 19. Training provided.

All staff work 5½-6 days a week. 3-8 month contracts. Meals and accommodation provided. All applicants must have a keen interest in working with children, be willing to work long hours and be able to provide good references.

Overseas applicants are welcome but must possess valid work documentation/visas, and be able to provide police clearance forms. Instructors should have a high level of English and other staff should communicate well in English. It is company policy to personally interview/assess each candidate individually.

To receive an application form and further information, apply to the Recruitment Department at the above address.

PGL TRAVEL: Alton Court, Penyard Lane (874), Ross-on-Wye, Herefordshire HR9 5NR (tel 01989-767833). Over 3,000 staff needed to assist in the running of children's activity centres throughout the UK. Europe's largest provider of adventure holidays for children has offered outstanding training and work opportunities to seasonal staff for over 40 years.

GROUP LEADERS required to take responsibility for small groups of children and ensure that they get the most out of their holiday. Min. age 20. Previous experience of working with children necessary.

GENERAL STAFF. To help with stores, site cleaning, kitchen, driving (car, PCV or LGV), administration, coffee bar, nurses (RGN or SEN), etc. Min. age 18.

Pocket money from £36 per week, with B & L provided. Vacancies available for short or long periods between February and October. Overseas applicants eligible to work in the UK welcome. Requests for application forms to the Personnel Department at the above address.

PRIME LEISURE ACTIVITY HOLIDAYS LTD: 4A Chawley Lane, Cumnor Hill, Oxford OX2 9PX (tel 01865-865300; fax 01865-865433; e-mail prime.leisure@btinternet.com). Runs multi-activity holidays and day camps for children aged 4-14 in centres in Oxfordshire, Berkshire, and Hertfordshire. The company is committed to providing safe and fun holidays for all young children.

SITE LEADERS (8). £200 + per week. Qualified teachers with camp experience preferred.

SECOND IN CHARGE (8). £110 per week. Preferably third-year trainee teachers with coaching and camp experience.

SENIOR INSTRUCTORS. £85 per week. Should have experience/qualifications in tennis, swimming ASA Bronze Medallion, (trampolining BTF), first aid, art, etc.

TRAMPOLINING INSTRUCTORS. £90 per week.

TRAINEE INSTRUCTORS. £60 per week. Applicants should have an interest/qualifications in sports and/or arts and crafts.

Staff needed for April and from the end of July and August. Free B & L provided. Overseas applicants considered subject to language ability and relevant qualifications. Interview sometimes necessary. Applications from January to Personnel at the above address.

Events and Exhibitions

AFAR EXHIBITION SERVICES LTD: Suite 6, Craven Hall, Sackville Street, Skipton BD23 2PB (tel 01756-797877; fax 01756-797677).

EXHIBITION STAFF, TRAFFIC MANAGEMENT STAFF, PORTERS, CLEANERS, SECURITY STAFF (18) to work nationwide at exhibitions, shows, and fairs. Some work is indoor and some outdoor. Wages £42.50 per day. To work 8am-7pm, 4-10 days at a time. Min. period of work 4 days. Accommodation is available at bed and breakfast cost for staff who do not live locally.

Applicants must be over 18. Overseas applicants considered. Interview not always necessary. Applications to Mrs Caroline Goulden.

THE CRAFT MOVEMENT: PO Box 1641, Frome, Somerset BA11 1YY (tel 01373-813333; fax 01373-813636). An events organiser specialising in premium quality craft/design shows. Its offices are based in Somerset, but the shows take place in various venues in London and Winchester.

PORTERS (6-8 per show). Wages £3.50-£4.00 per hour. Needed 2 days per show. Must be at least 17.

STEWARDS (2-4 per show) Wages £3.50-£5.00 per hour. Needed 3 days per show. Must be at least 17.

CASHIERS (2-4 per show). Wages £3.50-£5.00 per hour. Needed 3 days per show. Must have previous retail experience and be at least 17.

LEAFLET DISTRIBUTORS (2-4). Wages £5.00 per hour. Needed 3 days per show. Must be at least 17.

Staff are needed for various weekends throughout the year. Accommodation not provided. Overseas applicants with a reasonable standard of English are required. Interview not always necessary. Applications to Gillian McInnes from March/April.

EVENTS MANAGEMENT (UK) LTD: 6 Quarry Park Close, Moulton Park, Northampton NN3 6QB (01604-499662; fax 01604-790445). An outdoor events company that supplies staff and manages events such as the British Formula 1 Grand Prix, outdoor concerts at the National Bowl, and various horse racing fixtures.

STEWARDS, PROGRAMME SELLERS, TICKET SELLERS, CAR PARK ATTENDANTS, SECURITY STAFF (1000 + at peak of summer). Wages £3.00-£3.85 per hour. Period of work varies from 1 morning to 1 week. Min. period of work 1 day between March and Christmas. Accommodation available if necessary with a small charge for food.

Applicants must be over 18, and willing to work long hours outdoors. English speaking overseas applicants with work authorisation considered. Applicants will be required to phone to be interviewed, details will be sent out with application forms. Applications at any time of year to the Operations Manager.

PROMOTIONAL SUPPPORT LTD: 276 Chase Road, Southgate, London N14 6HA (tel 0181-886 7009; fax 0181-886 0078). A promotional company that organises roadshows, exhibitions and events and supplies promotional staff for clients such as Van Den Burgh's and other blue chip clients.

TEMPORARY PROMOTIONAL CONTRACTS available. Wage varies from £40-£60 per day. To work 8-10 Hours a day. No accommodation available. Min. period of work 1 day at any time of year.

Applicants should have bubbly, outgoing, attractive personalities. Overseas applicants considered. Interview preferred, but not necessary. Applications at any time to Chola at the above address.

SPECIAL EVENT ORGANISERS (UK) LTD: F23 Langley House, Langley Mill, Nottinghamshire NG16 4AN (tel 01773-534414; fax 01773-534414). Offers opportunities at various holiday centres around the UK.

POOL LIFEGUARDS (50). Wages £120-180 per week. To work approx. 40 hours a week. Must be over 18 and have National Pool Lifeguard qualification.

SPORTS ORGANISERS (10). Wages £120 + per week. Must be over 18 and have Sports Leader qualifications.

Accommodation is available free of charge. Min. period of work depends on starting date between March and November. Overseas applicants with the relevant qualifications are considered. Applications from January to Alan Scaife or Carol Hadwick.

Holiday Centres and Amusements

BOURNE LEISURE GROUP LTD: Normandy Court, 1 Wolsey Road, Hemel Hempstead, Hertfordshire HP2 4TU (tel 01442-241658). Over 20 holiday parks in resorts in the UK.
Five hundred team members needed. Competitive wages and full training provided for positions listed below. Accommodation is available, where appropriate, for which a small charge may be made. Previous experience is not essential. Applicants should have an outgoing personality and smart appearance, and be prepared to work flexible hours. Min. age 18. Vacancies arise between March and October.
BAR TEAM MEMBERS, RECEPTIONISTS and LIFEGUARDS who are available for the whole season (Easter and May-September) should write for an application form or send details to Mr Steve Mullings, Personnel and Training, at the above address. (For shorter periods see below).
CHILDREN'S ENTERTAINERS, ENTERTAINMENT TEAM MEMBERS and SPORTS ORGANISERS preferably available March to October. For further information contact Tommy Dee, Entertainment Office, Hopton Holiday Village, Hopton, Great Yarmouth (tel 01502 731603).
BAR TEAM MEMBERS, RECEPTIONISTS, SITE WORKERS, CATERING TEAM MEMBERS, LIFEGUARDS and SHOP ASSISTANTS who are available for a min. period of 8 weeks. Contact the park of their choice, from the following list:
Allhallows Holiday Park, Allhallows on Sea, Kent (tel 01634-270385).
Berwick Holiday Centre, Berwick on Tweed, Northumberland (tel 01289-307113).
Burnham on Sea Holiday Village, Marine Drive, Burnham on Sea, Somerset (tel 01278 783391).
Cala Gran Holiday Park, Fleetwood Road, Fleetwood, Lancs (tel 01253-872555).
Church Farm Holiday Village, Pagham, West Sussex (tel 01243-262635).
Greenacres Holiday Park, Morfa Bychan, Porthmadog, Gwynedd (tel 01766-512781).
Haggerston Castle Holiday Park, Beal, Berwick on Tweed, Northumberland (tel 01289-381333).
Hopton Holiday Village, Hopton on Sea, Great Yarmouth, Norfolk (tel 01502-730214).
Kiln Holiday Park, Marsh Road, Tenby, Dyfed, Wales (tel 01834-844121).
Lakeland Holiday Park, Flookburgh, Grange over Sands, Cumbria (tel 015395-58556).
Lydstep Beach Holiday Park, Lydstep Haven, Tenby, Dyfed, Wales (01834-871871).
Marton Mere Holiday Park, Mythop Road, Blackpool, Lancs (01253-767544).
Pendine Holiday Village, Pendine, Dyfed, Wales (tel 01994-453398).
Orchards Holiday Park, St Osyth, Clacton on Sea, Essex (tel 01255-820651).
Quay West Holiday Park, New Quay, Dyfed, Wales (tel 01545-560477).
Rockley Park, Rockley Sands, Poole, Dorset (tel 01202-679393).

Seton Sands Holiday Centre, Longniddry, East Lothian, Scotland (tel 01875-813333).
Thorpe Park, Humberston, Cleethorpes, South Humberside (tel 01472-813395).
Wemyss Bay Holiday Park, Wemyss Bay, Renfrewshire, Scotland (tel 01475-520812).

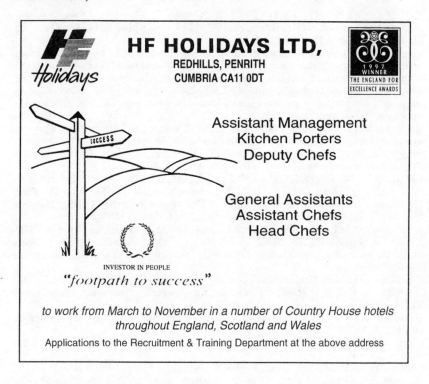
HF HOLIDAYS LIMITED: Redhills, Penrith, Cumbria CA11 0DT (tel 01768-899988; fax 01768-899323). A non-profitmaking organisation which owns 20 Country House hotels based in the National Parks of England, Scotland and Wales. A good opportunity to make friends and enjoy time off by joining guests for their walking and social programme.
ASSISTANT MANAGERS. Responsible to management for efficient organisation and smooth function of all household duties. Experience essential.
GENERAL ASSISTANTS. For domestic work in household and dining room. Training provided.
KITCHEN PORTERS. To assist chefs with the cleaning of utensils and maintaining cleanliness of kitchen. Involves the preparation of vegetables and salads. Training given.
ASSISTANT CHEFS. Previous experience preferable though positions are suitable for students undertaking first appointments after college.
DEPUTY CHEFS. Practical experience required. Responsible for kitchen in Head Chef's absence.

HEAD CHEFS. Practical experience of catering for up to 100 covers is essential.

Rates of pay vary from £80 to £215 per week according to position plus full board and accommodation. Season lasts from March to November plus Christmas and New Year. Applications to Recruitment and Training Department at the above address.

Hotels and Catering

ANGLO CONTINENTAL PLACEMENTS AGENCY: 21 Amesbury Crescent, Hove, East Sussex BN3 5RD (5 lines tel/fax 01273-705959; e-mail anglocont@applied-tech.com). A friendly agency established in 1988 and based on the South Coast. The office is open from 8.30 to 5.30 Mon-Fri. Au Pairs and hotel staff placed all over England. Only works with professional agents.

CHEFS, COMMIS CHEFS, CHEFS DE PARTIES, WAITERS, WAITRESSES, RECEPTIONISTS etc required. Positions available in all aspects of the hotel industry.

Live-in positions available. Staff wanted from New Zealand, Australia and South Africa. Previous work experience essential. Min. period of work 6 months. Work on fruit farms and in factories also available.

Applications including c.v. and 4 IRCs to Sharon or Donna at the above address.

CHOICE HOTELS — EUROPE: 112-114 Station Road, Edgware, Middlesex HA8 7BJ (tel 0181-233 2001; fax 0181-233 2080; email admin@friendly.u-net.com). Owns, manages and franchises over 240 hotels on 13 European countries. Assistance can be offered with finding jobs in Europe, but posts are primarily for the UK.

ROOM ATTENDANTS (50), WAITERS/WAITRESSES (50), BAR STAFF (30), COOKS/CHEFS (35), KITCHEN/HOUSE STEWARDS (30), RECEPTIONISTS (40). Minimum wage for 39 hour week for all positions is £140.40. All staff work a 5 day week of 35-39 hours. Accomodation is often available. Min. period of work 4 months, as full training given. Positions open all year and in all parts of the UK.

Applicants should have a smart appearance, pleasing personality, reasonable English, and be at least 18. Priority given to those with previous hotel experience. Applications to Francoise Bernandon, Recruitment Administrator at Choice Hotels.

COUNTRYWIDE HOLIDAYS: Head Office: 1st Floor, Grove House, Wilmslow Road, Didsbury, Manchester M20 2HU (tel 0161-448 7112; fax 0161-448 7113). Countrywide Holidays runs 6 guesthouses throughout Britain located in places of outstanding beauty in the Lake District, North Yorkshire, and the Peak District. It has been established for over 100 years.

CUSTOMER SERVICE STAFF (10-15) wanted for varied opportunities in housekeeping and food service duties. Wages £80 per week plus board and accommodation. To work approx. 5½ days a week. Staff required from mid April to September; minimum period of work 3 months. Experience in hotel work valuable but not essential. Foreign applicants need to have English of at least an intermediate standard.

Applications from February to Leslie Woolhouse, Facilities Manager, at the above address.

FOCUS: Komtech House, 255/257 London Road, Headington, Oxford OX3 9EH (tel 01865-308488; fax 01865-742235). Focus has four branches around the country which will organise 14 camps in 1999. Focus provides exciting learning activities for diverse groups of people and aims to encourage the personal development of all individuals involved in its programmes. Works in residential and non-residential settings using a variety of team-based, challenging activities and community projects.
COOKS (2)per project. Wages £50 per nine day camp.
ADMINISTRATORS (8). £55 for three weeks work prior to the camp and £35 for an 11 day camp.
  To work on residential projects and camps based in Oxford, Cambridge, Leicester or Nottingham. FOCUS camps are for teenagers with limited opportunities and adults with either a physical or a learning disability. Min. age 18. To work 9 days per camp either in the Easter or summer holidays. Overseas applicants who speak English welcome. Apply from February for the Easter camps and from May for the summer camps to Charlotte Dix at the above address. All applicants must be available for an interview. For further information on volunteer opportunities with Focus consult the voluntary work chapter.

FRIENDLY HOTELS PLC: Premier House, 10 Greycoat Place, London SW1P 1SB (tel 0171-222 8866). Runs 56 hotels in the UK.
ROOM ATTENDANTS (50), WAITERS/WAITRESSES (40), BAR STAFF (15), HOUSE AND KITCHEN STEWARDS (30). Average basic wage £100 + per week. To work 37½ hours per week with opportunities for overtime. Min. age 18. Should have a neat appearance and good personality. Min. period of work 4 months. B & L often available. Overseas applicants eligible to work in the UK and with hotel school training welcome. Applications at any time of year to Mr Brian Worthington, Personnel Director, at Friendly Hotels plc.

GREAT ADVENTURES: Grafham Water Centre, Perry, Huntingdon, Cambridgeshire PE18 0BX (tel 01480-810521; fax 01480-812739). Provides activity and special interest holidays with centres in Cambridgeshire, Derbyshire and Gloucestershire.
CATERING ASSISTANTS (10). £170 per week plus food and accommodation. Must have food hygiene certificate. To work 40 hours per week from May to July; min. period of work 2 months. Work also available for 10 months. Overseas applicants welcome; note all candidates must be available for an interview. Apply from January to Mr Philip Robson at the above address.

MILL HOUSE INNS PLC: Century House, Westcott Venture Park, Westcott, Aylesbury, Buckinghamshire HP18 0XB (tel 01296-652600; fax 01296-652626). Owns a current estate of 60 managed houses all over the UK. Most are located in wonderful countryside settings with a focus on casual family dining.
BAR STAFF (20), WAITING/TABLE SERVICE STAFF (20), KITCHEN PORTERS (10), CHEFS (20, RECEPTIONISTS/ADMINISTRATION STAFF (5). Wages depend on site location. All staff work a 48 hour week.
  Accommodation available, but not at places of work, at a cost already deducted from pay. Full training is provided. Min. period of work 8 weeks between March and October. Overseas applicants are considered, but must be proficient in written and spoken English and have necessary work authorisation. Applicants should have a neat appearance and a pleasant personality.
  Applications from March to Nick Thompson, Personnel Manager.

MONTPELIER EMPLOYMENT AGENCY: 34 Montpelier Road, Brighton, Sussex BN1 2LQ (tel 01273-778686; fax 01273-220359). Specialises in positions away from Brighton, and runs a full countrywide service. The agency has been established for 34 years and particularly seeks experienced hotel staff such as chefs and restaurant and reception staff.
ALL TYPES OF CATERING STAFF required for positions in hotels and restaurants throughout Britain. Wages negotiable. Usually 5½ days per week. Previous hotel and catering experience essential. Overseas applicants must already be resident in the UK with valid work authorisation. Min. period of work 12 weeks from May/June to September/October. Applications from April/May to the Montpelier Employment Agency.

THE LAKE DISTRICT
Come and find your Oasis...
Set in stunningly beautiful Lake District Countryside, Oasis Lakeland Forest Village is one of the UK's premier leisure resorts. Our aim is to provide unforgettable breaks with the highest standards of service and friendliness in a superb setting.
We are looking for individuals who are smart, reliable, enthusiastic, motivated and have excellent references.

Catering Staff, Chef's, Lifeguards, Instructors and many other positions
Contact: HR, Oasis Lakeland Forest Village, Temple Sowerby, Cumbria, CA10 2DW

THISTLE HOTELS: 2 The Calls, Leeds LS2 7JU (tel 0113-2439111; fax 0113-244 0379).
There are over 90 Thistle and Mount Charlotte Hotels within the UK, most of which require staff in most departments. The length of employment is negotiable but involves a minimum of 3 months. Wages are calculated on an hourly basis and vary from hotel to hotel. Some live-in accommodation is provided, but is not available in all hotels.
All nationalities are welcome, but non-European nationals must possess a work permit before applying. Applicants must be over 18 years of age, and fluent English is essential. All applications should be sent to the Recruitment Administrator, Group Personnel Department at the above address.

TOWNGATE PERSONNEL LTD.: 65 Seamoor Road, Westbourne, Bournemouth, Dorset BH4 9AE (tel 01202-752955; fax 01202-752954). A recruitment agency which specialises in the hospitality industry, but also recruits permanent management staff and experienced operational staff for seasonal positions (March-October).
SILVER SERVICE WAITING STAFF (50). £120-£180 per week.
CHEFS: All Grades (50). £120-£250 per week.
To work in various hotels throughout the UK mainland, the Channel Islands and the Isle of Man. To work a 6 day week. Previous experience essential. Also required:
HOTEL RECEPTIONISTS (20) for hotels on the Channel Islands. £120-£180 per week. To work 6 day week. Hotel reception experience a must.
All staff required for a minimum of 6 months between April and September.

Accommodation included. Overseas applicants welcome. Applications from March to James Tucker, Operations Manager, at the above address.

YHA: National Recruitment Department (Hostel Staff) PO Box 11, Matlock, Derbyshire DE4 2XA.
SEASONAL ASSISTANT WARDENS needed to help run the YHA's 240 youth hostels in England and Wales. Work is available for varying periods, between February and October each year. Min. age 18. Assistants undertake a variety of tasks including cleaning, catering and reception work. Experience in one or more of the above areas is essential as are enthusiasm and excellent customer service.

All posts are subject to a face-to-face interview at applicants expense, at the hostel where the vacancy arises. Valid work permits will be required from non EU nationals. Recruitment takes place from December until May. For an application form send an A4 (324mm x 229mm) size s.a.e. marked VW1 to the above address.

Medical

FOCUS: Komtech House, 255/257 London Road, Headington, Oxford OX3 9EH (tel 01865-308488; fax 01865-742235). Focus has 4 branches around the country which will organise 14 camps in 1999. Focus provides exciting learning opportunities for diverse groups of people and aims to encourage the personal development of all individuals involved in its programmes. FOCUS works in both residential and non-residential settings using a variety of team-based, challenging activities and community projects.
NURSES (2) per project. Wages £50 per 9 day camp. To work on a summer camp based either in Oxford, Cambridge, Nottingham and Leicester. FOCUS camps are for teenagers with limited opportunities and adults with either a physical or a learning disability. To work 9 days per camp either at Easter or in the summer. Minimum age 18. Overseas applicants who can speak English welcome.

Apply by February for the Easter camp or by May for the summer camp, to Charlotte Dix at the above address. Note all applicants must be available for an interview or have recent references. For further information on volunteer opportunities see the voluntary work section.

PGL TRAVEL Alton Court, Penyard Lane (874), Ross-on-Wye, Herefordshire HR9 5NR (tel 01989-767833). Europe's largest providers of adventure holidays for children have offered outstanding training and work opportunitities for seasonal staff for over 40 years.
NURSES (RGN, EGN. or equivalent) to work at residential children's activity holiday centres throughout the UK. Vacancies can be for periods of anything from one week to ten months. Free B & L supplied plus £75 per week. Suitably qualified overseas applicants who are eligible to work in the UK welcome. Full details and an application form can be obtained from the Personnel Department at the above address.

Outdoor

HARVESTING OPPORTUNITY PERMIT SCHEME (GB): YFC Centre, NAC, Stoneleigh Park, Kenilworth, Warwickshire CV8 2LG (tel 01203-696589; fax 01203-696559).

HOPS(GB) has a limited number of work permits available for full time students born and studying in Central and Eastern Europe on HOPS (GB) registered farms to pick fruit/vegetables/flowers/hops between May and November for a minimum of 10 weeks. Most jobs start between 1 May and 12 June. HOPS (GB) has a limited number of work permits available. For 2000, students to be born in the years 1975 to 1979 inclusive, not in their graduation year should apply. Agricultural students preferred.

Self-catering accommodation is provided on the farm. Wages according to the British Agricultural Wages Board. HOPS (GB) charges an administration fee (including insurance).

Information/application forms available from the above address between August and October in the year before the planned visit. Note applicants should be applying in 1999 for the 2000 summer season.

Sport

GREAT ADVENTURES: Grafham Water Centre, Perry, Huntingdon, Cambridgeshire PE18 0BX (tel 01480-810521; fax 01480-812739). Runs special interest and activity holidays and courses with centres in Cambridgeshire, Derbyshire and Gloucestershire.
ACTIVITY INSTRUCTORS (20) wanted for canoeing, windsurfing, sailing, archery, climbing and mountain biking. Must have N.G.B. qualifications. £170 per week plus food and accommodation. To work 40 hours per week from May to July; min. period of work 2 months. Positions also available for 10 months. Overseas applicants welcome; note interview is required. Apply from January to Mr Philip Robson at the above address.

HF HOLIDAYS LIMITED: Redhills, Penrith, Cumbria CA11 0DT (tel 0181-905 9556). A non-profitmaking organisation which owns 20 Country House Hotels based in the National Parks. An excellent opportunity to demonstrate leadership skills while having fun.
WALKING LEADERS are required by Britain's leading walking holiday company that caters for all types of walkers. Applicants may choose how often and when they want to lead the walking holidays (from 2-30 weeks per year). Accommodation, travel expenses and approx. £15 per week equipment allowance will be provided. Students can be employed for the Easter or Summer periods at £60 per week.

Candidates should be experienced walkers with leadership potential, fully competent in the use of map and compass, considerate and tactful. Assessment courses are held during the winter (difficult for applicants living abroad) so early application is essential. For an information pack contact the Walking Department at the above address.

OUTWARD BOUND TRUST: Watermillock, Nr. Penrith, Cumbria CA11 0JL (tel 0990-134227; fax 017684-86983; e-mail enquiries@outwardbound-uk.org; web page outwardbound-uk.org). A registered charity (no. 313645) with three residential centres in Wales, the Lake District and Scotland.
TUTORS required to encourage people of all ages and backgrounds to examine themselves and to take responsibility for their own development. Wages on application. Applicants must have the following qualifications: Summer MTLB Award, SPA, BCU 3 Star, RYA Level II and a valid First Aid Certificate. Staff are required all year round. Please write, enclosing current c.v., to the Divisional Managing Director (Personal Development) at the

above address. The Outward Bound Trust also provides outdoor skills and qualification courses.

PGL TRAVEL: Alton Court, Penyard Lane (874), Ross-on-Wye, Herefordshire HR9 5NR (tel 01989-767833). Over 3,000 staff needed to assist in the running of children's activity centres throughout the UK. Europe's largest provider of adventure holidays for children has offered outstanding training and work opportunities to seasonal staff for over 40 years.

QUALIFIED INSTRUCTORS required to teach canoeing, sailing, windsurfing, pony trekking, hill walking, fencing, archery, judo, rifle-shooting, fishing, motorsports, arts and crafts, drama, English language and many other activities. Pocket money £36-70 per week with full B & L provided. Min. age 18. Vacancies available for short or long periods between February and October. Overseas applicants eligible to work in the UK welcome. Requests for application forms to the Personnel Department at the above address.

Language Schools

ANGLO EUROPEAN STUDY TOURS LTD.: 8 Celbridge Mews, London W2 6EU (tel 0171-229 4435; fax 0171-792 8717). Runs summer courses for 10-18 year olds all over the UK, offering general English plus sports, entertainments and excursions.

TEACHERS OF ENGLISH AS A FOREIGN LANGUAGE (200 +) to teach overseas students for 19 hours a week, Monday to Friday, at centres all over the UK. Wages £165-£200 per week. Residential and non-residential posts available. To work July-August.

No age limits but applicants need a TEFL qualification (RSA or Trinity) and a degree. Applications to Carolyn Morris, Director of Studies, at the above address.

ARDMORE ADVENTURE LTD: Berkshire College, Burchetts Green, Maidenhead, Berkshire SL6 6QR (tel 01628-826699; fax 01628-829977; e-mail mailbox@ardmore.org.uk).

ENGLISH LANGUAGE TEACHERS required to teach 3-6 hours per day Monday to Friday; 15 children per class. Teachers required to administer, test and prepare lessons for and teach pupils participating in the English language course. Applications considered from qualified TEFL teachers and those who have suitable experience or related English or teaching qualifications. For further details contact Ardmore Adventure at the above address.

EF INTERNATIONAL LANGUAGE SCHOOLS: EF International School of English, 74 Roupell Street, London SE1 8SS (tel 0171-401-8399; fax 0171-401-3717). A multi-national group of 9 companies and non-profit organisations. Offices in 34 countries offer educational services to 200,000 participants per year.

TEMPORARY ACTIVITIES AND ADMINISTRATION ASSISTANTS required from June-August. To help organise trips and events, or work in the accommodation department. Must be responsible, enthusiastic and capable of ensuring the overseas students at the schools enjoy their time fully. Posts are available in London, Brighton, Hastings, Cambridge and London. Applications to the School Manager at the above address.

ENGLISH LANGUAGE AND CULTURAL ORGANISATION: Lowlands, Chorleywood Road, Rickmansworth, Herts WD3 4ES (tel 01923-776731; fax 01923-774678; e-mail efl@elco.co.uk). Three centres based in Rickmansworth in Hertfordshire, Newland Park in Buckinghamshire, and Ardingly College in Sussex.
EFL TEACHERS (20-30). To work from July 4-August 23; min. period of work three weeks. Must have either a degree, PGCE, RSA or Trinity qualifications. Salary £200-£300 per week. Accommodation is provided free of charge. Applicants should normally be available for an interview.
   Contact Tony Thompson at the above address from February 1999.

EURO ACADEMY LTD.: 77a George Street, Croydon CR0 1LD (tel 0181-681 2905/6; e-mail EUROACADEMY@btinternet.com; fax 0181-681 8850).
EFL TEACHERS for work in July and August in schools mainly in the south of England but also in the Midlands. The job involves both teaching and running activities, with groups of up to 15 students. Wages from £185 to £250 per week; no accommodation available. Applicants must be hold at least P. GCE or Cert TEFL qualifications.
   Applications to the above address.

INTERNATIONAL HOUSE HASTINGS: ILC Ltd., White Rock, Hastings, East Sussex TN34 1JY (tel 01424-720100; fax 01424-720323; e-mail ilc@compuserve.com; Web site http//www.ilcgroup.com).
TEACHERS OF ENGLISH AS A FOREIGN LANGUAGE (60) wanted for July and August. Wage £165-£280 per week. 26 hours teaching a week. CELTA (formerly CTEFLA) certificates required.
SOCIAL ACTIVITY ORGANISERS (200 nationwide) required during July and August. Wage: basic £100-£140 per week. Work includes running a full activity programme: discos, excursions, sports, local visits etc. Applicants should have common sense, flexibility, and a good sense of fun.

INTERNATIONAL LANGUAGE CENTRES (UK) Ltd: White Rock, Hastings TN34 1JY (tel 01424-720100; fax 01424-720323; e-mail ilc@compuserve.com; Web site http//www.ilcgroup.com). Runs language schools at up to 40 locations throughout Great Britain.
TEACHERS OF ENGLISH as a foreign language (500) wanted for July and August to teach adults and assist with a programme of social activities and excursions. Many residential posts available. Salary £150-£200 per week. Cambridge CELTA (formerly CTEFLA) certificate required. Applications from January to Personnel Department at the above address.
SPORTS AND SOCIAL ACTIVITIES ORGANISERS (200 nationwide) required during July and August. Wage: basic £100-£140 per week. Undergraduates and graduates min. age 20. Qualifications in sports coaching, first aid, arts and crafts etc. an advantage. Accommodation available in many locations. Work includes running a full activity programme: discos, excursions, sports, local visits etc. Applicants should have common sense, flexibility and a good sense of fun. Overseas applicants with a sufficient knowledge of English considered.

INTER-NATIONAL QUEST CENTRES: 9 Stradbroke Road, Southwold, Suffolk IP18 6LL (tel 01502-722648; fax 01502-722645). Work available in

language centres in Canterbury, Cardiff, Edinburgh, London, Oxford, Reading, Southampton, Loughborough and Worcester. The agency has been established for 21 years, and only offers work if vacancies actually exist.
EFL TEACHERS (200). £9 per hour for EFL certificate holders, £8.50 otherwise. 17 hours per week. No accommodation provided. Undergraduates studying modern languages, teachers, B.Ed. or PGCE, desirable; EFL an advantage but not essential.
ACTIVITY LEADERS (70). £140 per week. Full board provided. Min. age 19. Sport or drama experience an advantage.

Staff required from mid June to July and August but only those taken on in July kept on for August; min. period of employment 2 weeks. Applicants must have a standard of English as high as a native speaker. Interviews are carried out in Cardiff, Edinburgh, London and Southampton. Successful candidates must attend an induction session for which they are paid. Teachers attend a training session, and activity leaders attend an introduction session by the Directors.

Applications from April to Anna Maria McCarthy, Director of Studies, at the above address.

NORD ANGLIA INTERNATIONAL:10 Eden Place, Cheadle, Cheshire SK8 1AT (tel 0161-491 8415; fax 0161-491 4410).
ENGLISH TEACHERS (300 +). £64-£246 a week; to teach and lead activities. Should be graduates, with TEFL qualification and some experience.
ACTIVITY MONITORS (30 +) to lead activities. £80-£150 per week.
COURSE DIRECTORS (20 +). £230-£350 per week. Graduates, experience and Dip. TEFLA.
ACTIVITY CO-ORDINATORS (20 +) to lead activity monitors. £180-£280 a week. Need some similar experience.

Applications to Anna Fox, Recruitment Manager, at the above address.

OISE YOUTH LANGUAGE SCHOOLS: OISE House, Binsey Lane, Oxford OX2 0EY (tel 01865-792799; fax 01865-792706). Work available throughout the Midlands, South and West of England.
TEACHERS to teach English as a foreign language to small groups of foreign students. Must be qualified EFL teachers with experience.
ACADEMIC DIRECTORS. Qualified EFL teachers with organisational ability.
LEISURE DIRECTORS to run a pre-planned leisure programme and teach half a timetable.

Period of work Easter and July/August. Applicants must be graduates amd native English speakers. Some residential courses available. Details from the Recruitment Administrator, OISE.

PGL TRAVEL: Alton Court, Penyard Lane (874), Ross-on-Wye, Herefordshire HR9 5NR (tel 01989-767833). Europe's largest provider of adventure holidays for children has offered outstanding training and work opportunities to seasonal staff for over 40 years.
EFL TEACHERS required during July and August to work at children's activity holiday centres throughout the UK. Free B & L is supplied plus a wage of £100 per week. Full details and application forms from the Personnel Department at the above address.

PRIMARY HOUSE GROUP: 8A Summerley Street, London SW18 4ET (tel/fax 0181-947 6397; email abhod43@aol.com). The Group is an association of administrators, with a central office in London, who organise and co-ordinate EFL teacher training course worldwide.

STUDENTS required to build Primary House's network of organisers in the UK and internationally. Work is available both in the summer and throughout the academic year. For more information contact the Group Registrar, at the above address.

YES EDUCATION CENTRE: 12 Eversfield Road, Eastbourne, East Sussex BN21 2AS (tel 01323-644830; fax 01323-726260; e-mail engish@yes.co.uk). EFL TEACHERS. Wages £150-£350 per week for adult and junior schools in Eastbourne, and Junior schools in Abingdon, Brighton, Hastings, Oxford, Seaford and Maidenhead.

Staff required in July and August. No accommodation provided. Relevant teaching qualifications and previous experience required. Applications to Ms Hilary Mehew, Vice Principal and Director of Studies for Eastbourne, and Mrs Brigid Simcox, Course Director External Centres, for the other towns.

Vacation Traineeships

Accountancy, Banking and Insurance

BARCLAYS BANK PLC: Campus Recruiting, 54 Lombard Street, London EC3P 3AH.

Barclays operates in over 70 countries, and its global reach extends to all the worlds major financial centres. The company invests millions of pounds in training and IT.

Barclays offers work placement opportunities to undergraduates who are in their penultimate year and considering a career in business management with Barclays. Application forms may be obtained from college careers services or from the above address. Overseas applicants eligible to work in the UK will be considered if they speak and write English fluently and are studying for an honours degree at a university or business school. The closing date for applications will be notified to University Careers Services in the Autumn Term.

ERNST & YOUNG: Graduate Recruitment, Becket House, 1 Lambeth Palace Road, London SE1 7EU (freephone 0800-289208; web site www.ernsty.co.uk).

Ernst & Young is one of the world's largest professional services firms. They serve clients from 674 offices in over 30 countries. From most of their 24 offices in the UK the firm offers students in their penultimate year at university the opportunity to work for a period of up to six weeks. The scheme consists of a one week induction course followed by around five weeks practical work experience in a number of their departments. the scheme provides and excellent insight into a career with Ernst and Young.

Applicants should have a minimum of 22 UCAS points and possess the determination to build a successful business career. For further information and an application form contact your careers service or ring the above freephone number.

KPMG: 8 Salisbury Square, Blackfriars, London EC4Y 8BB (tel freephone 0500-664655; e-mail www.kpmg.co.uk).
KPMG runs vacation programmes offering an insight into the workings of a leading business advisory firm; it shows both the opportunities available to graduates and how a major City firm operates. KPMG offers on a national basis vacation experience to students of any degree discipline in their penultimate year at university. The length of the programmes vary and they may include workshadowing partners, managers and both qualified and trainee business advisors.

KPMG also offer a *Skills for Life* programme for those in their first year of study which involves a two day residential course aiming to provide a series of both personal and professional skills to aid career development; these are run at a variety of universities from late September.

For further details contact the Graduate Recruitment department at the above address.

MIDLAND BANK PLC: St Magnus House, 3 Lower Thames Street, London EC3R 6HA.
Midland Bank plc runs a summer executive training scheme offering 15-20 second-year undergraduates with an interest in the financial sector eight weeks working within the retail banking network. Placements are based on senior clerical positions and include a project relevant to the particular requirements of the branch. A competitive salary will be paid for a period from July to September. Traineeships are located across the country within the branch network. Accommodation is not provided. Work experience is only offered to a certain number of universities each year which will be determined by the Graduate Recruitment Manager. The selected universities may rotate every other year. For further information contact the Graduate Recruitment Manager at the above address.

PRICEWATERHOUSE COOPERS: Southwark Towers (L18), 32 London Bridge Street, London SE1 9SY (tel 0808-100 1500; fax 0171-939 3030).
Pricewaterhouse Coopers is the world's largest professional services organisation, providing a full range of business advisory services including auditing, business advisory, tax and management consultancy services.

The firm has a large number of vacation placements and shorter courses available throughout the country mainly during July and August for undergraduates who have already developed an interest in a career with a leading firm.

Students must be in the penultimate year of their degree with a proven track record of academic achievement and a clear indication of strong personal skills.

Applications should be made before Easter to the National Recruitment Department at the above address.

Business and Management
FIRST LEISURE PLC: Empress Buildings, 97 Church Street, Blackpool, Lancashire (tel 01253-293002).

First Leisure Corporation Plc, the owners of Blackpool Tower and Winter Gardens, is the largest privately owned leisure, entertainments and social facilities company in the country. It specialises in the provision of leisure, social and recreational amenities in a number of Britain's leading resort towns.

The company offers a wide range of vacation placements which are ideally suited to students seeking to explore a possible career in the leisure and recreation management industry. Candidates do not require a specific degree background but should be bright, motivated, and show an interest in the workings of the leisure industry. Positions range from General Assistant to Senior Supervisor. Job offers will depend on the candidate's experience and qualifications. Most work, however, is in bars, catering, amusements and retail trading.

A large number of seasonal positions is available throughout all sections of the company; the normal period of employment is from April to September (although there is some business in October and November). Wages are reviewed annually and are commensurate with experience, and position. Positions are open to all students currently at further education establishments, but as accommodation cannot be provided local candidates are preferred.

Work locations are at the following sites: The North, Central and South Piers; the Savoy and Clifton Hotels and the Tower and Wintergardens in Blackpool; Llandudno Pier, Llandudno; the South Parade Pier in Southsea; the Eastbourne Pier in Eastbourne and the Trecco Caravan Park at Trecco Bay, Wales. Applications to the General Managers of the above businesses (addresses available from the Personnel and Training Manager at the above address, or preferably, from the Yellow Pages).

UNILEVER UK: PO Box 1538, Slough PDO, SL1 1YT (tel 01541-543550; e-mail recruit.unileveruk@unilever.com; web site www.uniq.unilever.com).
Unilever is a global business employing over 250,000 people with a turnover of over £30 billion. It is a fast moving consumer goods organisation which specialises in foods and home and personal care products.

The Unilever Summer Programme offers penultimate year students 8-10 weeks of work experience in a UK business during the summer vacation. Working with managers, participants will be involved in real projects, tackling issues of genuine importance to the organisation and gaining a clear appreciation of the challenges and opportunities which exist within a global organisation.

These placements are open to students from all disciplines for vacancies in the following areas: Brand and Customer Management (marketing and sales), Information Technology, Commercial Management (accountancy, logistics and finance), and Personnel and Employee Relations. Applicants for Manufacturing and Supply Chain (manufacturing and engineering) and Product Development should have a relevant degree.

Further details and application forms will be available from the Careers Advisory Service or by calling 0541-543550 from mid November 1998. Closing date is February 26th.

The Law

EVERSHEDS: Senator House, 85 Queen Victoria Street, London EC4V 4JL (tel 0171-919 4500; fax 0171-919 4919; e-mail gradrec@eversheds.co.uk).

A large commercial law firm with branches in London, Birmingham, Cardiff, Copenhagen, Derby, Ipswich, Jersey, Leeds, Norwich, Nottingham, Manchester, Monaco, Moscow, Newcastle, Paris and Teeside.

Offers 100 two week summer placements shadowing solicitors at offices across the UK. Open to law penultimate/non-law final year undergraduates or graduates only. Candidates should have obtained or be expecting at least a 2.1 degree in any subject. Salary varies according to region.

Apply on EAF to the National Graduate Recruitment Officer by the end of February 1999 at the above address.

Public Sector

THE ARMY: Freepost, CV37 9GR (tel 0345-300 111).

Although the Army does not offer vacation training as such, it does run the Short Service Limited Commission (SSLC) or Gap Year Scheme, which is open to students who wish to take a year out after leaving school and before taking up a firm place at University. It is aimed at students of high academic ability who demonstrate a responsible and mature attitude and show leadership potential.

Successful candidates attend a 3 week course at Sandhurst and are commissioned into their chosen Corps or Regiments as 2nd Lieutenants, on a special rate of pay of £11,187. They serve for a minimum of four months and a maximum of 18 months. There is no subsequent obligation to serve in the Army.

Applicants must undergo a rigorous selection procedure, which begins with an advisory interview with a Schools Liaison Officer. This can be arranged through the Schools Careers' Staff or by writing to the above address. Applicants must have been resident in the UK for five years and must be a British or Commonwealth citizen.

THE CIVIL SERVICE: More than 60 departments and over 100 executive agencies, employing around 480,000 people make the Civil Service on of the largest employers in the UK.

A number of Government Departments and Agencies will offer vacation opportunities for students in 1999; details are published in a booklet - *Vacation Employment for Students 1999* available from your Careers Service, or Civil Service Careers (tel: 0117-982 1171; note that this number is for despatch of copies only; please do not call it for further information on vacation work).

Students are advised to apply early as most opportunities have deadlines for applications early in 1999. Further information on careers in the Civil Service is available from Careers Services and also via the internet: http://www.cabinet-office.gov.uk/fsesd

LOCAL GOVERNMENT STUDENT SPONSORSHIP (LGSS): Local Government Opportunities (LGO), 78-86, Turnmill Street, London, EC1M 5QU (tel 0171-296 6600; fax 0171-296 6666). LGO is a promotional and careers information service for local authorities. They operate the national careers enquiry service, the LGSS, and the vacancy information service on the internet called *Jobsearch*. These services are designed to provide job and information seekers with details on potential opportunities in local government. They do not operate a recruitment service, and are provided by the Local Government Management Board.

The Local Government Student Sponsorship Scheme offers structured paid work experience placements to higher education students who complete their studies in the summer of 1999. These are specifically designed to introduce individuals to the management of a local authority while they undertake a worthwhile project for at least five weeks during the summer.

Applications are invited from committed students who are able to demonstrate a genuine interest in working in local government. Although no specific degree discipline is required for many of the opportunities on offer, the competition for places is very fierce. To ensure success, candidates will have to demonstrate a good understanding of the challenges facing local authorities.

Students will receive a minimum training allowance of £120 per week and are given the opportunity to compete for further generous cash prizes when they complete and submit a satisfactory management report. The application period is November 1998-April 1999. For an application form and further details, please telephone the coordinator Carol Lee on 0171-296 6508 or write to him at the above address.

POST OFFICE: The Assessment Consultancy, Coton House, Rugby, Warwickshire CV23 0AA.

The Post Office Finance Vacation Scheme offers 10 traineeships for 6 weeks over the summer. It gives penultimate-year undergraduates, who are hoping to pursue a career in Accountancy, an opportunity to gain career-related work experience and training, whilst completing a 'real-life' project.

Vacancies occur nationwide, and in all of the Post Office businesses. Students studying any degree subject will be considered, although good A level grades (24 UCAS points) or equivalent qualifications are asked for. Overseas applicants eligible to work in the UK will be considered. The salary is approximately £200 per week, plus London weighting if applicable.

Applications for the Finance Vacation Scheme should be made by the start of February on a standard application form to the above address, quoting the reference VACWORK both on your application form and on the envelope.

Applications for any other vacation work in The Post Office should be made to the Personnel Manager at local Royal Mail or Post Office Counters offices.

Science, Construction and Engineering

BRITISH STEEL DISTRIBUTION: PO Box 4, Bridgenorth Road, Wimbourne, Wolverhampton WV5 8AT (tel 01902-891186; fax 01902-891169).

Offers around 12 placements to Engineering and Business Studies Graduates. Work is available in the Easter, Summer and Winter vacations. Ideally, students should work 3 months over the summer. Annual rate £9,000 pro rata appropriate to period of work.

Applications should be made to the Personnel Officer.

CHRISTIANI & NIELSEN LTD: Orion House, Tachbrook Park, Leamington Spa, Warwickshire CV34 6RQ (tel 01926-886666; fax 01926-886656).
Christiani & Nielsen Ltd, a firm of building and civil engineering contractors, offers training placements to students at both its sites and regional offices. As the positions are not organised on a formal basis, the number, length and timing of the placements varies considerably from year to year. The posts are open to students who are studying Civil Engineering at university or a college of further education; they are generally in the south, the midlands or Wales. Wages are fixed according to the student's year of study.
Applications should be made on an ad hoc basis to Mr D. Price, Personnel Manager, to arrive between May and June.

GEC GRADUATE RESOURCING: West Hanningfield Road, Great Baddow, Chelmsford, Essex CM2 8HN.
Employing over 125,000 people worldwide and with a turnover exceeding £11 billion the General Electric Company plc is a world force in electronics and engineering. GEC technologies span a wide range of electrical, electronic, mechanical and communication engineering activities in commercial, consumer and defence markets. These include: space and satellite telecommunications, medical imaging equipment, domestic appliances, integrated circuits, navigation and security. GEC companies provide the systems and equipment for these products and services to customers across the world.
Vacation training opportunities exist within at the major divisions including GEC-Marconi, GPT and the Industrial Group. The majority of places are in engineering, although there are a small number of commercial placements. Those interested can find out further information from their Careers advisor or any of the professional engineering institutions. Applicants can write to the above address for an information pack on current opportunities within the group.

GKN PLC: PO Box 55, Redditch, Worcestershire B98 0TL (tel 01327-588893; fax 01527-533467; e-mail grad-rec@gknghq.co.uk).
Every year GKN offers 20 engineering experience placements to penultimate year degree students of Mechanical, Aeronautical, Manafacturing or Materials Engineering. Salary is £200 per week
Placements last for 12 weeks over the summer and take place all over the UK. Accommodation is not provided, but trainees can be given help in finding somewhere suitable.
Overseas applicants are considered. Applications by 31st December 1998 to Mrs S. Grymer.

IBM (UK) LTD: PO Box 41, North Harbour, Portsmouth, Hampshire, PO6 3AU.
IBM runs a summer programme which has positions around the country, but predominately in Hursley (near Winchester), Warwick, Basingstoke and South Bank. Each new recruit receives training and induction and can go on to work in all areas of the business, including professional services, consultancy, marketing, administration and software and hardware development. These placements last between 2 and 3 months and the salary depends on status and experience. IBM welcomes applications from students of all degree disciplines who are in the penultimate year of their course, and by the end of their

placement students are in an excellent position to be considered for IBM's graduate programme. Please apply by contacting the Student Employment Officer at the above address. Overseas applicants should apply to IBM's head office in their own country, making it clear that they wish to be considered for vacancies in the UK; this is because they will be better able to judge your qualifications. Any suitable applicants will then be forwarded to the UK.

IMI PLC: PO Box 216, Witton, Birmingham B6 7BA (tel 0121-356 4848; fax 0121-356 2877).
IMI normally offer four traineeship positions a year involving engineering project work such as the design and building of test rigs, solving of technical problems and creation of technical manuals at their premises in the West Midlands, Yorkshire, Oxfordshire and in Bristol. These positions last for between 7 and 12 weeks during the summer vacation. The wage paid depends on how many years the applicant has been at university, but should be in the region of £750 per month; accommodation will be provided for the first 14 nights by which time trainees are expected to have arranged their own accommodation.
Applicants must be studying mechanical, manufacturing or electrical engineering at university. Applicants from abroad will be considered; German speakers are especially welcome.
Applications should be sent to Sarah Jackson, Manager, IMI Graduate Trainees and Students, at the above address.

NATIONAL INSTITUTE OF AGRICULTURAL BOTANY: Huntingdon Road, Cambridge CB3 0LE (tel 01223-342234; fax 01223-342206; e-mail N.NIABPSNL@PVRO.MAFF.AC.UK).
Vacation work involving working in fields, laboratories, etc. is offered to about 30-50 applicants a year. A small number of placements are also offered, usually for the summer vacation or for 6 or 12 months, at regional trial centres and the head office. £130 per week. Accommodation not provided although lists of accommodation are available. Applications from April/May for summer work or November/December for longer placements, to the Personnel Assistant at the above address.

ROLLS-ROYCE PLC: P.O. Box 31, Derby, DE24 8BJ (tel 01332-244369; fax 01332-513929).
Rolls-Royce designs and manufactures engines that power civil and military aircraft and supplies power systems providing energy to communities worldwide. Their engines are also found in navy vessels and Britain's nuclear submarines.
Rolls-Royce Plc currently offer the following forms of traineeships:
VACATION TRAINEES for attachments in engineering, commercial, manufacturing, procurement, marketing, personnel and logistics. Ten weeks are spent in a department which is of relevance to the course the applicant is studying. Training takes place over the summer vacation which precedes the final academic year. Students complete an individual project or contribute towards a major piece of work within the department.
INDUSTRIAL TRAINEES for placements usually during the final training period of a sandwich course. The number of attachments will be influenced by business requirements. Twelve month placements in finance usually include

three attachments within the company. Attachments in manufacturing or research may last 6 or 12 months and trainees may be required to undertake one major project in one department.

Help is given in finding accommodation and placements are in Derby, Bristol, Ansty, the North East, or Scotland. Apply by the end of November to the Company Recruitment Officer at the above address quoting CRO/0065.

London and Home Counties

Berkshire
Buckinghamshire
Hertfordshire

London
Surrey

London: if you want to move to London to work during the summer season think first about where you are going to live. While rented accommodation is not difficult to find the price is likely to be high and staying for only a short period may prove difficult. However, there are several youth hostels, and you may be able to find a cheap deal among the 'Accommodation to Rent' columns of the city's many newspapers and magazines. In addition to numerous local papers there are several publications which are not associated with any particular area. The main ones to look out for are: *TNT* and *Southern Cross* (both free), the *Evening Standard* (daily) *Time Out* and *Loot.* These publications also carry job advertisements. Vacancies arise most commonly in retail, secretarial, hotel, restaurant and domestic work. The chance of finding a job will be increased if you are flexible as to where you can work, so consult the local paper in several different districts.

Various Jobcentres in London have special Temporary Sections. The Jobcentre at 1-3 Denmark Street, London WC1 (tel 0171-853 3253) specialises in temporary, casual and some full-time vacancies. The Hammersmith Jobcentre (Glen House, 22 Glenthorne Road, W6 0PP; tel 0181-210 8100; fax 0181-210 8181) offers a wide range of temporary work, including retail, administrative and construction jobs. Their vacancies are not just for Hammersmith, but also for Ealing, Kensington and Chelsea. They also keep lists of vacancies with the local Borough Council—these tend to be clerical and administrative posts. In addition, they have a special Euroadviser, to provide advice for people going to work in Europe, and for European Citizens coming to work in the UK.

There are also hundreds of private employment agencies, especially along Oxford Street. The South of the River Agency (128c Northcote Road, SW11; tel 0171-228 5086) recruits staff for any jobs private householders might require, from babysitting to barbecue staff. Drake International (branches at

5 Regent Street SW1, tel 0171-437 6900; 44 South Molton Street; 62-63 Fenchurch Street; 43 Maiden Lane) covers a range of fields, including secretarial, industrial, driving and catering, for both permanent and temporary positions. Many such agencies advertise in *TNT* magazine.

In terms of vacation traineeships, prospects are particularly good for anyone interested in accountancy or law. In addition, many big companies have their head offices in London, so a variety of other opportunities are also available.

Home Counties: in the comparatively prosperous Home Counties job prospects can be fairly good over the summer. In particular, there is a demand for staff among marquee erectors and events organisers. The Jobcentre in Reading has access to jobs at the Ascot and Windsor races and other events both in the city and elsewhere in the region. Epsom, Newbury and Sandown are the other main racecourses in the area; it is worth contacting these at any time of year.

Reading is a major source of longer term summer employment in the Home Counties. Finding rented accommodation here is surprisingly easy too. Office, domestic, retail and packing work tends to be the most common, though it's worth approaching the local authority, which runs various summer programmes. Vacancies tend to be most numerous in the earliest months of the year. Try looking in the *Reading Evening Post* (daily), the *Reading Chronicle* (weekly) and the *Newbury Weekly News*.

Windsor is a busy tourist town all year round, but especially over the summer. Temporary work may be available at the Leisure Pool as well as at the local hotels and river boat companies. McDonalds are among the largest employers of temporary staff. The Jobcentre in Maidenhead (tel 01628-844900) has a wide range of vacancies, both full-time and part-time, permanent and temporary, and in a variety of occupations. The weekly *Maidenhead Advertiser* has jobs pages.

In Luton, north of London, there is a high demand for factory workers, who may need forklifting qualifications. Jobs at the airport are available, but may require a driving licence. Various other types of work are also available, including manual labour, caring, and catering, for an average wage of around £3.50.

Business and Industry

ADVENTURE BALLOONS: Winchfield Park, London Road, Hartley Wintney, Hants RG27 8HY.
OFFICE STAFF (1/2) to work from 8.30am-5.30pm Monday-Friday. Wage £200 per week; no accommodation available. Period of work from March to October. Applicants need computer experience and a good telephone manner.

Applications to the Manager at the above address.

AGW TRADES: 288 Chase Road, Southgate, London N14 6HF (tel 0181-882 8074; fax 0181-886 5303).
SHOPFITTERS. Minimum wage £9.50 per hour. Previous experience necessary.
LABOURERS. Minimum wage £4.50 per hour. Minimum age 18. Site experience required.

TRADE MATES. Minimum wage £5.00 per hour. Minimum age 18. Site experience necessary.
ELECTRICIANS. Minimum wage £9.00 per hour. JIB approved.
PLUMBERS. Minimum wage £9.00 per hour. Previous experience required.
  Hours vary for all positions. Staff required all year round to work in the London area; minimum period of work 1 day. Accommodation available sometimes. Overseas applicants welcome — especially Australians, Kiwis and South Africans. Applications can be made by phone at any time.

ANGEL INTERNATIONAL RECRUITMENT PLC: HQ 4 Union Street, London Bridge, London SE1 1SZ (tel 0171-940 2000; fax 0171-940 2018). Angel was founded in 1965 and adheres strictly to the codes of practice laid down by its professional bodies. Open 7am-6pm Monday to Friday with branch offices in London, Essex, Hampshire, Kent and Surrey. Work may be offered in catering environments, throughout the year for chefs, cooks, waiting and general catering and kitchen assistants. Pay may vary between £3.60 and £10.50 per hour dependent on experience. Work may also be offered to experienced office staff with 50wpm typing; to warehouse and factory staff; to experienced computer personnel and to experienced or qualified nurses and carers.
Applicants from abroad should note that placements can only be made after arrival in the UK; Angel cannot enter into correspondence prior to arrival in the UK. Work can usually be offered within 2-3 days of arrival. Angel cannot assist with accommodation. Apply to the office in person or by phone on arrival in London.

CATCH 22: 199 Victoria Street, London SW1E 5NE (tel 0171-821 1133). Employment agency covering Central London.
GENERAL INDUSTRIAL STAFF for temporary jobs such as furniture moving, driving, warehouse and message-running. Flexible hours but usually 8 hours a day and preferably 5 days a week. Possibility of overtime.
  No B & L available. Min. age 18. Must be adaptable to different environments and have a good level of English. Work available all year round. Min. period of work 3 months. Apply by phone to the above number.

HARRODS LTD: Knightsbridge, London SW1X 7XL (tel 0171-730 1234, ext 2211).
SALES STAFF, CLERICAL STAFF, SELLING SUPPORT STAFF to cover the July Sale, from October to December and from December to January to cover the Christmas and January Sale. Applicants must be a minimum of sixteen years old, be eligible to work in the UK, and based within the London region. Fluent spoken English is essential. Interested applicants should visit the Harrods Recruitment Centre, 11 Brompton Place, SW1X. Opening hours Monday-Friday from 9.30am-1.30pm, Monday 1.30-3.30pm, Wednesday 1.30-6.30pm and Thursday 1.30-5.30pm.

INSIDE COMMUNICATIONS LTD: 9 White Lion Street, London N1 9XJ (0171-837 8727; fax 0171-837 7124). An exhibitions and publishing company; part of the Mirror group. The London office employs over 60 staff in sales, editorial, administration and publishing.
TELEPHONE TICKET HOTLINE STAFF (6-8) to deal with ticket sales for the National Self Build Home Show at Alexandra Palace in London. The work involves taking ticket orders, filling in payment details, giving details of

seminar programmes and sending out tickets. Wages £5 per hour. To work 9.00am-5.30pm Monday to Friday. No accommodation is available. Min. period of work 1 month between August 1st and September 17th.

Must have a good telephone manner and good handwriting. Interview to be conducted by telephone. Applications in May to Margaret Stapley.

MAIN EVENTS: Unit 5, Island Farm Avenue, West Molesey Trading Estate, West Molesey, Surrey KT8 0UZ (tel 0181-941 2411; fax 0181-941 4710).
STAFF (up to 10) required to set up and man inflatable equipment, including bouncy castles, at events, activity days etc. £5 per hour. Work is on an ad hoc basis; hours and dates cannot be guaranteed but depend upon company's contracts at a particular time. Min. age 21. Must be able to deal with people and have a sense of fun. First-aid qualification an advantage. No accommodation available; applicants should ideally live locally. Overseas applicants with a good level of English welcome. If possible applicants should be able to attend an interview. Applications at any time to Mr James Feary, Main Events.

RESEARCH EUROPE LTD: Suite C, 4 Warple Way, Tech West House, Acton, London W31 0UE (tel 0181-743 4242; fax 0181-743 3298). Established in 1994, the company employs 200-250 people and continues to expand annually. Its parent company is based in Princeton in the USA.
FREELANCE TELEPHONE INTERVIEWERS (5-10 to conduct telephone interviews in another language (Spanish, Italian, German, French, English). Wages £5/6 per hour. To work 8am-4pm, 9am-5pm, 4-8pm or 5-9pm. No accommodation is available. Min. period of work 1 month. No contracts are offered as work is on a project to project basis.

Applicants must have a good phone manner and excellent communication skills. They must also be professional, intelligent, polite and flexible. Min. age 18.

Overseas applicants with a good understanding of spoken and written English are considered. Interview necessary. Applications to Dennis Dwyer.

VAUXHALL AFTERSALES: Griffin House, Osborne Road, Luton LU1 3YT (tel 01582-426311; fax 01582-426446).
WAREHOUSE OPERATIVES (90); duties include manual function shift work. Wages were £5.89 per hour in 1998, plus shift premium if applicable. To work 38 hours a week. Staff needed from July for 6-10 weeks. Work may also be available at Christmas. No accommodation is available. Applicants must be over 18.
Applications to the Personnel Dept. TW4 from October onwards.

WETHERBY STUDIOS: 23 Wetherby Mansions, Earls Court Square, London SW5 9BH (tel 0171-373 1107).
MALE PHOTOGRAPHIC MODELS. Wages £75-£100 cash for 3-hour sessions. Dozens needed throughout the year. No accommodation available. Should be aged 18-40 years, but physique is more important than age. While more than half the models used are slim, it can be difficult to find men who have worked on their chest and arm definition, which is required if picture sessions promoting leisure wear are planned. Moustaches and beards permissible. No modelling experience necessary. Applicants must supply snapshots to show how they photograph facially and physically. Follow-ups are frequent, depending on the photographers' reactions to the first test shots.

Overseas applicants welcome, but must speak fluent English. Applications to Mr Mike Arlen, Director, Wetherby Studios.

WILLIAM HILL ORGANIZATION LTD: 1-5 Morris Place, Finsbury Park, London N4 3JG (tel 0171-705 5338). One of the largest betting organisations in the country with over 1500 branches; summer opportunities may lead to a career.
CASHIERS to work various flexible hours in betting shops during the summer (days and evenings), including Saturdays. Positions in London only. Min. age 18. Training will be given. Period of work 10-16 weeks between April and August. Applications between January to March to the Recruitment Office, William Hill Organization.

Children

ACTION HOLIDAYS LTD: Robinwood, Jumps Road, Todmorden, Lancashire OL14 8HJ (tel 01706-814554). Runs multi-activity holiday centres in Surrey and Berkshire for children aged 5-15 years.
STAFF required to look after children in all departments of the holiday camp: instructors, supervisory and general support staff. For details of work see entry in the Nationwide chapter.

ADVENTURE & COMPUTER HOLIDAYS LTD: P.O. Box 183, Dorking, Surrey RH5 6FA (tel and fax 01306-881299). A small, friendly company with 15 years experience in running activity holidays for children aged 4-13. Based in a school in the Surrey hills, with an activity centre in Cornwall.
CAMP LEADERS, TEACHERS required for day and residential camps. £130-£160 per week. Day camp staff to work 9am-5pm; on residential camps staff work longer hours, depending upon requirements. Min. age 21. Qualifications or experience with children preferred. Period of work April to August (mostly July-August), min. period one week. Free accommodation is provided on residential camps. Day camp staff need to live in London or Surrey area. All applicants should be able to attend an interview. Applications any time to Ms Sarah Bradley, Director, at the above address.

EXPERIENCE UK LTD: Poolside Manor, Lyndhurst Gardens, Finchley, London N3 1TD (tel 0181-349 1945; fax 0181-349 9057; e-mail enquiry@experienceuk.demon.co.uk). Staff needed for children's holiday camps: day camps operate in Edgware and Finchley and a residential camp takes place in Suffolk.
LEADERS for activity programmes at daycamps amd residential camp. Applicants preferred with qualifications in first aid, life saving arts/crafts and sports.
COOKS, KITCHEN ASSISTANTS with appropriate qualifications to cater for 130 children and adults on the residential camp.
Accommodation provided. To work mid July to August. Wages subject to negotiation. Good references essential. Applications to The Operations Co-ordinator at the above address.

THE GROVE: Carshalton, Surrey SM5 3AL (tel 0181-770 6616; fax 0181-770 6655). Six playschemes for 5-11 year olds run by the London Borough of Sutton.
ASSISTANT PLAYLEADERS (30). Up to £5.46 per hour. To work 36 hours

a week, Monday to Friday. Min. age 18. Vitality and enthusiasm essential, relevant experience plus a knowledge and understanding of children's needs desirable. Staff required throughout school holidays, approx. 6 weeks in summer (July to September) (also Christmas, Easter and half term holidays). Min. period of work is the duration of the relevant playscheme's operation. No accommodation provided. Applicants must be available for interview. Applications from September (closing date 30 April) to Personnel, Education Department, at the above address or ring 0181-770 6528/9.

NORTH HERTFORDSHIRE DISTRICT COUNCIL: Council Offices, Gernon Road, Letchworth, Hertfordshire SG6 3JF (tel 01462-474333; fax 01462-474500).
PLAYLEADERS (10). Wages were £175 per week in 1998.
SENIOR PLAYWORKERS (12). Wages were £157.50 per week in 1998.
PLAYWORKERS (50). Wages were £140 per week in 1998.
   Duties include general supervision, health and safety, planning of activities and creating a fun and happy environment to play in. All staff work 35 hours a week, Monday to Friday. To work 21 July-27 August, depending on summer holidays.
   Applicants must be over 18. Experience of working with children aged 5-11 is essential. Teacher/Nursery nurse training/qualifications are an advantage. Applications to Sue Topping.

ONLY CONNECT: Cambridge House, 131 Camberwell Road, London SE5 7JZ (tel 0171-701 0769; fax 0171-703 2903). A charity which runs services for people with learning disabilities in the London borough of Southwark.
PLAYWORKERS (35). £31-£37 per day. To work from 7.45am to 3.45pm. Must have relevant experience and be over 16. Work is available from July 28th to August 30th; min. period of work 3 weeks. Accommodation is not available.
   Applications from June 5th to the Play and Respite Care Manager at the above address. All applicants must be available for an interview.

PGL TRAVEL LTD: Alton Court, Penyard Lane (874), Ross-on-Wye, Herefordshire HR9 7AH (tel 01989-767883). Over 3,000 staff needed to assist in the running of activity centres in Surrey and Hertfordshire. Europe's largest provider of adventure holidays for children has offered outstanding training and work opportunities to seasonal staff for over 40 years.
QUALIFIED INSTRUCTORS in canoeing, sailing, windsurfing, pony trekking, hill walking, fencing, archery, judo, rifle shooting, fishing, motorsports, arts and crafts, drama, English language and many other activities. Min. age 18 years.
GROUP LEADERS to take responsibility for small groups of children and ensure that they get the most out of their holiday. Min. age 20 years. Previous experience of working with children necessary.
   From £36-70 per week pocket money and full B & L provided. Vacancies available for short or long periods between February and October. Requests for application forms to the Personnel Department at the above address.

RUNNYMEDE BOROUGH COUNCIL: Civic Offices, Station Road, Addlestone, Surrey KT15 2AH (tel 01932-705436; fax 01932-855135).
SPLASH DIRECTOR to take overall responsibility for organising activity scheme, including managing staff, for a group of 280 children aged 11-16. To

work for 3 weeks in August. Wages £700 total. No accommodation. Hours: 8.45am-5pm Mon-Fri. Supervisory experience preferable.

SPLASH INSTRUCTORS (14) to organise activities and supervise off-site coach trips. Dates and hours as above. Wages £480 total.

PLAYSCHEME & PLAY PLUS SCHEME DIRECTORS (12) to be responsible for organising schemes for 30-60 5-7 year olds and up to 40 8-11 year olds. To work for 4 weeks in August. Wages £660 gross total. Hours 9am-4pm Monday to Friday.

INSTRUCTORS (29) to organise activities on above playschemes and supervise coach trips. Wages £530 gross total. 9am-4pm Monday to Friday.

ASSISTANTS (22) for the above playschemes. Wages £390 gross total. Same hours as for instructors and to assist with same duties.

All posts above are non-residential. No overseas applicants. Applications to Linda Jacks, Leisure Development Officer, at the above address.

WOKING BOROUGH COUNCIL: Civic Offices, Gloucester Square, Woking, Surrey GU21 1YL (tel 01483-743805; fax 01483-750585).

PLAYSCHEME ASSISTANTS (60) to organise and lead activities for groups of children, assist the leader and ensure safety of children at all times. Wages £3.95 per hour in 1998 but may change for 1999. Applicants should be aged at least 18.

PLAYSCHEME LEADERS (8) to organise and co-ordinate a day to day programme of varied activities for 5-15 year olds; duties include administration, money collection, and taking responsibility for keyholding and staff. Wages £5.25 per hour in 1998, but may change for 1999. Should be aged at least 18 with previous experience of working with children and of organising; any children-related qualifications would be advantageous.

To work from 9am-4pm, Monday-Friday. Period of work from approx. July 27-approx. August 28. Possession of first aid qualifications desirable.

Applications to Rachel Harrison, Sport and Play Development Officer at the above address.

Holiday Centres and Amusements

BEALE PARK: Lower Basildon, Reading, Berkshire RG8 9NH (tel 0118-9845172; fax 0118-9845171). A non profit-making charitable trust which offers leisure activities and birdwatching.

TICKET SELLERS (2). Wages £4.00 per hour. To work full and/or part time over the summer months. No accommodation is available. Period of work May-September. Min. period of work July/August. Some experience in working with the public and handling cash is preferred. Interview necessary. Applications from May to Andrew Howard.

CHESSINGTON WORLD OF ADVENTURES: Leatherhead Road, Chessington, Surrey KT9 2NE (tel 01372-729560; fax 01372 725050). The fifth most popular tourist attraction which charges admission fees in the UK. A leading theme park in the South of England (12 miles from London) it incorporates a long established zoo; it offers a fun and lively working environment with many benefits.

RIDE ASSISTANTS to assist with the loading and unloading of visitors.

GAMES STAFF to man one of the side shows or work in the arcades.

CATERING STAFF to work in one of the many varied catering units.

SHOP ASSISTANTS to serve visitors with souvenirs and gifts.
ADMISSIONS STAFF to work at the main entrance, welcoming visitors to the park.
All positions to work 40 hours per 5 day week including weekends and bank holidays. Hourly rate of pay with full training provided at induction. Applicants must be aged between 16 and 55. No experience is necessary but you must be enthusiastic and enjoy working as part of a team. EU and Commonwealth nationals welcome. Apply to the above address from December to January.

LEGOLAND WINDSOR: Winkfield Road, Windsor, Berkshire SL4 4AY (Human Resouces Department tel 01753-626150/154). LEGOLAND Windsor is a theme park dedicated to the imagination and creativity of children, where the kids are king. It draws on the inspiration of the world famous LEGO toys and models.
The operating season lasts from March to November during which over 700 staff are employed in the following positions:
TICKET SELLERS, GUEST SERVICES ASSISTANTS, RETAIL ASSISTANTS, ATTRACTIONS ASSISTANTS ON RIDES AND PLAYSCAPES, GROUNDS CLEANERS, CATERING ASSISTANTS, GARDENERS, USHERS, STAGE TECHNICIANS, COSTUME TECHNICIANS, NURSES AND SECURITY OFFICERS. Pay starts from £4.35 per hour (£3.35 per hour if under 18 years old). In return for dedicated commitment to work, benefits include excellent training opportunities, social events and discounted bus passes.
To work an average of 40 hours per week with some part time work available. Accommodation not provided but free accommodation service available to those employees seeking local accommodation. Overseas applicants must be EU citizens or have a valid work permit before applying. Fluent English essential. Minimum age 16. No previous experience necessary.
Applicants must have a passion for serving others, an exuberant personality and a natural affinity with children. To be part of the LEGOLAND team, staff need to be willing to work hard and have fun whatever the weather (many positions involve working outside).
Call the Human Resources Department for an application form. Applications received from the preceding December.

THE SHERLOCK HOLMES MUSEUM: 221B Baker Street, London NW1 6XE (tel 0171-738 1269; fax 0171-224 3005).
VICTORIAN MAIDS (2) to receive visitors attending the museum. Minimum age 24; knowledge of other languages would be an asset.
SHERLOCK HOLMES LOOKALIKE to dress up as Sherlock Holmes and give out promotional literature to tourists. Must be slim, at least 6' tall and well spoken.
Wages £40 per day; no accommodation available. Period of work from May to September. Applications to John Aidiniantz, Co-manager, at the above address.

TENT CITY LTD: Old Oak Common Lane, East Acton, London W3 7DP (tel 0181-743 5708/0181-749 9074).
ASSISTANTS (50) required to work for five-week periods each from 1 June to 7 September. Free food and accommodation is provided, plus £33 pocket money per week. Some expenses paid and organised trips. Duties include

working in snack bar and reception, maintenance, cleaning, putting up and taking down of tents, organising residents' social events, providing help and information for residents.

Must be aged over 18. No special qualifications required, just honesty, energy and a sense of fun. Overseas applicants particularly welcome. Applications to Tent City Ltd at the above address. IRC or stamped s.a.e. is required for response.

THORPE PARK: Staines Road, Chertsey, Surrey KT16 8PN (tel 01932-577120; fax 01932-566367; e-mail thorpepark@mail logo.co.uk). Leisure park attracting 1 million guests each year requires large numbers of staff to work in the following areas:
RIDE OPERATORS (200), RETAIL STAFF (60), CLEANERS (100), GUEST SERVICES (30), LANDSCAPE (12), FARM (8), PERSONNEL (10). All staff to work approx. 8 hours a day, 5 days a week. Wages were £4.00 per hour in 1998. All staff must be outgoing and enthusiastic. Staff required from February to October; minimum period of work 3 months. Some accommodation available. Overseas applicants with a high standard of spoken English considered. Applications from the end of January to the Personnel Department, Thorpe Park.

THE TUSSAUDS GROUP, LONDON SITES: c/o Madame Tussauds, Marylebone Road, London NW1 5LR (tel 0171-487 0200; fax 0171-465 0860).
VISITOR SERVICES ASSISTANTS, but also RETAIL ASSISTANTS, CATERING ASSISTANTS, HOUSEKEEPING ASSISTANTS, CAFE ASSISTANTS and PHOTOGRAPHERS (approx. 40) to work for Madame Tussauds. Required to work from late June to mid September for £736.75 per month. To work 40 hours per week, five days out of seven on a rota basis, including weekends. Eight hour shifts between the hours of 8am and 8pm. Experience of work with the public is essential. Min. age 18.
EXHIBITION GUIDES, PHOTOGRAPHERS, and HOUSEKEEPERS (approx. 15) to work for Rock Circus. Required for same time period and hours as above. Shifts would be between 11.40am and 9.40pm. Wages as above. Experience of work with the public is essential. Min. age 18.

THE ZOOLOGICAL SOCIETY OF LONDON: Regent's Park, London NW1 4RY (tel 0171-586 6251; fax 0171-586 5743; e-mail 101333.360@compuserve.com).
TOILET ATTENDANTS (4). Wages £194 per week. To work a 10 day rostered fortnight, working alternate weekends with 1 day off a week.
GROUNDSPEOPLE (8). Wages £194 per week. To work a 10 day rostered fortnight, working alternate weekends with 1 day off a week.
GARDENER (1). Wages £180 per week. To work Monday-Friday. Must have gardening qualifications.
SALES ASSISTANTS (22). Wages £210 per week. Full and part-time positions available. To work 10 day rostered fortnight, working alternate weekends with 1 day off per week. Must have retail references for past 2 years.
ANIMAL KEEPERS (8). Wages £215 per week. To work every weekend with 2 days off in the week. Must have animal qualification or some experience of working with animals.

Period of work April to September. Applications to Marcia Latty.

Hotels and Catering

BLOOMSBURY PARK HOTEL: 126 Southampton Row, London WC1B 5AD (tel 0171-430 0434; fax 0171-242 0665). A 95 bedroom hotel with a restaurant and 2 bars.
WAITING STAFF, BAR STAFF (3). Wages £160.00 per week gross. To work 39 hours a week. Accommodation is available at a cost of £40.00 per week. Min. period of work 6 months between March and September. Applicants must be over 18. No experience is necessary.
Uniform, meals on duty and on-the-job training are provided. Selected staff will attend training courses. Overseas applicants with good English condidered. Interview necessary. Applications from February to Mr McEwan Smith or the Personnel Manager.

BRIGGENS HOUSE HOTEL: Briggens Park, Stanstead Abbotts, near Ware, Herts. SG12 8LD (tel 01279-829955; fax 01279-793685).
CASUAL WAITING, BAR and BANQUETING STAFF. £3.30 per hour. Period of work May to October. Min. age 18 and experience essential. Overseas applicants welcome. Applications to the Manager at the above address.

COPTHORNE HOTEL: Cippenham Lane, Slough, Berkshire SL1 2YE (tel 01753-516222; fax 01753-516237).
WAITING STAFF (3/4), BARTENDER. At least £4.72 per hour with free uniform and meals. To work 37½ hours on shift work per week with the possibility of overtime. Applicants must be at least 18 with hotel qualifications or experience. To work from June to September; min. period of work three months. Temporary accommodation available. Overseas applicants with valid working visas welcome.
Apply from April to the Personnel Manager at the above address. Note that all applicants must be available for an interview.

GARFUNKELS: 103 Charing Cross Road, London WC2H 0BP (0171-457 7582; fax 0171-494 28721; e-mail 106404.3075@compuservecom). A restaurant chain with branches in Bath, Cambridge, Sutton, Kingston, Edinburgh, Glasgow, Heathrow Airport, Gatwick Airport, and all over London.
WAITING STAFF and KITCHEN STAFF. Flexible hours; wages to be arranged. Staff required throughout the year, mainly between June and September. Minimum period of work 3 months. Accommodation not available. Kitchen staff must have good knowledge of food hygiene. Foreign applicants with high standard of spoken English considered. All applicants should be available for interview. Applications all year round to the Manager of the appropriate branch.

HARRIS EMPLOYMENT: 21 Great Chapel Street, London W1V 3AQ (tel 0171-287 2663).
Offers a wide range of bar, waiting, cook and chef positions in pubs, hotels and catering outlets. Some positions offer accommodation. Min. period of work 6 months. Previous experience preferred; references and work permits required. Overseas applicants welcome. All applicants must be conversationally fluent in English. Apply to Lisa Webb at the above address.

HILTON NATIONAL HOTEL: Seven Hills Road South, Cobham, Surrey KT11 1EW (tel 01932-864471; fax 01932-868017). A 140 bedroom busy 4 Star

hotel, set in 40 acres of woodland, with conference facilities for 300 people and a leisure centre.
RESTAURANT AND BAR STAFF (4), CONFERENCE AND BANQUET- ING PORTERS (2). Wages £126.00 (gross) per week, live-in. To work 37½ hours a week over 5 days, and some overtime (either early or late shifts) depending on business. Must be over 18, with a good level of English. Some experience preferred.
ROOM ATTENDANTS (4). Wages £126.00 (gross) per week, live-in. To work 37½ hours a week over 5 days, 8.00am-4.00pm. Must be over 18, and able to understand and speak basic English.

Min.period of work 2 months between May and August. Overseas applicants considered. Telephone interview sufficient if applicants enclose a photo with their application. Applications as soon as possible to Deborah Buckland.

HOLIDAY INN GARDEN COURT: Tilling Road, Brent Cross, London NE2 1LP (tel 0181-201 8686; fax 0181-967 6372). Owned by Bass, the hotel is part of the Holiday Inn chain.
FOOD AND BEVERAGE ASSISTANTS (2/3) to perform bar and waiting work. Wages £4.00 per hour.
RECEPTIONIST (1) to greet and check in guests. Wages £4.00 per hour.
HOUSEKEEPING ROOM ATTENDANTS (2) to clean rooms. Wages £4.00 per hour.

All staff work 30-40 hours a week depending on business. Accommodation is available at a cost of £60 per week inclusive. Min. period of work 4 months between April/May and September.

Applicants must be over 19. Overseas applicants who are suitably qualified and speak English well are considered. Interview may be necessary if applicants are in the UK. Applications to Gerald Malone from January.

HOLIDAY INN MAYFAIR: Berkeley Street, London W1X 6NE (tel 0171-493 8282; fax 0171-412 3008). A busy 4 star hotel situated in Mayfair which caters for business and leisure clients.
ROOM ATTENDANTS (5) to clean 10 rooms a day to a high standard. Wages £168 per week. To work 5 days a week according to a rota. No accommodation is available. Min. period of work 6 months between April and November.
Commitment and enthusiasm are more important than experience. Overseas applicants with work authorisation are considered. Interview necessary. Applications should be made after arrival in the UK to the Personnel Department.

INTERNATIONAL HOTEL: 163 Marsh Wall, London E14 9SJ (tel 0171-712 0100; fax 0171-7120102). The hotel is situated opposite Canary Wharf, and has 442 bedrooms, 3 restaurants, a nightclub, and a healthclub.
ROOM ATTENDANTS (10). Wage £3.55-£4.00 per hour.
WAITING STAFF (5). Wage £3.50-£4.50 per hour.
RESTAURANT SUPERVISORS (2). Wage £5.00 per hour.
CONFERENCE AND BANQUETING HEAD WAITER (1). Salary £11,000 per annum.

All staff to work 40 hours a week, with 2 days off. No accomodation is available, but staff receive free meals on duty, uniforms, use of the health club at discounted rates, and staff rates at hotels in the same group.

Staff required immediately. Overseas applicants welcome. Interview necessary. Applications to Joanne Usher as soon as possible.

JARVIS ELCOT PARK HOTEL: Elcot, Newbury, Berkshire RG20 8NJ (tel 01488-658100; fax 01488-658288). A 75 bedroomed hotel with 9 conference rooms and a leisure club set in 16 acres of countryside.
RESTAURANT ATTENDANTS (1-2). Wage £3.50 per hour if living in, £4.05 if living out. To work 39 hours over 5 days a week. Accommodation subject to availability at a cost of £21.45 per week (1998 figure). Meals and uniform provided. Paid overtime. Min. period of work 2 months between May/June and August/September.
Applicants must be over 18 with some experience of restaurant work. Interview necessary, but can be conducted over telephone. Overseas applicants entitled to work in the UK considered.
Applications from March to the Personnel and Training Manager.

JUNIPER HALL FIELD CENTRE: Old London Road, Mickleham, Dorking, Surrey RH5 6DA (tel 01306-883849; fax 01306-742627). A residential and environmental outdoor centre.
DOMESTIC/CENTRE ASSISTANTS (up to 4) for general kitchen/serving work. £73.06 gross per week plus free B and L in single rooms. To work approx. 8 hours a day with 2 variable days off. Work available all year round; min. period of work 3 months. No special qualifications required, but should preferably be aged 18-28. Overseas applicants welcome. All applicants must have valid working visas. Applications to the Bursar at the above address.

KENSINGTON FORTE POSTHOUSE: Wrights Lane, Kensington, London W8 5SP (tel 0171-368 4019; fax 0171-368 4056). A 550 bedroomed hotel serving international professional clients.
CHAMBER STAFF (10), BAR STAFF (3). Wage for both positions £180 for 39 hours a week. No accommodation available. Min. period of work 3 months between June and September.
Overseas applicants welcome. Interview necessary. Applications from May to the Personnel Officer.

LONDON HOSTELS ASSOCIATION LTD: 54 Eccleston Square, London SW1V 1PG (tel 0171-834 1545; fax 0171-834 7146). Established in 1940, recruits residential staff for 10 London hostels run for young employed people and full time bona-fide students.
GENERAL DOMESTIC STAFF to do housework and help in kitchens. Wages paid weekly with free B & L provided. Opportunities to attend courses and improve English skills. Hours: average of 30-39 hours per week (mornings and evenings). Min. period of work 3 months throughout the year. Jobs available all year round, long stays welcome.
Min. age 18 years. Common sense and willingness to tackle variety of jobs required. EEA applicants eligible to work in the UK welcome. Applications should be sent 2 months before date of availability to Mr T. Perkins, Personnel Manager, London Hostels Association.

MAYDAY TEMPORARY CATERING STAFF: See below for addresses.
Arranges catering jobs to suit all levels of experience.
CHEFS. £5.40-£7.25 per hour plus holiday pay.
WAITING STAFF. £4.50-£5.50 per hour.

BAR STAFF. £4.50 per hour.
DELI ASSISTANTS. £4.00 to £4.50 per hour.
KITCHEN PORTERS. £4.00 per hour.
Temporary and permanent positions available all year round. Overtime is available for evening and weekend work and employees are paid weekly. Applicants should telephone any of the offices listed below or come directly to their nearest office from Monday to Thursday between 10am and 12pm: 2 Shoreditch High Street, London E1 6PG (tel 0171-377 6416) (City); 21 Great Chapel Street, Soho, London W1V 3AQ (tel 0171-439 3009) (West End); 35 Goldhawk Road, Shepherds Bush, London W12 8QQ (tel 0181-749 9300) (West London). Bar Staff should call in at the West End branch or telephone 0171-287-2663. All applicants must have a valid work permit.

MAYFAIR INTER-CONTINENTAL HOTEL: Stratton Street, London W1A 2AN (tel 0171-629 7777; fax 0171-629 7504). A 5 star deluxe hotel in London's West End with 287 bedrooms. Part of the Inter-Continental Hotels and Resorts chain.
WAITING STAFF (10). Wages £4.90 per hour plus tips. To work 40 hours a week.
ROOM ATTENDANTS (15). Wages £5.00 per hour. To work 40 hours a week.
No accommodation is available. Min. period of work 1 month between June and September. All applicants must be over 18 and have a minimum of 6 months previous experience.
Overseas applicants with work permits considered. Interview necessary. Applications to the Personnel Department.

MOUNT ROYAL HOTEL: Bryanston Street, Marble Arch, London W1A 4UR (tel 0171-629 8040; fax 0171-629 0628).
WAITER/WAITRESS. Experience in catering essential.
BARTENDER. Min. age 18 years. Bar experience essential.
All staff to work 30-40 hours a week in shifts. Wages approx. £4.28 gross per hour. Uniform and meals on duty provided. Period of work June to September. Must have excellent presentation. Overseas applicants considered, provided they speak fluent English. All applicants must be available for interview. Applications from May to Ms B. Duffy, Personnel Department, at the above address.

NORFOLK PLAZA HOTEL: 29/33 Norfolk Square, London W2 1RX (tel 0171-723 0792; fax 0171-224 8770). An 87 bedroom, 3 Star hotel by Paddington Station in London W2. The majority of clients are Europeans on short leisure breaks in London, with a mixture of local UK Corporate customers. The hotel employs approx. 40 staff.
HOTEL RECEPTIONISTS (2). Wages £42.30 (gross) per 8-hour shift, with 5 shifts per week, plus weekly tips. Uniforms, meals and other benefits provided free but no accommodation available. Period of work June to end of September. Min. age 20. Applicants must be able to speak English and a Western European language fluently; knowledge of another language would be an advantage. Experience of working on a computer database system and telephone switchboard essential. Overseas applicants welcome. Two weeks' training will be provided for successful applicants. Applications should be sent to Mr Ali Muttawa, General Manager, at the above address.

THE PENDLEY MANOR HOTEL: Cow Lane, Tring, Herts. HP23 5QY (tel 01442-891891; fax 01442-890687). A 4 star 71 bedroom country house hotel and conference centre set in 35 acres of countryside.
CONFERENCE/BANQUETING WAITING STAFF (10-20) to help serve at weddings, conferences and dinner dances. To earn £3.50-£4.00 per hour with the possibility of tips, but no accommodation available. To work mainly Fridays, Saturdays and Sundays, but with some weekday work. Period of work June-August. Should preferably have experience of silver service/hotel work, be at least 17 years old, clean with a smart appearance and a good attitude to customer care; own transport an advantage.
Applications to Sally Francis, Personnel Manager at the above address.

ROYAL WESTMINSTER HOTEL: 49 Buckingham Palace Road, London SW1W 0QT (tel 0171-834 1821; fax 0171-931 7542; e-mail roywestminster@cix.co.uk). A four star central London hotel, with 134 bedrooms, a brasserie style restaurant and a popular bar.
WAITING STAFF (4) to wait at tables. Wage £175.00 per week plus tips. To work 39 hours over 5 days a week. Shared accommodation available at a cost of approx. £47.50 per week. Min. period of work 3 months between end of June and end of September.
Applicants must be over 18. Experience not necessary, but interview required. Overseas applicants with excellent English considered.
Applications early in 1999 to the Personnel Department.

SELFRIDGE HOTEL: Orchard Street, London W1H 0JS (tel 0171-408 2080; fax 0171-629 8849).
WAITING STAFF (2) to work in the hotel's busy Orchard Terrace brasserie-style restaurant; plate service. Wages of £162 per week plus gratuities. To work 6.30am-3pm or 3-11.30pm, 5 days out of 7. Applicants should have 6 months' previous waiting experience, good social skills and be smart and presentable.
ROOM ATTENDANTS (2) to clean 14 bedrooms and bathrooms per day. Wage £167 per week. To work from 8am-4pm, 5 days out of 7. Applicants should be hard working with good social skills and a flexible attitude. Some experience of working in housekeeping preferred.
Must be available for 4 months minimum. No accommodation available. Applications to Steven Brown, Personnel and Training Manager, at the above address.

STAKIS LONDON METROPOLE: Edgware Road, London W2 1JU (tel 0171-616 6474; fax 0171-616 6471). A cosmopolitan four star hotel with 668 bedrooms in central London.
WAITING STAFF (4). £180 per week. To work either 39 hours full time or 25 hours part time over 5 days per week. Min. age 18. Must have previous experience with a good command of the English language.
ROOM ATTENDANTS (15). £180 per week. To work 39 hours per week full time over 5 days. Must have good customer care skills, previous experience, and basic ability to read and write English.
LUGGAGE PORTERS (2). £170 per week. To work 39 hours over 5 days per week. Must have good customer care skills, smart appearance and a good command of the English language.
RECEPTIONIST (1). £209 per week. To work 39 hours over 5 days per week.

Must have previous experience and good command of written and spoken English.

Staff required from May to October; min. period of work June to September. B & L available at £47 per week subject to availability. Staff have free meals on duty and are provided with uniforms.

Overseas applicants welcome but must be available for a telephone interview. Apply from April 1st to the Personnel Department at the above address.

STAKIS HOTEL NEWBURY: Oxford Road, Newbury RG20 8XY (tel 01635-247010; fax 01635-247077). A 4 star hotel which has 112 bedrooms, a restaurant, bar and leisure club. Catering for business and leisure clients, it is located 3 miles from the town centre on the M4 junction.

RESTAURANT STAFF (6), BAR STAFF (3), HOUSEKEEPING STAFF (3). Wages £3.72 per hour. Positions are full-time or part-time, 5-39 hours a week. Accommodation is available at a cost of 50p per hour worked. Period of work 1st June to 30th September.

Applicants must be over 16. No experience necessary. Overseas applicants with good English are considered. Interview necessary. Applications to Amanda Palmer at any time of year.

STAKIS ST ANNE'S MANOR HOTEL: London Road, Wokingham, Berkshire RG40 1ST (tel 0118-977 2550; fax 0118-977 2526; e-mail personnel-.manager@st.Annes.stakis.co.uk). A four star 160 bedroom luxury conference based hotel, set in 25 acres of gardens.

BAR PERSONS, ROOM ATTENDANTS, BANQUETING/RESTAURANT WAITING STAFF. Wage for all positions approx. £4.00 per hour. To work hours as required. Accommodation may be available for £20 per week, inclusive of bills and food. Min. period of work 3 months.

Staff should be at least 16 years old; training will be given. An interview is necessary. Overseas applicants with knowledge of English considered. Applications to Emma James, Personnel Manager.

SWAN HOTEL: The Hythe, Staines, Middlesex TW18 3JB (tel 01784-452494/454471; fax 01784-461593).

WAITING STAFF (1). £140 per week plus tips. Min. age 18.

BAR STAFF (2). £140 per week. Couple preferred. Min. age 18.

KITCHEN PORTER (1). £125 per week. Min. age 16.

COMMIS CHEF (1). £160 per week. Some experience or basic training is required.

GENERAL ASSISTANTS (2). £140 per week. Couple preferred. Must be able to do a variety of jobs, including bar and restaurant work.

Wages quoted above will vary according to age, experience and qualifications. Staff to work 5 days per week, with some split shifts. Some overtime available. Accommodation provided free of charge. No experience is necessary unless otherwise stated. Min. work period 6 weeks but commitment of 6 months preferred. Positions available all year round. Applications (with photograph) to Mr & Mrs Kothe, at the above address.

TOWN & COUNTY CATERING: All England Lawn Tennis and Croquet Club, Church Road, Wimbledon, London SW19 5AE (tel 0181-947 7430; fax 0181-944 2253). The company hold the contracts for the public and hospitality

areas at most of the prestigious events of the Season, including the Wimbledon Tennis Championships and the Buckingham Palace Garden Parties.
MANAGERS, CHEFS, PORTERS, WASHING UP STAFF, CATERING ASSISTANTS, SILVER SERVICE, PLATE WAITING & BAR STAFF (1,200 in all) needed to work at the Wimbledon Tennis Championships between June 20 and July 5. Hours of work and rates of pay by arrangement. Applicants must be aged at least 18 and have good communication skills. Some items of uniform are supplied and staff must supply the rest.
   Applications should be sent to the Recruitment Office at the above address.

VINCENT HOUSE: 5 Pembridge Square, London W2 4EG (tel 0171-229 1133). Residential club for business people.
GENERAL ASSISTANTS required to help with housekeeping, restaurant and porterage. Wages £83-£97 per week, dependent on age, plus free B & L. To work average of 35 hours per week. Ages: 18-25 years. Work available all year round but employment is for a minimum period of 4 months. Overseas applicants welcome. Applications to Mr B. Bucher, Vincent House.

WOODLANDS PARK: Woodlands Lane, Stoke D'Arbernon, Cobham, Surrey KT11 3QB (tel 01372-843933).
HOTEL STAFF to work 40 hours a week. Wages from £4 an hour; company discounts plus use of the leisure and health facilities are also included. Uniform provided. Minimum period of work 6 months all year round. All positions are live-in. Overseas applicants with a high standard of English welcome. Applications at any time to Tina Downing, Area Personnel Manager, at the above address.

Medical

ANCHOR CARE ALTERNATIVES: 206 Worple Road, Wimbledon, London SW20 8PN (tel 0181-946 8202; fax 0181-944 7431). Cares for the elderly and disabled in their own homes throughout the UK.
LIVE-IN CARE WORKERS. Wages from £249 per week.
DAILY CARE WORKERS. Wages from £5.50 an hour.
   Staff required all year round to care for mainly housebound people. Minimum period of work 2-3 months. Duties include personal care, cooking, housekeeping, laundry, shopping and companionship. Overseas applicants authorised to work in the UK welcome. Applicants must be friendly with a caring attitude. Applications 2-3 weeks before work is required to the Senior Area Manager at the above address.

UNIVERSAL CARE: Chester House, 9 Windsor End, Beaconsfield, Buckinghamshire HP9 2JJ (tel 01494-678811/678503; fax 01494-671259). Aims to enable the elderly and disabled to remain in thier own homes for as long as possible.
RESIDENTIAL CARERS/COMPANIONS (20), to live in with elderly and/ or disabled clients. £250-£300 per week. Hours according to requirements of position. Must have a caring attitude and be at least 20 years of age. Staff required year round; min. period of work three months. Placements are for periods of two weeks and carers provide assistance with basic household tasks such as cooking, shopping and light housework. Companionship is particularly

important and in some cases personal care is required. Overseas applicants fluent in English with a valid work permit welcome.

Apply year round to Sharon Chilton at the above address. All applicants must be available for an interview.

Outdoor

CAM VALLEY PLUMS: 39 Chiswick End, Meldreth, Royston, Herts. SG8 6LZ (tel 01763-262964/260332; fax 01763-260332).
FRUIT PICKERS (6) for work in September. Wages at piece-work rates; to work 5-7 days per week. Caravan accommodation available. Applicants must be aged 18 and over.

Applications to T.J. Elbourn, Manager at the above address.

SERCO LTD: Oak Lodge Depot, Richmond Park, Surrey TW10 5HS (tel 0181-948 0168; fax 0181-948 0169). Staff needed to look after 2,300 acres of parkland.
SEASONAL GARDENERS/ESTATE WORKERS (up to 4) for general basic gardening duties and labouring duties. To work 5 days per week, Monday-Friday. Period of work April-October. Possession of a driving licence an advantage but not essential.
LITTER PICKERS (up to 5) to empty bins and pick up litter. Will involve work every other weekend (with weekdays off in lieu), some evenings and on public holidays. Required around the year. Driving licence essential.

Wages £4.36 per hour; to work 40 hours per week. No accommodation available. All applicants must be aged over 18 and have a National Insurance number. The working environment is pleasant, but staff must be prepared to work hard in all weathers.

Applications to Nigel Hampton, Manager at the above address.

Sport

CONTESSA RIDING CENTRE: Willow Tree Farm, Colliers End, Ware, Hertfordshire SG11 1EN (tel 01920-821 792/496; fax 01920-821496). A riding school and competition yard with a particular interest in dressage. Set in a rural area 30 miles north of London, with easy access to Cambridge and Stansted Airport. Has a large indoor and outdoor school and highly qualified staff.
STABLE HELPERS to perform general yard duties including mucking out, grooming, tack cleaning and horse leading. Horses range from novice to grand prix standard. Pocket money, riding and self-catering accommodation are provided; if the applicant has riding teaching qualifications then a salary may be negotiated. To work from 8am-5pm (beginning at 8.30am on two days) over $5\frac{1}{2}$ days per week. Applicants must be aged 17; qualifications and experience preferred.

To work throughout the year, especially around the holiday periods. Minimum period of work one month. Applicants preferably should be available for an interview. Brochures available. Apply year round to Tina Layton at the above address.

EXSPORTISE LTD: PO Box 191, Reigate, RH2 8YT (tel 01293-862849; fax 01293-863006).

HOCKEY, TENNIS, CRICKET, GOLF, SWIMMING AND FOOTBALL COACHES (10). £100-£200 per week plus B & L. Qualifications essential. Applicants must be willing to work all hours and organise evening entertainments. Opportunity to make extra money by doing airport pick-ups. Min period of work 5 weeks between 12 July and 30 August.
Interviews will be held. Applications from now on to the Course Co-ordinator, at the above address.

Language Schools

ENGLISH CENTRE FOR INTERNATIONAL STUDENTS: Hampstead Garden Suburb Institute, Central Square, London NW11 7BN (tel 0181-455 8176; fax 0181-455 4448). An adult education centre with a large provision for EFL.
SUMMER SCHOOL EFL TEACHERS to teach levels from elementary to advanced, and participate in a social programme. Wages £17 per hour. All summer school teachers are part time, and teach a flexible timetable of about 6-15 hours a week, Monday to Friday. Accommodation could be arranged in local homes at a cost of £70-80 per week.
   Min. period of work 4 weeks from 5th July-27th August. Applicants must hold an RSA Dip TEFLA or equivalent. An interview is necessary. Applications from 1st February to Georgie Raman.

EUROACCENTS/YOUTH SERVICE SCHOOLS: 16/20 New Broadway, London W5 2XA (tel 0181-566 2188; fax 0181-566 2011; e-mail languages@euroaccents.co.uk). Organises language courses (mainly English) for foreign students. In addition to accommodation and tuition, students are offered a full programme of daily activities.
SOCIAL ORGANISERS (1/2). Wages £150-£200 per week. To work long hours. Min. period of work 8-10 weeks between April/mid May and the end of August. Accommodation available.
   Applicants should be aged 20-25. Experience is useful but not necessary. Overseas applicants with good English considered. Interview necessary.
   Applications from January/February to Mr G. Gerosa.

EXCEL ENGLISH: The Hall, 8 Muswell Hill, London N10 3TD (0181-365 2485; fax 0181-442 1143; e-mail info@exceleng.demon.co.uk). A language school which teaches English as a Foreign Language to students from all over the world.
ASSISTANT SOCIAL ORGANISERS (1/2) to assist with the summer social programme and take students on outings. Some general administration work and airport meeting work may be involved. Wages £5 per hour. To work 5-7 hours a day, Monday to Friday, with occasional Saturday work.
   No accommodation is available. Min. period of work 4 weeks from 28th June to 27th August. Applicants must be over 18. No experience is necessary, but applicants must be outgoing and friendly, and be educated to at least A level standard.
   An interview is necessary. Applications from April to Judy Loren.

FRANCES KING SCHOOL OF ENGLISH: 5 Grosvenor Gardens, London SW1W 0BB.
ENGLISH LANGUAGE TEACHERS (30) to teach up to 30 hours per week at various centres, plus optional leading of groups and taking part in activities

with students; residential centres may require extra duties. Pay on an hourly basis, with accommodation included at centres outside London. Period of work from the first week of July-last week of August. Must hold RSA/ Cambridge TEFL certificates plus a minimum of one years experience. Applications to R. Stewart, Director of Studies, at the above address.

HAMPSTEAD SCHOOL OF ENGLISH: 553 Finchley Road, Hampstead, London NW3 7BJ (tel 0171-794 3533; fax 0171-431 2987; e-mail hampstead@compuserve.com.). The school has an average of 350 foreign students, and enjoys a reputation for excellence. Staff pride themselves on treating each student as an individual.
STUDENT GROUP LEADERS (6-8) to guide foreign language students around London and take care of them while on route to and during their evening engagements. Wages of £5.00 to £6.00 per hour; flexible hours ranging from 15 to 40 hours over mainly afternoons and evenings. Work would suit undergraduates aged 19 and over who have successfully completed at least one year of an university course. To work from last week of June to the end of August, some to September 5. Applicants should be energetic, enthusiastic and like dealing with people. No accommodation provided. Applicants must be available for interview. Applications to Jill Sieff, Principal, at the above address.

HEATHFIELD SUMMER SCHOOL: Ascot, Berkshire SL5 8BQ (tel 01344-885197; fax 01344-882235). A girls' boarding school with first class facilities set in beautiful grounds just outside Ascot, near Windsor. Excellent conditions of employment for experienced staff. British Council recognised.
EFL TEACHERS (2-3) to teach 20 lessons and participate in social/residential programme at a girls' summer school. Period of work from July 10-August 7; wages from £220 per week. Must be aged at least 21 and TEFL qualified. Applications to The Director, at the above address.

KING'S SCHOOL OF ENGLISH (LONDON): 25 Beckenham Road, Beckenham, Kent BR3 4PR (tel 0181-650 5891; fax 0181-663 3224; e-mail info@kingslon.co.uk; www.kingslon.co.uk). The only year round recognised school in Beckenham. Takes around 150-250 students from all over the world. Established in 1966.
EFL TEACHERS (APPROX 10) to work from mid June to end of August for 16-32 lesson per week programmes (min 4 weeks) mainly for learners aged over 16. Only RSA Cambridge qualified applicants to apply from January.
TRAVEL MANAGER & ASSISTANT for the organisation of leisure programme including evening work and weekends, and airport transfers. Must have a good knowledge of attractions in London and South East England. Knowledge of Italian or Spanish or Russian an advantage. Suitably qualified overseas applicants with good English considered. Interview essential.
    Salaries by negotiation. Applicants must be EU Citizens or have work permits. Applications to the Principal at the above address.

SELS SCHOOL OF ENGLISH: 64 Long Acre, Covent Garden, London WC2E 9JH (tel 0171-240 2581; fax 0171-379 5793). Located in fashionable Covent Garden near the Opera House, the school teaches English at all levels to foreign adults in groups of 5-9 and on a one-to-one basis.
ASSISTANT to work in the tea room and clean premises. Wages £4.50 per hour. To work 5-9 hours per day, Monday to Friday and alternate weekends.

Period of work by arrangement. Ages: 18-30 years. Knowledge of Portugese, Spanish or Italian useful.
CLERKS/SECRETARIES. £5+ per hour. To work approx. 30-40 hours per week. Must have typing and word processing experience.
  Long period of employment preferred. Applications to Mr Y. Raiss, Sels School of English, at the above address.

SUPERSTUDY UK: 1-3 Manor Parade, Sheepcote Road, Harrow HA1 2JN (tel 0181-861 5322). Teaches all levels of English to all nationalities, specialising in general English and conversation in a friendly atmosphere. Five minutes walk from Harrow-on-the-Hill Underground station.
EFL TEACHERS (2-4). £10.88 per hour, exact hours of work to be arranged. Minimum period of work 2-4 weeks between 1 July and 31 August. Accommodation not available. RSA/UCLES, CTEFLA and first degree required.
  Applications as early as possible to Alice Ryder at the above address.

TASIS ENGLAND AMERICAN SCHOOL: Coldharbour Lane, Thorpe, Surrey TW20 8TE. Set in 35 acres; approx. 30 minutes train journey from London, the school runs a summer programme for American and International students.
COUNSELLORS. To supervise sports and activities such as visits and trips all over England, and act as teaching aides. Driving licence necessary.
TEACHERS. To teach English as a foreign language and traditional high school maths and English courses. Must be familiar with the American educational system.
  Wages according to relevant experience. B & L provided. Applicants must have a standard of English as high as that of a native speaker and completed at least one year at university. Applications, including c.v., should be sent by 15 March to Mr David West, Director of Summer Programmes, at the above address.

WARNBOROUGH COLLEGE: Friars House, London SE1 8HB (tel 0171-922 1200;fax 0171-922 1201; e-mail admin@warnborough.edu; website http://www.warnborough.edu). A dynamic and forward thinking institution, dedicated to providing quality educational opportunities to students around the world.
TEACHERS OF ENGLISH as a foreign language. Payment at an hourly rate. To teach beginner, intermediate and advanced levels. Must have university degree, TEFL qualification and experience. Applications to the Director, English Language Programme, Warnborough College.

Vacation Traineeships

Accountancy, Banking and Insurance

ARTHUR ANDERSEN: 1 Surrey Street, London WC2R 2PS (tel 0171-438 3000; fax 0171-438 3150).
The Arthur Andersen Summer Vacation Programme aims to provide students

with an insight into the accountancy profession and the various opportunities that it can offer. The firm offers approximately 25 students the opportunity to work in their offices for 8 weeks during the summer vacation. Most places are in the London Office, although some vacancies exist in regional offices as well. The programme consists of a two-week residential course in book-keeping, auditing, tax and microcomputer skills followed by two three-week placements in both the Assurance and Business Advisory (A&BA) and Tax Consultancy practice.

Applicants should be entering their final year at university and have a strong academic record. Trainees are paid weekly plus overtime and expenses. Salaries are set on an annual basis, in 1998 the salary was £260 per week. Successful performance during the placement will result in students going straight to final interview stage should they wish to apply for a full-time position in their final year. To apply, complete the application form inside the back cover of their graduate brochure and return it, after January 1, to Kathryn Lovell, Graduate Recruitment Manager, at the above address.

CITIBANK: P.O. Box 16086, London EC1M 4LE.
Citibank is one of the largest consumer and corporate banks in the world, spanning 100 countries, with over 90,000 employees and assets in excess of $310 billion. The company offers Summer Associate positions to students in their penultimate year. Approximately 50 students are taken on each year to work in a variety of departments. Students do not need to be from any specific discipline. Positions last for approximately two months and the placement would typically involve working on a key project. Students, who through their placement and assessment demonstrate that they have the qualities Citibank are seeking, will be made early offers of employment. Salary in 1998 was £350 per week.

Applications should be sent by 6th March to the Graduate Recruitment Manager at the above address.

INSTIUTE FOR FISCAL STUDIES: 7 Ridgmount Street, London WC1E 7AR (tel 0171-291 4800; fax 0171-323 4780; e-mail mailbox@ifs.org.uk).
IFS is an independent research institute which specialises in the economic analysis of public policy, especially the field of taxation policy. It aims to bridge the gap between purely academic research and issues of practical policy. The research is largely orientated towards microeconomic analysis, and has a strong quantitative flavour.

The institute makes use of major UK surveys of households, individuals and firms in order to analyse the impact of taxation and other public policies on individuals' and companies' behaviour. Research is disseminated through conferences, publications, the journal *Fiscal Studies* and other journals. IFS aims to provide impartial information from a politically independent standpoint.

IFS offers approx. 3 placements which last for 6 weeks in the summer in London. Trainees can expect to work with a research team on a particular project. Tasks involve the preparation and analysis of data, the conducting of literary searches, and writing up search results. Applicants should have a minimum of 2 years undergraduate experience in Economics or a closely related subject. The salary in 1998 was £200 per week. No accommodation is provided.

Overseas applicants entitled to work in the UK are considered. Applications including a CV and covering letter should be sent to Roger Markless. Applicants should check web site for details early in 1999.

JAMES AND COWPER CHARTERED ACCOUNTANTS: Phoenix House, Bartholomew Street, Newbury RG14 5EF (tel 01635-35255; fax 01635-40500; e-mail rpooles@jamescowper.co.uk).
James and Cowper offer accountancy traineeships over the summer vacation. Work involves preparing accounts for sole traders, partnerships and limited companies, and assisting with audits. The traineeships are open to under-graduates only, who are studying Accountancy degrees and interested in pursuing a chartered training contract when they complete their degree. A competitive salary is offered.

One traineeship is offered in Reading and two in Newbury. No accommoda-tion is provided but assistance is given in finding lodgings. EEA and EU applicants who will be able to continue work when they qualify will be considered.

Applications by May to Mrs R. Pooles, Personnel Manager.

Law

ALLEN & OVERY: One New Change, London EC4M 9QQ (tel 0171-330 3000; fax 0171-330 9999).
Allen & Overy, an international city-based law firm, offers vacation placements to about 80 undergraduates (both Law and non-Law students) in their penultimate year of study. The placements last for three weeks between late June and early September. The salary is £200 per week.

Applications should be sent by 31st January 1999 to Mimi Lee-Denman at the above address.

ASHURST MORRIS CRISP: Broadwalk House, 5 Appold Street, London (tel 0171-638 1111; fax 0171-972 7990; e-mail jane.ahern@ashursts.com).
Offers 50 placements which involve work-shadowing solicitors, undertaking research and simple drafting. A programme of talks and tours is arranged, together with opportunities to meet members of all legal departments. Trainees spend each week in a different department. Applicants must be university students who have completed at least their second year, or graduates. Any discipline. A subsistence allowance is paid.

The company has two intakes of students each summer. Individual placements last for 3 weeks. No accommodation is provided. Placements are based in London. Overseas applicants considered. Applications including CV and covering letter to Jane Ahern between January 1st and February 28th.

BEACHCROFT STANLEYS: 20 Furnival Street, London EC4A 1BN (tel 0171-242 1011; e-mail ef@beachcroft.co.uk).
Beachcroft Stanleys offers work experience in a legal environment for undergraduates who wish to pursue a career as a solicitor. They offer 15 places to 2nd year law or 3rd year non-law University undergraduates with a good academic record. There is a series of two/three week placements, running from June till August. The placements will involve working with and shadowing a solicitor; one week in a contentious seat and the second in a non-contentious seat. The salary is £175 per week.

Applications should be sent between January 1 and February 28 to Ms Emma Falder at the above address.

CAMERON McKENNA: Mitre House, 160 Aldersgate Street, London EC1A 4DD.
Cameron McKenna, a UK and international law firm, offers two week placements to students during Easter and Summer. Positions are open to second and final year law students or final year non law graduates who expect to achieve at least a 2:1 degree. The firm is distinctive, unstuffy and approachable, and is looking for creative, bright, commercially aware, committed people who have the potential to contribute to its future success.

For an application form and further details please call 0845-3000 491. The closing date for applications is Friday 26th February 1999.

CLIFFORD CHANCE: 200 Aldersgate Street, London EC1A 4JJ (tel 0171-600 1000; fax 0171-600 5555).
Clifford Chance is a leading international law firm offering a full range of legal services to businesses, financiers and governments. There are four schemes during the Easter and summer vacations for students in their second and third year of undergraduate studies. The two week placement provides and insight into the practical side of law and a structured programme of lectures, case studies, and visits to city institutions. The salary in 1998 was £200 per week.

Applications should be made by February 26th, 1999, to Anne Niblock, Recruitment and Development Manager, at the above address.

LINKLATERS: 1 Silk Street, London EC2Y 8HQ (tel 0171-456 2000; fax 0171-456 2222).
Linklaters is a leading international law firm with a well-established reputation for commercial work on a national and international scale. The firm offers about 75 placements on schemes located in London, organised at Christmas, Easter and in the summer (2 weeks at both Christmas and Easter and 2 schemes of 4 weeks in summer). In the summer students get to work in two different departments for 2 weeks each. The placements are open to students in their penultimate year at university. The salary is £190 a week. Help can be given finding accommodation.

Applications for the Christmas scheme should be made in October/November, and in January/February for both the Easter and Summer schemes, to Jane Leader, Graduate Recruitment Officer, at the above address.

STEPHENSON HARWOOD: One, St Pauls Churchyard, London EC4M 8SH (tel 0171-329 4422; fax 0171-606 0822).
Stephenson Harwood offer 21 students the opportunity to spend 2 weeks work-shadowing solicitors. Trainees spend 1 week each in 2 different departments. Applicants must be 2nd year Law undergraduates or 3rd year non-Law undergraduates. Salary is £175 per week.

Placements last 2 weeks and take place from the last fortnight in June to the end of July in the firm's St Pauls Office. No accommodation is provided but help can be given in finding it.

Applications by the end of February to the Graduate Recruitment Department.

WILDE SAPTE: 1 Fleet Place, London EC4M 7WS (tel 0171-246 7000).
Wilde Sapte, a major international law firm based in the City, runs information weeks during the summer. The programme includes a full course of lectures and an extended legal case study demonstrating the work of several departments. Applicants must be studying Law at university and should be

applying for the summer before the start of their final year of studies. Salary is approx. £160 a week.

Applications, enclosing a c.v., should be sent by 31st January to Nicola Graham, Recruitment Officer, at the above address.

Media and Marketing

INDEPENDENT TELEVISION:
A limited number of work experience placements are sometimes available with the regional ITV companies. Vacancies are rarely known in advance and demand constantly outstrips supply.

Applicants must be students on a recognised course of study at a college or university; their course must lead to the possibility of employment within the television industry (ideally, work experience would be a compulsory part of the course); and the student must be resident in the transmission area of the company offering the attachment, or in some cases, attending a course in that region. However, opportunities may occasionally exist for students following computing, librarianship, finance, legal, administrative or management courses. Suitably qualified applicants from overseas are considered.

Placements vary in length from half a day to several weeks or months, depending upon the work available and the candidate's requirements. Students do not normally receive payment from the company, although those on courses of particular relevance to the industry are paid expenses. Students from sandwich courses who are on long-term attachments may be regarded as short-term employees and paid accordingly.

Applications should be sent to the Personnel Department of the applicant's local ITV company. General information on working in the television industry can be obtained from Skillset, the industry training organisation, on 0171-534 5300.

MERIDIAN RECORDS: PO Box 317, Eltham, London SE9 4SF (tel 0181-857 3213).
Meridian Records is a small record company specialising in the recording and production of classical records.

In 1999 the company will be seeking one or two candidates who can demonstrate motivation and a keen interest in music. No other particular qualifications are required, although applicants should have a general interest in all aspects of running a record company. An ability to read music is useful but not essential. The successful candidate(s) will participate in a wide variety of tasks including the preparation of art work, accounting, recording, editing and the maintenance of machines, buildings and grounds.

The traineeships are unpaid, though the company may be able to offer accommodation on its premises. The placements run for a varying number of weeks during any of the three main vacations. Overseas applicants will be considered. It is the policy of Meridian Records to only employ non-smokers.

Applications should be sent to Mr John Shuttleworth, Director, at the above address.

Science, Construction and Engineering

BINNIE, BLACK & VEATCH: Grosvenor House, 69 London Road, Redhill, Surrey RH1 1LQ (tel 01737-774155; fax 01737-772767).

Binnie, Black & Veatch is a civil engineering consultancy specialising in water supply, public health and environmental engineering. Much of their work involves bringing treated drinking water and sewage treatment facilities to the developing world.

Each year the firm takes two pre-university trainees for up to twelve months. These students will normally have Mathematics and Science A levels and will be preparing to read Civil Engineering, Mathematics, Physics or Applied Science. The firm also offers placements over the summer to two or three undergraduate students of Civil Engineering. These traineeships last for up to ten weeks and take place in the firm's Hydraulics and Computer Departments. Suitably qualified applicants from abroad will be considered.

In 1998 those on summer placements were paid £190 per week and pre-university trainees about £8,750 p.a.

Applications should be sent to M.E. Hannah, Human Resources Director, by Easter.

DATA CONNECTION LTD: 100 Church Street, Enfield, Middlesex EN2 6BQ (tel 0181-366 1177; e-mail recruit@datcon.co.uk; web site http://www.dat-con. co.uk).

Founded in 1981, Data Connection is a leading British software development company with a world-wide reputation for developing complex high quality software. Customers include the development laboratories of organisations such as Hewlett Packard, IBM, Lotus Microsoft and Sun. The company has around 170 employees and is based in North London, with satellite offices in Edinburgh, Chester, and Washington DC.

Vacation work is offered to exceptional students with an interest in the development of complex software. Applicants typically have all A grades at A level. Data Connection provides complex and challenging programming assignments, with help and support. A salary of £1,000 per month and subsidised accommodation in the Company House is offered. Many vacation students go on to join Data Connection as full-time employees; some receive sponsorship while still at University.

Interviews are held all year round. However, as vacancies are limited it is best to apply in the autumn term. For more details contact Justine McLennan at the above address, or apply on-line following the links from the web site.

INTEX MANAGEMENT SERVICES: 6 Dencora Business Park, Booth Drive, Wellingborough, Northamptonshire NN8 6GR (tel 01933-402255; fax 01933-402266; e-mail ims.europe@virgin.net). IMS is a specialist market research company in the electronics industry, with offices in the UK and the US.

ASSISTANTS (2) to help market research and senior research analysts in the production and promotion of global research studies. Applicants should be electronic engineering undergraduates. Wages depend upon experience. To work 40 hours a week. No accommodation is available. Min. period of work 10 weeks between July and September.

Overseas applicants with good spoken and written English considered. Applications from April to Linda Barratt.

M. W. KELLOGG LTD: Kellogg Tower, Greenford Road, Greenford, Middlesex UB6 0JA (tel 0181-872 7000).
M. W. Kellogg Ltd specialises in petrochemical engineering, construction and Project Management. It offers traineeships during the summer vacation mainly for engineers to carry out process, construction and equipment work. Occasional IT positions are available. Applicants should be studying for a degree in either Chemical or Mechnical engineering, or Construction.
Trainees will be paid £6 per hour. Placements take place at the head office in Greenford. Help is usually given with finding accommodation, but students must pay for their own board and lodging. Applications should be sent from April or May to the Recruitment Officer at the above address.

LOGICA: Freepost 21, London W1E 4JZ (tel 0171-446 2333).
Logica is a leading international computer systems, software and consultancy company with activities worldwide. It operates from offices in 22 countries worldwide and has completed projects in over 60, and is committed to making technology work for its customers, who include some of the world's leading international organisations. It offers vacation work placements during the summer, based in its offices in central London and the South East. A large proportion of Logica's work is systems integration. It is likely that on joining the company, trainees will work on a project at the systems implementation stage. This involves programming to build, develop and integrate the system to meet client requirements. Implementation can involve teams of between two and 100 people working on a system, and can last for a few months to several years.
Logica is interested in applicants in their penultimate year at university or college, preferably within either computing or a logical/numerate discipline, with a keen interest in information technology. Suitably qualified EEA applicants welcome.
Accommodation is not provided. Applications should be submitted on a Logica application form for industrial placements by March and addressed to the Graduate Recruitment Officer at the above address.

SIR ROBERT MCALPINE LTD.: Eaton Court, Maylands Avenue, Hemel Hempstead, Herts HP2 7TR (tel 01442-233444).
Sir Robert McAlpine is one of the UK's major building and civil engineering contractors, undertaking projects such as industrial plants, marine works, power stations, offices, theatres and leisure complexes.
University students reading degrees in construction-related subjects, or 'A' level students considering degrees, are offered employment lasting a minimum of 8 weeks during the summer. Students assist site engineers working on various major construction sites throughout the country. The salary varies according to experience and qualifications and assistance in finding lodgings is provided. Approximate number of vacancies will be between 20 and 50.
Applications should be made to Mr T.B. Hill, Technical Personnel Manager, at the above address.

MADGE NETWORKS LTD: Wexham Springs, Framewood Road, Wexham, Slough SL3 6PJ (tel 01753-661652).
Madge Networks Ltd runs a vacation training scheme for students at their Research and Development Centre in South Buckinghamshire. The placements involve programming and design work and the student is given a specific project to complete under supervision.

The company is looking for students from a good university who are reading Computer Programming or Electronic Engineering and are at the top of their academic field. The company is, however, most interested in students who can show they have successfully completed projects and programmes outside of the requirements of their academic course. The chosen candidates will be expected to work for a minimum of two months over the summer vacation and will earn a salary in the region of £275 per week.

Applicants should contact the Recruitment Manager at the above address.

MERCK, SHARP & DOHME LTD.: Hertford Road, Hoddesdon, Hertfordshire E911 9BU (tel 01992-467272; fax 01992-468175).

Merck, Sharp & Dohme Ltd., one of the world's largest research-based pharmaceutical companies, offers non-first year university students possible vacation traineeships in the following departments: Business Planning, External Affairs, Finance, and Sales Administration. Training takes place over the summer for 8 weeks at the Head Office, Hoddesdon. For accommodation trainees will be given the telephone numbers of nearby university halls of residence and local estate agents. Applications to Melanie Burns, Human Resources, at the above address.

METEOROLOGICAL OFFICE: London Road, Bracknell, Berkshire RG12 2SZ (tel 01344-856032; fax 01344-856021).

The Meteorological Office provides the National Meteorological Service including weather forecasts, observations and climatological data. Scientists also carry out research into the improvement of weather forecasting and the consequences of long term climate change. Over the summer the company offers placements to university students entering their third year of Mathematics, Physics, Computing or a related subject. The students work at the Bracknell head office, for a period of 8-12 weeks. The salary is £11,583 p.a. The Met. Office, as part of the Ministry of Defence, cannot employ overseas students.

Applications should be sent by 20th January to the Recruitment Section at the above address.

S. B. TIETZ & PARTNERS: 14 Clerkenwell Close, Clerkenwell, London EC1R 0PQ (tel 0171-490 5050; fax 0171-490 2160).

An independent civil, structural and traffic engineering consultancy based in lively Clerkenwell.

S. B. Tietz offers summer placements to students from university or college who are studying Civil Engineering or related disciplines. All trainees will gain first-hand experience of structural and civil engineering. Suitably qualified applicants from abroad, preferably from Germany and France, will be considered. Salary will be discussed at interview.

Applications should be sent by April to A.K. Moores, Partner, at the above address.

SCOTT WILSON KIRKPATRICK & CO LTD: Scott House, Basing View, Hampshire RG21 4JG (tel 01256-461161).

A dynamic multi-disciplinary international consulting group involved in engineering, transportation planning and environmental planning projects throughout the UK, Europe, and world markets.

The company has a regular requirement for Civil Engineering students who have completed at least one year of their University course to undertake summer vacation work based in their Basingstoke offices. Opportunities are available within their Maritime, Highways and Transportation sections.

Applicants should have a genuine interest in their subject, be adaptable, and show initiative. Duties and duration of placement may vary considerably depending on the workload at the time. Applications should be made in April to Mr A. Morton, Head of Personnel, at the above address.

The West Country

Cornwall
Devon
Dorset
Gloucestershire
Somerset
Wiltshire

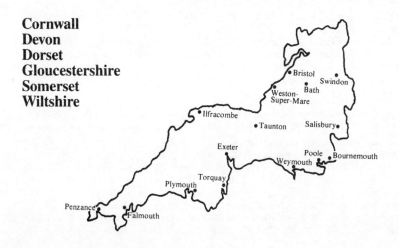

The coasts of Dorset, Devon and Cornwall are scattered with hotels which need staffing during the summer season. The South West tourist trade was particularly badly hit by the recession, but the demand for staff in catering and retail is now gradually picking up.

The largest employers of temporary staff are the many holiday camps in the region: Pontins has several centres in the South West, Butlins reopens its refurbished Family Entertainment resorts at Easter and there are a further two camps in St Ives and Hayle. The Jobcentre in Penzance recruits for local caravan parks during both Easter and summer, as well as for employers on the Scilly Isles. Recruitment for the Scilly Isles' particularly long season begins in January. In and around Penzance there are often vacancies for chefs and kitchen/service staff.

There may well be a demand for agricultural workers and fruit pickers at the strawberry farms around Camborne or in Penzance, home to one of the largest bulb farms in the area.

There is a Hotel and Catering Jobshop, with vacancies ideal for students, within Bournemouth Jobcentre. The Jobcentre, which deals with the West Dorset area, also advertises a variety of other summer jobs, including work as gardeners and beach workers.

Vacancies in Taunton in Somerset are mainly for office and retail work, but there is a need also for fruit pickers, general agricultural workers and production workers, many of whom are recruited through temping agencies. It is important to apply early because the demand is high among students. Some temporary jobs are advertised in the *Tele-Admart* and the *Somerset County Gazette* and Somerset Council also has a relief register of temporary workers for the summer. Temporary jobs are also advertised in the town's two Colleges.

Bristol is one of the few other areas away from the coast where there is an extensive demand by retailers for more staff over the summer.

Children

ADVENTURE AND COMPUTER HOLIDAYS: P.O. Box 183, Dorking, Surrey RH5 6FA (tel 01306-730716).
CAMP LEADER to organise activities for children on residential holidays in Cornwall. Wages £160 per week. Min. age 25. To work over the summer holidays; also opportunities at Easter. Must have qualifications or experience working with children. Applications to Ms S. Bradley, Director, at the above address.

ROCKLEY POINT SAILING SCHOOL: Hamworthy, Poole, Dorset BH15 4LZ (tel 01202-677272; fax 01202-668268). A watersports centre operating all year round offering residential sailing courses for children, teaching sailing, windsurfing, canoeing and powerboating.
CHILD CARE ASSISTANTS (4). £60 a week plus free B & L. Min. age 19. Some experience of looking after children is needed as staff must take responsibility for groups of children attending the courses. Min. period of work 6 weeks between March and September. Overseas applicants welcome. Applicants must be available for interview. Applications from January to Peter or Lis Gordon, Rockley Point Sailing School.

Holiday Centres and Amusements

BEE WORLD AND ANIMAL CENTRE: Stogumber Station, Taunton, TA4 3TR (tel 01984-656545).
ASSISTANTS for tea rooms. £3.00 per hour.
BEE HELPER, ANIMAL HELPERS (2): minimal wages but good work experience.
To work for 8 weeks or less during the school holidays. Applications should be made to Mrs R. K. S. Bolton at the above address.

CHATSWORTH CENTRE: Ulwell Road, Swanage BH19 1LG (tel 01929-422122; fax 01929-421075).
KITCHEN STAFF (6). £60 per week, live-in. No experience required.
ACTIVITY INSTRUCTORS (4) from £75 per week, live-in. All relevant national qualifications required.
Period of work March to October. Overseas applicants welcome. An interview will be conducted by telephone. Applications from February to the Manager at the above address.

HAVEN LEISURE LTD: Bideford Bay Holiday Village, Bucks Cross, Bideford, Devon EX39 5DU (tel 01237-431331; fax 01273-431649).
LIFEGUARDS (4). £3.60 per hour. Must hold National Pool Lifeguard qualification.
CATERING ASSISTANTS (4), BAR ASSISTANTS (4) £3.24 per hour.
Wages given above are 1998 rates. All staff to work 39 hours a week. Posts occur between Easter and end of October. Min. age 18 years. An ability to deal with people is essential. Accommodation available at a cost of £23.40 per

week. Anglophone overseas applicants will be considered. Applications from January to the Personnel Manager, Haven Leisure Ltd.

SALCOMBE REGIS CARAVAN PARK: Salcombe Regis, Sidmouth, Devon EX10 0JH (tel/fax 01395-514303). A very busy caravan park set in rural Devon; no discos etc.
SHOP/RECEPTION STAFF (2). Wages £4 per hour. To work 2-5 hours a day, 6/7 days a week. Must be computer literate, smart in appearance and personable.
ASSISTANT WARDENS/COMMUNITY CLEANERS (2). Wages £4 per hour. To work 2-5 hours, 6/7 days a week. Must be reliable and adaptable.
    Period of work mid June-end August. Accommodation possibly provided. Overseas applicants with good English will be considered. Applications at any time to Derek or Faye.

WESTERMILL FARM HOUSE: Exford, nr Minehead, Somerset TA24 7NJ (tel 01643831-216). Campsite, six self-catering cottages and farmhouse cottage on 500-acre farm by a river in the middle of Exmoor National Park.
FARM CAMPSITE ASSISTANTS (2). Wages specified on application. Long hours, with 1 day off a week. Large caravan provided, meals with family. Duties include signing people in and out, cleaning showers and toilets, working in shop, grass cutting and weeding, checking and cleaning cottages, log cottage painting and some domestic jobs including cooking.
    Must be conscientious, intelligent and hard working, with a practical nature. One assistant needed from mid-May, the other from the beginning of July; one to work until early September, the other to early October. Overseas applicants welcome. Applications and further details (enclosing s.a.e./IRC) from January to Mrs O.J.C. Edwards at the above address.

Hotels and Catering

ANCHOR HOTEL AND SHIP INN: Porlock Harbour, Somerset TA24 8PB (tel 01643-862753; fax 01643-862843). Attractive hotel 10 yards from water's edge in a small picturesque harbour set in the beautiful scenery of Exmoor.
BAR STAFF. Min. age 18. Experience preferred. Min. period of work July to September.
KITCHEN ASSISTANTS, SILVER SERVICE WAITING STAFF. Min. age 17. Min. period of work July to September.
    All staff receive approx. £125 a week for 5 days' work. Split shifts including weekends. B & L available at £25 per week. Applications in writing, enclosing s.a.e., from January to the Personnel Department, The Anchor Hotel and Ship Inn.

AZTEC HOTEL: Aztec West, Almondsbury, Bristol BS32 4TS (tel 01454-201090; fax 01454-202593). A busy 4 star hotel with 129 bedrooms and 21 meeting/syndicate rooms. Old style design and philosophy aims to make guests feel welcome.
BAR STAFF (2). Must be over 18.
WAITING STAFF (2). Must be over 16.
    Both positions receive wages of £86 per week. To work 24 hours a week. No accommodation is available. Min, period of work 4 weeks between April and September.

Overseas applicants with good language skills considered. Interview necessary. Applications from January to Joanne.

BOURTON LODGE HOTEL: Whiteshoots Hill, Bourton on the Water, Glos. GL54 2LE (tel 01451-820387; fax 01451-821635; e-mail bourton@star.co.uk). A small family run hotel situated outside a village and suited to peaceful study and country activities such as walking or cycling.
WAITING/BAR ASSISTANT. Duties to include serving in the restaurant in the evening, working in the bar, serving afternoon teas and reception work. To work split shifts over a five day week, with main duties over weekends. Wages by arrangement; some live-in accommodation may be available. To work either from the end of the summer term to the beginning of the winter term, or all year by arrangement. Applicants must be aged 18, non smokers and have a smart appearance.
  Applications to Brian Miles, Director at the above address.

COLLAVEN MANOR HOTEL: Sourton, Devon EX20 4HH (tel 01837-861522; fax 01837-861614). A small 4 Crown country house hotel with 9 bedrooms. The hotel is recommended in the *Good Hotel Guide*.
WAITER/WAITRESS (1). Wages £3.50 per hour.
HOUSEKEEPING PERSON/RECEPTIONIST (1). Wages £3.50 per hour.
KITCHEN ASSISTANT (1). Wages £3.50 per hour.
SOUS CHEF (1). Wages £4.50 per hour.
  All staff must be adaptable and flexible, and prepared to assist in the general running of the hotel. Applicants must be over 16. Accommodation is provided.
  Period of work June to September. Overseas applicants who speak English considered. References must be provided if an interview is impossible. Applications from December to Mrs J. Mitchell.

DEVON BEACH HOTEL: The Esplanade, Woolacombe, Devon EX34 7DJ.
RESTAURANT, CHAMBER and KITCHEN STAFF, PORTERS (6). From £85 a week plus free B & L. To work 48 hours a week. Some experience preferred but not essential. Min. period of work 8 weeks between May and October. Applications from March to the Hotel Manager.

FAIRHAVEN SEA FRONT HOTEL AND RESTAURANT: 40 The Esplanade, Weymouth, Dorset DT4 8DH (tel 01305-760200).The Hotel is part of a family owned group of hotel and restaurants in Weymouth. Weymouth is a holiday resort on the South coast with a sandy beach and 17th century harbour.
WAITING STAFF (5), CHEFS AND GRILL COOKS (3), KITCHEN ASSISTANTS (2). Wages by arrangement plus tips. To work 6 days a week. Meals provided and accommodation may be available. All staff must be available from the end of May to September. Some jobs are suitable for overseas students wishing to perfect their English. Send applications (with photograph) from March onwards to the Manager, Fairhaven Hotel.

FARWAY COUNTRYSIDE PARK: Colyton, Devon EX13 6JL (tel 01404-871367/871224).
ASSISTANT COOK; wage £2.75 per hour. To work from 10am-4.30pm.

WAITING STAFF (2); wage £2.25 per hour. To work 10am-4pm.
Period of work for above positions July-September.
GENERAL AGRICULTURAL ASSISTANT(S) (1 or 2) to work from 10am-4pm. Wages £2.25 per hour. To work July-September; also vacancies during the Easter holidays.
Applications to Ms Christine Harding, Partner, at the above address.

FORTE HERITAGE HOTELS: St John Street, Salisbury, Wiltshire SP1 1SD (tel 01722-327476; fax 01722-412761). A 3 star 68 bedroom hotel catering for tourists, business guests and leisure breaks. Situated in the centre of Salisbury opposite the Cathedral.
WAITING STAFF needed from May to December to work in the restaurant, bar and lounge area, and to provide room service. Wages £3.60 per hour including accommodation plus any tips. To work on a shift basis 7-10.30 am, 11am-3pm or 6.30-10.30pm; to work 30 hours over a 5 day week, with no overtime given. Applicants should have a basic knowledge of the work and be aged over 18.
Applications to Craig Moore, Catering Manager at the above address. The hotel should also be needing chefs, a kitchen porter and chamber staff; for details of these positions contact Mr Morris McNiall, Head Chef, or Mrs Patricia Hall, Head Housekeeper.

GLOBE INN: Frogmore, Kingsbridge, South Devon TQ7 2NR (tel 01548-531351).
COOKS, KITCHEN HELP, WAITING ASSISTANT, BAR STAFF. Wages specified on application. Accommodation is available, terms to be negotiated. To work approx. 40 hours a week: mornings, lunchtimes and evenings, with one full day a week off. Period of work June to September. Min. age 18. Overseas applicants eligible to work in the UK and with good English welcome. Applications before 1 May to Mr and Mrs Duncan Johnston.

GRAFTON TOWERS HOTEL: Moult Road, Salcombe, South Devon TQ8 8LG (tel 01548-842882). A quiet, family run hotel, situated on the edge of Silcombe, with magnificent views over the estuary. Renowned for its home cooking and relaxed, comfortable atmosphere.
GENERAL ASSISTANTS (4). £120 per week plus gratuities. To work 45 hours per week either in the restaurant or servicing rooms and in the laundry. Applicants must have an outgoing personality and be prepared to work hard. Board and accommodation provided free of charge. To work from mid March to mid October; min. period of work May to September. English speaking overseas applicants welcome. Applicants may be required for an interview although this could possibly be done over the telephone.
Applications from February to Julian Huxtable, Proprietor at the above address.

HOOPS INN: Horns Cross, Bideford, Devon EX39 5DL (tel 01237-451222; fax 01237-451247). A 13th century 2 star historic inn and hotel with 12 rooms, close to the coastal path. Renowned for its cooking and traditional coaching inn atmosphere.
GENERAL ASSISTANTS for duties including waiting, housekeeping, kitchen and bar work. 40-45 hours per week. Miniimum age 18. Experience preferred.

CHEFS also needed. Experience essential.
Staff required for Spring, Summer and Winter Season. Accommodation available. Applications including recent photograph to Mrs Gay Marriott at the above address.

HUNTSHAM COURT: Huntsham Valley, near Tiverton, Devon EX16 7NA (tel 01398-361 365; fax 01398-361 456). A country manor hotel which specialises in group hire for parties, conferences and weddings. A gothic Victorian house set in a remote countryside loocation, it has a reputation for being different and unique.
WAITING STAFF (2-4), CHAMBER STAFF (2-4), EXPERIENCED CHEFS/COOKS (2), CARPENTER/TRADESMEN. Wages from £70 to £130 a week inclusive of accommodation and meals. Applicants must have some knowledge of English, a neat appearance, and be a team worker.
    Min. period of work 12 weeks, staff required all year round. Applications with photo and s.a.e./IRC to Andrea Bolwig, Director, Huntsham Court.

KNOLL HOUSE HOTEL: Studland Bay, near Swanage, Dorset BH19 3AH (tel 01929-450450; fax 01929-450423). A country house holiday hotel superbly located in a National Trust Reserve overlooking Studland Bay. Independent and family run, it has a reputation for service and care of its guests, many of whom return annually.
WAITING STAFF (6-10) for dining room including wine service. £108 per week.
HOUSEKEEPING STAFF (6-10). £108 per week. No experience required.
GENERAL ASSISTANTS (2-3) to care for children. £108 per week.
CHEFS (4). Salary dependent on experience. 706/1 or equivalent not always necessary.
    All staff to work 39 hours with two days off per week. Free B & L available in single rooms. A happy disposition and a good attitude are more important than experience. Min. age 17 years. Positions available for a min. 8 weeks between March to October. Easter and summer vacation positions also available, as well as further positions not mentioned here but only available for the entire season. EU applicants with good spoken English welcome. Interview is not always necessary. Apply from the start of the year to the Staff Manager, Knoll House Hotel.

LAND'S END AND JOHN O'GROATS COMPANY: Land's End, Sennen, Penzance, Cornwall TR19 7AA (tel 01736-871501; fax 01736-871812). A leading tourist attraction in Cornwall located in a spectacular setting. It comprises various exhibitions and trading units which operate throughout the year. In winter the operation is reduced.
CATERING PERSONNEL, RETAIL STAFF for various jobs at Land's End from Spring to early Autumn. Wages by arrangement; hours depend on the level of business. Applicants should be aged over 16, those with previous experience preferred.
    Applications to J. Bond at the above address.

LIMPLEY STOKE HOTEL: Lower Limpley Stoke, Near Bath BA3 6HZ (tel 01225-723333; fax 01225-722406)
WAITERS (3), CLEANER, CHAMBER STAFF (3), BAR STAFF (3), NIGHT PORTER, GENERAL ASSISTANTS (2). Wages to be discussed

depending on position applied for and previous experience. Period of work by arrangement.

Applications to Nick Gray, Managing Director at the above address.

LUCKNAM PARK HOTEL: Colerne, Chippenham, Wilts SN14 8AZ (tel 01225-742777; fax 01225-743536). A four star hotel with a one Michelin star restaurant, set in 500 acres of parkland, 7 miles from the historic town of Bath.

RESTAURANT STAFF (2-4). Restaurant experience essential.

LOUNGE BAR STAFF (1-2).

All staff to work full time, shift hours. Min. age 18 years. Min. period of work 4 months between April and December. Accommodation available for £40 per week. All staff are entitled to use the hotel's extensive leisure spa facilities. Overseas applicants with good spoken English welcome; applicants in England will be required to attend an interview. Personality and appearance of the staff should reflect the high class nature of the hotel.

Applications to Clare Proffitt at the above address.

MR & MRS I.S. MACDONALD: The Flat, 1 Barton Road, Woolacombe, North Devon (tel 01271-870752). Fish and chip takeaway in a popular resort, a few minutes' walk from the sea.

COUNTER ASSISTANTS (3). £145-£150 per week, on an hourly basis. Serving takeaway food, some general cleaning when preparing food and shutting shop. Need little training but lots of sympathy.

ASSISTANT FRYER. Training given. £170-£180 per week, on an hourly basis.

All staff to work 48 hours per 6-day week. Free B & L in comfortable flat with excellent facilities. Min. period of work 6 weeks between May and September. Must have pleasant appearance and sense of humour. Excellent English essential. Applications (enclosing s.a.e. and photograph) from March to Mr & Mrs I.S. MacDonald at the above address.

MILL ON THE BRUE ACTIVITY CENTRE: Trendle Farm, Bruton, Somerset BA10 0BA (tel 01749-812307; fax 01749-812706). An outdoor pursuits company offering over 30 activities such as canoeing and climbing. The centre is one hour's journey from Bath and Bristol, and has many young, energetic staff.

DOMESTIC STAFF (2-3). No experience necessary.

KITCHEN ASSISTANT (1-2). Experience preferred.

All staff to work 35 hours per week. Wages £65 per week plus full B & L in attractive staff accomodation. Min. period of work 7 weeks between January and December. Overseas applicants welcome. All applicants should be available for interview. Full on the job training provided. Applications from December to Ruth Braithwaite at the above address.

NARRACOTT GRAND HOTEL: Beach Road, Woolacombe, Devon EX34 7BS (tel 01271-870418). 100 bedroom hotel with extensive leisure facilities situated in a small coastal village near a surfing beach surrounded by National Trust land, and overlooking Woolacombe Sands.

WAITING STAFF, PORTERS, KITCHEN STAFF and ROOM STAFF. Wages specified on application. Short period of work between February and

January. Longer periods possible. Applications, including details of work experience and photo, to Mr Wyld, Narracott Grand Hotel.

THE NOEL ARMS HOTEL: High Street, Chipping Campden, Gloucestershire GL55 6AT (tel 01386-840317; fax 01386-841136). A company owned 3 Star hotel/coaching inn in the Cotswolds. Generally guests are from Europe, America, Australia or the UK, and stay about 3 days.
RESTAURANT STAFF to work a 5 day week serving dinner, breakfast and/ or lunch.
HOUSEKEEPING STAFF to work a 5 day week from 9am-5pm.
GENERAL ASSISTANT(S), KITCHEN STAFF to work hours as required on a 5 day week.
BAR STAFF to work lunchtimes and evenings during a 5 day week. Must be aged at least 18.
RECEPTION STAFF to work a 5 day week either from 7.30am-3.30pm or from 3pm-finish.
   Wages by arrangement; live-in accommodation provided or accommodation may be arranged locally. Period of work from April to October. Applications to E. Jobson, Assistant Manager, at the above address.

NORFOLK ROYALE HOTEL: Richmond Hill, Bournemouth, Dorset BH2 6EN (tel 01202-551521; fax 01202-299729). A luxury 4 star hotel owned by the English Rose Hotels Group.
BAR STAFF, ROOM ATTENDANTS, WAITING STAFF. Wages £4 per hour. Part-time, full-time or casual work available for all positions. Previous experience essential.
KITCHEN PORTERS. Wages £3.50 per hour. Full-time positions only.
   No accommodation is available. Staff are required around the year for periods of 6 weeks or longer (although less time will be considered).
   Overseas applicants with work permits are considered. Interview necessary. Applications at any time to Sally Sayers.

PENKERRIS: Penwinnick Road, St. Agnes, Cornwall TR5 0PA (tel 01872-552262). Attractive detached house with garden.
GUEST HOUSE ASSISTANT required, to work on an au pair basis. Afternoons free to visit the beach or explore the cliff walks. Accommodation provided in exchange for help. Wages according to duties and season. The guest house is open throughout the winter. Min. work period 3 months; longer preferred, but 3 weeks acceptable over Christmas and Easter. Overseas applicants welcome: the job is ideal for students wishing to perfect their English. Applications a.s.a.p. to Mrs Dorothy Gill-Carey at the above address.

RISING SUN HOTEL: Harbourside, Lynmouth, North Devon EX35 6EG (tel 01598-753223; fax 01598-753480; e-mail: RISINGSUNLYNMOUTH@EASYNET.CO.UK).
GENERAL ASSISTANT (2) for waiting in the restaurant, bar work, chambermaiding and washing up duties. Wages £120 per week plus board and lodging. To work 39 hours a week. Staff required from April to September (inclusive); minimum period of work 2 months. Minimum age 19. Suitably qualified foreign applicants welcome.
   Applications as soon as possible to Mr Hugo Jeune, at the above address.

RIVIERA HOTEL: Burnaby Road, Alum Chine, Bournemouth, Dorset BH4 8JF (tel 01202-763653; fax 01202-299182). A large family holiday orientated hotel based 20 minutes walk from the centrew of Alum Chine and 2 minutes walk from the beach.
WAITER/WAITRESS (2). £90 per week plus tips live-in. To work 36 hours/6 days per week. Experience required. Min. age 18.
CHAMBER STAFF (2). £85 per week live-in. To work 36 hours/6 mornings per week. Experience preferred.
  Wages may be increased depending on experience. Min. work period 3 months between March and November. Min. age 18. All applicants must have a friendly personality and the ability to smile. Previous experience preferred. Overseas applicants eligible to work in the UK welcome. Send applications with s.a.e in February to the General Manager, Riviera Hotel.

ROSKARNON HOUSE HOTEL: Rock, Wadebridge, Cornwall PL27 6LD (tel 01208-862875/862329).
GENERAL ASSISTANT (1/2). Min. £80 for working 45 hours basic a week, plus overtime. To work 6 days per week. Any catering or housekeeping knowledge useful.
ASSISTANT COOK, KITCHEN PORTER. Wages and hours negotiable.
  Free B & L provided. Min. period of work 6 weeks from 25 May to 12 October. Work also available for 2-4 weeks at Easter. Overseas applicants eligible to work in the UK welcome. Applications in late March to Mr Veall at the above address.

ROYAL BEACON HOTEL: The Beacon, Exmouth, Devon EX8 2AF (tel 01395-264886; fax 01395-268890). Georgian Coaching House overlooking the sea, known for its old world charm and high standard of service.
CHAMBER STAFF (2), RECEPTIONISTS (2), BAR STAFF (2), KITCHEN ASSISTANTS (2), PORTER (1). Pay by arrangement. To work 38 hours per 5-day week. Deductions made for B & L. Min. work period 4 months between 1 April and 31 October. Also vacancies at Christmas, lasting 3-4 weeks. French, Spanish and German applicants welcome. Applications to Mr D.J. Larke, Royal Beacon Hotel.

THE ROYAL CASTLE HOTEL: 11 The Quay, Dartmouth, Devon TQ6 9PB (tel 01803-833033; fax 01803-835445).
WAITERS/WAITRESSES (4-6), BAR STAFF (4-6). Wages £4.00 per hour. To work 40 hours over 5 days a week. Accommodation is available at a cost of £32.50 per week. Min. period of work 16 weeks between Easter and November.
  An interview is not always necessary. Staff do not need experience, just a bright personality, the right attitude, and the ability to work and play hard. Applications about 3 weeks prior to desired start to the Duty Manager.

THE ROYAL YORK AND FAULKNER HOTEL: The Esplanade, Sidmouth, South Devon EX10 8AZ (tel 01395-513043; fax 01395-577472).
WAITING STAFF. To work 37¾ hours per week.
BEDROOM CLEANERS/DINING ROOM RELIEF. To work 39¼ hours per week.
  All staff to work 5½ days a week. Applicants must have white shirt, black trousers/skirt, black shoes. All staff should have common sense, a pleasant

manner, smart appearance, a sense of humour and be willing, conscientious, adaptable and trustworthy. Good rates of pay; further details on application. Live in accommodation available. Staff needed from early March to the end of October. Min. period of work 4 months. Full-time employment available to suitable applicants. Applications preferably in January/February, with photograph, c.v. and two references, to Mr Peter Hook, Managing Director, The Royal York and Faulkner Hotel.

SUNNYDENE HOTEL: 11 Spencer Road, Knyveton Gardens, Bournemouth, Dorset BH1 3TE (tel 01202-552281). A family run hotel with 11 bedrooms situated midway between Boscombe and Bournemouth and catering for a wide range of customers.
GENERAL ASSISTANT. £45 a week plus free B & L. To work 6 days a week in split shifts: 8am-1pm and 4.30-8pm. Assistants must be prepared to help with any aspect of hotel work including cooking, cleaning, waiting on tables, and bedroom work. Must like children, and have a very even temper, lots of patience and a lively sense of humour.
   Min. period of work 10 weeks between mid July and mid September. Must be prepared to stay at least until 11 September. Overseas applicants welcome. Applications from March enclosing a recent photograph and s.a.e./IRC, to Mrs L.H. Hackett, Proprietor, Sunnydene Hotel.

SWALLOW HIGHCLIFF HOTEL: St Michael's Road, Westcliff, Bournemouth BH2 5DU (tel 01202-557702; fax 01202-292474). A four-star hotel overlooking the sea.
HOTEL STAFF: summer work available in the restaurant and housekeeping departments. No accommodation available. Previous experience essential. Those interested should contact Juliet Pull, Personnel Manager, at the above address for an application form.

SWALLOW ROYAL HOTEL: College Green, Bristol BS1 5TA (tel 0117-925 5100; fax 0117-925 1515). A 242-room hotel next to the cathedral, which aims to provide a friendly and flexible customer service in keeping with the decor and setting of the hotel.
VARIOUS HOTEL AND CATERING STAFF. £3.50-£3.95 per hour. To work 5 days a week on a rota, including weekends and bank holidays. Accommodation is not provided. Should have hotel or restaurant experience or be college trained. Overseas applicants welcome, but all candidates must be available for interview. Applications to Claire Edwards, Personnel and Training Manager, at the above address.

THE THREE HORSESHOES: Branscombe, near Seaton, Devon EX12 3BR (tel 01297-680251). Family-run country pub near the coast.
BAR STAFF, KITCHEN ASSISTANT and WAITING/GENERAL ASSISTANT. £100 per week plus free accommodation. To work 40 hours per week. Period of work from June to October. Applicants should be of smart appearance and have a friendly manner. Applications in April to Mr J. Moore at the above address.

TORS HOTEL: Lynmouth, North Devon (tel 01598-753236; fax 01598-752544). A 3 star 4 crown 33 bedroom hotel stituated on the North

Devon coastline with stunning seaviews across the Bristol Channel to Wales.
SILVER SERVICE WAITING STAFF. £125 a week. Experience or the ability to learn required.
CHAMBER PERSON, PORTERS, KITCHEN PORTERS. £125 a week. To work 39 hours a week. No experience needed.
   All staff work 6 days a week. Free B & L provided. Bonus paid on completion of season. Send applications with details of previous experience and photograph a.s.a.p. to the Manager, the Tors Hotel.

TIVERTON HOTEL: Blundells Road, Tiverton, Devon EX16 4DB (tel 01884-256120; fax 01884-258101).
RESTAURANT STAFF (2) to work in the restaurant/banqueting area.
KITCHEN ASSISTANT to prepare food in the kitchen.
   To earn £90 per week for a 40 hour, 5-day week; accommodation provided. Needed to work from May to September. Must be aged over 18 years.
   Applications to Rhys Roberts, General Manager at the above address.

TRALEE HOTEL LTD: West Hill Road, Bournemouth BH2 5EQ (tel 01202-556246; fax 01702-295229). A busy 100 bedroom holiday and conference hotel.
WAITER/WAITRESS (1). To work 39 hours a week over 6 days plus overtime. Must have experience and be over 18
KITCHEN PORTER (1). To work 39 hours a week over 6 days plus overtime. Must be over 18. No experience necessary.
ROOM ATTENDANT (1). To work 30 hours a week over 6 days with no overtime. Must be over 18. Experience preferred.
BAR ATTENDANT (1). To work 40 hours a week over 5 days and overtime. Must have qualifications and experience and be over 18.
GENERAL ASSISTANT (1). To work 40 hours a week over 5 days. Must be over 16. Experience preferable.
   All positions receive wages of £3.50 per hour. Accommodation is available at a cost of £28.50 per week. Min. period of work 12 weeks between April and December.
   Staff should be professional, courteous, co-operative and flexible. Overseas applicants considered. Interview necessary. Applications to the Personnel Department 4 weeks prior to intended arrival.

TWO BRIDGES HOTEL: Warm Welcome Hotels, Two Bridges, Dartmoor, Devon PL20 6SW (tel 01822-890581; fax 01822-890575). A 29 bedroom hotel in the middle of Dartmoor with a busy pub trade restaurant and function suite for weddings, dinners and conferences. Friendly working atmosphere.
BAR ASSISTANT, WAITING STAFF (4), RECEPTION ASSISTANT: to work a 5 day week of approx. 40 hours, with extra time available.
HOUSEKEEPING STAFF (2) to work approx. 30 hours per week.
   Required from the beginning of July to the end of October. Wages of £3.25 per hour if living out (or some limited opportunities for living in, wages negotiable) plus tips. Previous experience and qualifications not necessary, but bar assistant must be aged over 18. Applications with recent photograph to Mr. Ross Greig, Personnel Manager, at the above address.

WATERSMEET HOTEL: Mortehoe, Woolacombe, Devon EX34 7EB (tel 01271-870333; fax 01271-870890). A 3 star high quality country house hotel with 25 bedrooms set on the National Trust's North Atlantic Coastline and overlooking a sandy beach.
RESTAURANT/BAR STAFF (2), HOUSEKEEPING STAFF (2), KITCHEN STAFF (2). 40-42 hours per week over 6 days. £60 a week including B & L. Min. age 18 years. Experience an advantage. Min. period of work 2 months between May and October. Applications, with c.v. and photograph, from January to Mr Neil Bradley at the above address.

WOOLACOMBE BAY HOTEL: Woolacombe, Devon EX34 7BN (tel 01271-870388; fax 01271-870613). A family hotel situated near 3 miles of golden sands and a surfing beach.
WAITING STAFF, ROOM STAFF, KITCHEN STAFF, BAR STAFF, PORTERS. £3.08 per hour (live-in). To work 44 hours per week. B & L provided. Min. age 18. Min. work period 4 months between Easter and October. Staff are also required over Christmas and New Year (22 December to 2 January approx.). Applications from March to The Manager, Woolacombe Bay Hotel.

Outdoor

AVON VALLEY FARM: Bath Road, Keynsham, Bristol BS31 1TS. A large, friendly and busy pick-your-own farm, with staff-picked fruit sold through the farm shop.
SOFT FRUIT PICKERS (10) required from 1 June-1 August. Piece work rates (approx. £3.21 per hour). Flexible hours between 6am and 8pm, 7 days depending on size of crop and weather. Sites for own tent and equipment available (60p daily for showers etc). All employees must be prepared to pick. Min. age 16 years. National Insurance card required on arrival. Non EU applicants welcome, but must apply via Concordia or HOPS for work permit and placement, and not directly to farm. Apply, with s.a.e. and telephone number, to Mr J.F.P. Douglas at the above address.

J. F. COLES T/A V. T. COLES: Stephens Farm, Spaxton, Near Bridgwater, Somerset TA5 1BU (tel 01278-671 281).
PEA AND BEAN PICKERS (20). Piece work rates, hours 7am-4pm. Minimum period of work 6 weeks between June and September. Accommodation: own tents required, water and portaloos available. No experience necessary. Overseas applicants welcome. Applications from end of May to Mr and Mrs Coles at the above address.

K. S. COLES LTD.: Cheston House Farm, Cheston, Wellington, Somerset TA21 9HP (tel 01823-664244; fax 01823-660325).
PEA PICKERS (60 or more). Approx. mid June to end August. Piece work at £2 per 21lb picked. 5-6am start; 4.30pm finish. Minimum age 18. Applications to Mrs C.M. Coles, Director, at the above address.

THE COURTS: Holt, Trowbridge, Wiltshire BA14 6RR (tel 01225-782340).
GARDENER (1). To work with two others maintaining an important National Trust garden. £4.00 per hour. To work variable hours from March 1 to September. Min. period of work one month, although preference will be

given to someone who can work for the whole season. Min. age 20. Applicants should be motivated with some experience. Overseas applicants welcome, present employees speak French and Italian to help with any language difficulties. No accommodation available.

Apply from March 1 to Mr Troy Smith, Head Gardener, at the above address. Note that it is preferable for candidates to be available for an interview.

CUTLIFFE FARM: Sherford, Taunton, Somerset TA1 3RQ (tel 01823-253808).
FRUIT PICKERS (30+) to pick strawberries, raspberries, runner beans, plums, etc. Wages at piece work rate plus bonuses. Some accommodation may be available in caravans. Period of work late May to early August. Min. age 18. Overseas applicants welcome, provided they have obtained the necessary work visa. Applications to A.P. & S.M. Parris at the above address.

M.J. DAVISON: Ploddy House, Newent, Gloucestershire GL18 1JX (tel 01531-820240).
ASSISTANTS (20) to work as members of teams planting, harvesting and packing salad crops and vegetables. The teams normally consist of British and foreign students working 6 days a week when necessary. Wages generally at an hourly rate of £3.21 per hour at age 20+ years, but also some piece work. Normal working hours 7.30am-4.30pm with lunch and coffee breaks. Accommodation either limited self-catering at £15 per week or on a camp site with cooking, washing and toilet facilities and a tv room at £5 per week. Min. age 18; must enjoy outdoor work and must be from the EU. Applications to M.J. Davison, Owner, at the above address.

MR J.F.P. DOUGLAS: Avon Valley Farm, Bath Road, Keynsham, Bristol BS31 1TS.
FRUIT PICKERS (around 20) to work from the beginning of June to mid August. Wages at piece rates. Flexible working hours between 6am and 10pm, 7 days per week (no overtime). Camping with own equipment only. Min. age 16 years, National Insurance cards will be required on arrival. Some supervisory positions may be available, depending on competence. Non EU applicants welcome, must apply via Concordia or HOPS for work permit and placement, and not directly to farm. Applications to Mr J. Douglas at the above address. Please enclose a s.a.e. and tel. no.

ELWELL FRUIT FARM: Waytown, Bridport, Dorset DT6 5LF (tel 01308-488283). A small family run farm, open for pick-your-own soft fruit from mid-June. Close to pub, and 3/4 miles from market town, harbour and beach.
APPLE AND PEAR THINNERS AND PICKERS (10). Agricultural hourly rate of pay (£3.21 per hour gross in June 1998). Accommodation is limited (4-6 people) at a charge of £20 per week per person sharing. No camping at farm, however, tourist camp sites are nearby (2 miles). Min. age 18. Wet weather clothing is essential.EEC applicants are welcome but must have a good understanding of the English language. Two periods of work, each approx. 4-5 weeks. Thinning- June to early July. Picking- September. (Exact dates dependant on season, weather, size of crop, etc.).

Applications from mid June onwards to Caroline or William Jackson at the above address.

FORDE ABBEY FRUIT GARDENS: Forde Abbey, nr Chard, Somerset TA20 4LU.
HELPERS required in soft fruit and pick-your-own business for fruit picking. Wages at standard agricultural rate and/or piece work rates, according to job. Must be hard workers, prepared to work early shifts and Sundays. Job most suited to students. Some accommodation and camping facilities available. Period of work mid-June until the end of July. Early applications recommended. Apply in writing (with s.a.e.) to Mrs J. Kennard, Forde Abbey, at the above address.

HAYLES FRUIT FARM LTD: Winchombe, Cheltenham, Glos. GL54 5PB (tel 01242-602123; fax 01242-603320). A farm in a rural setting in the Cotswold Hills.
FRUIT PICKERS (10) to work 8am to 4pm, picking apples, pears, plums or nuts. Piecework rates, approx. £20-£35 per day. No experience necessary. Min. period of work 3-5 weeks between August and end of September. Min. age 21 years. No accommodation provided. Campsite available. Applications from 1 July to Mr Martin Harrall at the above address.

MICHAEL H. KEENE & SON LTD: The Moat, Newent, Gloucestershire GL18 1JG (tel 01531-820363). A family run company which grows apples for supermarkets. Situated in an attractive tourist area within easy reach of shops in Cheltenham and Gloucester.
APPLE PICKERS (12) required for careful hand-picking, starting 1 September. Payment is by recognised hourly rates. To work from 8am to 4pm. Instruction will be given in how to pick carefully. A campsite with showers, toilets and electric cooker is available, but must bring own tent, cooking utensils, wet-weather clothes and boots. There is some mobile home accommodation — please check for availability. A sitting area with TV also provided. No dogs allowed. Please note that applicants from outside the EEA must have permits to work in the UK.
   Call 01531-820363 or 01531-820503 in early August to confirm starting dates.

MANOR HOUSE HOTEL: Castle Coombe, Chippenham, Wiltshire SN14 7HR (tel 01249-782206; fax 01249-782159).
GARDENERS (2) for general gardening duties including mowing, hedge cutting, planting and watering. Wages £130 per week; no accommodation available. To work from 8am-4pm, Monday-Friday. Work available around the year. Minimum age 16. Applications to A.R. Tilbury, Head Gardener, at the above address.

NEWTOWN FARM: Newent, Gloucestershire GL18 1JX (tel 01531-820240).
ASSISTANTS (20+) to plant and cut lettuce. Wages at Agricultural Wages Board rates or piece work. To work 5-6 days a week when required. Early start necessary, often 6am. Accommodation provided on a campsite with shower and toilets; some self-catering accommodation also available at a charge.

Period of work May to October: preference given to those who can start in May. All applicants must be over 18 and physically fit. EU/EEA nationals and overseas applicants with Work Permits welcome. Applications, enclosing s.a.e., to Mr J. Davison at Ploddy House, Newent, Glos. GL18 1JX.

NORTH PERROTT FRUIT FARM: North Perrott, Crewkerne, Somerset TA18 7SR (tel 01460-73451; fax 01460-77685).
APPLE AND PEAR PICKERS (20). To work 6-8 hour days with some weekend work. Piece work rates, approx. £25-£40 per day depending on ability. Min. age 18 years. Must be strong, hard-working and enjoy the outdoor life. Work available between 28th August-10th October. Camping allowed. Regretfully, applicants from outside the EU cannot be accomodated. Applications to Mr J. Hoskyns, North Perrott Fruit Farm.

SHERBORNE CASTLE ESTATES: Digby Estate Office, 9 Cheap Street, Sherborne, Dorset DT9 3PY (tel 01935-813182; fax 01935-816727). A privately owned estate which has been in the same family ownership for nearly 400 years. Sherborne Castle is a Grade 1 listed building.
GARDENING/GROUNDS STAFF. Approx. £120 per week. Mondays to Fridays 8am-4.30pm. Min. age 20. Accommodation probably available. An interest in gardens/plants essential. Min. period of work one month between June and September. Applicants must be available for interview. Applications any time to Mr W.N.C. Beveridge at the above address.

Sport

KNOWLE MANOR & RIDING CENTRE: Timberscombe, Minehead, Somerset TA24 6TZ (tel 01643-841342; fax 01643-841644). The centre is based in Exmoor National Park.
RIDING INSTRUCTOR to work 5½ days a week. Salary £100 per week. Applicants must have B.H.S.A.I.
RIDE LEADERS (2) to work approx. 35 hours a week. Salary £70 per week. Experience with horses essential. Recommended B.H.S. Riding and Road Safety. Mature outlook also needed. Minimum age 18.
DOMESTIC HELPERS (3) to clean and to perform waiting duties in hotel. Wages £70 per week. To work approx. 35 hours a week. No experience necessary but applicants must be cheerful.
  Minimum period of work for all positions July to end of August or preferably September. Board and accommodation is provided free of charge. Suitably qualified foreign applicants welcome. Applications from April onwards to Sue Lamacraft at the above address. Interviews will be held for all the above positions.

MENDIP OUTDOOR PURSUITS: Laurel Farmhouse, Summer Lane, Banwell, Weston-super-Mare BS24 6LP (tel 01934-820518). A multi-activity mobile centre established in 1987 for clients aged 8 years and above. Training available in safety, education, technical skills and NVQs.
INSTRUCTORS. £150+ per week. Min. age 21.
  All instructors to work 5 days per week. Must hold qualifications in outdoor pursuits. Accommodation is **not** provided. Min. period of work 2 weeks between June and September. Overseas applicants able to communicate well

in English welcome. All candidates must be available for interview. Applications from March to J. Hayward at the above address.

MILL ON THE BRUE ACTIVITY CENTRE: Trendle Farm, Bruton, Somerset BA10 0BA (tel 01749-812307; fax 01749-812706). INSTRUCTORS (12). £50-£70 per week plus B & L for 45 hours' work. Min. age 19. BCU, First Aid, Bronze Medallion, RLSS Lifeguard, SPSA and experience of working with children preferable but not essential. Min. period of work 7 weeks between January and December. Applicants should be prepared to attend a 24 hour selection day and attendance at 9-day training compulsory. Overseas applicants welcome. Long term instructors given chance to gain qualifications. Applications from December to R. Braithwaite, Mill on the Brue Activity Centre.

ROCKLEY POINT SAILING SCHOOL: Hamworthy, Poole, Dorset BH15 4LZ (tel 01202-677272; fax 01202-668268). A watersports centre which operates all the year round, teaching sailing, windsurfing, canoeing and powerboating.
SAILING INSTRUCTORS (40). £40-£50 a week plus free B & L. To work 6 days a week. Min. age 18. Min. qualification RYA Level 5 or thorough knowledge of sailing. Min. work period 6 weeks between March and September. Overseas applicants welcome. Applicants should be available for interview. Applications from January to Peter or Lis Gordon, Rockley Point Sailing School.

WEST-ANSTEY FARM EXMOOR: Dulverton, Somerset TA22 9RY (tel 01398-341354). A working farm and stables adjoining open moorland four miles from Dulverton, the nearest town.
RIDING ASSISTANTS (2). Must be able to take out rides and lead beginners when necessary. Hours vary depending on schedule of activities. Min. age 16. Must be fairly light, a good rider and with experience of going on riding holidays or of conducting treks and caring for ponies, horses and people. Sense of fun, helpfulness and a cheerful disposition essential. Must also be willing to help indoors when necessary.
  Pocket money plus B & L provided. Applicants must be non-smokers and able to get on with both adults and children. Accommodation only available for females. Work available all year round. Min. work period 8-10 weeks. Applications with a contact phone number and photograph a.s.a.p. to the Proprietor, West-Anstey Farm Exmoor.

Language Schools

ANGLO-CONTINENTAL EDUCATIONAL GROUP: 33 Wimborne Road, Bournemouth BH2 6NA (tel 01202-557414; fax 01202-556156).
TEACHERS OF ENGLISH (up to 100) for English language summer courses for adults. To teach 20, 25 or 30 lessons per week. Cambridge CELTA/Dip. TEFL or equivalent qualifications required, plus experience of TEFL.
TEACHERS OF ENGLISH (20) for 8-16 year olds in residential and non-residential schools. TEFL or equivalent qualifications preferable, but candidates with enthusiastic and outgoing character may also be considered.
HOUSE STAFF (6) for residential junior centre. To work 6 days per week, mostly in the afternoons and evenings. Experience with children needed.

SPORTS STAFF (8) on both residential and non-residential junior courses. Cert.Ed/PGCE preferable; experience with children essential.

In 1998, salaries were £140-£240 per week according to qualifications and experience. No accommodation, except on some residential junior courses. Min. age 23. Period of work between 1 June and 30 August. Applications from the beginning of March to Ms J. Haine, Anglo-Continental Educational Group.

CHANNEL SCHOOL OF ENGLISH: Country Cousins Ltd., Bicclescombe, Ilfracombe, Devon EX34 8JN (tel 01271-862834; fax 01271-865374).
EFL TEACHERS (3) to work July 3-August 11. Wages £10.20 per hour; to work 24 hours per week. Must have TEFL qualification and should have experience with the age range 11-16. Applications to John Swan, Director, at the above address.

CONQUEST TOURS LTD.: 13 Victoria Road, Bath BA2 3QY (tel 01225-448252; fax 01225-442375; e-mail rebecca@con-ster.demon.co.uk). A small specialist summer school operator which also leases houses for summer holidays. Located in the beautiful holiday resort of Bath.
EFL TEACHERS (10-15). Must speak English to the standard of a native, with TEFL qualification. Min. age 20. £9 per hour for 15-20 hours a week, £200 for 5½ days a week.
SPORTS LEADERS (5-10). Fun loving and energetic, sports leaders should be qualified with life-saving certificate and first aid. Min. age 20. £150-200 for 5½ days a week.
SUMMER SCHOOL MANAGERS (2-5). Management experience, good interpersonal skills and a dynamic personality essential. Min. age 30. £300 for 6 days a week.
CLEANERS (1-2). Energetic, conscientious and able to work on own initiative. Car desirable. £4.50 per hour for 15-30 hours a week, £150 for 40 hours a week.
MAINTENANCE STAFF (1-2). Must be practical,strong, able to use tools and work on own initiative. Carpentry experience and car desirable. £5.00 per hour for 15-30 hours a week, £200 for 40 hours a week.
AU PAIR/MOTHERS HELP/HOUSEKEEPER (1-2). Pleasant and flexible person required to look after house and children. Ability to cook and keep house essential. £45 per week (accommodation included) for 40 hours a week, September-June.
Staff required from early July to late August. Min. period of work 3 weeks. Accomodation available in house share for £40 per week. All applicants must have a good command of the English language. Applications from early 1999 to Rebecca Merriam at the above address. Please enclose a c.v.

DORSET ENGLISH LANGUAGE INSTITUTE: Wessex House, 9-11 Gervis Place, Bournemouth BH1 2AL (tel 01202-316611; fax 01202-318811). A British Council recognised small language school which runs junior and adult summer courses in July and August. Encourages a close relationship between staff and students. Situated in the centre of a seaside town ½hour from the New Forest, and 1½hour's train journey from London.
EFL TEACHERS(1-5) to work 9am-5pm. E.F.L. 2 year's experience required.
ACTIVITY LEADERS (2). 4 hours a day. 2 year's experience required.

RECEPTIONIST (1/2). To work 9am-5pm. Min. age 19. GCSEs required. Staff wanted from July to September. Min. period of work 1 month. Accommodation not available. Overseas applicants welcome. Applications from 1st June to the Administration Manager at the above address.

THE ENGLISH COUNTRY SCHOOL: 18 Riverside, Winchcombe, Cheltenham, Gloucestershire GL54 5JP (tel/fax 01242-604067). A British Council accredited English language summer school in Kent, for children and teenagers.
ENGLISH TEACHERS (8) to teach English and assist with sports and crafts. Wages £260 per week live-in, with time off. Must have EFL qualifications, and/or PGCE/BEd.
SPORTS ORGANISERS (2). Wages £260 per week live-in, with time off. Must have relevant sports coaching qualifications.
   Min. period of work 3 weeks between mid July and mid August. Interview necessary. Applications from April to the Director.

HARROW HOUSE INTERNATIONAL COLLEGE: Harrow House Drive, Swanage, Dorset BH19 1PL (tel 01929-424421; fax 01929-427175).
EFL TEACHERS (20) to teach up to 40 lessons per week, 9am-5pm, June-August; payment of at least £6.50 per 45 minute lesson. Possibility also of helping with evening activities and one full day excursion every two weeks, both paid extra. No accommodation is available but assistance may be given in finding it. Applicants must have EFL teaching experience, be at least 21 years old and have some knowledge of foreign languages. Applications to Andrew Kirby, Principal, at the above address.

MIDLAND SCHOOL OF ENGLISH STUDIES LTD: 62 Littledown Avenue, Queens Park, Bournemouth, Dorset BH7 7AS (tel 01202-303265; fax 01202-303265).
TEACHERS (up to 10). Wages £209-£305 per week. Hours approx. 9am-5pm Monday to Friday, including one excursion day a week and one extra-curricular evening. Most weekends off. Must have at least a B.Ed, preferably with TEFL. Should be keen, able to discipline large groups and enjoy team work.
   No accommodation provided but free lunches usually available. Min. period of work 3 weeks in either July or August. Contractual problems make it difficult for positions to be offered to overseas applicants. All applicants must be available for interview. Applications a.s.a.p. to Miss A. Burton, Director, Midland School of English Studies Ltd.

MILLFIELD SCHOOL HOLIDAY VILLAGE: Street, Somerset BA16 0YD (tel 01458-445823).
TEACHERS (approx. 30). To teach specialist activities, including sports, creative arts and English as a Second/Foreign Language. Rates of pay depend on qualifications and experience but not less than £104 a week. Normally 5-hour day but some evening and weekend work expected. To work 6 days per week. B & L available in exchange for evening/weekend duties. Min. period of work 1 week between 28 July and 15 August.
   Young teachers or final year college students preferred, PE specialists especially welcome. Governing bodies' coaching qualifications (for sport) essential. Overseas applicants with equivalent qualifications considered.

Applications a.s.a.p. to Mr Douglas Humphrey, Development Manager, or Mrs Carolyn Steer, at the above address.

RICHARD LANGUAGE COLLEGE: 43-45 Wimborne Road, Bournemouth, Dorset BH3 7AB (tel 01202-555932; fax 01202-555874; e-mail enquiry@rlc.co.uk).
TEACHERS of EFL (20). £240-258 per week depending on qualifications and experience. Hours 8:30am-4:30pm Monday to Friday. Teaching 6 or 7 lessons per day, of 45 minutes to adults of mixed levels and different nationalities, in classes of about 10 students. Must have first degree in foreign languages/ English literature and RSA Prep. Certificate in TEFL.
Help can be given in finding accommodation. Min. work period 2 weeks between 1 June and 30 August. Applicants from America, Canada, New Zealand and Australia will be considered. Applications from 31 March to the Director of Studies, Richard Language College.

TRYTHALL ENGLISH LANGUAGE CENTRE: The Duchess of Albany Building, Ox Row, Salisbury, Wiltshire SP1 1EU (tel 01722-412711; fax 01722-414604; e-mail: TELCEng@aolcom; http://www.telc.co.uk). Small but expanding language school in the centre of Salisbury. Offers English tuition to groups of international students in a friendly work environment.
EFL TEACHERS (5). £7.50-£10 per hour. To work mornings and some afternoons. Applicants must be TEFL qualified with experience teaching multi-lingual groups.
SOCIAL ACTIVITY ORGANISERS (2). £4-£5 per hour. To work afternoons and some weekends. Applicants must have proof of organisational skills. Minimum age 18.
Staff required from July-August. Board and accommodation is not provided. Enthusiasm and energy needed. Applications from March to Steven Richards at the above address.

Vacation Traineeships

Law

BURGES SALMON SOLICITORS: Narrow Quay House, Narrow Quay, Bristol BS1 4AH (tel 0117-902 2725; fax 0117-902 4400; e-mail lisa-.head@burges-salmon.com).
Burges Salmon offer summer work experience placements to those wishing for a training contract. Trainees can gain real experience from lawyers and rotate around different departments. The company offers 24 places each year. Although mature students may be selected, 2nd year university Law students and 3rd year university non-Law students are generally chosen. Applicants from colleges of Further Education are considered if their A levels are excellent, and their application is of a high standard.
A salary of £100 per week is offered. Placements last for 2 weeks and take place at Head Office in Bristol. A list of recommended accommodation can be distributed to trainees. Overseas applicants are considered.

For a placement in the summer of 1999, applicants are recommended to attend an open day on either 19th or 26th March. Applications should be sent to arrive before March 5th to Miss Lisa Head, Graduate Recruitment Co-ordinator.

WILSONS SOLICITORS: Steynings House, Fisherton Street, Salisbury SP2 7RJ (tel 01722-412412; fax 01722-411500; e-mail cd@wilsons-solicitors.co.uk). Wilsons offers summer placements for 10-14 students. Applicants should be either Law students or university students considering a career in law. Salary is £60 per week. Placements occur in June-July at Head Office, and last for 2 weeks. No accommodation is provided.

Applications by March to Carole Davidson.

Science, Construction and Engineering

DAVIES, MIDDLETON & DAVIES LTD.: Phoenix Estate, Caerphilly Road, Cardiff CF4 4XH (tel 01222-623317; fax 01222-617575).

Davies, Middleton & Davies, a firm of civil engineering and building contractors, has places for one or two trainees to act as assistants to site engineers in the South West. For further details see the Wales chapter.

RAYCHEM LTD: Cheney Manor, Swindon, Wiltshire SN2 2QE (tel 01793-573869; fax 01793-573746).

Raychem Ltd specialises in the design and development of radiation chemistry techniques for commercial applications and applied technologies for industrial use. It has invested large amounts of research money into the treatment of plastics by high energy electronic beam radiation.

The company offers vacation placements to students reading for degrees in Chemistry, Physics, Electronics, Electronic, Mechanical or Manufacturing Engineering and Materials Technology, although other scientific disciplines may also be appropriate. Experience is useful but not essential. Positions are available between June and October and are based in Swindon.

Applications should be sent by the end of March to Mrs Christine Hill, Personnel Administrator, at the above address.

The South Coast

Channel Islands
Hampshire
Isle of Wight

Kent
East Sussex
West Sussex

Hotel and catering jobs should not be too hard to come by along the southern coast as long as you begin your search in good time. In Hastings, for example, many hotels open just for the holiday season and vacancies are generally for unskilled workers. Early enquiries are advisable in view of the likely difficulties in finding accommodation. Holiday camps in the area, such as the Coombe Haven Holiday Park or Camber Sands Leisure Park, always need seasonal summer staff. For details of work in the Hastings area contact Hastings Jobcentre on 01424-784332/784336.

Holiday camps in West Sussex always need seasonal staff too. Bognor Regis Jobcentre is the main contact for Butlins, the largest employer in region, with a special 'Butlins Hotline' to deal with application forms (tel 01243-224206). Butlins is just one of the many holiday camps along the South Coast, others include Sussex Beach Holiday Village, Sussex Coast Holiday Village, Church Farm Holiday Village and Pontins Ltd in Hastings. Most of these provide live-in accommodation as well.

Eastbourne has roughly ten times as many hotels as Hastings, and hotels always have a problem recruiting staff. A large number of seafront kiosks also need staffing throughout the summer. Eastbourne also hosts an annual Airborne Week which attracts hundreds of thousands of visitors and staff are always needed.

As well as work connected with the tourist industry, southern England is a good area for agricultural work, particularly in the hop fields and orchards of Kent (the 'Garden of England') during September. Around Ramsgate on the south Kentish coast, greenhouses require people to pick tomatoes for much of the summer season. Thanks to technology and new crops, it is possible to find agricultural work at any time of year. Wages are not bad, but be prepared for an early morning start. Seasonal jobs of this kind are advertised in the Ramsgate Jobcentre.

The South Coast is one of the principal centres for English language schools, which require teachers, youth leaders and supervisors. The majority of schools can be found at coastal resorts: Hastings, Bexhill, Eastbourne, Brighton, Hove and Bognor Regis, and in Tunbridge Wells and Canterbury inland.

Sporting activities, including the Farnborough Air Show in September generate a short-term requirement for staff to help with catering and car parking. In Southampton, exhibiting companies employ canvassers during the weeks running up to the Boat Show at Olympia in London. Southampton Jobcentre can be contacted at 61-64 High Street, Southampton for more information.

Both Jersey and Guernsey have thriving tourist industries, and the fact that Jersey is exempt from VAT, capital gains tax or inheritance tax means that financial services thrive there. However, potential jobseekers should be aware that Jersey retains the right to deport non-UK Nationals; even EEA/EU citizens need a work permit before they can be employed in the Channel Islands.

Business and Industry

CHILSTONE GARDEN ORNAMENTS: Victoria Park, Fordcombe Road, Langton Green, Kent TN3 ORE (tel 01892-740866; fax 01892-740249). Manafacturers of reconstituted stone architectural items and garden ornaments.
WORKSHOP HELPERS (2) to help with the mixing, etc. Must be strong and energetic.
OFFICE ASSISTANT to help with general office duties. Typing would be an advantage.
Wages and hours by arrangement. Interesting and varied work available throughout the year. Applicants must find own accommodation. Applications to the Manager at the above address.

FLETCHERS: 1 Sudley Terrace, High Street, Bognor Regis PO21 1EY (tel 01243-821417; fax 01243-841200). To work in a refreshment kiosk in a large public park serving drinks, snacks and fast food.
SALES ASSISTANTS (2) required. Period of work from 20th March to 30th September. Must be available to work for the summer season. Wages £3-£3.25 per hour for a minimum of 30 hours per week. Applicants must be over 20 and able to cook fast food. Accommodation is not available. Overseas applicants must speak a high standard of English. Interview is necessary. Applicants should apply from January 1st to R.H.Gowdies or Jane Brown at the above address.

ORDNANCE SURVEY: Romney Road, Maybush, Southampton, Hampshire SO16 4GU (tel 01703-792665; fax 01703-792583).
STAFF needed throughout the year for temporary administrative work. Wages £4.50-£4.90 per hour. Good keyboard skills required. No accommodation is available.
Commonwealth or EEA Nationals are considered. Applications should be made to the employment agency Barker Personnel Services, at 23 Burlington House, Portland Terrace, Southampton SO14 7EN.

Children

EMBASSY SUMMER SCHOOLS: 44 Cromwell Road, Hove, East Sussex BN3 3ER (tel 01273-207481; fax 01273-208527). Organises English language/ activity summer schools for 8-14, 12-16 and 16-19 year olds at schools, colleges and universities around the UK. Courses combine practical language learning with activities and excursions.
ACTIVITY STAFF to organise a variety of afternoon, evening and weekend activities. Salary £100 per six day week. Full board and accommodation provided at residential centres. Age 20-30 years old. Should ideally have coaching qualification/experience, but not essential; applicants with summer school/camp experience preferred. All applicants must speak English as well as a native English speaker, have a lively personality, initiative, be flexible, hardworking and able to work under pressure. Applications from March/April to the Recruitment Manager, at the above address.

PIED PIPER HOLIDAY CLUBS: PO Box 2902, Brighton BN1 8US (tel 01273-504485).
STUDENTS/TEACHERS to organise activities for 4-14 year olds on day camps in Surrey and West Sussex in July and August. No accommodation available. Working hours 9am-5pm, Monday to Friday. Min. age 18. First Aid/ Life Saving qualifications an advantage.
    Applications with c.v. and s.a.e. to the above address.

RUSHMOOR LEISURE: Council Offices, Rushmoor Borough Council, Farnborough Road, Farnborough, Hampshire GU14 7JU (tel 01252-398745).
PLAYLEADERS needed every school holiday to help organise a daily programme of activities and events for children aged 5-11. Wages £4.00-£4.50 per hour. Accommodation is not available. Hours: 9.30am-4.30pm or 8:30am-5:30pm (with a break for lunch) from Monday to Friday. Period of work 26th July-27th August, i.e. 3 or 5 weeks depending on the playscheme. Min. age 18. Applicants should have experience of working with children and be good organisers. Sports coaching qualifications and arts and crafts skills would be an advantage. 2 day training course provided. Applications by March 1999 to D.A. Wall at the above address.

Holiday Centres and Amusements

ATHERFIELD BAY HOLIDAY CAMP: Chale, Ventnor, Isle of Wight PO38 2JD. Small family owned holiday centre providing holidays for school parties, families and the over 50s. Situated 8 miles from Ventnor on a cliff top, in 14 acres of grounds, and on own foreshore.
WAITING STAFF (8). Basic wage £76 a week, plus tips.
KITCHEN PORTERS (8). Basic weekly wage £84.
BAR STAFF (2). Basic wage £84 per week. Overtime available.
SNACK BAR ASSISTANTS (4), STILLROOM ASSISTANTS (2). Basic weekly wage £84.
    All staff to work approx. 39 hours a week. Free B & L. Experience not essential but must have friendly personality. Use of camp facilities when off duty. Min. age girls 16, boys 17. Training given. Employment from 5 May to early October. Min. period of work 16 weeks.
    Applications, which must include a s.a.e. for a quick reply, from 15 March to Mrs M. Williamson, Atherfield Bay Holiday Camp.

BUCKLEYS YESTERDAY'S WORLD: 89/90 High Street, Battle, East Sussex TN33 0AQ (tel 01424-774269; e-mail 1005532731@compuserve.com). Tourist attraction incorporating a museum of shops and social history and a gift shop selling nostalgic items. Situated opposite the Abbey Gatehouse at Battle.

CUSTOMER CARE ASSISTANTS (3) wanted to work variable hours including one day at weekends. Wages £3.35 per hour. Must be smart and reliable with a pleasant personality and the ability to deal well with customers. Min. age 15. To work between Easter and September during Easter/Whitsun/ Summer vacations. No accommodation available.

Apply to the Manager from March to Whitsun, at the above address. Note all applicants must be available for interview.

HARBOUR PARK LTD: Seafront, Littlehampton, West Sussex BN17 5LL (tel 01903-721200; fax 01903-716663). A family amusement park situated on the sea front with rides and attractions for all ages, a restaurant, burger bar and ice cream parlour.

CASHIERS. To work 5/6 days a week including weekends. Min. age 18 and experience of handling cash desirable.

RIDE OPERATORS. Min. age 18. Accommodation available for all posts. Period of work June to September; min. period of work 6 weeks.

CATERING PERSONS. Min. age 18 years.

For all posts starting rate of pay £2.50 per hour. Overseas applicants eligible to work in the UK welcome. Applications to the Operations Director at the above address to be received by the end of April.

SAUSMAREZ MANOR: St Martin, Guernsey, Channel Islands G Y4 6SG (tel 01481-35571; fax 01481-35572).

EXPERIENCED COOK to cater for dinner parties of up to 20 people, and/or HOUSEKEEPER required for father and two student sons. To do housework and shopping on a regular basis and clean the Manor House which is open to the public. Hours: 3 per day at £3 per hour plus free lodging. Afternoons and most evenings free. Period of work May to October although it is understood that one person may not be able to work the entire period. Should ideally have experience of working en famille. Overseas applicants welcome. Interview necessary, but can be conducted by phone. Early application is advised and appreciated because applicants generally either come back the following year or send a friend beacause they enjoy it so much. Apply between January and April to Peter de Sausmarez at the above address.

SUSSEX BEACH HOLIDAY VILLAGE: Earnley, nr Chichester, West Sussex PO20 7JP (tel 01243-671213).

BAR STAFF (8). To work split shifts. Min. age 18 years. Must have experience and be trustworthy with money.

COUNTER ASSISTANTS (3) and GROUNDS PERSON. Experience not essential, training provided.

All staff receive free B & L and £2.00 per hour (plus tips as for bar and waiting staff). Hours: 39 over 6 days. Min. work period 5 weeks between March and November. Must be adaptable, trustworthy and of smart appearance. Overseas applicants eligible to work in the UK and with good English welcome. Applications to Mr Alan Chamberlain, Deputy General Manager, Sussex Beach Holiday Village.

Hotels and Catering

ALBION HOTEL: Freshwater Bay, Isle of Wight PO40 9RA (tel 01983-753631).
GENERAL ASSISTANTS. To work 5½ days a week, with split shifts for breakfast, lunch and dinner. Wages by arrangement. All meals provided free. Applicants should be aged 18-25 years. Some experience desirable. Applicants must be available for the whole season from Easter until the end of October. Applications from February to the Manager, The Albion Hotel.

ANCHOR INN: Barcombe, nr Lewes, Sussex BN8 5BS (tel 01273-400414). A small smuggling inn built in 1790 situated in a riverside setting providing a high standard of cuisine, accommodation, boat hire and pleasant service. Family owned and run by a classic car and jazz enthusiast. Friendly atmosphere.
GENERAL ASSISTANT (1) and KITCHEN ASSISTANT (1). £55 per week plus tips and free B & L. Two days off per week. Min. age 17. Must be a hard worker and have a pleasant manner. Staff required to cover period from mid-May to mid-September, period of work 8 weeks. Non-smokers essential. EEA applicants welcome. Applications in March/April to Mrs J.S. Bovet-White, The Anchor Inn.

ASHFORD INTERNATIONAL HOTEL PLC: Simone Weil Avenue, Ashford, Kent TN24 8UX (tel 01233-219988; fax 01233-647743).
ROOM ATTENDANTS (6). £3.36 per hour. To work 40 hours per week, 5 days out of 7 on a rota which includes weekends. No experience necessary but should preferably be aged at least 18.
WAITING STAFF (4). Wages variable, £3.53 per hour. Working hours variable, as and when required. Min. age 18. No qualifications necessary but previous experience beneficial.
  Accommodation is not available and own transport necessary since public transport is not available. Period of work June/July to September/October; min. period to be discussed at interview. Overseas applicants welcome, provided they have valid work permit, accommodation and good English. Write for an application form from April/May to the Personnel and Training Department at the above address.

BOTLEIGH GRANGE HOTEL: Hedge End, Southampton SO30 2GA (tel 01489-787700; fax 01489-788535). Country house-style hotel set in its own picturesque gardens and lakes, close to Hedge End town, and enjoying good communication links to Southampton/Winchester.
WAITING STAFF (2), KITCHEN ASSISTANT (1). Wages by arrangement plus tips. To work 45 hours, 5 days a week. Period of work June to December. Accommodation available. Applicants should be presentable and have pleasant personality. Overseas applicants must be able to speak fluent English. Applications to the Manager at the above address.

BRANDSHATCH PLACE: Fawkham Valley Road, Fawkham, Kent DA3 8NQ (tel 01474-872238; fax 01474-879652).
HOTEL STAFF to work 40 hours a week. Wages from £4.00 an hour; company discounts plus use of the leisure and health facilities are also included. Uniform provided. Minimum period of work 6 months all year round. All positions are live-in. EU applicants with a high standard of English

welcome. Applications at any time of the year to Loretta Finch, Area Personnel Manager, at the above address.

CAREYS MANOR HOTEL: Lyndhurst Road, Brockenhurst, New Forest, Hampshire SO42 7RH (tel 01590-623551; fax 01590-622799). A 3 star hotel with 79 bedrooms, 2 restaurants, and a health and fitness club with 380 members. Employs 130 staff.
RESTAURANT STAFF (3) to work a 50-60 hour week.
KITCHEN STAFF (2) to work a 50 hour week.
   Both positions receive wages of £160-£200 per week. Board and lodging is available for £35 per week, plus £2 Community Charge. Min. period of work 1st July to 15th September. Applicants must be over 16 and have qualifications. Overseas applicants considered.
   Applications from April to S.G. Elliott.

THE CASTLE KEEP HOTEL: Kingsgate, Broadstairs, Kent CT10 3PQ (tel 01843-865222; fax 01843-865225; e-mail thecastlekeep@hotmail.com).
SNACK BAR ASSISTANT (1) to prepare sandwiches, teas, coffees, etc. To work 8 hours, 5 days a week. Should have some experience.
BREAKFAST CHEF (1) to cook and order breakfast supplies and keep the kitchen clean. To work 6 hours a day, 6 days a week. Should have some experience.
GARDENER (1) to deal with garden maintenance. To work 8 hours a day, 5 days a week. Should have some experience.
POOL MAINTENANCE PERSON (1) to work 8 hours a day, 5 days a week. Should have some experience.
MAINTENANCE PERSON (1). Duties to include light carpentry and/or plumbing and/or electrical and/or painting work. To work 8 hours a day, 5 days a week.
CLEANER (1). To work 8 hours a day, 5 days a week. Some experience helpful, but not necessary as training can be given.
RECEPTIONIST (1) to care for guests, deal with reservations, answer the telephone etc. To work 8 hours a day, 5 days a week. Experience is not necessary as training can be given.
BAR PERSON (1) to serve customers and clean bar. To work 8 hours a day, 5 days a week. Should have some experience.
CHEF (1) to order supplies, cook main meals and keep kitchen clean. To work 6 hours day, 5 days a week. Should have experience.
HEAD WAITER/WAITRESS (1) to serve customers and maintain restaurant cleanliness. To work 7 hours a day, 5 days a week. Should have experience.
WINE WAITER (1) to work 6 hours a day, 5 days a week. Should have experience.
ENGLISH TEACHER (1) to teach English as a second language. To work 8 hours a day, 5 days a week.
   Staff required from June 30th onwards. All staff receive £40 pocket money per week, shared accommodation, breakfast and dinner. Applications to J. Ben, Supervisor.

CONGRESS HOTEL: 31-41 Carlisle Road, Eastbourne, Sussex BN21 4JS (tel 01323-732118; fax 01323-720016).
STAFF required to work 37½ hours over 5½ days per week. £100 per week plus B & L. Min. age 18 years. Period of work March to November. Min. period of work 6 months. Applications to Sandie Howlett, Director, Congress Hotel.

HOTEL DES PIERRES: Mont de la Greve de Lecq, St Ouen, Jersey, Channel Islands JE3 2DT (tel 01534-481858; fax 01534-485273). A 16 bedroom private hotel on Jersey's North Coast catering for approx. 35 guests. The hotel is in a quiet area located one minute from the beach and coastal walks, and 30 minutes from St Helier by bus/car. CHAMBER STAFF/LAUNDRY PERSON (1), CHAMBER STAFF/WAITING STAFF/BAR STAFF (2), DISHWASHER/SERVING ASSISTANT (1). Wages £440 per month. COMMIS CHEF (1). Salary and bonus to be advised on application. All staff work 42 hours a week over 6 days. Min. age 20. Min. period of work 5 months between April and October. Binding contract given. Accommodation is available free of charge.

Applicants must be clean, conscientious and punctual. Experience is necessary, as is the ability to work under pressure and be polite to guests at all times. High standard of work expected. Overseas applicants who speak English are considered, although work permits in Jersey are restricted. Interview not necessary, but photo and references are essential.

Applications to Mr or Mrs Flath, Managers, from February.

DRAM O'APPLES CIDER HOUSE: Pump Bottom Farm, Birdham Road, Chichester, West Sussex PO20 7EH (tel/fax 01243-773828).
WAITING ASSISTANT, BAR ASSISTANT, KITCHEN ASSISTANT to work for a privately owned cider house on a cider-producing farm catering for the holiday and local trade. Wages of £3.25 per hour plus tips; no accommodation available. Shift work from 10am-6pm, Tuesday-Sunday. Period of work from May 19th to September 7th.
Applicants should be aged at least 18, good communicators with personality, mature, honest, literate and numerate; cooking skills an advantage.
Applications to Mr Julian Moores, Owner, at the above address.

DUKE OF NORMANDIE HOTEL: Lefebvre Street, St. Peter Port, Guernsey GY1 2PJ (tel 01481-721431; fax 01481-711763). 3 crown hotel catering for guests in a friendly, informal, homely way. 1 minutes walk from the town.
CHAMBERMAIDS, PLATE SERVICE RESTAURANT STAFF AND BAR WAITERS. Salaries by negotiation. Live-in accommodation provided. Hotel experience essential. Permanent positions available. Applications any time to the Manager, Duke of Normandie Hotel.

FARRAR'S HOTEL: 3-5 Wilmington Gardens, Eastbourne, East Sussex BN2 4JN (tel 01323-723737; fax 01323-732902).
ROOM ASSISTANTS (2) to work from 8am-2pm. Wages of £3.50 per hour plus tips.
DAY PORTERS (2) to work from 10am-2pm and 5pm-9pm. Wages of £3.50 per hour plus tips.
RESTAURANT STAFF (2) to work from 7-11am and 6-9pm. Wages £3.50-£4.00 per hour.
Needed to begin work as soon as possible. Minimum age 20. Applications to the Manager at the above address.

FARRINGFORD HOTEL: Bedbury Lane, Freshwater Bay, Isle of Wight PO40 9PE (tel 01983-752500; fax 01983-756515).
SILVER SERVICE WAITING STAFF (3/4). Previous silver service experience preferred.
KITCHEN ASSISTANTS (2). No experience necessary.
Wages £100 per week.Free accommodation and meals. Min. age 18 years. Min. period of work 10 weeks at any time of year. Overseas applicants with reasonable English considered. Interview not necessary.
Applications with recent photo to Mr & Mrs Cerise, Managers, Farringford Hotel, at any time.

GRAND HOTEL: Grand Parade, St. Leonards, Hastings, East Sussex TN38 0DD (tel 01424-428510).
GENERAL HOTEL WORKERS (2) to clean bedrooms and work in the laundry and kitchen. Wages £3 per hour. Accommodation available for one person only. Period of work July and August. Overseas applicants welcome. Applications to Mr Peter Mann at the above address.

GREENHILLS HOTEL AND RESTAURANT: St. Peter's Valley, St. Peter, Jersey JE3 7EL (tel 01534-481042; fax 01534-485322).
NIGHT PORTER, DAY PORTER, BAR ASSISTANT, WAITING STAFF (2), KITCHEN STAFF (2), RECEPTIONIST to work a 42 hour, 6 day week. Wages of at least £140 per week. Period of work by arrangement. Min age 18. Applications to the Manager at the above address.

GREENWOOD LODGE HOTEL: Roseville Street, St Helier, Jersey JE2 4PL (tel 01534-67073; fax 01534-67876). A family run hotel close to the town and beach, with an outdoor swimming pool: registered for 60 guests and children.
WAITRESSES/GENERAL ASSISTANTS (3). Some cleaning involved. Wages £110 per week. To work 40 hours over 6 days a week. Experience in hotel and bar work useful. Preferably under 27 years of age.
CHEF (1) to cook mainly English meals. Wages £180 per week. To work 40 hours over 6 days a week. Must be imaginative. Preferably under 40 years of age.
KITCHEN PORTER (1) to keep the kitchen clean and pick vegetables. Wages £130 per week. To work 42 hours over 6 days. Preferably under 30.
Accommodation is available at a cost of £33 per week. Min. period of work 6-7 months between March/April and end October. Applicants must be flexible, efficient and conscientious, and able to work as part of a team. Suitable overseas applicants considered. A telephone interview, CV and photo are required. Applications from January to Mrs S.K. Snow.

HIGHFIELD COUNTRY HOTEL: Route d'Ebenezer, Trinity, Jersey JE3 5DT (tel 01534-862194; fax 01534-865342). Situated 4 miles from St Helier, the hotel is a short distance from beaches on the North Coast.
SECOND CHEF (1). Wages £180.00 per week. Must be over 20 and hold a 7061/2 qualification.
DINING ROOM STAFF (2). Wages £160.00 per week. Must have experience and be over 20.
BAR PERSON (1). Wages £160.00 per week. Must have experience and be over 20.

PORTERS (2). Wages £160.00 per week. Must have experience and be over 20.
RECEPTIONISTS (2). Wages £180.00 per week. Should be computer trained. Must be over 25.
All positions work 42 hours a week. Accommodation is available free of charge. Period of work 25th March to 31st October. Overseas applicants considered. Interview not necessary.
Applications from January/February to David Cord.

HOSPITALITY INN: South Parade, Southsea, Portsmouth, Hants PO4 0RN.
SILVER SERVICE STAFF. To wait on customers from table d'hote and a la carte menus, and serve at functions and banquets. Previous silver service experience not essential as full training will be given.
WAITING STAFF (3) to serve breakfast, lunch and dinner and work at functions as required.
ROOM ATTENDANTS (2) to be responsible for cleaning guest bedrooms, bathrooms and corridors.
Wages vary according to age and experience, plus tips. To work 5 days per week in shifts. Min. period of work 12 weeks. Accommodation available. Overseas applicants welcome. Applications to the Personnel Manager at the above address.

KINGSWAY HOTEL: Marine Parade, Worthing, West Sussex BN11 3QQ (tel 01903-237542; fax 01903-204173).
GENERAL ASSISTANTS. Min. £90 per week plus free B & L. To work at least 39 hours a week. Duties include restaurant, bar and stillroom work. Min. period of work 12 weeks between June and September. Min. age 18. Applications, enclosing a stamped s.a.e., to the General Manager, Kingsway Hotel.

LA BARCA RESTAURANT AND GUEST HOUSE: The Bulwarks, St Aubin Harbour, St Aubin, Jersey JE3 8AB (tel 01534-44275; fax 01534-852939). The Italian restaurant is small but efficient, and provides silver service.
WAITERS/WAITRESSES (4). Wages £160.00 per week. Must be over 20, and speak English.
CHAMBER ASSISTANT (1). Wages £150.00 per week.
BARMAN (1). Wages £170.00 per week. Must have some experience.
Accommodation is available at a cost of £20.00 per week. Hours by arrangement: to work 7 days a week. English speaking overseas applicants are considered. Period of work March 1st to November 30th. Min. period of work summer season. Interview may be required, but depends on CV.
Applications as soon as possible to the Manager.

L'ANCRESSE BAY HOTEL: L'Ancresse Bay, Guernsey GY3 5AJ (tel 01481-46664; fax 01481-43493; e-mail lancress@guernsey.net). A friendly, family run hotel which has 25 bedrooms. The 4 Crown hotel overlooks a beautiful bay. There is an excellent bus service to St Peter Port.
WAITERS/WAITRESSES (3), BARPERSON (1), RECEPTIONIST (1), CHAMBER STAFF (3), KITCHEN PORTERS (2). Wages £100 + per week after tax, insurance, board and lodging for a 42 hour, 6 day week. Some

overtime. **Accommodation is in staff quarters situated behind hotel. Min. period of work 9 weeks between mid April and mid October.**
Applicants should preferably be 18-28, pleasant and hard-working. Experience is desirable but not essential. Overseas applicants with reasonable spoken English accepted. Telephone interview necessary.
Applications to John Sims after January 5th.

HOTEL L'HORIZON: St Brelade's Bay, Jersey, Channel Islands JE3 8EF (tel 01534-43101; fax 01534-494450). A 4 star 107 bedroom hotel, located in one of the island's bays.
TERRACE WAITERS (5). To work a 6 day week.
ROOM ATTENDANTS (10). To work a 5 day week.
WAITERS/WAITRESSES (20) for all levels of work. To work a 5 day week.
RECEPTIONISTS (5). To work a 5 day week.
   All positions receive wages of £140 per week tax free. All applicants must be presentable, with good English, good customer care skills and have relevant experience. Some accommodation is available for £90 per month inclusive. Min. period of work 6 months between April and September.
   Uniform and free meals provided. All applicants must have worked within a similar customer care environment before. Overseas applicants who have good English considered. Interview not necessary. Applications from March to Andrew Cox, Personnel and Training Manager.

LAKE HOTEL: Shore Road, Lower Bonchurch, Ventnor, Isle of Wight PO38 1RF (tel 01983-852613). A small hotel in a quiet location.
CHAMBER STAFF (2). To work 39 hours a week. Shifts: 7.30am-12.30pm and 6.30-8.30pm.
WAITING STAFF (2). To work 43 hours a week. Shifts as above.
   All staff work 6 days for £95 a week, plus free B & L. Some experience required, and applicants should have a sense of humour, be tidy and polite, and be able to work quickly and under pressure. Overseas applicants with good English welcome. Min. period of work 3½ months between May and end of October. No replies for shorter periods of work. Applications from January to Mr Wyatt, Lake Hotel.

LITTLE HODGEHAM: Smarden Road, Bethersden, Kent (tel 01233-850323).
GENERAL ASSISTANT (1) to work in an upmarket guest house. To wait on tables, clean rooms, mow grass, clean the pool, etc. Wages £60 a week plus free B & B. Bicycle may be borrowed (guest house not near shops). Applicants will only be considered if they are available to work for a min. of 3 months from April/May to September 1. Applicants must be honest and clean, with good manners and speech. Gardening and/or catering experience an advantage. A cordon bleu chef will receive a higher wage (after a trial week). Applicants from the USA, Canada and Eastern Europe are welcome only if they have working visas. Please make sure you have read the above details before applying. Applications a.s.a.p. to Miss Erica Wallace at the above address.

LONSDALE, SMITH'S, EDEN AND PALM COURT HOTELS: 51-61 Norfolk Road, Cliftonville, Margate, Kent CT9 2HX (tel 01843-221053; fax 01843-299993). A family run group of private hotels. Hotels have indoor

heated swimming pools and sports facilities. All rooms are en suite and have telephones, colour TVs and tea and coffee making facilities.
RESTAURANT STAFF/ROOM ATTENDANTS (4). Wages £45 per week including food and accommodation. To work 40 hours over 5 days a week (usually on split shifts) with no overtime. Must be over 18. Min. period of work 3 months between May and September.

Overseas applicants considered. Interview not necessary. Applications from January to Mrs Ann Smith.

MORVAN FAMILY HOTELS: 57 Rouge Bouillon Street, St Helier, Jersey JE3 9LA (tel 01534-873006; fax 01534-876424). A company in operation for 42 years which runs 5 hotels in Jersey.
STAFF required for various posts ranging from head chefs through to chamber staff. Wages by arrangement; accommodation is available at a cost of £30 per week. Min. period of work 6 months between March and October.

Overseas applicants considered. Interview not necessary. Applications from January to Adrian T. Gordon.

OCKENDEN MANOR HOTEL: Ockenden Lane, Cuckfield, Haywards Heath, West Sussex RH15 5LD (tel 01444-416111; fax 01444-415549).
COMMIS WAITERS/WAITRESSES to work in the restaurant and bar and at functions. Wages of at least £80 per week plus tips and accommodation; to work split shifts over a 5 day week.

Period of work by arrangement around the year. Applicants must be aged at least 18 and have restaurant experience; silver service experience desirable.

Applications to Claire Catliff, Assistant Manager, at the above address.

OLD COURT HOUSE HOTEL: Gorey Village, Grouville, Jersey JE3 9FS (tel 01534-854444; fax 01534-853587; e-mail OCHHOTEL@ITL.NET). A 3 star, 58 bedroom establishment located in the Channel Islands opposite the beach and on a frequent bus route into St. Helier. Lively village location with plenty of amenities.
SILVER SERVICE WAITER/ WAITRESS (6). £170 for 42 hours per week over 5½ days. Previous experience is essential.
COMMIS WAITERS (2). £150 per week. Hours as above. Training will be given.
HALL PORTERS (2). £150 per week. Hours as above. Bar experience is an asset.
CHAMBERMAIDS (5). £140 for 42 hours over 6 days per week. Previous experience is essential.
BREAKFAST CHEF (1), CHEFS DE PARTIE (2). £180 for 42 hours over 5½ days. Experience in a similar position essential.

Min. age 18. Positions available from May to late September/October; min period of work May-September inclusive. Shared accommodation available in twin rooms with private bathrooms for £35 per week. Overseas applicants are welcome; an interview is not necessary. High standards of work and appearance are expected. Apply from March/ early April to Mr R.A.D. Smale, Manager or Mr. P. Winch, Restaurant Manager at the above address.

PORTELET HOTEL: St Brelade, Jersey, Channel Islands JE3 8AU (tel 01534-41204; fax 01534-46625). A family hotel, situated on the coast, catering for 160 guests.

HALL PORTERS (2), COMMIS BARMAN (1), COMMIS WINE WAITER (1). From £140 a week. To work 42 hours per week over 6 days. Min. age 18. Full-board accommodation is available at £30 a week. Period of work May to October; min. 4 months. EEA applicants with a good knowledge of English considered. Applications from April onwards to Mr Mario Dugini, Manager, at the Portelet Hotel.

HOTEL REX: St Saviours Road, St Helier, Jersey JE2 4GJ (tel 01534-31668; fax 01534-66922). Established 40 years ago, the hotel is 5 minutes from St Helier.
RECEPTIONISTS (2). Wages £145 per week. Must have computer experience.
DAY PORTER (1). Wages £135 per week. Should have some experience.
WAITERS (2) and WAITRESSES (2). Wages £135 per week. Must have silver service experience.
COMMIS CHEF (1). Wages £136 per week. Must be experienced.
  All staff work 42 hours a week. Accommodation is available at a cost of £35 per week. Staff share accommodation, with a max. of 2 per room. Uniforms are supplied by the hotel. Min. period of work 6 months between April and October.
  Interview necessary. French and Italians are encouraged to apply. Applications form 1st March to N. Berenguer, Hotel Manager.

ROC ANNICK GUEST HOUSE: La Rue des Boeufs, St Mary, Jersey JE3 3EQ (tel 01534-862272; fax 01534-865709; e-mail annick@Super.net.uk). A quiet country guest house with 11 bedrooms.
WAITRESS/CHAMBERMAID (1) to work alongside proprietor. Wages £135 per week. To work 34 hours over 7 days a week. Accommodation is available at a cost of £32.50 per week. Min. period of work 6 months from May to October. Experience is preferred.
  Overseas applicants with perfect English considered. Interview preferred. Applications from April to Anne Coote.

ROCKLANDS HOTEL: St. Lawrence, Isle of Wight PO38 1XH (tel 01938-852964; fax 01983-852964).
KITCHEN, BEDROOM, RESTAURANT and RELIEF ASSISTANTS. Wages approx. £100 per week plus board and lodging. To work 8 hours per day. Period of work by arrangement between March and late November. Previous experience is not necessary.
  Applications should be sent with a c.v. to M. Exposite or B. Robertson-Walker at the above address.

THE ROYAL HOTEL: Belgrave Road, Ventnor, Isle of Wight PO38 1AS (tel 01983-852186; fax 01983-855395).
WAITING STAFF (4/5), CHAMBER STAFF (4/5), KITCHEN PORTERS (2/3). £100-£120 per week. To work at least 45 hours per week. Training available. Accommodation provided at no extra cost. Staff required from April to October; min. period of work the three months of July, August and September. Overseas applicants welcome, members of staff from France, Spain and South Africa already employed.
  Interview required or trial work period is necessary. Applications from March 1st to the Personnel Manager/General Manager at the above address.

ROYAL ESPLANADE HOTEL: Ryde, Isle of Wight PO33 2ED (tel 01983-562549; fax 01983-563918). Run by Shearings Hotels, the hotel has an 11 month season and is closed in January. It offers various benefits of working for a large company.
WAITING STAFF, KITCHEN PORTERS, CHAMBER STAFF, BAR STAFF. From £2.70 per hour plus tips. To work 39 hours per week. Max. age 28 years. All staff work 6 days per week. Free B & L. No experience needed. Full in-house training is given. Applications enclosing photograph to Mrs C. Davies, General Manager.

SEYMOUR HOTELS OF JERSEY: 1 Wharf Street, St Helier, Jersey JE2 0ZX (tel 01534-875926; fax 01534-780726). The largest hotel group in the Channel Islands, with 5 hotels catering for all aspects of the leisure, business and conference markets.
RECEPTIONISTS (20). Wages were £170 per week in 1998. Some previous experience is required. Computer skills and languages are an advantage. Must be over 18.
WAITING STAFF (35). Wages were £160 per week in 1998. Some positions require specific skills eg. silver service. Must be over 18.
BAR STAFF (15). Wages were £160 in 1998. Previous experience needed. Must be over 18.
COMMIS CHEFS, CHEFS DE PARTI, SOUS CHEFS (20). Wages were £150-£200 in 1998. Applicants must have experience relevant to the level of the position.
ROOM ATTENDANTS (20). Wags were £135 per week in 1998. Some experience would be useful.
PORTERS (10). Wages were £140-£160 in 1998. Some experience would be useful.
All staff work 42 hours a week over 5/6 days. Accommodation is provided at a cost of £31.35 per week. Min. period of work 6 months between March/April and end October. Full training is provided where appropriate. There are opportunities for career development and permanent employment.
Applicants should be UK/EEC citizens, with a basic level of spoken English. Interview necessary, but may be conducted by telephone. Applications from February to Mrs S. Armes, Group Personnel Training Manager.

STAKIS ARUNDEL HOTEL: Yapton Road, Walberton, West Sussex BN18 OLS (tel 01243-551215; fax 01243 552481).
CASUAL BANQUETING STAFF for silver service lay ups and clear downs, customer care etc. To work as and when business requires (mainly weekends and evenings).
CASUAL KITCHEN PORTERS (3) to see to the cleanliness of the kitchen, washing pots, plates etc.
Wages £3.50 per hour. Period of work by arrangement, but to begin work as soon as possible. Applicants should be aged at least 18. Applications to Joanne Cox, P & T Manager, at the above address.

STOCKS ISLAND HOTEL: Sark, via Guernsey, Channel Islands GY9 0SD (tel 01481-832001; fax 01481-832130; e-mail stocks@sark.net). Sark is a small rural island 20 miles from France; fishing, farming and eco-tourism provide the main local occupations. Stocks is a traditional old farmhouse and home of the Amorgie family.
SILVER SERVICE WAITING STAFF for general waiting and some cleaning

duties in two award-winning restaurants. Must possess silver-service skills, a pleasant personality and caring attitude.

KITCHEN PORTER for general kitchen cleaning duties and some vegetable preparation in two high quality kitchens with a brigade of qualified chefs. Must work extremely cleanly, efficiently and quickly. Overseas applicants considered.

BISTRO STAFF for general waiting and cleaning duties in busy but informal Bistro restaurant. Must be attractive with pleasant personality and very good references. The ability to work quickly, cleanly and efficiently are essential.

Wages £125 per week, tax-free with no deductions. B & L provided. Private medical health cover provided. To work maximum of 60 hours per week over 6 days. Eighteen members of staff required to work from April until October, with four additional workers between June and September. Overseas applicants welcome but must speak the standard of English of a native. Preferred age group 20-35. Sark is an isolated and unspoilt island. Applicants must be able to adapt to the unique working environment. For further details contact Mr Paul Armorgie, Stocks Island Hotel and Restaurants.

Outdoor

ADRIAN SCRIPPS LTD.: Moat Farm, Five Oak Green, Paddock Wood, Tonbridge, Kent TN12 6RR (tel 01892-832406; fax 01892-832721).

HOP PICKERS. Approx. £150 a week. Work involves mechanical picking of hops for a period of 4-5 weeks from 1 September.

PIECEWORK FRUIT PICKERS to pick apples and pears growing on small trees for 4-5 weeks from early September.

Self-catering accommodation provided. Min. age 18. For more details write to Adrian Scripps Ltd. at the above address, enclosing s.a.e, after 1 June. Please note that no bookings are taken before July 1.

AGGS FARMS: The Garden House, Merrywood Lane, Pulborough, Sussex RH20 3HE (tel 01903-742116).

FRUIT PICKERS (3) to work from 5-16 September. 9am-4.30pm per day. Wage of £3.20 per hour. No accommodation available. Applications to S. Hanbury, AGGS, at the above address.

APPLE PIE FARM: Cranbrook Road, Cranbrook, Kent TN17 4EU (tel 0181-948 8132). Set in an area of outstanding natural beauty, the farm is about 20 minutes walk from Cranbrook. Minicabs are available nearby.

APPLE PICKERS (30). Wages in line with the current rate for casual work. During the height of the season (September to October) applicants may work as many hours as required by the employer or crop. Simple accommodation is provided free of charge. No qualifications necessary. Overseas applicants welcome. Staff required from August to October. Applications to Mr J. Pollitzer at the above address.

S.C. AND J.H. BERRY LTD: Gushmere Court Farm, Selling, Faversham, Kent (tel 01227-752205/752838). A family run farm in a beautiful area of Kent, which grows a range of crops to sell to supermarkets, wholesalers and brewers.

HOP PICKERS/DRIVERS/OAST CREW (5). Wages at standard Agricultural Wages Board Rates. There may also be employment for an additional 4 workers to be paid piece work rates. To work a standard 39 hours per week, plus at least 16 hours overtime. Longest hours are expected of the oast crew. Work cannot be guaranteed during wet weather. Self-catering accommodation in caravans available for approx. £10 a week: blankets, pillows and separate kitchen, lounge and shower facilities are provided, but applicants should bring their own sleeping bags, towels, etc. as well as Wellington boots and waterproof clothing.

Workers are needed for the entire period between 21 August and 20 September. Applicants should be students over 18 years old. EEA applicants considered. Possession of a driving licence would be an advantage. Applications (with s.a.e. or IRC) should be sent from 1 May to Mr J.P.S. Berry at the above address.

BRAMSHOT HOUSE: Fleet, Hampshire GU13 8RT (tel 01252-617304). A family who need help with their large garden, chickens, ducks, general repairs and maintenance. Would suit anyone wanting a working holiday. 45 minutes by train from London.

GARDENERS/PAINTERS/CARPENTERS (1-2). £20 pocket money per week. Flexible working arrangement averaging 3-5 hours per day. Plenty of free time for sightseeing. Self-contained fully furnished flat provided, also produce from the garden when available and use of bicycle, tennis court and swimming pool. Some skill in painting, gardening or carpentry essential. Overseas applicants welcome. Applications to Mrs P.A. Duckworth at the above address.

W. BRICE & SON LTD: Mockbeggar Farm, Higham, Rochester, Kent ME3 8EU (tel 01634-717425; fax 01634-717891). A farm with an International Camp close to London. Lots of work for all skills. Entertainment programme.

FRUIT PICKERS AND PACKERS (up to 400). Weekly wages according to piece work rates. To work up to 8 hours a day, 6 days per week. Minimum period of employment four weeks.

Caravans and campsite available at £15.00 per person per week to include use of farm kitchen, showers and other facilities. Period of work May to October, but the busiest time is June 1 to July 10. New pickers are not normally accepted after August 1st. EEA applicants or overseas applicants with work permits welcome.

Applications, with s.a.e. please, to the above address.

BROGDALE FARM: Brogdale Road, Faversham, Kent ME13 8XZ (tel 01795-535286; fax 01795-531710). Home of the national fruit collections and centre for the conservation and evaluation of fruit crops.

FRUIT PICKERS (6-10). To work from June until the end of October harvesting fruit crops and trials. Min. age 17.

FRUIT FARM WORKERS (2). To work from June to November: general farm work including nursery production and propagation. Min. age 18; must have some previous experience or college qualifications.

To work a basic 39 hour week. To be paid agricultural wages board rates plus bonus. Accommodation may be available. Min. stay 8 weeks. Applications to Dr D.Pennell, Director, at the above address.

J.I.B. CANNON & SON: Roughway Farm, Tonbridge, Kent TN11 9JN (tel/fax 01732-811284). A farm located only 30 minutes from London, yet set in the quiet and picturesque county of Kent.

FRUIT PICKERS (20). To work 7 or 8 hours a day. Piecework rates. Min. age 18.
   Period of work 20 June - 20 July. Applicants must be from the E.U. or eligible to work in the U.K. Accommodation available at cost of £1.50 per day. Stamina is vital as work is outside and of a physical nature. Applications from April enclosing s.a.e. or IRC to G.B. Cannon, Roughway Farm.

CHARRINGTON FRUIT FARMS: Old Cryals, Cryals Road, Matfield, Tonbridge, Kent TN12 7HN (tel 0189-272 2372; fax 0189-272 3311).
FRUIT PICKERS (6-10). Casual rate paid, flat rate during harvest time. Minimum age 18 years. Min. period of work 1 week between end of August and first week of October. No accommodation available so applicants should live locally. Must be healthy and willing to work hard and for long hours when the weather permits. Overseas applicants welcome but must have work permit and visa if coming from non EU countries. Please apply, from July, to Charrington Fruit Farms at the above address.

S.H. CHESSON: Manor Farm, Oldbury, Ightham, Sevenoaks, Kent TN15 9DG (tel/fax 01732-780496). Situated approx. 64km from London. Approx. 2km from station and shops.
FRUIT PICKERS (20) to work 6 days per week picking strawberries (June-Sept) and apples/pears (Sept/Oct). Hours of work vary depending on the nature of the job. Start time 6.30am-8.00am; finish 2-5pm. Day off alternate Sat/Sun. Wages: piecework in region of £100-£150 per week. Minimum work period 4 weeks between 1 June and 10 October. Campsite charges £11.20 per week; kitchen, showers, laundry, tv/video room, canteen, outdoor recreations, outings and entertainment provided. Bring your own tent. Minimum age 18. EU/EEA citizens welcome. Non EU/EEA citizens must apply for necessary work permit through Concordia. Apply in writing for an application form, from March 1 to Mr A.T.Chesson, at the above address. All applicants must enclose a s.a.e.

EDWARD VINSON LTD: Ratling Court Farm, Aylesham, Near Canterbury, Kent CT3 3HN (tel 01304-840427; fax 01304-840582). Located between Canterbury and Dover, the farm is ideally situated near to the train station at Adisham on the Dover to Victoria London line
FRUIT PICKERS (up to 50) to pick strawberries for supermarket outlets. Wages at piece work rates; average earnings are between £20 and £30 per day. Working hours 6am-1pm plus some evening picking, 6 days a week. Private campsite available on farm for use of students. Period of work from early June to late September. Applications to Mr R. Dunkling, Office Manager, at the above address.

ELPHICKS FARM: Scuffits, Hunton, Maidstone, Kent ME15 OSB (tel 01622-820758).
APPLE PICKERS (6). Wages at Agricultural Wages Board rate. To work 8-9 hours per day. Caravan accommodation provided. Min. age 19 years. Period of work end of August to end of September. Overseas applicants must have valid working visas. Applications (enclosing s.a.e. or IRC) to be sent no earlier than 1 April and no later than 31 May to Mr S.S. Day, Elphicks Farm.

EWELL FARM: Edward Vinson Ltd., Graveney Road, Faversham, Kent ME13 8UP (tel: 01795-530335; fax 01795-591415). A friendly fruit growing company with 6 farms.
PICKERS (15) to harvest strawberries from June-September, and apples and pears from September 1-28, approx. Payment at piece work rates; average £23-£40 per day. To work 8 hours per day, 6 days per week. Accommodation available for approx. £3 per day. Strawberry picking is hard work, but there is good money to be earned by fit pickers. Only people with valid work permits should apply. Applications to Mr C. Rose, Farm Manager, at the above address.

S. FERMOR: Oakdene Farm, Sutton Valence, Maidstone, Kent ME17 3LS (tel 01622-843332; fax 01622-843332). Small fruit farm.
FRUIT PICKERS (10). Paid at piecework rates.
To work Monday-Friday; possibly 7 days per week. Basic accommodation available. Min. period of work 1 week between May and September. Min. age 18. Overseas applicants welcome. Applications including s.a.e at any time to Mrs J. Fermor at the above address.

GASKAIN'S LTD: Norham Farm, Selling, Faversham, Kent ME13 9RL (tel 01227-752239; fax 01227-751265)
FRUIT PICKERS (100), FRUIT PACKERS (20) required to pick and pack strawberries, cherries, plums, apples and pears. Wages at piecework rates and Agricultural Wages Board daily rate. 8.30am-4.30pm, 7 days per week when necessary. Min. period of work 3 weeks between 20th May and 6th October (June and September most labour required). Site for own tent available at approx £2.50 per week. Toilets, showers, kitchen/mess room on site. Age 18 yrs and above preferred. Overseas applicants welcome but those from outside the EEA must hold a valid work permit. Applications to the Office Manager at the above address.

H.E. HALL & SON LTD: Little Pattenden, Marden, Kent TN12 9QL (tel 01622-831376; fax 01622-831654).
FRUIT PICKERS (10). Paid piecework based on £4 per hour. 8am-3pm, Mon-Fri, but flexible hours and days dependent on weather and crop. Basic self-catering accommodation available at no cost. Min. period of work 1 day between mid August and mid October. Min. age 20. No previous experience essential but it is useful. Male and female staff welcome. Overseas applicants considered if work authorisation is in order and English is spoken.
Applications from June onwards to Peter Hall by telephone.

HEATON & HUNT (SOFT FRUIT GROWERS): Boundary Farm, Maidstone Road, Hadlow, Tonbridge, Kent TN11 OJH (tel 01732-851184; fax 01732-850640). Situated half a mile from the shops of Hadlow and connected to Tonbridge and Maidstone by frequent buses.
RASPBERRY/BLACKBERRY PICKERS AND PACKERS (30). Some general farm work. Wages at Agricultural Wages Board piece rates. Picking and packing takes place 7 days a week. Pickers are expected to work 5 or 6 days a week, from 6.30am-4.30pm approx. Days off by arrangement. Min. age 18 years. Friendly campsite available with mess room, kitchen, bicycles, tv, telephone and hot showers. Min. period of work 4 weeks between 1 July and 31 October. Overseas applicants welcome but those from outside the EEA

must hold a valid work permit. Applications to Alexander Hunt Esq., at the above address.

HILL FARM ORCHARDS: Droxford Road, Swanmore, Hampshire SO32 2PY (tel 01489-878616). Pleasantly situated between Portsmouth and Southampton, with shops and pubs nearby. Picks soft fruits (mainly raspberries) for high class outlets.
SOFT FRUIT PICKERS (up to 30). Required June to July.
APPLE PICKERS (up to 50). Required September to October.
  Pay as set by Agricultural Wages Board and piece work rates at the height of the seasons. Hours: 8.00am-4pm Monday to Friday, with occasional weekends. Min. fee campsite available. Min. period of work 1 week. Applicants must be eligible to work in the UK. Applications by post to Mr Paul Roberts, Farm Manager, at the above address: by mid-April for soft fruit pickers, by August for apples.

HUGH LOWE FARMS LTD: Barons Place, Mereworth, Maidstone, Kent ME18 5NF (tel 01622-812721). Farms growing quality strawberries and raspberries for local markets and supermarkets.
SOFT FRUIT PICKERS (50). Piece work rates. To work 6 days per week. Min. age 18. Campsite with facilities provided: bring own tent, sleeping bag and cooking utensils. Busy but pleasant working conditions. Work available from late May to September (late May arrivals particularly welcome). EEA nationals welcome. Write for application form, enclosing s.a.e., to the above address. Please do not expect a reply to applications until after 15 April.

IAN T. LINCH: Haven Farm, North Street, Sutton Valence, Maidstone, Kent ME17 3HS (tel 01622-842222).
FRUIT PICKERS (8). Payment at piece work rates, variable working hours. Period of work June to October. Free accommodation available in 2 caravans sleeping four. Applicants must be authorised to work in the UK. Applications to Mr I.T. Linch at the above address.

LANGDON MANOR FARM: Seasalter Road, Goodnestone, Faversham, Kent ME13 9DA (tel 01795 530035).
SOFT FRUIT PICKERS & AGRICULTURAL WORKERS required to pick and pack all types of soft fruit to a very high standard. Minimum age 18. Pickers will be trained and should be hard working and conscientious. Min. work period of 3 weeks between mid May and October. Pickers especially welcome in June. Hours 6am to 3pm with some work in evenings. Piecework rates paid.
  Accommodation available in mobile homes, cost £14 per week; or if you bring your own tent £7 per week. Facilities include showers, toilets, mess room, kitchen, bus to shops. Group outings, discos and barbeques organised. English lessons given 2 nights per week. Easy access to London (by train 50 minutes). Early booking advised; notification of acceptance March. Overseas applicants welcome but those from outside the EEA must hold a valid work permit. Applications to the above address enclosing a s.a.e. or IRC.

LAUREL TREE FRUIT FARM: Boar's Head, East Sussex TN6 3HD (tel 01892-661637 or 01892-654011; mobile 0468-980308; fax 01892-663417).
PICKERS (20) for top fruit picking (apple and pear). Wages £3.10 per hour, to work 6 hours per day. Period of work depends on harvest, but probably 20

days between 25th August and 30th September (approx). No accommodation available. Overseas applicants with valid working visas welcome. No interview necessary. Applications from 20th August onwards to Robert Booker (mobile phone 0468-980308) or evenings at the above number.

H. MOUNT AND SONS LTD: Woolton Farm, Bekesbourne, Canterbury, Kent CT4 5EB (tel 01227-830525; fax 01227-831969).
FRUIT PICKERS/FARM WORKERS (10). To pick raspberries, strawberries, blackberries, apples, pears and do plantation work. Wages at hourly or piece work rates. To work 8 hours per day. Min. age 18. Staff required from May 15th to September 30th, min. period of work 4 weeks. Accommodation available. Full cooking and washing facilities available. Overseas applicants with valid working visas welcome.
   Applicants must be available for interview. Applications from May 1st to Mrs Rosemary Mount at the above address.

MURDOCH & ALLFREY LTD: Clock House Farm, Coxheath, Maidstone, Kent ME17 4PG.
SOFT FRUIT PICKERS/PACKERS. Wages £25-£40 per day: piecework rates for picking. No qualifications required. Accomodation with showers and other facilities provided. Applications accepted only from those able to commence work prior to 15 June. Min. period of work 3 weeks. Overseas applicants welcome, but those from outside the EEA must hold a valid work permit. Applications from 1 January to Mr R.K. Pascall at the above address.

R.H. NIGHTINGALE & PARTNER: Gibbet Oak Farm, Appledore Road, Tenterden, Kent TN30 7DH (tel 01580-763492; fax 01580-763938).
APPLE/PEAR PICKERS (up to 15) to work from 25 August to 30 September. 5-9 hours per day, depending on ripening of crops. Payment at piecework rates. Applicants should be fit, willing and able; age not important. Overseas applicants welcome, but those from outside the EU must hold a valid work permit. Applications to P.J. Nightingale at the above address.

PERRYHILL ORCHARD: Bolebroke Lodge, Edenbridge Road, Hartfield, East Sussex TN7 4JJ (tel 01892-770595).
FRUIT PICKERS (8-10). To work 4-8 hours per day picking mainly apples and top fruit. Wages £20-£45 per day. Must be aged at least 18 and have plenty of common sense. Work available during August, September and October. Please apply to Mr J. Smith at the above address.

PLATTINUMS LTD: PO Box 265, Sevenoaks, Kent TN15 8ZX (tel 01787-248330). The largest growers of Kentish cobnuts in the UK. The base from which picking and packing takes place is Hadlow in Kent.
COBNUT PICKERS (20) for manual picking of nuts into weighed units. Wages at piecework rates apply, averaging out at £4.50 per hour. Pickers work 8 hours a day, 7 days a week. Min. period of work 2 weeks between mid August and mid October. Accommodation is available at a cost to be arranged.
   Overseas applicants are considered. Interview not necessary. Applications from late May to Mr R. Clark or Mr A. Hunt.

SANDBANKS FARM: Edward Vinson Ltd., Graveney, Near Faversham, Kent ME13 9DH (tel 01795-539452; fax 01795-539509).
FRUIT PICKERS to work June-October. Wages at piecework; £15-£50 per day possible, depending on ability. No accommodation available. Hours

flexible, but typically 7am-3pm; weekend work available, but time off as needed without restrictions. Applicants should be at least 16 and reasonably healthy. Applications to Mr Phil Armstrong, Farms Manager, at the above address.

SPELMONDEN ESTATE CO. LTD: Spelmonden Farm, Goudhurst, Kent TN17 1HE. Situated on the A262 between Lamberhurst and Goudhurst. Nearest train station is Marden on the line from Ashford to Charing Cross. All fruit is supplied to supermarkets so must be picked with great care.
HOP, APPLE, PEAR, PLUM AND COBNUT PICKERS. August 27th to early October for 45 hours or more per week. Pay between £154 - £204 (depending on exemption from tax and N.I.) Self catering accomodation in 2/3/4 bedrooms plus TV room, showers etc. Cost £10 per week. Overseas applicants with valid work permits welcome to apply. Applications in writing only from May 1st (enclosing s.a.e.) to the Managing Director at the above address.

SUNRISE FRUITS: The Street, Stourmouth, nr. Canterbury, Kent CT3 1HY (tel 01227 721977; fax 01227 728633).
STRAWBERRY PICKERS (50) to work from 1 June to end of September. No min. period of work. Payment daily at piecework rates, wages can be £25-£30 per day. 8 hours work weekdays, 5 hours at weekends. Accommodation may be available. No experience or qualifications needed but applicants should be willing workers and have a good sense of humour. Min. age 16. Overseas applicants welcome only if a work permit (if required) is produced. Applications from the end of March or early April to Richard Burt at the above address.

TANGMERE AIRFIELD NURSERIES LTD: Tangmere Airfield, Tangmere, Chichester, West Sussex PO20 6GB (tel 01243-533696; fax 01243-778506). A young dynamic horticultural company, which grows green, red, orange and yellow peppers to a very high standard for supply to the major high street supermarkets.
SEASONAL STAFF required to work in a progressive business. Excellent rates of pay are offered, and good working conditions in one of the most modern and clean nurseries in Europe. No accommodation provided. Minimum period of work 4 weeks between May and September. Overseas applicants in possession of the necessary work permits considered. All applicants must be available for interview. Apply from the end of March by phoning the switchboard/reception on 01243-533696.

THOMAS NEAME (MACKNADE): Macknade, Faversham, Kent ME13 8XF (tel 01795-532216).
HARVEST WORKERS (6) to pick fruit and vegetables and perform other farm work, including some heavy work, from June to October. Payment at basic agricultural rate of £3.21 per hour or at a piece rate. Accommodation for some available in self-catering cottages; tents may be required for September and early October. Applicants from abroad must already be legally entitled to work in the UK. Applications to Mrs P. Cuomo at the above address, enclosing a s.a.e.

H. W. TWYMAN: Reynolds Place, Littlebourne, Canterbury, Kent CT3 1QJ (tel 01227-721257) Situated 4 miles from Canterbury, near Littlebourne village.
APPLE PICKERS (30). Wages paid at piecework rates. 7 hours a day. Min. period of work 1 week in September. Accommodation not available. Overseas applicants welcome. Min. age 16.
Applications at any time to Mr S. Twyman by telephone.

WAKELEY BROTHERS (RAINHAM, KENT) LTD: Spade Lane, Hartlip, Sittingbourne, Kent ME9 7TT (tel 01634-263355; fax 01634-265011).
FRUIT PICKERS required. Period of work from 1-30 September. Wages based on Standard Agricultural Rate or piecework. Applicants must be hard working and available for the whole period.
Accommodation (hot showers, TV room, etc.) provided on a self catering basis. Applications to Mrs Sarah Bing, at the above address.

R.J. WALKER: Little Postern, Postern Lane, Tonbridge TN11 0QU (tel 01732-353290).
APPLE PICKERS (5) to work for three weeks during September. Piecework rates. Min. age 18. No accommodation available. Please apply by mid-August to Mr Walker at the above address.

WAPSBOURNE MANOR FARM: Sheffield Park, Uckfield, East Sussex TN22 3QT (tel 01825-723414; fax 01825-722451; e-mail info@wapsbourne.demon.uk). A working holiday company offering a variety of activities including volleyball, tennis, and theme parties.
AGRICULTURAL, INDUSTRIAL and SERVICE INDUSTRY WORKERS (150). Minimum £3 per hour for manual work with higher rates for more skilled workers. To work six days per week between 35 and 72 hours. Applicants must be students aged between 17 and 27 with good social skills who enjoy life and have plenty of spirit.
Staff required year round; min. period of work eight weeks. Accommodation is available in mobile homes, with all facilities including cafe and satellite TV. Overseas applicants with valid working visas welcome. Applications from October to the Recruitment Manager at the above address. Note: applicants may be required for an interview.

L. WHEELER & SONS (EAST PECKHAM) LTD.: Bullen Farm, East Peckham, Tonbridge, Kent TN12 5LX (tel 01622-871225; fax 01622-872952). A hop farm within an hour's journey of London. Local facilities such as shops and pubs are available.
APPLE PICKERS (20). 6 hour day, 5 days a week.
HOP PICKERS (20). 8-9 hour day, 5 days a week.
Approx. £3.20 per hour with the possibility of bonuses. Minimum period of work 5 weeks between 23 August and 30 September. Accommodation available with just a charge for electricity. Overseas applicants authorised to work in the UK welcome. Applications from June to the Manager at the above address.

WILLIAMSON FRUIT FARMS: Manor Farm, Great Whelnetham, Bury St Edmunds, Suffolk IP30 OUQ (tel 01284-386278).
RASPBERRY, STRAWBERRY, BLACKBERRY, APPLE AND PEAR PICKERS (8) to work from 1st July to 30th September approx.

Payment at piecework rates; to work Monday-Friday 9am-3.30pm with possibility of weekend work. Campsite with cooking facilities, fridge and deep freeze, washrooms and lounge with television available. Applicants should be aged over 18. Applications to G. Williamson, Secretary, at the above address.

Sport

CALSHOT ACTIVITIES CENTRE: Calshot Spit, Fawley, Hampshire SO45 1BR (tel 01703-892077; fax 01703-891267; e-mail ccsccal@hants.gov.uk; web site http://www.hants.gov.uk.calshot). One of the biggest outdoor adventure centres in Britain.
ACTIVITY INSTRUCTORS (10) to work March to October. Wages £170 per week. Applicants must be over 21 and have experience and qualifications in dinghy sailing, canoeing, windsurfing, etc. Experience in skiing or climbing or other outdoor activities an advantage. Applications from September for following year.
VISITING INSTRUCTORS to work all year round for single sessions, days, weekends. Must be fully qualified applicants over 18. Activities include dinghy sailing, canoeing, windsurfing, powerboating, rock climbing, skiing, and snowboarding.
SUMMER HELPERS to assist with activities and pastoral care of youngsters aged 8-16. To work July/August. Applicants must be over 18.
High levels of training and staff development are undertaken. Good opportunities exist for internal promotion. Applications to Calshot Activities Centre at the above address.

MEDINA VALLEY CENTRE: Dodnor Road, Newport, Isle of Wight PO30 5TE (tel 01983-82596; e-mail mvcentre@compuserve.com; fax 01983-825962).
SEASONAL TEMPORARY RYA DINGHY SAILING INSTRUCTORS needed from the end of July to August. Must have RYA dinghy sailing instructor qualifications. Applications to Peter Savory.

Language Schools

CICERO LANGUAGES INTERNATIONAL: 42 Upper Grosvenor Road, Tunbridge Wells, Kent TN1 2ET (tel 01892-547077; fax 01892-522749; e-mail cicero@pavilion. co.uk; Website http://www.cicero.co.uk).
EFL TEACHERS (5) to teach English as a foreign language to students of many nationalities (average age 25). Salary £8-£9 per hour. Hours of work variable. Period of work mid July to end of August, min. period of employment 4 weeks. Accommodation is not available. Applicants must have a degree and TESOL/CTEFLA qualifications. Experience also important. Punctuality and a professional attitude are essential. Applications from April to the Director of Studies, Cicero Languages International.

CONCORDE INTERNATIONAL SUMMER SCHOOLS LTD: Arnett House, Hawks Lane, Canterbury, Kent CT1 2NU (tel 01227-765537; fax 01227-762760). Concorde International has been organising summer schools for over 25 years in prestigious locations in the south of England. They have a high return rate of students and teachers.

EFL TEACHERS (approx. 150). To teach in summer schools, must have a standard of English as high as a native speaker. Wages £210-£275 a week depending on course. An average working week consists of 15 hours tuition and supervising 5 hours of activities, but weeks vary according to individual programmes. Both residential and non-residential positions are available. Applicants should have the RSA CTEFLA or Trinity College certificate TESOL or PGCE in an appropriate subject, and some summer school experience.

DIRECTORS (approx. 8) to ensure the smooth running of the centre and liaise with Head Office, the local host family organiser and the group leader. Other duties include holding staff meetings and weekly in-house training sessions, briefing teachers and standing in for them if required. Wages £400 a week. Both residential and non-residential positions are available, depending on the centre. Applicants must hold a RSA Dip. TEFL or Trinity College diploma in TESOL and have a minimum of 5 years' summer school experience.

ASSISTANT DIRECTORS OF STUDY (approx. 6) to ensure the smooth running of the centre, liaise with Head Office, oversee the daily routine and give support to staff, in addition to 15 hours' tuition a week. Wages £260 + a week. Positions are residential and non-residential. Applicants must hold RSA Dip. TEFL and have several years' teaching experience.

CENTRE MANAGERS (approx. 8) to ensure smooth running of the social programme and take care of the students' health and welfare. Other duties include liaising with Head Office, and regular staff at the centres. Positions are residential. Applicants should hold a qualification in leisure management. Period of work June, July and August for all positions. Applications to the Vacation Course Director at the above address.

EAST DENE CENTRE: Bonchurch Village Road, Ventnor, Isle of Wight (tel 01983-852374; fax 01983-856007). A residential centre for teaching programmes and linguistic courses.

TUTORS to provide lessons in conversational English during the mornings, and to assist leaders with running pre-set afternoon leisure activities. £125 a week plus full B & L. Flexible hours. Tutors required April, July and August. Kitchen and catering assistants sometimes also needed. EEA applicants will be considered. Send a full c.v. with s.a.e. to the East Dene Centre, at the above address.

EASTBOURNE SCHOOL OF ENGLISH: 8 Trinity Trees, Eastbourne, E.Sussex BN21 3LD (tel 01323-721759; fax 01323-639271; e-mail english-@esoe.co.uk). Runs language courses for students aged 16 and over from all around the world. The freetime programme is lively and varied.

ASSISTANT SOCIAL ORGANISER (1). Responsible post suiting someone energetic, enthusiastic and reliable. Some experience with overseas students an advantage. Min. age 20. To work 6 days per week (flexi-time) for £200 per week. Required from mid June to mid September. Accommodation not available. Interview necessary. Applicants should apply with a c.v. to Dorothy S. Rippon, Principal, from early 1999 at the above address.

EMBASSY SUMMER SCHOOLS: 44 Cromwell Road, Hove, East Sussex BN3 3ER (tel 01273-207481; fax 01273-208527). Organises English language/ activity summer schools for 5-17 year olds at schools, colleges and universities

around the UK. Courses combine practical language learning with activities and excursions.
ACTIVITY STAFF to organise a variety of afternoon, evening and weekend activities. Salary £100 per 6 day week. Full board and accommodation provided at residential centres. Age 20-30 years old. SHould ideally have coaching qualification/experience, but not essential; applicants with summer school/camp experience preferred. All applicants must speak English as well as a native English speaker, have a lively personality, initiative, be flexible, hardworking and able to work under pressure. Applications from March or April to the Recruitment Manager, at the above address.

ENGLISH LANGUAGE CENTRE: Friars Gate Farm, Marden Hill, Crowborough, Sussex TN6 1XH. Has run fully residential courses since its foundation in 1967. The centre has a reputation for thorough immersion in English culture, many supervised activities and excursions, good pastoral care and knowledgable and dedicated staff.
ENGLISH TUTORS (3) to teach English from a set syllabus to small groups of overseas students aged 12-19. Salary £120 a week plus B & L and travel. Lessons for 3 hours 5 mornings per week, plus supervision of excursions, sports and social activities. Time off by arrangement. Must have genuine interest in country life and young people and be well-dressed, with a sense of responsibility and authority. Non-smoking, native English speakers only. Age: 20-50 years. Min. period of work 3 weeks from 27 March-16 April, and 26 June to 27 August. Applications in writing to the Director at the above address.

GREYLANDS SCHOOL OF ENGLISH LTD: 315-317 Portswood Road, Southampton, Hampshire SO17 2LD (tel 01703-315180; fax 01703-586684).
AU PAIR/SCHOOL ASSISTANT to do up to 5 hours of housework a day, inclusive of cooking twice a week, 5 days a week, plus 1½ hours work at the school. To receive £35 per week and full accommodation plus 1½ hours language classes four mornings a week, plus one excursion a week. To work from May or June until late August/early September.
    Applicants should be aged over 18, non smokers, nationals of an EU country or eligible to work in the UK and hard workers with outgoing personalities. Applications to Eleanor Ann Gough, Principal, at the above address.

HARVEN SCHOOL OF ENGLISH: The Mascot, Coley Avenue, Woking, Surrey GU22 7BT (tel 01483-770969; fax 01483-7400267). A private organisation providing full-time intensive courses in English as a foreign language with a comprehensive social programme for adults and juniors in pleasant surroundings.
QUALIFIED EFL TEACHERS (10), SPORTS/SOCIAL ASSISTANTS (2) to work for an English language school in June, July and August. Salary according to qualifications and experience; no accommodation provided. To work from Monday-Friday or Saturday from 9.30am-4pm approx. and some evenings for the social programme. Applicants should have relevant qualifications and experience. Applications to Sarah Michelotti, Director of Studies, at the above address.

HASTINGS ENGLISH LANGUAGE CENTRE (HELC): St Helens Park Road, Hastings, East Sussex TN34 2JW (tel 01424-437048/441549).
EFL TEACHERS (10) £130-£230 for 15-24 hours per week. Degree and

CELTA (or equivalent) required. Staff wanted from mid June to September. Min. period of work 4 weeks. Accommodation not available. Applications from middle of April to Hastings English Language Centre at the above address.

ITS ENGLISH SCHOOL: 43-45 Cambridge Gardens, Hastings TN34 1EN (tel 01424-438025; fax 01424-438050). A small, professional, language school situated in the centre of Hastings and recognised by the British Council.
EFL TEACHERS (4). £135 for 15 hours work per week, £270 for 30 hours work per week. Must have Trinity College or RSA Certificate in TESOL/TEFLA.
No accommodation available. Min. period of work 4 weeks between 22 June and 6 September. Overseas applicants with a standard of English as high as that of a native speaker welcome. All applicants must be available for interview. Applications from 1 April to John Palim or Richard Clemenson at the above address.

KENT SCHOOL OF ENGLISH: 3, 5, 10, 12 Granville Road, Broadstairs, Kent CT10 1QD (tel 01843-868207; fax 01843-860418; e-mail kse@adept-.co.uk). Founded in 1972 by the present principal. A dynamic, energetic, enthusiastic and friendly place to work.
VACATION ENGLISH LANGUAGE TEACHERS AND ACTIVITY LEADERS (25). £180-£250 per week, with possible supplement for outstanding candidates. To work 5 mornings plus 4 afternoons and evenings per week or 3 afternoons, 3 evenings and Saturdays. Must be graduate students with TEFL experience, although exceptional undergraduates will be considered. Required from Whitsun to late June at Easter and July to August in the summer.
No accommodation is available. Applicants must enclose a c.v. and photograph, and telephone if coming from abroad. Applications welome at any time from Autumn 1998 to Chris McDermott, Director of Teaching, at the above address.

PASSPORT LANGUAGE SCHOOLS: 37 Park Road, Bromley, Kent BR1 3HJ (tel 0181-466 5925; fax 0181-466 5928). Runs language programmes in different centres from Ormskirk to Worthing for students mainly from Europe and the Far East. Courses take place throughout the year, but summer is the busiest time.
TEFL TEACHERS. Required at various centres throughout Britain to teach international students ages 11-17 and assist with afternoon and evening leisure activities. Min. age 21. Applicants must have RSA/UCLES or Trinity College Certification in TEFL or be state qualified teachers with EFL experience. Training day is held. Approx 15-30 hour, 5 day week for 2-10 weeks between July and August. Salary £130-£300 per week depending on experience and position. Board and accommodation provided in residential schools. Teachers must arrange own travel and insurance.
Applicants must have a standard of English as high as that of a native English speaker. Apply to the Director of Studies at the above address.

REGENCY SCHOOL OF ENGLISH: Royal Crescent, Ramsgate, Kent CT11 9PE (tel 01843-591212; fax 01843-850035). A British Council recognised school and a member of ARELS.
TEMPORARY EFL TEACHERS (15). Guaranteed 14 hours of teaching per

week, but up to 28 hours usually available. Must hold at least a Trinity College or RSA Certificate. £9.05 per hour.
ACTIVITY LEADERS (3). £100 per week for 20-30 hours' work. Must be sporty and enthusiastic.
Min. period of work 6 weeks between June and September. Overseas applicants with a standard of English as high as that of a native speaker considered. The school has hotel accommodation but this is often full during the summer. Applications from April to Jocelyn Flaig, Director of Studies, Regency School of English.

RICHARD LEWIS COMMUNICATIONS: Riverdown House, Warmford, Hants SO32 3LH (tel 01962-771111; e-mail jasondominici@crossculture.com); fax 01962-771050). An international company committed to providing training solutions in the areas of language, cross culture and communication skills. The company operates in 5 continents, and offers career opportunities to travel.
ENGLISH TEACHERS to work from June to September. Wages approximately £250 per week depending on experience/qualifications, with food and accommodation provided. To teach from 9am-5pm; will also be expected to attend dinner daily and perform one evening duty such as escorting a trip to a pub or the theatre a week. Applicants should have a university degree, RSA/Trinity TEFL certificate and at least 1 year's teaching experience.
Applications to Jason Dominici, Director at the above address.

STAFFORD HOUSE SCHOOL OF ENGLISH: 8/9 Oaten Hill, Canterbury, Kent CT1 3HY (tel 01227-452250; fax 01227-451685; e-mail enquiries-@staffordhouse.com). The summer school has mixed nationality classes with a max. of 15 students per class. Ages 12-adult. Emphasis is on productive skills and fluency-based activities.
TEFL TEACHERS (35). 15 hours teaching per week plus 1 Saturday excursion every 2 weeks and 4 afternoon or evening activities every two weeks. Rates of pay on application. Min. period of work 1 week between June and September. TEFL qualifications such as RSA/Trinity Certificate or RSA/Trinity Diploma required. Reliability, energy and enthusiasm are essential.
Applications from April to Mike Turner at the above address.

Vacation Traineeships

Travel and Tourism
HOTEL HOUGUE DU POMMIER: Castel, Guernsey, Channel Islands (tel 01481-56531; fax 01481-56260).
Hotel Hougue du Pommier does not offer formal traineeships, but certain positions are open to students of Catering hoping to develop their skills and gain valuable work experience. The positions are mainly in the restaurant.
B & L is provided free of charge. Applicants are not required to attend an interview. Further details about jobs available from Mr Steven Bone, General Manager, at the above address.

Science, Construction and Engineering

GIFFORD AND PARTNERS: Carlton House, Ringwood Road, Woodlands, Southampton SO40 7HT (tel 01703-813461; fax 01703-813462; e-mail mail@giffeng.co.uk).

Gifford and Partners is a firm of consulting engineers particularly interested in the design of building and highway structures and in marine works worldwide. Each summer the firm takes on up to six students to work in its Head Office and in the regional office in Chester. Student engineers work within a design team in a multidisciplinary consultants design office. Disciplines include civil, structural, building services, environmental and geotechnical engineering; also land surveyors and archaeologists.

Traineeships last for up to three months and are open to students reading Civil or Structural Engineering at university. Suitably qualified applicants from abroad are welcome. The salary in 1998 was £150 a week.

Interested candidates should contact Mr Bruce Cozens, Personnel Manager, by 1 March.

East Anglia

Cambridgeshire
Essex
Norfolk
Suffolk

East Anglia is not one of the most promising of areas in which to look for temporary summer employment. However, Norfolk and Cambridgeshire are major agricultural areas and fruit picking, packing and processing work provide comparatively good prospects. King's Lynn, Wisbech and East Dereham (near Norwich) are the principal centres.

In and around King's Lynn the *Lynn News* and *Lynn Advertiser* carry general job advertisements. Factory work is the main source of summer employment in the town, as local food factories employ temporary production operators between June and September. Private employment agencies do not seem to deal with much unskilled temporary work, so concentrate on the Jobcentre: in King's Lynn it keeps a register of people looking for temporary work, though you are still advised to check in person on a regular basis. Nowadays there are only a limited number of temporary jobs available for students, as priority is given to the local unemployed or students whose permanent home is King's Lynn. A lot of this work is governed by the weather, and is therefore irregular. King's Lynn Jobcentre can be contacted at Lovell House, St Nicholas Street, King's Lynn PE30 1LR. The *Eastern Daily Press*, which is circulated throughout Norfolk and in northern Suffolk, also lists general job vacancies.

Temporary tourism and holiday-related jobs are most easily found in Hunstanton, Cromer, Lowestoft and above all Great Yarmouth which, after

Blackpool, is Britain's major entertainment resort. Vacancies are less plentiful than they were a few years ago, but opportunities are still there if you apply in good time. You can contact Great Yarmouth Jobcentre at Copperfield House, The Conge, Great Yarmouth NR30 1EJ. Hunstanton seems to have ridden the storm more successfully than other resorts, and a number of large hotels consistently require staff. While some live-in accommodation is provided by employers in Hunstanton, this is harder to come by in King's Lynn and Wisbech (where rented lodgings are also in short supply). Wisbech Jobcentre (tel 01945-585931) has general job adverts in the *Fenland Citizen*, which comes out every Wednesday, and the *Wisbech Standard*, which comes out every Friday. Temporary factory work for local large employers and lots of seasonal picking/packing work is available as well as many vacancies requiring skilled workers that cannot be filled.

As a major tourist attraction and language school centre, a number of associated jobs can be found in Cambridge. The town's Jobcentre (Henry Giles House, 73-79 Chesterton Road, Cambridge CB4 3BG) usually has summer opportunities for catering staff and jobs teaching English as a foreign language. There is also agricultural work available in the area picking soft fruits and later in the year, picking potatoes. A major local agricultural contractor uses the Earl of Derby pub car park on Hills Road as a pick-up point in the early morning for those wanting work. The contractor also offers agricultural work on a camping basis in many parts of England. The *Cambridge Evening News* newspaper advertises job vacancies on Wednesdays.

Felixstowe, on the Suffolk coast, is usually a good source of temporary work; Felixstowe Jobcentre is at 29-31 Hamilton Road, Felixstowe, Suffolk IP11 7AZ. Ipswich Borough Council and Suffolk County Council usually need to recruit temporary staff over the summer too.

Business and Industry

GRAND UK HOLIDAYS: Aldwych House, Bethel Street, Norwich NR2 1NR (tel 01603-619933; fax 01603-616316). Britain's largest coach tour operators catering exclusively for the over 55s in over 140 resorts and destinations.
COURIERS (25). £140 net per week plus optional excursion and tips. To work on eight-day coach tours. Applicants must be friendly and have an outgoing personality and the ability to relate to those over fifty-five. Accommodation and food provided. Staff needed from May to September. Applications to the above address.

Children

KIDS KLUB: The Lodge, The Hall, Great Finborough, Stowmarket, Suffolk IP14 3EF (tel 01449-675907; fax 01449-771396; e-mail www.kidsclub.com).
ACTIVITY SUPERVISORS (30). Salary at least £90 per week. Min. age 18.
ACTIVITY INSTRUCTORS (15). Salary at least £125 per week. Must have National Governing Body awards. Min. age 18.
MATRONS (4). Salary at least £150 per week. Must have first aid or nursing qualifications. Min. age 21.
GENERAL ASSISTANTS (4). Salary at least £75 per week. Min. age 16.

All positions are for 6 days per week. Staff are required from March 1st or July 1st to August 31st. Min period of work 4 weeks. Accommodation is available for no extra charge.

Applicants from overseas welcome; a phone or personal interview is required. Applications from January to Mike Garling at the above address.

Holiday Centres and Amusements

BANHAM ZOO: The Grove, Banham, Norfolk NR16 2HE (tel 01953-887773). Situated between Attleborough and Diss on the B1113 Norwich to Bury St Edmunds Road.
CATERING STAFF & RETAIL ASSISTANTS required from Easter to September. Wages on application. Apply in writing to Mr Simon Lane at the above address: applicants considered will be invited for interview. Please note: no accommodation available.

COLCHESTER ZOO LTD: Maldon Road, Stanway, Colchester, Essex CO3 5SL (tel 01206-331292; fax 01206-331392; e-mail colchester.zoo@btinternet.com).
RETAIL STAFF (12), CATERING STAFF (12), SITE CLEANERS (4), FACE PAINTERS (3), GARDENERS (2). Wages at least £3 per hour for all positions. No accommodation available. Apply to Mr and Mrs Tropeano at the above address. Note all applicants must be available for interview.

ENGLISH HERITAGE: Hazelrigg House, 33 Marefair, Northampton NN1 1SR (tel 01604-730320; fax 01604-730321). A governing agency of the Department for Culture, Media and Sport, which manages historic buildings and ancient monuments.
SEASONAL PART-TIME CUSTODIANS (25) to work up to 36 hours per week.
SEASONAL FULL-TIME CUSTODIANS (30) to work 45 hours per week including lunch break.

Main duties include customer service, visitor management, retail sales/merchandising, site presentation, health and safety and site marketing and promotion. Wages for both positions £4.87 per hour (pay award pending). Positions are available at various locations across the Midlands and East Anglia. No accommodation is available.

Min. period of work mid March to 31st October. Applicants should be aged 16-58 and have at least 6 months previous experience of dealing face to face with the general public in a service, leisure or retail environment. Overseas applicants with valid work authorisation are considered. Interview necessary.

Applications from 4th January to Victoria Souter (HRLO) (tel 01604-730333).

MOLE HALL WILDLIFE PARK: Widdington, Saffron Walden, Essex CB11 3SS (tel/fax 01799-540400; e-mailMolehall@aol.com). A wildlife park with deer, llamas, otters, monkeys, wild fowl and a butterfly house in a 20 acre garden and meadow.
ANIMAL WARDENS (2-3) to work a 40 hour week; accommodation and pocket money provided. Minimum period of work 2 months between April

and November. Applicants must be aged at least 16; foreign applicants will be considered, but must speak reasonable English.

Applications should be sent to John Doe at the above address.

PETER PAN'S ADVENTURE ISLAND: Southend on Sea, Essex SS1 1EE (tel 01702-468023; fax 01702-601044).

RIDE OPERATORS, CATERING ASSISTANTS to work from May to September. Wages, hours, periods of work etc. by arrangement.

Applications to Marc Miller at the above address.

Hotels and Catering

THE BRUDENELL HOTEL (REGAL): The Parade, Aldeburgh, Suffolk, IP15 5BU (tel 01728-452071; fax 01728-454082). Regal is a new company that owns 100 hotels. The Brudenell Hotel is one of the smaller ones with 47 bedrooms, and is very old and right on the sea front.

WAITERS/WAITRESSES (4). Wages £3.00/£4.00 per hour. To work approx. 40 hours a week. Must be over 18.

BAR PERSON (1). £3.00/£4.00 per hour. To work approx 40 hours a week. Experience necessary. Must be over 18.

SUPERVISORS (2). Wages £3.50-£4.50. To work approx. 40 hours a week. Must be over 20 and have at least 1 year's waiting experience.

HOUSEKEEPING PERSON (1). Wages £3-£3.50 per hour. To work 20-30 hours a week. Must be over 16.

A wide variety of work is available, mainly on shifts. Staff will be trained in-house to wine taste, stock-take etc. Staff can learn about other departments than their own if they wish. Accommodation is available at a cost of 50p of the hourly wage.

Min. period of work 2 months between 1st June and 30th September. Suitably qualified overseas applicants considered. Interview necessary, at least over the telephone.

Applications to the Restaurant and Bar Manager.

THE CRESTA COURT HOTEL: Church Street, Altrincham, Cheshire Wa14 4DP (tel 0161-927 7272; fax 0161-926 9194; web site www.cresta-court.co.uk). A busy 3 star hotel with 140 bedrooms and banqueting facilities for up to 350 people. The hotel is just outside Manchester city centre, with easy access by Metrolink.

FUNCTION BAR STAFF (6). Wages £3.60 per hour. Part-time positions with flexible hours. Must be over 18.

FUNCTION WAITERS/WAITRESSES (6). Wages £15.50 per session. Part-time postions with flexible hours. Must be over 16.

RESTAURANT STAFF (3). Wages negotiable. To work flexible hours. Must be over 16.

No accommodation is available. Min. period of work 1 month between June and September. Applicants must be clean cut, honest, reliable, friendly and motivated. Training may be offered.

Overseas applicants considered. Interview necessary. Applications at any time to Mr Warrington.

KENTWELL HALL: Long Melford, Sudbury, Suffolk CO10 9BA (tel 01787-310207; fax 01787-379318). A redbrick Tudor mansion in rural Suffolk offering re-creations of Tudor domestic life. Staff on the 20th century side ensure smooth running of event for the public.

RETAIL AND CATERING STAFF (10) to serve in a temporary shop/ restaurant in a marquee during C16th re-creations; duties also include marshalling school parties. Wages by arrangement; must make own arrangements for accommodation. Minimum age 16; applicants need a pleasant manner and to be fit as they will be on their feet all day.

Period of work 3 weeks in June/July. Applications should be sent to Mary Fitzgerald, Administrator, at the above address.

THE LODGE HOTEL: Old Hunstanton Road, Hunstanton, Norfolk PE16 6HX (tel 01485-532896; fax 01485-535007). A Grade II listed Hotel close to a beach with 16 ensuite bedrooms; popular with bird watchers and golfers.

WAITER and BAR PERSON. Required for 20-40 hours per week from early July to late September. Salary £3-£3.50 per hour. Must have some relevant experience. Min. period of work 6 weeks; accommodation is not provided. Overseas applicants welcome. Applicants should apply as soon as possible to Mr A.G.Best, Proprietor, at the above address.

OASIS LEISURE CENTRE: King's Lynn & West Norfolk Borough Council, Central Promenade, Hunstanton, Norfolk PE36 5BD (tel 01485-534227; fax 01485-534227).

CATERING ASSISTANTS (6). Experience of fast food service required, plus basic food hygiene certificate. Wages £3.60 per hour. To work up to 47 hours, 6 days per week. Period of work April to October. Accommodation is not available. Overseas applicants with fluent English welcome. Applicants should be available for interview. Applications from February onwards to Russell Wilson, Senior Duty Officer, at the above address.

SWYNFORD PADDOCKS HOTEL: Six Mile Bottom, Newmarket, Suffolk CB8 OUE (fax 01638-570283).

WAITING STAFF (2): must have experience of silver service restaurant work.

COMMIS CHEF: must have experience of kitchen work.

Wages of £110 per week, with accommodation included. To work 10 shifts per 5 day week: split shifts breakfast-lunch/lunch-dinner. Period of work from June to September. Applicants should be aged at least 18. Applications to Mr. A. Perry, Manager, at the above address.

WHITE HART HOTEL: Market End, Coggeshall, Essex CO6 1NH (tel 01376-56165Y; fax 01376-561789).

WAITING STAFF (2-3) to work split shifts to cover breakfast, lunch and dinner. Wages and period of work by arrangement; accommodation available for two people. Applicants need a good standard of English and to be aged 18 or over. Applications to Alison Shaw, Manager at the above address.

Medical

CHRISTIES CARE LTD.: The Old Post Office, High Street, Saxmundham, Suffolk IP17 1AA (tel 01728-605000; fax 01728-604483; e-mail christies.care@virgin.net; web site www.christiescare.co.uk). Founded in 1987, the company provides live-in care to people in their own homes throughout the Eastern region and Greater London.

CARERS (50) for live-in positions with clients in their own homes. Clients are all dependent adults with many different ailments who need varying degrees of care such as incontinence management, hoist work for paraplegics, experience with dealing with dementia and the bedridden; all need home help with cooking, shoppong and housekeeping. Salary £220-£320 per 7 days. Staff required all year round; minimum period of work 7 full days. Applicants must have previous experience of care work, be over 18, and able to work legally in the UK. Applications to the Recruitment Department at the above address.

Outdoor

ANGLIA ALPINES: St Ives Road, Somersham, Huntingdon, Cambridgeshire PE17 3ET (tel 01487-840103; fax 01487-840096). A modern wholesale nursey supplying herbs and alpines to garden centres throughout the UK. Approx. 1 hour by train from London.
NURSERY WORKERS (8). Wages from approx. £3.30 per hour upwards. Flexible hours but min. of 30 hours a week. Preference given to those with horticultural experience. Overseas students welcome. Min. work period 2 months between March and June (July to September for those who have started earlier). Applications to the General Office, Anglia Alpines.

BOXFORD (SUFFOLK) FARMS LTD.: Hill Farm, Boxford, Sudbury, Suffolk CO10 5NY. (tel 01787-210348; fax 01787-211106). Situated in beautiful countryside within an hour's train journey from London.
FRUIT PICKERS and FRUIT PACKERS required to work on farms and packhouse situated on the Suffolk/Essex border. The work involves the picking and packing of soft and top fruit (strawberries, raspberries, apples etc). The season is from June to July for soft fruit and the middle of August to the end of October for apples. Hours of work and wages are variable subject to the crop and weather. Self catering caravan accommodation is available and the camp has toilets, showers, laundry facilities and TV. Workers must be over 18 years old with a liking for outside work and with valid working visas and work permits. Transport will pick up in Colchester between 2pm and 3pm but it is essential that the farm is contacted 24 hours before arrival. Applications to the Personnel Manager by 1st June to the above address.

FIVEWAYS FRUIT FARM: Fiveways, Stanway, Colchester, Essex CO3 5LR (tel 01206-330244; fax 01206-330828; e-mail Elsanta1@aspects.net). A medium sized farm run by two brothers growing a great variety of crops. Situated in a rural oasis on the outskirts of Colchester with shops close by.
FRUIT PICKERS (17-22). Strawberry picking from May-September; apple picking from August but principally from September to October; orchard work and many semi-skilled jobs in propagation tunnels and French tunnels etc.; packing fruit for supermarkets. Wages at piece work rates, approx. £100-£170 per 5-7 day week. Hours flexible, start at 6am with hourly work also available. No overtime.
Minimum period of work 2 months. Meadow next to farm available for camping. New building with cooking facilities, microwave, shower room, toilets and large recreational areas with TV and indoor dormitories of necessary. Charge £15 per week. Supermarket, post office, off-licence and

launderette within a 5 minutes walk from the farm. Overseas students aged over 18 welcome.

Applications from the beginning of the year to Alistair Mead, c/o Fiveways Fruit Farm.

FRIDAYBRIDGE INTERNATIONAL CAMP: Fridaybridge, Wisbech, Cambridgeshire PE14 0LR (tel 01945-860255; fax 01945-861088).
GENERAL AGRICULTURAL WORKERS to pick strawberries and apples, cut broccoli and celery, and help with many other jobs. To work 5-6 days per week. Bed, breakfast, packed lunch and evening meal provided at a reasonable weekly charge. Should be aged 17-30.

Temporary staff vacancies also available for drivers, bar staff, shop staff, administrative staff, kitchen assistants and English teachers. Club, disco, swimming pool, tennis court, plus many other facilities provided. Vacancies available from end of May to end of October. Min. period of work 3 weeks. EEA students aged 16-30 welcome. Send s.a.e./IRC for brochure (applications on official forms only) to Dept. VW, Fridaybridge International Camp.

G'S FRESH SALADS: Barway, EL7, Cambridgeshire CB7 5TZ (tel 01353-727314; fax 01353-727255).
PRODUCTION OPERATIVES (30) required from 1st November to end of April to harvest and pack salad and vegetable crops. Must be fit and used to hard manual work. Wages at piecework rates (average £180 per week). Food and accommodation available on site for £55 a week. Average 10 hours per day; five and a half day week. Minimum age 19. Applications to Sharon Gudgeon, Hostel Personnel Manager, at the above address.

HEMINGSTONE FRUIT FARMS: Main Road, Hemingstone, Ipswich, Suffolk IP6 9RN (tel 01449-760482; fax 01449-760280).
STRAWBERRY PICKERS (50). To work 8am-3pm, 5 days a week (sometimes 6 or 7). Salary piece rate: up to 25p/lb.
APPLE PICKERS (100). To work 8am-3pm, 5 days a week. Salary piece rate variable, some casual hourly rates.
FRUIT PACKERS (20). To work 8am-4.30pm, occasionally earlier or later; paid casual hourly rates.
No experience required. Accommodation available in local bed and breakfast for £15 per night or on campsite for £3.50 per night. Overseas applicants welcome. Staff wanted for a minimum of three weeks between May to October. Peak months for work are June and September, low month is July.

Applications from April onwards to Christine Pearse at the above address.

INTERNATIONAL FARM CAMP: Hall Road, Tiptree, Essex CO5 0QS (tel 01621-815496).
FRUIT PICKERS. Pay at piecework rates (according to amount of fruit picked). Hours 8am-4pm Monday to Friday; some weekend work. Full B & L provided for approx. £50 a week. Age: 19-25 years. Min. work period 2 weeks between early June and mid-July.
Overseas applicants welcome, but places for non-EEA nationals are open only to full-time students who have not completed their studies. Applications to be

sent as early as possible to the above address: s.a.e. (or IRC if writing from abroad) essential for reply.

A. E. MARSHALL FARMS: Old Shields Farm, Ardleigh, Colchester, Essex CO7 7NE (tel 01206-230251; fax 01206-231825).
FRUIT PICKERS (20-40) to work from the end of May to mid/late September. Wages by arrangement, paid out weekly. To work from 8.00am-4.00pm, 6 days per week. Min. age 18 years. Camping and dormitory accommodation available for around 15 people, own equipment is required. Applications should be sent to Gail Marshall at the above address.

OAK TREE FARM: Hasketon, Woodbridge, Suffolk (tel 01473-735218).
STRAWBERRY PICKERS. Pay according to piece work rates. Min. 8 hours per day when picking, usually 6 days a week with Saturdays off. Campsite and hostel accommodation available. Min. age 18 years. Period of work 4 weeks from approx. 20 June, min. 3 weeks. Overseas applicants welcome. Applications before 1 April enclosing s.a.e. to Mrs R. Stephenson, Oak Tree Farm.

OUTBACK INTERNATIONAL: Pentney House, Narborough Road, Pentney, Norfolk PE32 1JD (tel 01760-337121; fax 01760-337061). F.P. Personnel and Personnel Recruitment require staff all year round for farm and production work in and around the Norfolk area.
PRODUCTION AND FARM STAFF to pack, cut and sort fruits, vegetables, meats and poultry. Wages £3.50 to £4.50 per hour according to piece work rates (approx. earnings £20-£70 per day). To work 8-12 hours a day, 5-7 days a week plus overtime. Accommodation is available on farm at £65 per week, and at factories at £75 per week. Cost includes 3 meals a day, transport and bedding.
   Min. period of work 3 weeks at any time of year. Main farm season is May-October. Applicants must be 18-35 years old. Overseas applicants with EU/EEA passport or work authorisation, and good English are considered. Interview not necessary. Applications with I.D. at least 2-3 weeks before arrival date to Tammy Blackmur.

R. & J. M. PLACE LTD: Church Farm, Tunstead, Norwich NR12 8RQ. Large soft fruit growers in the centre of the Broadland National Park.
FRUIT PICKING, weather permitting, details on application. Accommodation available for approx. £42 per week, including breakfast, in purpose-built dormitory blocks. Tents and caravans are not permitted. Must be in good health. No previous experience necessary. Social activities in camp include tennis, volleyball, badminton, basketball, football, pool and many other activities. Open between end of February and November. Overseas applicants welcome. Applications with s.a.e. to the Administrator, R. & J. M. Place Ltd.

C. & A. SANDERSON: Bramley House, Cox's Lane, Wisbech, Cambridgeshire PE13 4TD (tel 01945-583023).
STRAWBERRY PICKERS (8-10). Piecework rates. To work Monday to Friday and sometimes Sunday mornings. Pickers must be willing to work hard, with early start common. Free campsite, washroom with hot and cold water and toilet. Limited caravan accommodation also available at small charge.

Period of work approx. 3-4 weeks, commencing late June. Overseas applicants welcome. Applications to A. Sanderson, Bramley House.

F. TOOKE & SON: The Elms, Pullover Road, West Lynn, King's Lynn, Norfolk PE34 3LR (tel 01553-773281; fax 01553-773281).
APPLE PICKERS (20-25) for work September-October. Payment at piece work rates; to work from 6.30am-3.30 pm. No accommodation available. Applicants should be aged 18-70 and able to handle fruit carefully.
   Applications to Mrs J. Tooke, Partner, at the above address.

Sport

BRADWELL ENVIRONMENTAL & OUTDOOR CENTRE: Bradwell Waterside, nr Southminster, Essex CM0 7QY (tel 01621-776256; fax 01621-776378). A local authority-run high quality multi-activity residential centre for young people and adults. Based on the edge of the River Blackwater in Essex, it is an excellent site for all water and land based activities.
SAILING (6) and CANOEING (2) and ARCHERY INSTRUCTORS. Wages negotiable. To include B & L. To work approx. 8 hours per day. RYA Certificate desirable or BCU/GNAS. Min. work period 3 months between April and October inclusive. Applications in January/March to the Principal, Bradwell Sailing Centre.

OASIS LEISURE CENTRE: King's Lynn & West Norfolk Borough Council, Central Promenade, Hunstanton, Norfolk PE36 5BD (tel 01485-534227; fax 01485-533090).
POOL ATTENDANTS (12-14). Royal Life Saving Society bronze medallion essential, experience of leisure industry an advantage. Wages £3.60 per hour. To work up to 47 hours/6 days per week. Period of work April to October. Accommodation is not available. Overseas applicants with fluent English welcome. Applicants should be available for interview. Applications from February onwards to Russell Wilson, Senior Assistant Manager, at the above address.

SOUTHEND BOROUGH COUNCIL LEISURE SERVICES: PO Box 6, Civic Centre, Victoria Avenue, Southend-on-sea, Essex SS2 6ER (tel 01702-215604). Southend is a seaside resort town with many attractions for all age groups. The local authority arranges probably the largest playscheme in Essex with a dedicated team of staff.
BIZ SUPERVISOR AND LEADERS to organise and supervise a variety of sports, arts and games for 8-16 year olds at various council facilities in Southend. Wages £150 for the supervisor and £115 for the leader per week. Uniform is provided. Hours: 8.30am-3.30pm Monday to Friday. Period of work by arrangement during the Easter and summer holidays. Min. age 19. Applicants with coaching and first aid qualifications and experience of working with children preferred. Suitably qualified overseas applicants welcome. Applications to the Administration Section at the above address.

Language Schools

BRIAR SCHOOL OF ENGLISH: 8 Gunton Cliff, Lowestoft, Suffolk NR32 4PE (tel 01502-573781; fax 01502-589150). Runs holiday language courses for foreign language learners on the Suffolk coast. In business since 1960.
TEACHERS OF ENGLISH. From £6.80 per hour. To work up to 6 hours daily. TEFL qualifications or experience preferable. Applicants must possess either a degree or a teacher's certificate.
SPORTS INSTRUCTORS. From £4.80 per hour. To work up to 6 hours per day. Must hold at least an L.T.A. Part 1 certificate.
   Successful applicants for both jobs can earn extra pay by leading excursions on Saturdays to Norwich, Cambridge, London and other local places of interest. Min. period of work 3 weeks between end of June and end of August. Accommodation is not available. Teaching applications should be sent to Ms H. Sterne and Sports Instructor applications to Mr N. J. Doe, at the above address.

CAMBRIDGE ACADEMY OF ENGLISH: 65 High Street, Girton, Cambridge CB3 0QD (tel 01223-277230; fax 01223-277606). Situated in the leafy suburb of Girton, the Academy runs non-residential courses for teenagers and young adults, and residential courses for the 10-13 age group.
EFL TEACHERS to teach English to teenagers. Required for 3 week courses between July 15 and August 22; wages of approx £800 per course. The job involves 21-24 hours teaching a week. Must have RSA TEFL/Trinity College certificate or equivalent and experience. Applications to S.Levy at the above address.

EUROYOUTH LTD: 301 Westborough Road, Westcliffe, Southend-on-Sea, Essex SSO 9PT (tel 01702-341434; fax 01702-330104). Established in 1961 Euroyouth has wide experience in arranging private home stays in the UK and abroad. Suitable for groups and individuals, with an emphasis on language learning.
BRITISH TEACHERS required to teach English as a foreign language to continental students in Southend-on-sea. Easter and summer courses. Previous experience desirable especially in EFL or continental schools. Min. age 21 years. Please write enclosing s.a.e. giving details of experience, qualifications, and availability dates to Euroyouth Ltd at the above address.

STUDIO SCHOOL OF ENGLISH: 6 Salisbury Villas, Station Road, Cambridge CB1 2JF (tel 01223-369701; fax 01223-314944). The oldest and largest of the permanently-established Cambridge language schools, and a founder member of the ARELS organisation
EFL TEACHERS for young people's courses (age 10-14 and 15-17). Applicants should have CTEFLA, CELTA, TESOL and/ or EFL experience. Language background or primary training also an advantage.
ACTIVITY ORGANISERS for young people's courses (ages as above). Applicants should have interests/abilities in sport, art, music or drama, and need stamina, initiative and enthusiasm.
COURSE DIRECTORS AND ASSISTANT COURSE DIRECTORS (ages as above). Applicants should have good organisational and managerial skills. Some EFL or summer camp experience preferred.
   Residential and non-residential posts available, mainly between July and

August but also at other times of the year. Applications to Richard Mountford at the above address.

Vacation Traineeships

Science, Construction and Engineering

EASTERN ELECTRICITY PLC: PO Box 40, Wherstead Park, Ipswich, Suffolk TP5 2AD (tel 01473-553404; fax 01473-553523). One of Britain's leading integrated electricity and gas groups, with a turnover in excess of £3 billion per annum. Part of The Energy Group plc.
Eastern Group offers summer vacation employment around East Anglia. Positions arise on an ad hoc basis and may be in various departments. There is also the possibility of some Easter or Christmas placements. The salary is between £150 and £200 a week and although no accommodation is provided, Eastern Group offer assistance in finding suitable accommodation. Interested candidates should apply by March to the Graduate Recruitment Co-ordinator, Group HR, Eastern Group plc.

GARDLINE SURVEYS: Admiralty Road, Great Yarmouth, Norfolk, NR30 3NG (tel 01493-850723; fax 01493-852106). The largest independent company in Surrey, which operates a fleet of 6 fully equipped vessels. The vessels operate worldwide, covering Europe, the Far East and West Africa.
Gardline Surveys is involved in hydrographic and marine geophysical survey. The company offers a variable number of placements in several different fields, including Seismic/Hydrographic survey work for surveyors, geophysicists and electronic engineers; there will also be some office work. The company recruits a maximum of two trainees for each area.
Vacancies are open to students on relevant degree courses, with a preference for those in their second or third year of study. Overseas applicants are welcome. Trainees are based in Great Yarmouth from where they will be sent to work on survey vessels, mainly in the North Sea. Shared accommodation is sometimes available. The salary for 1998 was £6,972 p.a. pro rata, plus £26 per day field allowance.
Applicants should contact Dr K.P. Games, Geophysical Director, at the above address, preferably in the new year.

GEC-MARCONI RESEARCH CENTRE: West Hanningfield Road, Great Baddow, Chelmsford, Essex CM2 8HN.
In 1999 GEC-Marconi Research Centre intends to recruit about five undergraduates to work as laboratory assistants on projects supervised by research engineers and scientists during the summer. Candidates should be studying for degrees in Electronics, Electrical Engineering, Physics, Mathematics or Computing. The work lasts for 10 weeks and the salary is £148-£193 per week.
Further enquiries to Miss Alison Stephens, Senior Personnel & Training Advisor, at the above address. Applications should be made from March-May.

HARLOW CHEMICAL COMPANY LTD: Central Road, Templefields, Harlow, Essex CM20 2BH (tel 01279-436211; fax 01279-444025).
Harlow Chemical Company Ltd offers vacation traineeships to two students each summer. These are to work within Research & Development or Technical Service Laboratories. The placements last for 6-8 weeks and are open to university undergraduates reading for a degree in Chemistry or related subject. Accommodation is not provided. Applications should be made in April or May to the Personnel Manager, at the above address.

RAYTHEON SYSTEMS LTD: The Pinnacles, Harlow, Essex (tel 01279-407390; fax 01279-410413; e-mail < h3488@fir.cossor.com)
Each year Raytheon Systems offers 4-6 opportunities for students to work in hardware support and electronic engineering. On-the-job training will be provided. Applicants should preferably be students who have completed one year of their university course. Vacancies are generally for Engineering students, but occasionally non-science staff are needed. In 1998 the company paid students who had completed one year of their course £250, but stresses the exceptional ability of these employees.

Placements last all summer with the possibility of follow-on work at Christmas and Easter and are located at Harlow. The company can help arrange lodgings, but would prefer applicants to live locally.

Applications by February to Kevin Clay.

WOODS OF COLCHESTER: Tufnell Way, Colchester CO4 5AR (tel 01206-544122; fax 01206-574434).
A member of the GEC Industrial Group, Woods are the largest manufacturing company in Colchester with over 700 employees; they specialise in the design, manufacture, marketing and distribution of air handling equipment for a wide variety of industries including the mining, gas and construction industries.

The company is seeking three or four students to work for up to eight weeks over the summer. Work will include a variety of different tasks-some general, some specific-depending on the candidate's experience. Project work includes the design and development of new engineering systems, computer work, CAD development and other related duties.

Candidates should be first or second year degree level university students. They should be bright and motivated and show a keen interest in exploring engineering as a potential career. Degree students in Mechanical or Electrical Engineering are welcome to apply. The rate of pay is approx. £150 per week. Applicants who live locally are preferred.

Applications should be sent by April to C.T.Thomas, Training Manager, at the above address.

The Midlands

Bedfordshire
Cheshire
Derbyshire
Herefordshire
Leicestershire
Lincolnshire
Northamptonshire

Nottinghamshire
Oxfordshire
Shropshire
Staffordshire
Warwickshire
W. Midlands
Worcestershire

The Midlands region includes a number of large industrial towns, the most notable of which is Birmingham. Temporary jobs in these centres tend to involve warehouse and factory work or the retail trade; the main glut of vacancies arises from September onwards for the run up to Christmas. In addition, the larger local authorities, such as Birmingham and Coventry, take people on as playleaders and recreation assistants (Birmingham Jobcentre: Centennial House, 100 Broad Street, Birmingham B15 1AU). Some car dealers require people to deliver cars around the country, particularly in August, which is the beginning of the new year in the motor industry.

The tourist trade in the Midlands weathered the recession moderately well and there has been an increase in the number of seasonal vacancies over the last year or so. Tourism in the Midlands is concentrated in Warwick and Stratford-upon-Avon, the Cotswolds and Herefordshire. In this last county, the town of Ledbury is a good source of work, though rented accommodation is scarce (Ledbury Jobcentre: Crown Buildings, Bye Street, Ledbury, Herefordshire HR8 2AB). Hereford is likely to be a better base, with the *Hereford Times* (Thursday) and the *Hereford Admag* (Wednesday) both displaying local job vacancies; alternatively, contact the Hereford Jobcentre at Bath Street, Hereford HR1 2LG. In Staffordshire, Alton Towers Leisure Park takes on temporary ride attendants, shop staff and so on.

Fruit and hop picking jobs are available in the Vale of Evesham, Herefordshire and Lincolnshire, but in general the Midlands is an area where 'pick your own' farms are popular. Spalding and Boston in Lincolnshire are centres for agricultural packing. In Lincoln itself, most temporary jobs are in the retail or hotel trade. There is now a very strong retail trade in Lincoln with the Tritton Road area attracting several large new employers, the most recent being Debenhams. There are good opportunities for employment at the Lincolnshire Show, a two day event that is held yearly in mid June. To apply for work either visit the Lincoln Jobcentre (280 High Street, Lincoln LN2 1LL) or call 01522-342061/342065 in May or early June. The *Lincolnshire Echo* is the best local newspaper for job vacancies.

Oxford is a popular centre for language schools and there are opportunities not only for EFL teachers but also for sports instructors and social organisers. These and other jobs may be advertised in the *Oxford Times* (out on Friday) and the *Oxford Mail* (daily). Alternatively, for up-to-the-minute information on both jobs and accommodation look out for the coloured spreadsheet *Daily Information* (daily in term time, weekly during vacations) on noticeboards, in shop windows etc. There is, of course, competition for any summer jobs from those students at the University who choose to stay in Oxford for the summer.

The industrial heartlands of the Midlands provide plentiful opportunities for Vacation Traineeships, particularly in the field of science and engineering.

Business and Industry

MOBILE PROMOTIONS COMPANY: New Brook, Titchmarsh, nr. Kettering, Northants NN14 3DG (tel 01832-733460; fax 01832-735282).
DRIVERS—LIGHT COMMERCIALS (4), DRIVERS—HEAVY COMMERCIALS with HGV 1 (4), EXHIBITION STRUCTURE AND MARQUEE OPERATORS (6) to work at outdoor event promotions, exhibitions, and roadshows. Wages and hours vary with contracts. Min. period of work 2 months between March and October. Accommodation available whilst out on road/jobs.
Overseas applicants considered. All applicants must be able to attend an interview. Applications from March to Colin Allder or Robin Carlisle at the above address.

K.H. TAYLOR LTD.: The Freezing Station, Sheffield Road, Blyth, Worksop, Notts (tel 01909-591555; fax 01909-591713).
INSPECTION and QUALITY CONTROL PERSONNEL, PACKERS, STACKERS (approx. 50). Wages £4.34 per hour. To work 8 hours per day in shifts 6am-2pm, 2-10pm or 10pm-6am, Monday to Friday, with some weekend work available. No experience or qualifications needed. Must have own transport. Interview not necessary. Applications (quoting telephone number) from the beginning of June to K.H. Taylor Ltd at the above address.

Children

LEICESTER CHILDREN'S HOLIDAY CENTRE: Mablethorpe, Quebec Road, Mablethorpe, Lincolnshire LN12 1QX (tel/fax 01507-472444).
ACTIVITY LEADERS (12). KITCHEN/DINING ROOM STAFF (4). £58.00 per week.
COOK/CHEF. £85 per week.
To work a 6-day week. Free B & L provided.
ACTIVITY LEADERS required to organise. instruct and supervise an outdoor activities programme for children aged 7-12 years. Energy, enthusiasm and a good sense of humour essential.
Staff needed from beginning of May to end of August. Preference given to applicants able to work entire season. Min. age 18. Write for an application form (enclosing s.a.e.) from January to H. Eagle at the above address.

PGL TRAVEL: Alton Court, Penyard Lane (874), Ross-on-Wye, Herefordshire HR9 5NR (tel 01989-767833). Over 500 staff needed to assist in the running of activity centres in Shropshire, Oxford and the Wye Valley. Europe's largest provider of adventure holidays for children has offered outstanding training and work opportunities to seasonal staff for over 40 years.
QUALIFIED INSTRUCTORS in canoeing, sailing, windsurfing, pony trekking, hill walking, fencing, archery, judo, rifle shooting, fishing, motorsports, arts and crafts, drama, English language and many other activities. Min. age 18.
GROUP LEADERS to take responsibility for small groups of children and ensure that they get the most out of their holiday. Previous experience of working with children necessary.
All staff receive £36-£70 per week plus free B & L. Vacancies available for short or long periods between February and October. Overseas applicants eligible to work in the UK welcome. Requests for application forms to the Personnel Department at the above address.

ROBIN HOOD RIDING HOLIDAYS: Swan Lodge Ltd., Station Road, Upper Broughton, Melton Mowbray, Leics. LE14 3BH (tel 01664-823686; fax 01664-822346).
CAMP SUPERVISORS (3) to provide 24-hour supervision of children on riding holidays. Wages of £80 per week plus overtime, with free accommodation and riding. To work 5 days per week, hours by arrangement. Period of work July-August plus 2-3 weeks at Easter. Applicants should be aged at least 18; knowledge of first aid and previous experience would be advantages. Applicants need to have strong characters, with outward going personalities and good organisational skills.
Applications to Ian Jalland, Company Secretary at the above address.

ST JOSEPH'S HALL: Junction Road, Cowley, Oxford OX4 2UJ (tel 01865-711829; fax 01865-747791).
SOCIAL MONITORS (up to 6) needed for varying periods between mid May and the end of August. £180 per week plus bus pass and sweat shirt. To work 6 days and 3 evenings per week accompanying students on various activities: sports, social, cultural, excursions, night clubs etc., helping with airport transfers and performing basic administration work. Minimum age 19. No specific qualifications are essential but previous experience of being responsible for groups, knowledge of languages and Oxford, sporty character, would

all be useful. Personality is the most important quality. Applicants must be eligible to work in the UK. Applications to Kate Jennings, Social Organiser, at the above address.

Events

SHREWSBURY INTERNATIONAL MUSIC FESTIVAL: Suite 3, Victoria Court, Bexton Road, Knutsford, Cheshire Wa16 0PF (tel 01565-652667; fax 01565-652062; e-mail shrewsbury-fest@iftm.co.uk). SIMF will be in its 21st year in 1999. The annual event hosts a variety of amateur musicians and dancers from all over the world. The event is funded by the participating groups, and relies on local support to some extent. Events are held mainly in Shrewsbury's premier venues, but also in halls, churches and schools throughout Shropshire.

GROUP ESCORTS (5). The work is tiring and involves long hours, but is interesting and involves working as part of a team. Wages £40 per day. To work 24th June-2nd July and possibly longer. Applicants should be over 20, with an interest in music. No specific qualifications needed, but must be educated to at least A level standard, and have experience of handling groups with diplomacy, personality and efficiency.

OFFICE HELPER (1). Duties include photocopying/collating, and confirming arrangements over the telephone. Wages £4 per hour. To work in June: dates to be confirmed. Must be over 16, and have good numeracy and literacy skills and a logical mind.

Accommodation may be available, but applicants should preferably live near Shrewsbury for escort work, and near Knutsford for office work. Overseas applicants with reasonable English are considered. Interview preferred. Applications from January for escort work and April for office work, to Nichola Stokes.

Min. period of work 3 days between 6th and 13th August. Overseas applicants with good English are considered. Interview not necessary. Applications from March to Ian Harker.

Holiday Centres and Amusements

THE ABBEY COLLEGE: Wells Road, Malvern Wells, Worcs WR14 4JF (tel 01684-892300; fax 01684-892757).
ACTIVITIES STAFF/SPORTS STAFF. £110-£200 for 6 days work a week. Min. age 20.
WELFARE AND ADMIN. STAFF (3). £110 per week for 6 days work.

Sports qualifications and experience of summer schools preferred. Accommodation, meals and laundry facilities provided for all staff, plus free use of all sports and leisure activities and excursions. Work available from mid June to end of August. Overseas applicants welcome to work 4 weeks and get 2 weeks free English classes and accommodation free of charge. Applications from March to the Personnel Department at the above address.

AMERICAN ADVENTURE WORLD: Ilkeston, Derby DE7 5SX (tel 01773-531-521; fax 01773-716-140). The attraction offers employees a fun environment, plenty of training opportunities including NVQs, free entry to the Park, and a range of sports and social events.
RIDE OPERATORS (150). Wage £2.85-£3.30 per hour. Min. age 18.

ADMISSION ASSISTANTS (50). £2.30-£3.30 per hour. Min. age 16.
RETAIL ASSISTANTS (70). £2.30-£3.30 per hour. Min. age 16.
CATERING ASSISTANTS (120). £2.30-£3.30. Min. age 18. Food hygiene experience an advantage.
JANITORIAL ASSISTANTS (10). £2.20-£3.18 per hour. Min. age 16.
   Flexible working hours including weekends and Bank Holidays. Staff required from March to October. Accommodation not available. Overseas applicants with valid working permit welcome.
   Applications from February onwards to The Personnel Department at the above address. Interview necessary.

BUTLINS: Skegness, Lincolnshire PE25 1NJ (tel 01754-762311).
COOKS, CHEFS, KITCHEN ASSISTANTS, WAITING STAFF, CHALET CLEANERS, VENUE CLEANERS, BAR STAFF, SHOP/SUPERMARKET ASSISTANTS. Wages by arrangement; accommodation provided. Staff needed around the year; period of work by arrangement. Minimum age 18.
   Applications to Human Resources at the above address.

ENGLISH HERITAGE: Hazelrigg House, 33 Marefair, Northampton NN1 1SR (tel 01604-730320; fax 01604-730321). A governing agency of the Department for Culture, Media and Sport, which manages historic buildings and ancient monuments.
SEASONAL PART-TIME CUSTODIANS (25) to work up to 36 hours per week.
SEASONAL FULL-TIME CUSTODIANS (30) to work 45 hours per week including lunch break.
   Main duties include customer service, visitor management, retail sales/merchandising, site presentation, health and safety and site marketing and promotion. Wages for both positions £4.87 per hour (pay award pending). Positions are available at various locations across the Midlands and East Anglia. No accommodation is available.
   Min. period of work mid March to 31st October. Applicants should be aged 16-58 and have at least 6 months previous experience of dealing face to face with the general public in a service, leisure or retail environment. Overseas applicants with valid work authorisation are considered. Interview necessary.
   Applications from 4th January to Victoria Souter (HRLO) (tel 01604-730333).

THE OXFORD STORY: 6 Broad Street, Oxford OX1 3AJ (tel 01865-790055; fax 01865-791716).
OUTDOOR MARKETING STAFF (2) to work from June to September. Wages negotiable; to work flexible hours 3-4 days per week. Applicants should be aged at least 18 with good communication skills and outgoing personalities, be capable of approaching people and prepared to wear costumes if necessary.
   Applications to Jacquie Davison, Centre Supervisor, at the above address.

Hotels and Catering

ABBEY COLLEGE: Wells Road, Malvern Wells, Worcs., WR14 4JF (tel 01684-892300; fax 01684-892757; e-mail abbey@cix.compulink.co.uk; web site http:/www.abbeycollege.co.uk).

CATERING AND CLEANING STAFF (5) required to work 40 hours per week. Salary £100 per week. Relevant experience an advantage. Accommodation, meals and laundry facilities provided for all staff, and free use of all sports and leisure activities and excursions. Work available from mid June to the end of August. Overseas students are welcomed, to work 4 weeks and get 2 weeks free English classes and accommodation.

Applications from March to the Personnel Department at the above address.

THE BANBURY HOUSE HOTEL: Oxford Road, Banbury, Oxon OX16 9AH (tel 01295-259361; fax 01295-270954).

WAITING STAFF (3-4) and BAR STAFF (2) to serve food and beverages to customers, and be responsible for hygiene and general preparation. Areas of work include bar, restaurant, and function rooms. Various shifts and hours available. Min. rate of pay £3.75 per hour live out or £65 per week including meals and accomodation. Must be over 18.

ROOM ATTENDANTS (2) to service the guest bedrooms and public areas to a high standard; various days and shifts available. Min. rate of pay £3.63 live out or £65 per week including meals and accommodation.

Applications to Debbie Churchman at the above address.

THE BEAR HOTEL: Park Street, Woodstock OX20 1SZ (tel 01993-811511; fax 01993-813380). A 13th Century coaching inn with 44 luxury bedrooms, and a restaurant with 2 AA Rosettes for food and service.

WAITING ASSISTANT to work from July to October. Wages of £4.25; no accommodation available. Hours from 7am-3pm or 3pm-closing time, or to work split shifts; the working week is approximately 39 hours, depending on the requirements of the business.

Applications to Jane Jermyn, Operations Manager at the above address.

THE BRANT HOTEL: The Brantings, Groby, Leicester LE6 ODU (tel 01162-872703; fax 01162-321255). A traditional country inn set in a rural position, yet only minutes away from the city centre. Comprises a comprehensive bar and restaurant which open 7 days a week.

BAR STAFF (3), RESTAURANT STAFF (3) for full or part-time work June-September. Wages by arrangement. Minimum age 18.

Applications to D. Almond, Director at the above address.

CROWNE PLAZA HOTEL: Central Square, Birmingham B1 1HH (tel 0121-224 5020; fax 0121-224 5113).

FOOD AND BEVERAGE ASSISTANTS (5) to help clear tables and serve guests' meals. Wage £3.60 per hour. To work 40 hours a week.

HOUSEKEEPING ASSISTANTS (10). Duties include cleaning guests' rooms and public areas. Wage £3.70 per hour. To work 40 hours a week.

Staff are required from 1st of June to 31st September. No accommodation is available. An interview is required. Applications from 1st May to the Human Resources Manager.

ETTINGTON PARK: Alderminster, Stratford upon Avon, Warwickshire CV37 8BU (tel 01789-450123).

WAITING STAFF (2), HOUSEKEEPING ASSISTANTS (5). Wages £4 per hour; to work 40 hours per week, 5 days out of 7. Period of work April to October. Applicants must have previous experience of work in a similar establishment. Applications to Helen Wright, Regional P & T Manager, at the above address.

EYAM HALL: Eyam, Hope Valley, Derbyshire S32 5QW (tel 01433-631976; fax 01433-631603; e-mail nicwri@globalnet.co.uk)
GENERAL BUTTERY ASSISTANT(S) to work in a historic house.
GARDENER'S HELPER to work in a historic garden.
   Wages £3.50 per hour. Hours part or full time by arrangement; to work July-September inclusive. No qualifications needed except enthusiasm and common sense: training will be given.
   Applications to Ms N. Wright, Managing Partner at the above address.

GROVE HOUSE: Bromesberrow Heath, near Ledbury, Herefordshire HR8 1PE (tel 01531-650584).
GENERAL ASSISTANTS (1/2) to work in a guest house, providing general maintenance both in and out of doors. Also to work as an assistant on holiday courses for young children. Wages £25 per week including free B & L and outings on day off. Work available all year round for any length of time. Riding occasionally available. Applications with c.v. and photo, to Mrs E. M. Ross at the above address.

HOPCROFTS HOLT HOTEL: Banbury Road, Steeple Aston, Oxfordshire OX6 3QQ (tel 01869-340259; fax 01869-340865). Fifteenth-century coaching inn with 86 bedrooms, 9 conference suites and an AA Rosette restaurant.
WAITING STAFF for restaurant (plate service) and banqueting (silver service) work. £140 per week with meals on duty and accommodation provided. To work 39 hours per week over 5 days, in shifts. Min. age 18. Previous experience helpful.
PORTERING STAFF also required.
   Min. period of work 6 months. Overseas applicants with good English and experience welcome. An interview is not always necessary. Applications at any time to Ms W. Morley at the above address.

HOW CAPLE GRANGE HOTEL: How Caple, Herefordshire HR1 4TF (tel 01989-740208/740668; fax 01989-740301). Set in a rural location approx. 3 miles from the M50 motorway. Business is mainly party bookings and function trade.
CHEF/COOK (1-2). Approx. £120-£150 per week plus free B & L. To work approx. 40 hours per week. Min. age 18. No experience necessary but must be willing to work within other aspects of hotel work. Own transport absolutely essential. Staff needed between Easter to October and Christmas period. Applications to the Proprietor, How Caple Grange Hotel. Please telephone to check for vacancy availability.

JARVIS INTERNATIONAL HOTEL: The Square, Solihull, West Midlands B91 3QF (tel 0121-711 2121; fax 0121-711 5440). A busy 4 star conference, business and event hotel close to the N.E.C., airport and motorway network. Birmingham, Stratford, Warwick and the Cotswolds are all nearby. The hotel has 145 modern bedrooms and 25 conference rooms.
ROOM ATTENDANTS (10) to clean bed and bathrooms and prepare them for guests. To work 4-6 hours per day at times by arrangement 8am-8pm. Required for the summer from July 20th. Must be aged over 16.
BAR ASSISTANTS (10) to serve drinks, including serving wine at events and

parties. Hours by arrangement; will include some late nights. Required for the summer from July 20th; bar staff also required from November 16-January 12. Must be aged over 18.

RESTAURANT/BANQUETTE ATTENDANTS (10) to serve food at table in the restaurant and at parties. Hours by arrangement including some late nights. Required for the summer from July 20th; bar staff also required from November 16-January 12.

Wages £3.60 per hour with tips: no accommodation available. Applications to Linda D. Hurley, Personnel & Training Manager at the above address.

THE JERSEY ARMS HOTEL: Middleton Stoney, Oxon OX6 8SE (tel 01869-343234; fax 01869-343565).

HOUSEKEEPING ASSISTANT (1). Wages £125 per month. To work 45 hours over 5 days a week. Accommodation is provided. Min. period of work 1 month at any time of year.

Min. age 18. Applications to Mrs Livingston at the above address.

MOBILE PROMOTIONS CORPORATE EVENTS: Newbrook, Titchmarsh, Thrapston, Northamptonshire NN14 3DG (tel 01832-733460; fax 01832-732737).

CATERING STAFF/WAITING STAFF (6-10), HOSTS/HOSTESSES required to work at mainly outdoor events. Approx. £3.50 an hour, depending on job and experience. Hours and period of work variable between April and September.

No accommodation provided, except if working away. Overseas applicants welcome. All applicants must be available for interview. Applications from April to Gita or Robin Carlisle at the above address.

ORANGERY RESTAURANT: Charlecote Park, Wellsbourne, Stratford upon Avon CV35 9ER (tel 01789-470448).

GENERAL ASSISTANTS (60) to serve at the counter, prepare salad, wash up and clean. Wages £3.80+ per hour. Should have friendly, outgoing personality and a tidy appearance.

PASTRY COOK to make cakes, scones and sweets. Wage £4.20+ per hour depending on experience. Experience of working in a kitchen an advantage; must have a good knowledge of food hygiene and be able to work on own initiative.

The working week is Friday-Tuesday. Period of work June-October. Applications to Janet Darlow at the above address.

OXFORD THAMES FOUR PILLARS HOTEL: Henley Road, Sandford on Thames, Oxford OX4 4GX (tel 01865-334444; fax 01865-334400; e-mail enquiries@four-pillars.co.uk). A four star hotel.

CASUAL BAR STAFF (3) with bar experience.

CASUAL WAITING STAFF (3) with silver-service experience.

Wages for both positions £4.00 per hour. Working hours are varied. No accommodation is available. Min. period of work 4 months between June and September. Applicants must be over 18. Overseas applicants entitled to work in the UK considered. Interview necessary.

Applications from spring to Catriona Verrell, Assistant Manager.

PARK FARMHOUSE HOTEL: Melbourne Road, Isley Walton, Nr Derby DE74 2RN (tel 01332-862409; fax 01332-862364; e-mail info@parkfarmhouse-.co.uk). A small family run hotel with friendly young staff (mostly in their mid 20s) The hotel has 15 bedrooms, a function barn and a caravan park. Located next to Donington Park Motor Racing Circuit.
GENERAL ASSISTANT (1) to work mainly split shifts in all areas: bar, breakfast serving, evening waiting, washing up, room cleaning etc. Wages £3.30-£3.90 per hour. To work 41 hours over 5 days a week. Accommodation and meals on duty provided. Min. period of work 2 months between March and October.
   Previous relevant experience preferred but not essential. Overseas applicants with reasonable spoken English will be considered. Interview preferred, unless distance makes this difficult. Applications from February to John or Linda Shields.

PECKFORTON CASTLE: Stone House Lane, Peckforton, Nr. Tarporley, Cheshire CW6 9TN (tel 01829-260930; fax 01829-261230). A visitor attraction and a function/wedding venue located 12 miles east of Chester.
WAITING STAFF (5-10), BAR STAFF (2), KITCHEN ASSISTANTS (2) for weekend work between May and October inclusive. Wages of £5 per hour for Saturdays and functions or £4 per hour for Sundays. Hours approx 1-10pm on Saturdays and 10am-6pm on Sundays. Applicants should be aged over 18 and have previous experience.
   Applications to The Personnel Manager at the above address.

PEN-Y-DYFFRYN COUNTRY HOTEL: Rhydycroesau, Nr Oswestry, Shropshire SY10 7DT (tel/fax 01691-653700). A small family run hotel located 5 minutes from Oswestry.
GENERAL HOTEL WORKER (1), GENERAL KITCHEN ASSISTANT (1). Wages £3.50 per hour with accommodation provided. To work 4/5 days a week. Min. period of work 6 weeks between May and October.
   Overseas applicants considered. Interview necessary. Applications at any time to Miles Hunter.

PIPERS GROVE RESTAURANT: National Trust Enterprises Ltd., Snowshill Manor, Snowshill, near Broadway, Worcestershire WR12 7JU (tel/fax 01386-858685).
RESTAURANT ASSISTANTS (3) to serve customers, set and clear tables, wash up etc.
KITCHEN ASSISTANTS (3) to prepare meals (including occasional evening functions), tidy etc.
   Wages £3.80 per hour if over 21. To work 30-40 hours per week. Previous experience an advantage but not essential; applicants must be committed to the job and eager to succeed. Period of work from May to December.
   Applications should be sent to P.R. Boam, Restaurant Manager at the above address.

QUALITY HOTEL WARWICK: Chesford Bridge, Kenilworth, Warwickshire CV8 2LN (tel 01926-858331; fax 01926-858153).
HOUSEKEEPING/RESTAURANT STAFF (2-3). To work 5 days out of 7; salary £3.55 per hour. Accommodation is available at £22 per week. Staff are required all year round and no experience is necessary. Minimum period of

work 10 weeks. Applications to the Manager at the above address at any time.

THE RANDOLPH HOTEL: Beaumont Street, Oxford OX1 2LN (tel 01865-247481; fax 01865-791678). Oxford's premier hotel.
HOUSEKEEPING/RESTAURANT ASSISTANTS needed to work at The Randolph and The Eastgate hotels in Oxford, The Bear Hotel in Woodstock and The Upper Reaches in Abingdon. Wages £4 per hour for 30-39 hours over five days per week. No accommodation available. To work from June to September; min. period of work eight weeks. Overseas applicants with good English welcome. Minimum age 18.
Apply from April to Mrs Julia Makepeace, Human Resources at the above address.

SHILLINGFORD BRIDGE HOTEL: Shillingford Hill, Wallingford, Oxford-shire OX10 8LZ (tel 01865-858567; fax 01865-858636).
STAFF for all types of hotel work, full and part time. Varying rates of pay. Limited accomodation. Min. period of work 3 months.Applications to the duty manager at the above address.

WESTWOOD COUNTRY HOTEL: Hinksey Hill Top, Oxford OX1 5BG (tel 01865-735408; fax 01865-736536).
GENERAL ASSISTANTS (2). Min. £120 per week plus B & L. To work approx. 45 hours per 5½-day week. Hours by arrangement with flexible day off. Min. age 18. Tidy appearance required. Min. period of work 3 months between May and October. Overseas applicants welcome. All applicants must be non-smokers. Applications from February to Mr. Tony Healy, Proprietor, at the above address.

WHITE HART HOTEL: High Street, Chipping Norton, Oxfordshire OX7 5AD (tel 01608-642572; fax 01608-644143).
GENERAL ASSISTANTS (2) needed from June to September. £80 per week live-in. To work 30 to 40 hours per week in bar, kitchen, restaurant, housekeeping or reception areas. Smart appearance, friendly personality required. Minimum age 18. Applications to the Manager, at the above address.

THE WILD DUCK: Ewen, Cirencester, Glos GL7 6BY (tel 01285-770310; fax 01285 770924).
WAITING/BAR and GENERAL ASSISTANTS (2). To work 5 days per week for a rate of £3.50 per hour. Staff required from June to October; minimum period of work 6 weeks. Accommodation not available. Minimum age 18. Interview is necessary. Apply from May onwards to Tina Mussell at the above address.

Medical

OXFORD AUNTS: 2 George Street, Oxford OX1 2AF (tel 01865-791016/7; fax 01865-242606).
TEMPORARY POSITIONS for nurses and carers for the elderly and disabled. Experience and good references essential. Overseas applicants must have a good standard of English. Everyone must be able to attend an interview and provide three references.

Office Work

AUTO BUSINESS LTD: Carlton House, Gwash Way, Stamford, Lincolnshire PE9 1XP (tel 01780-481712; fax 01780-482383; e-mail autobusiness.compuserve.com). A small specialist publishing company producing publications for the motor industry.
RESEARCHERS (3-4) to write special reports etc, abstracting information from technical material provided. Wages by arrangement. Minimum period of work 2 months between June and September; working hours are flexible and the period of work does not need to be continuous. No accommodation available. Applicants do not need technical knowledge, but must have very good written English and up to date computer skills.
Applications to Ms Toni Lingard at the above address; an interview is not necessary but applicants need to submit samples of their written work.

Outdoor

C. DE ANGELIS & SON: 333 London Road, Wyberton, Boston, Lincs. PE21 7AU (tel/fax 01205-722891).
SOFT FRUIT PICKERS (100) required from 23 June for about 3 weeks.
PLUM PICKERS (50) required from 20 August for about 3 weeks. Includes ladder work.
APPLE PICKERS (50) required from 7 September for about 4 weeks. Includes ladder work.
To work variable hours from Monday to Friday. Camping available on site. Applications to the above address.

BADSEY FIELDS NRS LTD: Badsey Fields Lane, Badsey, Evesham, Worcestershire WR11 5EX (tel 01386-830944; fax 01386-833668).
GENERAL HORTICULTURAL WORKERS (10+) to work from June onwards. Wages at Agricultural Wages Board rates. To work a 40 hour week or as arranged. Min. age 16. Applications to P. Campagna, Director, at the above address.

T. W. & H. R. BRIGDEN LTD.: Pullens Farm, Ridgeway Cross, Near Malvern, Worcs. WR13 5JN (tel 01886-880-232; fax 01886-880-814).
FIELD SUPERVISORS (4) required to work with students, picking strawberries and raspberries. Wages paid at hourly rates for approx. 8 hours a day, 6 days per week (weather permitting).
ACCOMMODATION MANAGER to supervise foreign student workforce. From early June to mid/end August, staying for full period of time if possible. Accommodation may be available. Must have full clean driving licence; min. age 21. Applicants must speak English to the standard of a native speaker.
Applications at any time to Mrs Brigden at the above address. Interview necessary.

S. H. M. BROOMFIELD & SON: Elmbridge Fruit Farm, Addis Lane, Cutnall Green, Droitwich, Worcs WR9 0ND (tel 01299-851592; fax 01905-621633). A well-situated, thriving fruit farm dedicated to growing premium fruit (Best Midland Orchard winners 1995, 1996, 1997).
FRUIT PICKERS (20) to work from June 10th to October 20th. Piecework rates of pay (£3.60-£7 per hour according to working speed). To work 5 to 6 days per week. No experience or qualifications are necessary as full training is

given on site. Min. age 16; min. period of work varies depending on the season. Limited accommodation is available for £1 per night. Camping, toilet and washing facilities free.

Applications from May 25 to Colin Broomfield, Partner, at the above address.

J. M. BUBB & SON: Pave Lane Farm, Newport, Shropshire TF10 9AX (tel 01952-811497; fax 01952-825179).

TRACTOR DRIVERS (3). Must have clean driving licence and be experienced in tractor driving.

FORKLIFT DRIVERS (3). Must hold a fork lift certificate.

POTATO GRADERS/FLOWER PICKERS.To work 8 hours per day, 5-5½ days per week; overtime varies. Salary dependent on age, based on min. Agricultural Wages Board rates. Staff required for 20 weeks from June to October. A campsite is available for a charge of £10-£15 per week.

Overseas applicants with valid working visas welcome. Note: all applicants must be available for interview. Apply to Mrs C. Joyce at the above address.

H.J. AND S.J. FORTNAM: Fosbury Fruit Farm, Putley, Ledbury, Herefordshire HR8 2QR (tel 01531-670613).

FRUIT PICKERS (10). Wages according to Agricultural Wages Board rates. To work September 1st to October. Previous picking experience useful. Campsite available with showers and toilets.

AU PAIR (1). Standard rates paid. To work July 20th to September 4th. Must be a non-smoker, have previous experience and provide references. Accommodation available in farmhouse.

Overseas applicants entitled to work in the UK considered. Interview not necessary. Applications from Easter/April to Mrs F. Fortnam.

C. FRANCIS LTD: 13 Knight Street, Pinchbeck, Spalding, Lincolnshire PE11 3RA (tel 01775-723953). A small family company in the fens close to Peterborough. All strawberries are grown on a table-top system, so pickers do not need to bend down.

SOFT FRUIT and APPLE PICKERS (20). To work approx. 8 hours a day, 5 days per week. Staff needed from 8 June to 10 October. Min. period of work 4 weeks. Accommodation provided for weekly charge of £13 (tent) or £18 (caravan). Shower and cooking facilities included. Min. age 18. Overseas applicants with work permits welcome. Applications from 1 April to Mr Michael Bowser, at the above address.

JOHN HARGREAVES & SONS: Brook House Farm, Gedneydyke, Spalding, Lincs PE12 0AT (tel 01406-550246; fax 01406-550219).

SOFT FRUIT PICKERS (20-30). Rate of pay piecework 15p-30p per pound. To work 6 day week, flexible hours, lots of overtime.

SOFT FRUIT PACKERS (10). Piecework pay 20p-50p per tray. To work 6 days a week, long hours.

SUPERVISORS FOR SOFT FRUIT PICKERS: basic rate of pay £4.40 per hour; fixed overtime rate. To organise picking gangs, quality control of product, basic administration of piecework records. To work min. 7 hour day, 6 day week plus lots of overtime. Should have some experience of supervising people.

Accommodation for all workers in caravans on a campsite. Min. age for pickers is 16; 18 for supervisors. Period of work from mid June to mid September. Applications to Garth Baxter, Production Manager, at the above address.

HAYGROVE FRUIT: Redbank, Ledbury, Herefordshire HR8 2JL (tel 01531-633659; fax 01531-635969). Grows all soft fruits, for Marks and Spencer and other supermarkets. Almost all picking is done under tunnel protection from rain so full days and good crops are offered.
FRUIT PICKERS AND PACKERS. Many pickers are required over a long season. Good piecework rates offered to those willing to work hard. Friendly, cosmopolitan atmosphere, beautiful surroundings and 1 mile from town. Facilities provided include a campsite, showers and common room. Applicants must be over 19 and bring own tent. Work available from April to October. Experienced supervisors, tractor, lorry and HGV1 drivers also wanted. Foreign applicants welcome; applicants from outside the EU must have a valid work permit. Write (with s.a.e. or IRC) to Haygrove Fruit at the above address.

LEIGH SINTON FARMS AND NURSERIES: Lower Interfield, Nr. Malvern, Worcs. WR14 1UU (tel 01886-832305; fax 01886-833446).
CASUAL WORKERS (10-20). The work involves harvesting and preparing Christmas trees for wholesale and retail outlets. There is some indoor work but the majority is outdoors and in all weathers. To work from October to December; to work 39 hours per week plus overtime as required. Wages, accommodation etc. by arrangement.
Applications to B.J.P. McCarthy, Farm Manager at the above address.

LUBSTREE PARK FARM: The Humbers, Donnington, Telford, Shropshire TF2 8LW (tel 01952-604320; fax 01952-670307; e-mail lubstree.park@farmline-.com). A specialised producer of soft fruit. Much of production is under rain protection, including innovative table top strawberries. The farm prides itself on its facilities and good working relationship with its fieldworkers.
FRUIT PICKERS (150) for strawberry/raspberry picking/packing/field work. Piece work/day work. Accommodation in own tent or farm's mobile homes and dormitories. Superb facilities; hot showers, social and dining room, laundry room and toilets. Good atmosphere and satellite tv. Free transport to supermarket. Located near large town, but positioned in the country. Well paid work from May to November. All applicants must be over 18, EU nationals or students authorised to work in the UK and must book to confirm places well in advance. Application letters to Mr Ward at the above address.

MAN OF ROSS LTD: Glewstone, Ross-on-Wye, Herefordshire HR9 6AU (tel 01989-562853; fax 01989-563877). Situated in the Wye Valley, the farm supplies mainly to supermarkets.
FRUIT HARVESTERS (30) to pick strawberries, cherries, plums, apples and pears. Piecework rates. Hours according to crop needs, approx. 6-8 hours a day, 5-6 days a week. Min. age 18 years. Min. period of work 1 month between June and September (July is a quiet month). Accommodation available on campsite for £5 per week. Overseas applicants welcome, provided they have the necessary work permits. Applications from January to Anna Jackson at the above address.

MANOR FARM: Church Lane, Chilcote, Swadlincote, Derby DE12 8DL. FRUIT PICKERS required to pick mainly strawberries. Wages according to piecework rates. Working hours flexible but early start required, finishing usually by mid-afternoon. Accommodation on campsite available with toilet, showers and laundry facilities. Note that campers must provide their own tent and cooking equipment. Min. period of work one day between 10 June and end of September. Overseas applicants welcome. Applications from the beginning of March to Mrs Nicola Busby at the above address. Must apply in writing with a s.a.e. or no reply will be sent.

PENNOXSTONE COURT: Kings Caple, Hereford HR1 4TX (tel 01432-840289). A busy fruit farm with a multi-national atmosphere situated in a beautiful part of England.
STRAWBERRY PICKERS (35) from mid-May to end September.
RASPBERRY PICKERS (10) for month of July.
PLUM PICKERS (15) from mid-August to end September.
Wages on average £25-£30 per day, based on piecework rates. To work 6 days per week. Accommodation is limited. Some caravan accommodation may be available, though plenty of camping accommodation is available with full facilities. Applicants should be able to fit in with cheerful, friendly atmosphere. Min. age 18. Overseas applicants welcome. Applications for all pickers to be submitted, between April and first week in July and enclosing s.a.e. or IRC, to Mr N. J. Cockburn at the above address.

SIDDINGTON FARM: Leadington, Ledbury, Herefordshire HR8 2LN (tel 01531-632664; fax 01531-632232)
STRAWBERRY PICKERS (30). Piecework rates. Hours: 7am-2pm, Sunday to Friday inclusive. Campsite provided for those bringing their own camping and cooking equipment. Kitchen, TV room, toilets and showers are provided. No fruit picking experience necessary. Friendly working atmosphere. Period of work from first week in June for approx. 8 weeks. Overseas applicants eligible to work in the UK welcome. Applications to Mrs Houlbrooke at the above address.

STANLEY & PICKFORD: Rectory Farm, Stanton St John, Oxford OX33 1HF (tel 01865-351214; mobile 0976-302404; fax 01865-351679; e-mail S.and.P-@farmline.com). Runs a pick-your-own, and are suppliers of potatoes, strawberries, raspberries and other fruits.
FRUIT PICKERS (30) to pick mainly strawberries and raspberries approx. June 5-approx. August 5th. Wages at piece work rates. If the weather is suitable there is picking every day; hours of work are informal, but pickers can expect to work in the mornings and part of the afternoon. Accommodation is available on the farm in mobile homes and caravans with cooking facilities, communal room, showers etc. Previous experience would be an advantage.The farm employs field trainers to help staff pick correctly and efficiently.
Contact Mr R.O. Stanley, Partner, at the above address for a full information pack giving information on the work available, rates of pay, accommodation, training, accommodation etc.

STOCKS FARM: Suckley, Worcestershire WR6 5EH (tel 01886-884202; fax 01886-884110).
HARVEST WORKERS for harvesting hops by machine and fruit picking. Wages at usual agricultural rates. Self catering accommodation available.

Period of work from June to October. Applicants should like working in the countryside. Applications to Mr R. M. Capper, Stocks Farm, at the above address.

WITHERS FARM: Wellington Heath, Ledbury, Herefordshire HR8 1NF (tel/ fax 01531-632017).
CASUAL FARM WORKERS (10) for various jobs including driving, supervising and picking. Wages either £3.21 per hour (at the moment) or piecework; to work 6 days per week. Accommodation in tents or caravans at a cost of £5. Min. period of work 4 weeks between 25 May and 1 October. Applications from January to G. Leeds at the above address.

Sport

ANGLO WORLD OXFORD: 108 Banbury Road, Oxford OX2 6JU (tel 01865-515808; fax 01865-310068). A global English Language teaching organisation with schools and sales offices throughout the world, including seven schools in Britain and one in Ireland.
SPORTS INSTRUCTOR/LIFEGUARD for a well equipped summer school with first class sports facilites. Full time position from late June til late August; wages to be arranged. Some accommodation may be available. Overseas students with valid working visas welcome. Interview is necessary. Applications from March/April to the School Administrator at the above address.

NORTHFIELD FARM: Flash, nr Buxton, Derbyshire SK17 0SW (tel 01298-22543). BHS approved riding centre and working farm, situated in a small village. There is a post office and a pub 100 yards away. 30 horses are used, including an Andalusian stallion at stud, a few breeding mares and young stock.
TREK LEADERS (2). Approx. minimum pay £80 per week plus free B & L. To work 8.00am-5pm, 5½ days per week. Work available from April to September/October; min. work period July-August, preferably June also. Applicants must be competent riders, good with people and preferably car drivers; Riding and Road Safety Test and First Aid qualification also preferred. Must also be prepared to help out on the farm when needed. All applicants should be available for interview. Applications between March and May only (no applications before March) to Mrs E. Andrews, Northfield Farm, at the above address.

NORTH KESTEVEN SPORTS CENTRE: Moor Lane, North Hykeham, Lincoln LN6 9AX (tel 01522-883311; fax 01522-883355).
PART-TIME LIFEGUARDS required during all vacations. Must have RLSS Pool Lifeguard (PLG), preferably with spinal qualifications. Previous experience preferred. Approx. £4.00 per hour, with uniform provided. To work variable hours between 6.45am and 11pm including bank holidays. Application forms available from the centre.

PEAK DISTRICT HANG GLIDING CENTRE: York House, Ladderedge, Leek, North Staffordshire ST13 7AQ (tel 01538-382520).
GLIDING INSTRUCTOR(S) (1/2) to work from July to September. Wages £60 per day. Hours by arrangement. Must be experienced.

TELESALES ASSISTANT/SECRETARY. Wages and period of work by arrangement. Must have a good telephone manner.
Applications to Mike Orr at the above address.

SURFACE WATERSPORTS: Rutland Water, Whitwell Watersports Centre, Empingham, Leicestershire LE15 8BL (tel 01780-460464). Situated on 3,000 acres of inland water.
WINDSURFING INSTRUCTORS (2). £140 per week basic. To work min. 40 hours per week with possible overtime. No accommodation available. Must have RYA windsurfing or RYA sailing instructor's certificate and RYA sports boat handling or equivalent. Duties include rigging and de-rigging of sailboards and dinghies, windsurfing instruction and rescue work. Flexible attitude required. Min. period of work 2 months between April and September. Overseas applicants with good English, suitable qualifications and own lodgings are welcome. Applications from March to Mr Dave Hales, Proprietor, Surface Watersports.

Language Schools

THE ABBEY COLLEGE: Wells Road, Malvern Wells, Worcs WR14 4JF (tel 01684-892300; fax 01684-892757; e-mail abbey@cix.compulink.co.uk; web site http:/www.abbey.college.co.uk).
TEFL TEACHERS (15). £210-£310 per week. Must hold at least a RSA/ Trinity Prep. Certificate and have at least one year's experience. Previous summer school experience preferred. Accommodation, meals and laundry facilities provided. Work available from mid June to the end of August. All year positions also available. Min. period of employment 4 weeks. Free use of all sports and leisure activities and excursions open to all employees. Applications from March to Personnel Department at the above address. Interview necessary.

ANGLO WORLD OXFORD: 108 Banbury Road, Oxford OX2 6JU (tel 01865-515808; fax 01865-310068). A language school in North Oxford with a young and lively atmosphere.
SOCIAL ASSISTANTS (1-2). Minimum age 18. To assist the social organiser with arranging and promoting social events and sporting activities.
ACCOMMODATION ASSISTANTS (1-2). Minimum age 17; must have access to a car. To assist the accommodation officer, mainly by recruiting and inspecting new host families.
ADMINISTRATION ASSISTANTS (1-2). Minimum age 17. To undertake general administrative duties; computer literacy an advantage.
All jobs are on a full time basis with wages to be arranged. Some accommodation may be available in student residences; this is free if 'warden' responsibilities are undertaken.
Staff are required from May/June until the end of August, and an interview is necessary. Overseas students with valid working visas are welcome. Applications from March/April to the School Administrator at the above address.

EF LANGUAGE TRAVEL: Cherwell House, 3rd Floor, London Place, Oxford OX4 1AH (tel 01865-200720; fax 01865-243196; e-mail www.ef.com).
EFL TEACHERS, LEADERS, ACTVITY COORDINATORS needed to teach teenage overseas students and organize leisure activities between June

and the end of August. Teachers are paid £17 + per half day session (or £21 if with a TEFL qualification); leaders are paid £175 per week. Applicants should be university students aged at least 19; those with TEFL certificates preferred.
Applications to Otto Haas, Manager at the above address.

MS R. NEILSON: 2B Windsor House, Wake Green Road, Moseley, Birmingham B13 9SD.
ENGLISH TEACHERS (4) to work for 3 hours per day. Should be aged over 22 and hold a TEFL qualification
ANIMATEURS (4) to work for 6 hours per day. Must speak French and like working with children aged 12-18.
Wages by arrangement. Period of work from July to August. Applications to R. Neilson, Director at the above address.

OXFORD HOUSE SCHOOL OF ENGLISH: 67 High Street, Wheatley, Oxford OX33 1XT (tel 01865-874786; fax 01865-873351). Small, personal school near Oxford, catering for mixed nationality students (individuals and small groups only). A friendly working environment.
ADMIN/SECRETARIAL/SOCIAL ORGANISER (1) from June to September. Approx. £175 per week. 5 hour day; flexible but mainly 3 hours per morning Monday to Friday, plus two hours either afternoon or evening. Minimum age 20. Qualifications: knowledge of languages, first aid, secretarial and office skills.
ENGLISH TEACHERS (1-2) from July to the end of August. Wages: approx. £265 per week. 23 hours of class contact per week plus occasional supervisory/social duties. Min. RSA Certificate, TEFL or equivalent plus relevant experience.
Applications a.s.a.p. to Mr R.I.C. Vernede, Principal, Oxford House School of English.

SEVERNVALE ACADEMY: 25 Claremont Hill, Shrewsbury, Shropshire SY1 1RD. A small school running English courses for foreign students, both adults and juniors.
EFL TEACHERS (5-10). £150-£240 a week. To teach 15-27 hours per week over 4 days (not weekends). TEFL qualification (e.g. RSA/UCLES/TESOL certificate) and experience necessary. Period of work June to September. Applications from February to Mr J.W.T. Rogers, Principal, Severnvale Academy.

ST CLARE'S OXFORD: 139 Banbury Road, Oxford OX2 7AL (tel 01865-552031; fax 01865-310002; e-mail eduserv@stclares.ac.uk). An educational charity which operates a range of courses for students from around the world throughout the year and has residential premises in North Oxford.
EFL TEACHERS (20). To teach 15-26 hours per week. From £16 per hour. Must have Dip. TEFLA.
ACTIVITY STAFF (20). £185(+) per 40 hour week. Min. age 20 years. Experience of organising activities and sport essential.
Accommodation available free to those who chose to undertake pastoral activities. Min. period of work 3 weeks between June and September. All applicants must be available for interview. Applications from March to the Summer Staff Co-ordinator at the above address.

Vacation Traineeships

Accountancy and Insurance

NEWBY CASTLEMAN: West Walk Building, 110 Regent Road, Leicester LE1 7LT (tel 0116-254 9262; fax 0116-2470021).
The company offers vacancies for 2 students to experience working in a chartered accountant's practice. The work will involve assisting in accounts preparation and audit. Students at any level are invited to apply. Salary of £70 per week
  Placements last for 8 weeks in the summer and are located in Leicester. No accommodation is provided. Applications by 3rd March to M.D. Castleman, Partner.

WESLEYAN ASSURANCE SOCIETY: Colmore Circus, Birmingham B4 6AR (tel 0121-200 3003; fax 0121-200 2971).
The Wesleyan Assurance Society offers up to two placements in their actuarial department in Birmingham. Trainees assist student actuaries with project work, computer programming and general numerical work. Preference is given to university students in the penultimate year of a Maths-based degree course.
  The positions last for the length of the summer with existing holiday arrangements being honoured. The salary in 1998 was based on an annual rate of £8,000 p.a.
  Applications should be sent by 31st December, to Mr David Middleton, Financial Control Actuary, at the above address.

The Law

WRAGGE & CO: 55 Colmore Row, Birmingham B3 2AS (tel 0121-233 1000; fax 0121-214 1099; e-mail lucy-gibson@wragge.com).
Wragge and Co, a large commercial law practice, offers around 40 vacation traineeships each year to second and third year students of both law and non-law subjects. The work involves drafting, research, meeting clients, visits to court and analysing contracts.
  Placements will last for two weeks over the summer vacation. Trainees receive £100 for a 5 day week; help may be given in finding accommodation.
  Applications should be sent to Lucy Gibson, Graduate Recruitment and Training Manager, before February 12th.

Media

APPLEFORD PUBLISHING GROUP: Appleford, Abingdon, Oxon OX14 4PB.
Appleford Publishing Group is a specialist academic publisher majoring in Modern and Early Modern history and church history at Ph.D. level. It is a Christian organisation, normally only wanting those who share its Christian convictions and might eventually want to work for the company. The organisation would show employees round Christian publishing, book production and library (50,000 volumes) work. First or second year students

from pre-1980 universities and possibly interested in working with the Group on graduation are given preference. This opportunity is open to up to 3 applicants mainly during the summer vacation but occasionally also at Easter. Full board provided free with some payment for work, depending on what is done. Overseas applicants who are fluent in English and share the Evangelical Protestant convictions of the organisation, will be considered. Applications by February 1 for Easter work, by Easter for the summer vacation, to the Editorial Director at the above address. An interview is advisable. Please enclose full c.v. and a brief statement of interest.

VACATION WORK PUBLICATIONS: 9 Park End Street, Oxford OX1 1HJ (tel 01865-241978; fax 01865-790885).

Since its establishment in 1967 Vacation Work has become widely recognised as the leading publisher of employment directories and travel guides for young people. It currently features over forty titles in its catalogue including *The Directory of Summer Jobs in Britain, Work Your Way Around the World* and *Travellers' Survival Kit: USA and Canada.*

In 1999 the company will be looking for one or two people to work in an editorial capacity during the summer vacation. The work will involve assisting the editorial staff in the process of revising and up-dating the company's books. Duties are likely to include general secretarial and clerical work, organising mailings to featured organisations and editorial research and re-writing.

All candidates should be proficient at operating a word processor, and should be able to demonstrate an interest in or knowledge of the publishing business. Some writing or editorial experience is preferred. Applicants must be capable of working on their own initiative without direct supervision, although help and guidance will be given where necessary. They must be entitled to work in the UK and speak English as well as if it were their first language. The pay will be around £150 per week. Please note that no direct assistance can be given with finding accommodation. Applications should be sent to Mr Charles James at the above address around Easter in order to arrange an interview.

Science, Construction and Engineering

ALSTOM: Mechanical Engineering Centre, Cambridge Road, Whetstone, Leicester LE8 6LH (tel 0116-2015679; fax 0116-2015461).

The Whetstone site has been involved in gas turbines since Sir Frank Whittle worked there in the 1940s. The company aim to follow his innovative example to develop the technologies of the future. The Technical Centre is part of the ALSTOM group, specialising in engineering design, research and development. The company offers about four vacation placements for students who are studying for degrees in Engineering and related technical subjects at university. Trainees will work on specialised engineering projects and fulfil a variety of other duties. The majority of placements last for up to 10 or 12 weeks over the summer, with occasional vacancies during Christmas and Easter.

Pay is commensurate with the candidate's age and qualifications. Overseas applicants who do not require work permits will be considered.

Applications before April to Mrs V. Green, HR Administration, at the above address.

ALSTOM ENERGY LTD: Newbold Road, Rugby, Warwickshire CV21 2NH (tel 01788-531985; fax 01788-531658). ALSTOM Energy designs, manufactures, installs and commissions generating equipment for operation in power stations around the world.

ALSTOM Energy offers about 12 traineeships to students over the summer, involving work in engineering design, development and manufacture. The positions are open to 2nd year university students who are studying for a degree in Mechanical, Production or Aeronautical Engineering or Engineering Science. Candidates should be about to enter their final year of study. Opportunities may exist for sponsorship following a vacation placement. Suitably qualified overseas students will be considered.

The traineeships last for 8-12 weeks and take place at the company's Rugby site. The salary was around £182 a week in 1998.

Applications should be made by the end of January to Mrs M. James, Employee Development Officer, at the above address.

DERA: CIS/LS (Mal) Recruitment Centre, D307, DERA Malvern, St Andrews Road, Malvern, Worcestershire WR14 3PS (tel 01684-895642; fax 01684-894318).

Multi-disciplined teams are engaged in a broad spectrum of research, providing the principle focus for space research, satellite/land communications, imagery exploitations, parallel computing, software engineering, sensor technologies and command and control systems.

The Command and Information Systems, Sensors and Processing, and Land Systems (Malvern) Sectors of the Defence Evaluation Research Agency offers approx. 40-50 placements for students over the summer vacation as well as placements for those undertaking sandwich course industrial placements. Trainces are employed on Defence Research Science based projects at Malvern or Defford in Worcestershire.

The placements are open to undergraduates on Science or Engineering courses and last between 10 and 51 weeks. The salary for placements in 1998 was £750-£950 per month.

Application forms are available from 1 September at the above address and should be returned to Martin Felton, Student Liaison Officer, by 31 January.

GIFFORD AND PARTNERS: Carlton House, Ringwood Road, Woodlands, Southampton SO4 2HT (tel 01703-813461; fax 01703-813462).

Gifford and Partners is a firm of consulting engineers particularly interested in the design of building and highway structures and in marine works worldwide. Each summer the firm takes on students to work in its regional office in Chester. For further details see their entry in *The South* chapter.

ROVER GROUP LTD: International Headquarters, Warwick Technology Park, Warwick CV34 6RG (tel 01926-482473; fax 01926-482227). Rover Group is the UK's largest vehicle manufacturer, producing MGs, Rovers, Land Rovers and Minis. Rover is based around the Midlands with 40,000 employees.

Rover are seeking up to 120 students to work for 3 months during the summer vacation. Traineeships exist in product engineering, manufacturing, logistics, personnel, quality assurance, finance, purchasing and information technology.

Candidates should have completed the penultimate year of their degree course. Trainees may be based at any of the firm's plants at Oxford, Longbridge, Solihull, Swindon, Gaydon or at the Head Office in Warwick. Some assistance in arranging accommodation is available. The salary is c. £820 a month.

Applications should be sent to Rover Group Ltd. at the address above.

SHELL GLOBAL SOLUTIONS, THORNTON: P.O. Box 1, Chester CH1 3SH (tel 0151-373 5381; fax 0151-373 5899).

Shell offers a number of challenging research placements to high calibre university undergraduates in Physics, (Physical or Analytical) Chemistry, Materials Science, Mechanical Engineering, Electronics, Electrical Engineering, Mathematics, Statistics or Computer Science. Research covers areas of Fuels and Lubricants Technology, Analysis and Measurement Technology and Safety and Environmental Technology.

Overseas applicants are very welcome. To apply for these placements, contact the Personnel Department at the above address.

UNILEVER RESEARCH: Colworth Laboratory, Colworth House, Sharnbrook, Bedfordshire MK44 1LQ (tel 01234-781781).

Unilever Research offers a number of traineeships each year at its research centre in Bedfordshire. The company will be looking for students in their penultimate year of their course in the following, or related areas of study: Chemical Engineering, Computing, Chemistry, Consumer Science, Biological Sciences and Physics.

The company makes direct contact with a number of university departments, and students from these universities are selected after interview.

The North

Cumbria
County Durham
Greater Manchester
Isle of Man
Lancashire

Berwick-on-Tweed

Newcastle
Carlisle
Durham
Lake District
Middlesbrough
Scarborough
Douglas
York
Hull
Blackpool
Leeds
Grimsby
Liverpool   Manchester   Sheffield

Merseyside
Northumberland
Tyne and Wear
Yorkshire

While job vacancies in the tourist trade are scattered throughout the northern region, they are most abundant in the larger coastal resorts, the Yorkshire Dales and the Lake District.

The main resorts along the east coast are Bridlington, Filey, Whitby and Scarborough, Britain's fifth most popular seaside destination. Scarborough and Filey have a large number of seasonal vacancies, comparatively few of which have live-in accommodation. Further north lie South Shields, Whitley Bay and Berwick. As well as hotels and restaurants, amusement arcades are another source of employment, particularly in Bridlington. Live-in jobs are comparatively rare. South of Scarborough along the coast are four major holiday centres run by Haven Leisure Ltd; Primrose Valley, Blue Dolphin, Cayton Bay and Reighton Sands. Job Centres advertise vacancies and seasonal vacancies appear in the Scarborough Evening News six days a week (Thursday is the main day). Anyone interested in a seasonal position should contact either Scarborough Job Centre or the Personnel Department on 01442-230300 at Haven Leisure Ltd's Head Office in Hemel Hempstead. It is best to apply in January.

The principal tourist centre of the west coast is Blackpool, which has many vacancies for its many hotels, amusement arcades and fun parks. In addition Blackpool has an especially long season, remaining busy until the end of the illuminations in November. The *Blackpool Evening Gazette* offers a mailing service on request and has a special 'Jobs Night' edition every Thursday. Few jobs offer live-in accommodation and accommodation can be difficult to find during the summer months.

Morecambe, Fleetwood, Southport, Thornton, Cleveleys and Lytham St Anne's, also in Lancashire, are popular tourist haunts too. Hexham in Northumberland has opened a new golf course recently. It is also worth contacting the local Golf Clubs directly.

In the main tourist centres in the Lake District — Windermere, Bowness-on-Windermere, Ambleside and Grasmere — jobs are available in holiday camps as well as hotels. Unfortunately, unless you are lucky renting a room in the Lake District is likely to cost more than your weekly wage, so unless you are offered live-in accommodation or are willing to camp, the chances of saving much money are minimal. Hotels in the Lake District start advertising for staff about three weeks before Easter; wherever possible they will take on the same staff for the summer season too.

York and Harrogate are both on the tourist trail, and there is therefore a demand for extra hotel staff and shop staff. Your best chance of getting a job is to apply well in advance of the end of the student term. The York Races may offer opportunities for two or three days' work. Similarly a wide range of short-term work is usually available in July during the Great Yorkshire Show in Harrogate: jobs are advertised in the Jobcentre about a month beforehand. Three miles north of Ripon, the Lightwater Valley Theme Park takes on large numbers of seasonal staff which are also advertised in the Harrogate Jobcentre. In this area consult the *Yorkshire Evening Post* or *York Evening Press* for job advertisements.

Factory work provides a source of seasonal work in the North, with large factories recruiting extra people to work over the summer, mainly from June until September. They include Nestlé Rowntree and Terry Suchard in York and KP foods in Cleveland. Other factories to approach, either direct or through the local Jobcentre, are: Ben Shaws in Pontefract; Crystal Drinks Ltd in Featherstone; Unique Images in Bradford; and Glaxo Operations, Kerry Foods Ltd and Mono Containers in Durham. In the Durham area agencies such as Manpower usually recruit for this type of work.

The North has experienced rapid growth in call centre operations, predominately at Doxford Park in Sunderland. Companies such as London Electricity, One2One, Axiom, Littlewoods Home Shopping, Barclays and Subscription Services Ltd have relocated to this site. Other call centre operations throughout the region include Transco and BT call centre at North Tyneside, Abbey National at Stockton and Orange Telecommunications at Darlington. These operations are known to employ students on a temporary basis. There is usually a 3-4 week training period and most applicants need good keyboard skills and experience in customer care. Local job centres ahould be contacted for details.

Various local authorities, such as Gateshead, South Tyneside and Sunderland, may have work on playschemes or may need holiday cover in their many clerical departments. Newcastle and other large towns are the best places to try for retail jobs. The tourist trade in the Newcastle area is currently booming and it is a good place to look for work in the hotel and catering industry. Other places recommended for general summer work are Alnwick, Bamburgh, Corbridge, Haydon Bridge, Hexham, Seahouses, Barnard Castle, Durham and Redcar.

City Councils and Local Authorities are worth contacting to find out about significant forthcoming events which may need extra staffing.

Children

ACORN VENTURE LTD.: Acorn House, Worcester Road, Hagley, Stourbridge DY9 0NW. Multi-activity centres in the Lake District and elsewhere.
INSTRUCTORS. Must hold at least Instructor status with e.g. BCU or RYA, or have passed SPSA or MLTB assessment. Other nationally recognised coaching awards may be considered.
ASSISTANT INSTRUCTORS. Must be registered as training for the above award(s).
SUPPORT STAFF. Maintenance and/or catering. No experience necessary.
FULLY QUALIFIED NURSE.
Please note that all staff must be available from April/May to September: full period only. Application for further details by full c.v. only to the Personnel Department at the above address from 1 November onwards.

ACTION HOLIDAYS: Jumps Road, Todmorden, Lancashire OL14 8HJ (tel 01706-814554). Runs multi-activity holiday centres in Lancashire and elsewhere for children aged 5-15 years.
STAFF required to look after children in all departments of the holiday camps: instructors, supervisory and general support staff. For details of work see entry in Nationwide chapter.

NST ADVENTURE: Recruitment, Chiltern House, Bristol Avenue, Blackpool FY2 0FA (tel 01253-352525; fax 01253-356955; e-mail: nst@nstgroup.co.uk). A division of the NST Travel Group Plc.
OUTDOOR PURSUITS AND IT INSTRUCTORS (20) to instruct a range of outdoor activities and computing for children aged 9-13 years and to assist with evening programmes of entertainment. Wages £200 per month.
The following staff are required to work at a residential activity centre for children aged 9-13 in Lancashire.
CATERING MANAGER to oversee all catering arrangements. £400-£450 per month. Catering qualifications and experience required.
CATERING ASSISTANTS (5) to assist the catering manager. £200 per month. No previous experience required.
NURSE to provide nursing cover. £400-£450 per month. Must be a RGN.
Staff to work varied long hours, 6 days a week. All staff required between February and October; minimum period of work 3 months. Board and accommodation provided free of charge.
For more information and an application form contact the above address.

YMCA NATIONAL CENTRE: Lakeside, Ulverston, Cumbria LA12 8BD (tel 015395-31758; fax 015395-30015). The camp is set in 400 acres of woodland on the shores of Lake Windermere in the Lake District National Park, and is one of the largest camps in Europe.
DAY CAMP LEADERS (30). £15 a week during training, £20 thereafter plus travel expenses within Great Britain and free B & L. To work 5½ days a week, 9am-5pm. Min. age 18 years. Some experience of outdoor activities is advantageous and an interest in working with children necessary. The work involves leading groups of children aged 8-13 years in a wide range of activities, from environmental awareness to rock climbing. Min. period of work 8 weeks between early July and the end of August. Application forms available from October to Easter from Bridget Hadley, Day Camp Director, YMCA National Centre.

Holiday Centres and Amusements

ALLEN (PARKFOOT) LTD: Howtown Road, Pooley Bridge, Penrith, Cumbria CA10 2NA (tel 017684-86309). Family run caravan and camping park by Lake Ullswater, the second largest lake in the Lake District.
BAR STAFF working hours 6pm to midnight. Min. age 18 years.
KITCHEN ASSISTANTS (2) to help the head cook prepare meals, clear tables, operate the dishwasher and work the till. Hours 8am-2pm and 6-11pm.
COOK/CHEF to prepare cooked breakfasts, lunches and evening meals. Hours 8am-2pm and 6-11pm.
ADVENTURE SUPERVISOR (1) to run a children's action club from the Park. Activities include archery, tennis, baseball, volleyball, football, arts (raft making and crafts) and pool tournaments. Hours 9am-5pm Monday to Friday during school holidays.
NANNY/MOTHERS HELP (2) each to look after two school age children and help with household duties. Live in position. Must be able to drive.
Wages negotiable according to experience. Accommodation can be arranged in shared staff caravans. Period of work Easter, May Bank Holidays and from July to mid-September.
Applications, enclosing colour photo, details of work experience and dates of availability, to Mrs B. Mowbray or Mrs F. Bell, Parkfoot Caravan Park.

BLACKPOOL SEA LIFE CENTRE: The Promenade, Blackpool, Lancs. FY1 5AA (tel 01253-22445; fax 01253-751647).
CATERING STAFF (5-10), FRONT OF HOUSE STAFF (5), RETAIL STAFF (5). Wages £3.20 per hour. To work approx. 5 days, 40 hours per week; no overtime rates, but extra hours of work always available. To work from July 1st. Applicants should be aged over 16. Applications to Susan Lovery at the above address.

FARSYDE STUD & RIDING CENTRE: Robin Hood's Bay, Whitby, North Yorkshire YO22 4UG (tel 01947-880249; fax 01947-880877). The centre is set in 70 acres of grassland in the North York Moors National Park, and a short walk from the beach.
GENERAL ASSISTANTS (2) for support duties for residential riding holidays. £3 per hour for min. of 20 hours per week. Accommodation in house, cottage or caravan provided for £40 per week. Applicants must be willing, self-motivated, cheerful, non-smokers, adaptable, able to relate well to children and adults, and also enjoy country life. Min. period of work 6 weeks between May/June and September/October. Overseas applicants eligible to work in the UK and with basic English welcome. Applications to Mrs A. Green, Owner/Manager, Farsyde Stud & Riding Centre.

GUY'S THATCHED HAMLET: Canalside, St Michael's Road, Bilsborrow, Preston, Lancashire PR3 0RS (tel 01995-640010; fax 01995-640141; e-mail guysth@aol.com). A very busy family owned and run business comprising a restaurant, tavern, accommodation, cricket and bowling facilities, children's play area and conference facilities.
WAITING STAFF (5). Wages £135 per week. To work 40 hours over 5 days a week. Experience required. Must be over 16.
KITCHEN PORTERS (5). Wages £140 per week. To work 40 hours over 5 days. Must be over 16.

BAR STAFF (5). Wages £135 per week. To work 40 hours over 5 days. Must be over 18.
ROOM ATTENDANTS (2). Wages £100 per week. To work 30 hours over 5 days. Must be over 18.
CHEFS (2). Wages £240 per week. To work 40/45 hours over 5 days. Must have experience and be over 18.
   Accommodation available. Period of work May to October. Overseas applicants considered but must speak English. Interview necessary. Applications from Easter onwards to Angela Leach.

PLEASURELAND LTD: Pleasureland Amusement Park, Marine Drive, Southport PR8 1RX (tel 01704-532717; fax 01704-537936). An approved Investor in People and Positive Against Disability employer.
RIDE OPERATORS (60). Min. £3.10 an hour (1998 rate). Min. age 18.
RIDE ATTENDANTS (10). Min. £3.10 an hour. Min. age 17 years.
GAMES ATTENDANTS (14), CLEANERS for grounds (5). Min. £3.10 an hour. Minimum age 16 years.
TOILET CLEANERS (5). £3.50 per hour. Min. age 16 years.
CAR PARK ATTENDANTS (5). Min. £3.10 an hour. Min. age 18 years.
CATERING ASSISTANTS (40). Min. £3.30 per hour. Min. age 18 years.
ARCADE CASHIERS (6), ARCADE ATTENDANTS (12). Min. £3.20 per hour. Min. age 18.
CATERING SUPERVISORS (6). £3.40 per hour plus bonus. Must be over 18 and have some relevant experience.
   Pay rates currently under review for 1998 season and linked to ability/age/length of service. National Vocational Qualification (level II) offered in Mechanical Ride Operations and customer service, with others pending. All staff to work 5 or 6 days per week. No experience necessary unless otherwise stated as full training will be provided. Minimum period of work 1 day between March and April. No accommodation available but local B & Bs cost approx. £12 per night. Overseas applicants with a good standard of English considered. Applicants should be able to attend an interview. Applications between March and August to the Staff Services Department, Pleasureland Amusement Park.

RIPLEY CARAVAN PARK: Ripley, Harrogate, North Yorkshire HG3 3AU (tel 01423-770050).
ASSISTANT WARDENS (2) for general duties, including gardening, and cleaning shower block and swimming pool. Positions suitable for a mature couple. Wages specified on application. Period of work Easter to end of October. Accommodation not provided, but can bring own tent/caravan. Applicants must be able to attend an interview. Applications from early 1999 to Mr P. House, at the above address.

Hotels and Catering

BECKSIDE GUEST HOUSE: 5 Wordsworth Street, Keswick, Cumbria CA12 4HU (tel 01768-773093). A small guest house in the heart of the Lake District.
HOME HELP/BABY MINDER to work alongside proprietor in the mornings during breakfast serving and room cleaning, due to birth of proprietor's baby. Wages negotiable. To work 4 hours a day, 5 days a week.

Accommodation is available, at a negotiable cost. Min. period of work 10 months between February and December. No experience is required, but applicants should be sensible and reliable.

Applications from November to Mrs Helling.

THE BLACK BULL: Reeth, Richmond, North Yorkshire DL11 6SZ (tel 01748-84213). Small country pub and hotel in a beautiful National Park, offering a warm friendly welcome.

WAITING STAFF (2). Duties include preparation of salads and sandwiches and microwave cookery.

BAR ASSISTANT (1).

Wages £3.30 per hour for 39 hours a week basic, with some overtime possible. All staff have two days off a week. B & L available at a weekly charge of £15. Min. period of work Easter to Spring Bank Holiday or mid-July to mid-September. Applicants should preferably be available for interview. Applications enclosing s.a.e. from 1 January to Mrs E.M. Sykes, Proprietor, at the above address.

THE BLUE BELL HOTEL: Market Square, Belford, Northumberland NE70 7NE (tel 01668-213543; fax 01668-213787; e-mail bluebel@globalnet.co.uk).

RECEPTIONISTS (2) for telephone/reception duties from 8am-4pm or 4-11pm, 5 days per week. Wage by arrangement with variable tips. Should ideally be aged 21.

WAITING STAFF (2) to work from 7.30am-3pm or 6.30-11pm. Wages by arrangement plus good tips. Minimum age 18.

Accommodation provided. Period of work from April to November. Applicants for either position need commitment and dedication.

Applications to Paul Shirley, Partner, at the above address.

BRACKENRIGG INN: Watermillock, Penrith, CA11 0LP (tel 01768-486206). Rural lakeside hotel 5 miles from the nearest town.

GENERAL ASSISTANTS. Wages and hours by arrangement with 2 days off per week. Period of work from June to September. Min. age 18 years. Applicants must enjoy the countryside and be prepared to work very hard. Training is provided so experience is not necessary. Overseas applicants welcome. Applications to the Manager at the above address.

BRATHAY HALL TRUST: Ambleside, Cumbria LA22 0HP. A residential training centre situated on the north west shore of Lake Windermere.

DOMESTIC ASSISTANTS needed for general domestic work such as washing-up, cleaning rooms, assisting chefs, bar work. Wages £78.36 a week, including free B & L. Applicants must be prepared to work hard, up to 40 hours a week with 2 days off per week. Min. age 18. Staff needed all year round, min. period of work 3 months. Applicants must be prepared to attend an informal interview. Applications, in writing, to the Housekeeper at the above address.

BRIDGE HOTEL: Buttermere, nr. Cockermouth, Cumbria CA13 9U2 (tel 01768-770252; fax 01768-770215). A family owned hotel with 22 bedrooms, 6 apartments and a very busy bar located in a beautiful area of Wales which is popular with walkers.

WAITING STAFF (2) needed to work 40-50 hours per week; £3.25 per hour. Experience preferred, min. age 18.

BAR STAFF (2). Hours as above, £3.65 per hour.
Staff required from May to October; min. period of work 6 months. Accommodation available for £30 per week. Overseas applicants with high standard of English welcome. All applicants must be aged at least 18, have a love of the country, enjoy walking and be of a smart appearance; those with experience preferred. Own transport desirable.
Apply from March to Mr. John Milburn at the above address. No interview necessary.

CHADWICK HOTEL: South Promenade, Lytham St. Annes, Lancashire FY8 1NP (tel 01253-720061; fax 01253-714455).
RESTAURANT PERSONNEL (2). Wages £150-£165 per week depending on age and experience. To work 45 hours per week. Min. period of work 8 weeks at any time of year. No accommodation is available.
Overseas applicants are considered. Interview preferable but not necessary. Applications to Mr. Corbett at any time.

DERWENTWATER HOTEL: Portinscale, Keswick CA12 5RE (tel 017687-72538; fax 017687-71002). Diament Ltd. is an I.I.P. Company which won the International Environmental Award 1995 and and Excellence for People award. The hotel has 50 bedrooms/19 self-catering apartments and stands on the lake shore. Guests return to share the friendliness and enjoy the beautiful surroundings.
WAITER/ESS (2). £90-£110 per week. 5 days, 40 hours. Experience not essential.
BAR PERSON (1). £95-£120 per week. 5 days, 40 hours. Experience essential.
CHAMBERPERSON (1). £85-£110 per week. 5 days, 40 hours. Experience not essential.
Staff required for a minimum of 3 months between May and October. Accommodation available. Min. age 18. Overseas applicants with the ability to speak and understand English welcome. Applications from mid April to Mrs A. P. Aston at the above address, enclosing a stamped addressed envelope.

ENGLISH LAKES HOTELS: Low Wood, Windermere, Cumbria LA23 1LP (tel 015394-39459; fax 015394-34072).
WAITING STAFF (3) to serve breakfast, lunch and dinner. Wage £105.00 per week. To work 45 hours per week. Experience desirable but not essential; minimum age 18.
ROOM ATTENDANTS (3) to service the bedrooms of guests and other areas. Wage £103 per week. To work 40 hours per week. Experience not necessary.
CHEFS DE PARTIE (3) to work 45 hours per week. Wage £120 per week. Experience necessary.
COMMIS CHEFS (2) to work 45 hours per week. Wage £102.50 per week. Experience not necessary.
All positions are live-in; the above wages include accommodation and meals. To work five days out of seven including weekends. Period of work from May to October.
Applications to Lynn Riley, Deputy Group Personnel and Training Manager, at the above address.

THE FAMOUS SCHOONER HOTEL: Northumberland Street, Alnmouth, Northumberland NE66 2RS (tel 01665-830216).
GENERAL ASSISTANTS. Wages negotiable. There is a high tipping potential. To work 40-45 hours per week. Live in accommodation available. Min. work period 4 weeks between mid-June and mid-September. Overseas applicants with good English welcome. Applications a.s.a.p. to the Manager, the Schooner Hotel.

GEORGE WASHINGTON COUNTY HOTEL, GOLF AND COUNTRY CLUB: Stone Cellar Road, High Usworth, Washington, District 12, Tyne and Wear NE37 1PH (tel 0191-4029988; fax 0191-4151166). The hotel has 103 bedrooms, a restaurant and conference facilities for up to 200, a leisure club and an 18 hole golf course.
RESTAURANT WAITING STAFF, BAR STAFF. Wage negotiable. Min. age 18. Previous experience required. To work hours as required. No accommodation available. Staff needed from July to December. Min. period of work 4 weeks. Applicants must be available for interview. Applications from May to the above address.

M. B. & J. GOODWIN LTD: Low Skirlington Caravan Park, Skipsea, nr Driffield, Humberside YO25 8SY (tel 01262-468213/468466; fax 01262-468105).
BAR STAFF (2), RECEPTIONIST (1), KITCHEN STAFF (2), ENTERTAINER (1) to work on a holiday caravan site. Wages £130 per week or by arrangement. Normal hours, approx. 45 per week, including weekends and evenings. Free accommodation provided in a caravan. Period of work from June to September. Overseas applicants welcome. Applications to M. B. & J. Goodwin Ltd.

GRASMERE HOTEL: Grasmere, nr Ambleside, Cumbria LA22 9TA (tel/fax 0153943-5277). A very busy 12-bedroom hotel.
ASSISTANT COOK (1). £130 a week.
GENERAL ASSISTANT (1). £120 a week. Duties include waiting, bar work, housekeeping, reception, office work and some kitchen work.
   All staff work 40 hours, 5 days a week. Live-in accommodation available for women only: own room with TV provided. Min. age 21. Preferably college trained or at least 1 year's experience. Min. period of work 6 months, February to December. Overseas applicants with good knowledge of English welcome. Applications to Mr P. Riley, Proprietor, at the Grasmere Hotel.

HOLMHEAD FARM: Hadrian's Wall, Greenhead via Carlisle CA6 7HY (tel 016977-47402). A guest house on the Hadrian's Wall path with beautiful rural surrounding; positions therefore not suitable for socialites. Only 4 bedrooms to service and a clientele from all over the world, especially America.
GENERAL ASSISTANTS (1) required to help run a guest house. Wages £65 a week including B & L within a friendly home environment. Own mobile home with all facilities. To work up to 9 hours per day, 5 days a week with extra days off wherever possible. Duties include helping prepare and serve meals, washing up and cleaning rooms. Period of work Easter to 1 November. Min. period of work June to end of August. Min. age 18. No experience required. Overseas applicants with spoken English and the correct documentation welcome (owner speaks Norwegian). Candidates should be available for

interview, though if this is difficult references may suffice. Applications from January 1999 to P. Staff, Proprietor, at the above address.

THE HOTEL ST. NICHOLAS: St. Nicholas Cliff, Scarborough, North Yorks YO11 2EU (tel 01723-364101; fax 01723-500538). 144 bedroom hotel with own leisure facilities, conference and banqueting facilities, situated a few minutes walk from town centre, and on a cliff overlooking a beach.
ROOM ATTENDANTS (2).£3.20 per hour. To work between 33 and 39 hours over five/six days per week. Min. age 16. Similar experience preferred but not essential.
KITCHEN ASSISTANTS (2). £3.10-£3.20 per hour. To work approx. 39 hours over 5 days per week. Min. age 16. No experience or qualifications necessary.
WAITING STAFF (4). £3.0-£3.60 per hour depending on experience. To work between 39 and 50 hours per week with days off as required. No qualifications necessary but similar experience is essential. Min. age 18.

To work from early June to the end of September; min. period of work 6 weeks. No accommodation is available. Overseas applicants welcome. Interviews are not always necessary. Applications to Christine Leach from the beginning of February to the above address.

LADY ANNE MIDDLETON'S HOTEL: Skeldergate, York (tel 01904-611570; fax 01904-613043). Independent 52 bedroom hotel located in the city centre, with own health and fitness club, conference and event rooms.
WAITING STAFF (2). Up to £3.60 per hour. To work 39 hours per week. Min. period of work 3 months at any time of year. Accommodation is **not** available. Min. age 21. Overseas applicants welcome. All applicants should be able to attend an interview. Applications at any time to Mr M. Harrison at the above address.

LEASOWE CASTLE HOTEL: Leasowe Road, Moreton, Wirral L46 3RF (tel 0151-606 9191; fax 0151-678 5551; e-mail leasowe.castle@mail.cybase.co.uk). A 3 star hotel which conducts weddings, banquets and conferences.
WAITING, BAR, HOUSEKEEPING STAFF: wages, period of work etc. by arrangement. For further details contact K. Harding at the above address.

LEEMING HOUSE HOTEL: Watermillock, Ullswater, nr Penrith, Cumbria CA11 0JJ (tel 017684-86622; fax 017684-86443).
WAITERS/WAITRESSES (4). Experience needed.
BAR STAFF/PORTERS (2). Previous bar work experience required.
CHAMBER STAFF (4).
Salary for all staff from £113 a week. To work 5 days a week with consecutive days off. Accommodation provided (some shared) plus all meals. Ages: 18-35 years. Overseas applicants eligible to work in the UK and with good English welcome. Min. period of work from 1 April to 31 October. Applications from 1 February to the Personnel Manager, Leeming House Hotel.

LINDETH FELL HOTEL: Bowness-on-Windermere, Cumbria LA23 3JP (tel 015394-43286). A country house hotel set in magnificent grounds on the hills above Lake Windermere, offering good views and excellent cooking in a friendly atmosphere.

GENERAL ASSISTANTS (3). £150 a week plus free B & L. To work 40 hours a week. Duties include helping in the dining room, bedrooms and kitchen. Period of work 1 March to 15 November, min. period June to late October. Applicants must be available for interview. Overseas applicants in early 20s and with good English welcome. Applications from 1 January to P. A. Kennedy, Owner, at the above address.

MALLYAN SPOUT HOTEL: Goathland, near Whitby, Yorkshire (tel 01947-896486). Hotel with predominantly young staff, in beautiful quiet countryside.
WAITERS/WAITRESSES (2), KITCHEN/STILL ROOM ASSISTANTS (2), CHAMBER STAFF. £100 a week plus free B & L. To work 40 hours/5 days per week. Intelligent workers preferred. Work available all year. Overseas applicants considered. Applications with s.a.e. to Mrs Heslop, Mallyan Spout Hotel.

MOSS GROVE HOTEL: Grasmere, Cumbria LA22 9SW (tel 015394-35251; fax 015394-35691).
GENERAL ASSISTANT to work a maximum of 45 hours over a 5 day week. Wages £3 per hour, to live in. Period of work from July to early September. Applicants should be over 18, presentable, and be authorised to work in the UK. Applications to Martin Wood at the above address.

MOTEL LEEMING LTD: Bedale, North Yorkshire DL8 1DT (tel 01677-423611). Part of Leeming Service Area (A1/A684 Intersection).
GENERAL ASSISTANTS (2). To work 5 days a week. Must be hotel or catering students.
KITCHEN ASSISTANTS (3). Split and straight shifts over 5 days. Must be catering students.
RECEPTIONIST. Must have hotel experience.
SENIOR WAITING STAFF (2). Wages plus tips. Split shifts, 5 days a week. Must be hotel or catering student with experience of silver service.
OTHER WAITING STAFF (3). Wages plus tips. To work 5 days a week. Must have experience in silver service.
BAR STAFF (1). Split shifts, 5 days a week. Must have previous bar and cash handling experience.
SHOP ASSISTANTS (2). Straight shifts, 5 or 6 days a week. Must have cash handling experience.
CAFE ASSISTANTS (6). Straight and split shifts over 5 days.
CAFE ASSISTANTS-NIGHT SHIFT (2). Straight shifts, 5 nights a week.
   Wages to be arranged. B & L available. Min. age 18. Min. period of work 8 weeks between June and October. Applications from April to Mr C. A. Les, Motel Leeming Ltd.

NEWCASTLE AIRPORT MOAT HOUSE: Woolsington, Newcastle, Tyne and Wear NE13 8DJ (tel 0191-401 9988; fax 0191-4019972). The hotel is very accessible as it is moments away from the airport and minutes away from Newcastle town centre, the A1 and the Metro light railway.
CASUAL ROOM ATTENDANTS (10). To work approx. 20 + hours a week.
CASUAL EVENTS WAITERS/WAITRESSES (20), BAR STAFF (5). To work approx. 20-25 + hours a week. Wages by arrangement. No accommodation is available. Min. period of work 2 months between June and September.

Applicants must be over 16 and have a good general education. Overseas applicants considered. Staff must be flexible and prepared to work shifts and late shifts. Interview necessary. Applications from May to Miss Rosamund Young.

THE OLD KING'S HEAD HOTEL: Church Street, Broughton-in-Furness, Cumbria LA20 6HJ (tel/fax 01229-716293). A small family run hotel in a beautiful area of the country, remote from city life and with minimal public transport. Has 6 bedrooms and a busy restaurant serving an average of 100 meals per day in the busy season.
BAR PERSON (1). Wages £2.80 per hour.
WAITING STAFF (2). Wages £2.60 per hour.
GENERAL ASSISTANT (KITCHEN/LAUNDRY) (1). Wages £2.50 per hour.
All staff work flexible hours, either part-time or full-time, including evenings and weekends. Staff must work bank holidays. Must be over 18, capable, honest and reliable. Wages are dependant on experience and aptitude. Training available. Accommodation is available at a cost of approx. £20 per week. Employees are expected to work and assist in other areas as necessary, rather than observe strict job demarcation.
Min. period of work 2 months between Easter and October. Overseas applicants with understandable spoken English are considered. Applications from 1st March to Gary or Jackie McClure.

PATTERDALE HOTEL: Patterdale, Lake Ullswater, near Penrith, Cumbria CA11 0NW (tel 017684-82231; fax 017684-82440). A friendly family run, busy 57 bedroom Lake District hotel in beautiful surroundings.
CHEFS (2). £120 per week. To work 50 hours a week.
WAITING ON STAFF (3). £105 per week. To work 39 hours a week.
RECEPTIONISTS (2). £120 per week. To work 42 hours a week.
HOUSEMAIDS/PERSONS (2). £110 per week. To work 39 hours a week.
Experience not necessary unless applying for Chef's position. Min. age 17. Free B & L provided (own room with shared facilities). Opportunities for walking, climbing, etc. Min. period of work 6 months from March to December. Overseas applicants with good English welcome. Applications from early 1999 to Mr C. Tonkin, at the above address.

PREMIER HOTEL: 66 Esplanade, Scarborough, North Yorkshire (tel 01723-501062).
GENERAL ASSISTANTS, ROOM ATTENDANTS, COMMIS-CHEF required. Accommodation and all meals provided plus £50 per week plus gratuities. 8 weeks min.(not July and August only), must be able to work May and June, or June and July, or August and September, but applicants who can work for longer will be given preference. Overseas applicants very welcome. Applications for working in April, May and June or September and October are especially welcome. Please apply stating which post you wish to be considered for and giving details of any experience (not essential), to Mr and Mrs M. Simons at the above address.

QUALITY ROYAL HOTEL: 170 Ferensway, Hull HU1 3UF (tel 01482-325087; fax 01482-323172). A 155 bedroom city centre hotel which has a restaurant and large banqueting suites.
BAR PERSON, ROOM ATTENDANTS, COMMIS CHEFS, KITCHEN

PORTER (10). All positions at a wage of £3.30 per hour. Bar person and kitchen porter to work over 20 hours a week, other positions to work at least 16 hours. No accommodation is available.

Period of work June to December. No experience required. Bar person must be over 18. Overseas applicants with suitable English considered. Applications from June to the Personnel Manager.

QUEEN'S HOTEL: Main Street, Keswick, Cumbria CA12 5JF (tel 017687-73333). A 35-bedroom hotel in the heart of the Lake District.
CHAMBER STAFF (1), WAITING STAFF (1), BAR STAFF (2). £110 a week plus free B & L. To work 40 hours a week. No qualifications or experience necessary. Min. period of work 8 weeks between July and the end of August/September. Overseas applicants with good English welcome. Applications a.s.a.p. to Mr Peter Williams, Proprietor, The Queen's Hotel. Due to numbers only successful applicants will receive a reply.

QUEENS HEAD HOTEL: Main Street, Hawkshead, Cumbria LA22 0NS (tel 015395- 36271; fax 015395-36722). A busy hotel located in the hometown of Beatrix Potter.
WAITING STAFF (2), for general waiting duties plus some bar work as necessary. Staff required year round to work split shifts, 5 days per week. Min. period of work 3 months. Wages approximately £3.50 per hour; accommodation available, charge deducted from wages. Experience preferred. Overseas applicants welcome. Apply year round to Mr. A. Merrick at the above address.

SHARROW BAY HOTEL: Lake Ullswater, Penrith, Cumbria CA10 2LZ (tel 017684-86301/86483; fax 017684-86349). Luxury hotel and Michelin starred restaurant set in a tranquil postion on the edge of Lake Ullswater.
STILLROOM ASSISTANTS. Approx. £150 a week.
GENERAL ASSISTANTS. Min. £145 a week. To work in bedrooms.
All staff to work 50 hours/5½ days a week. Free B & L provided. Age: 17-30 years. Must have domestic interests and lots of common sense, and should enjoy living in the country and working as part of a team of perfectionists. Preferred period of work 9 months from early March to end of November. References required. Applications from January to the Manager, Sharrow Bay Hotel.

THE SHIREBURN ARMS HOTEL: Hurst Green, Clitheroe BB7 9QJ (tel 01254-826518; fax 01254-826208).
WAITING STAFF (2) to work over the summer between June and October. To live-in; wage £3.25 per hour plus tips. Split shift work, including weekends. Silver service; experience of working in a similar environment would be helpful. Applicants should be over 18, have common sense, be friendly and have a smart appearance. Applications to S.J. Alcock, General Manager, at the above address.

SWALLOW HOTEL: Tadcaster Road, York YO4 1QQ (tel 01904-701000; fax 01904-702308).
BAR STAFF (2). Min. age 18. Bar and customer care experience essential. Must have good communication skills, smart presentation and be flexible. Expected to provide own black and whites.

CHAMBER STAFF (2). Must have previous relevant experience. Uniform provided.
WAITING STAFF (3). Min. age 17 years. Experience in hotel silver service and customer care essential. Must be able to communicate well, be flexible and smart. Expected to provide own black and whites.
   All staff to work 30-40 hours per week. £3.50 per hour. No accommodation provided. Min. period of work 12 weeks throughout the year. Overseas applicants welcome provided they have a good grasp of the English language. All applicants must be available for interview. Phone or send a c.v. and covering letter advising availability from March to Gayle Enion at the above address.

SLALEY HALL: Slaley, Hexham, Northumberland NE47 0BY (tel 01434-676504). A 4 star hotel, golf resort and spa, set in 1,000 acres of Northumberland countryside.
CLUBHOUSE ASSISTANTS (5), WAITERS/WAITRESSES (10). Wages £3.50 per hour. To work 40 hours a week. Must be over 18. Min. period of work 4 weeks between May/June and October. Accommodation is available at £23 per week including breakfast, lunch and dinner.
   Overseas applicants who speak English considered. Interview necessary, but could be conducted over the phone. Applications from February to Michelle Smith or Bridget Fairless.

STAKIS LEEDS HOTEL: Millgreen View, Seacroft, Leeds, West Yorkshire LS14 5QF (tel 0113-273 2323; fax 0113-232 3018). A 101 bedroom hotel on the outskirts of Leeds city centre. Busy conference centre caters for functions of up to 200 people.
HOUSEKEEPING ASSISTANTS to work 9:30am to 1:30 pm, 5 days out of 7.
BAR STAFF and BANQUETING WAITING STAFF to work at weekends; overtime may be required.
   Wage for all positions is £3.58 per hour. Temporary accommodation can be provided. Period of work May to January.
   No experience is necessary. Applicants must be at least 16. Overseas applicants who speak English considered. Interview necessary. Applications at any time to the Personnel Manager.

THE VENTURE CENTRE: Lewaigue Farm, Maughold, Isle of Man IM7 1AW (tel 01624-814240). Adventure training centre giving introductory instruction in outdoor activities to children aged 9-15 years.
CATERING AND DOMESTIC STAFF. Free B & L. Min. period of work 5 months between March and August. Applications before March to Mr S. Read, Director, the Venture Centre.

WAREN HOUSE HOTEL: Waren Mill, Belford, Northumberland NE70 7EE (tel 01688-214581 fax 01668-214484). A 10 bedroom country house hotel on the coast near Holy Island, 60 miles south of Edinburgh.
WAITER/WAITRESS (1). Wages £3.00-£3.50 per hour. To work up to 40 hours a week. Must be at least 18.
CHAMBERMAID/KITCHEN HELP (1). £3.00-£3.50 per hour. To work up to 40 hours a week. Must be over 16.
RECEPTIONIST (1). Wages approx.£3.50 per hour. To work up to 40 hours. Must be over 18.

Accommodation available at a cost of approx. £20.00 per week. Min. period of work 4 weeks between June and October. Overseas applicants must be able to legally work in England.

Applications as soon as possible to Mrs Anita Laverack.

WEETWOOD HALL HOTEL AND CONFERENCE CENTRE: Otley Road, Leeds LS16 5PS (tel 0113-2306000; fax 0113-2306095; e-mail sales-@weetwood.co.uk). A four crown highly commended hotel and conference centre, which dates from 1625. White Rose Tourist Winner 1998.

WAITING STAFF (10), BAR STAFF (10), HOUSEKEEPING ROOM ATTENDANTS (5). All positions at a wage of £3.60 per hour. To work a 5/7 day week of 40 hours. Limited accommodation is available at £37.50 per week.

Min. period of work 2 months between July and October. Experience is preferred but not essential. Bar staff should be at least 18, other positions at least 17 years old. Interview necessary. Overseas applicant with fluent English considered.

Applications from March onwards to Jason Fox, HR Manager.

WILD BOAR HOTEL: Crook, Near Windermere, Cumbria LA23 3NF (tel 015394-45225; fax 015394-42498). A small friendly hotel with a large proportion of live-in personnel, surrounded by beautiful countryside.

WAITING ASSISTANT to work in the restaurant, split shifts. Wage £485 per calendar month.

PORTERING ASSISTANT to perform mainly work involving food, beverages and cleaning: to work straight shifts. Wage £435 per month.

Both jobs are live-in in own bedrooms with communal facilities, all found, with five days work out of seven. Period of work from May to the end of September/early October. Both jobs involve dealing directly with guests so pleasant and outgoing personalities are essential. Common sense is more desirable than previous experience. The hotel is in the country on a road without public transport so applicants need either own transport or a liking of rural surroundings.

Applications to Jon Bennett, Deputy Manager, of the Wild Boar Hotel at the above address.

Outdoor

T.C & B.J. BULMER: Kenyon Hall, Winwick Lane, Croft, Warrington WA3 7ED (tel 01925-763646). A friendly family run farm situated halfway between Manchester and Liverpool. All employees are regarded as part of the family.

FRUIT PICKERS/PACKERS (2), SHOPSTAFF (2). £3.20 per hour. To work variable hours over 7 days per week. Minimum age 20. Must be friendly, adaptable and able to do any of the numerous tasks on a fruit farm open to the public. Non-smokers only; must also have good mental arithmetic and be able to drive. To work from mid June to late July; min. period of work 5 weeks. Accommodation in a caravan available free of charge. Overseas applicants with good standard of English welcome.

Apply from January and before April to Mrs B. Bulmer to the above address. An interview is not always necessary.

FIELD AND LAWN (MARQUEES) LTD: Southlands, Leeds Road, Thorpe Willoughby, YO8 9PZ (tel 01757-210444). A young and enthusiastic company which takes a pride in its product and employees. Work hard, play hard atmosphere.

RIGGERS required to work long hours erecting marquees throughout the North of England. In exchange a high weekly wage is possible with payment of £3.60 per hour. Applicants would have to find accommodation near to Leeds or York. Riggers travel daily to place of work at Thorpe Willoughby. The work is very strenuous so fitness is essential. Overseas applicants, particularly from New Zealand, South Africa and Australia, welcome. Staff required from beginning of May through to end of September. Applications from 1 April through to end of September to the Operations Manager at the above address or telephone number.

Sport

ALSTON TRAINING & ADVENTURE CENTRE: Alston, Cumbria CA9 3DD (tel 01434-381886).
ASSISTANT OUTDOOR ACTIVITY INSTRUCTORS. Free B & L provided and free training given. Should have current driving licence. MLC or Canoe qualification useful. Domestic staff also required. Period of work 1 June to 30 September. For further details contact Mr Dave Simpson, Head of Centre, at the above address.

BROWN RIGG VENTURE CENTRE: Bellingham, Hexham, Northumberland NE48 2HR (tel 01434-220272).
RIDING, SAILING, CANOEING INSTRUCTORS AND FOOTBALL COACH. From £50 a week plus free B & L. Min. age 20. Overseas applicants with equivalent instructors' qualifications welcome.
GENERAL ASSISTANTS. £15-£30 a week. Min. age 17.
Free B & L provided. Min. period of work 4 weeks between May and October. Applications, stating relevant qualifications, to Mr Donald R. MacLeod, Brown Rigg.

CAMP WINDERMERE: Low Wray, Ambleside, Cumbria.
A charitable Outdoor Education camp for young people between the ages of 10-17 from schools and youth organisations.
QUALIFIED OUTDOOR PURSUITS INSTUCTORS/ASSISTANT INSTRUCTORS (12). Should have experience of working with young people in outdoor educational activities, be enthusiastic, willing to work hard and have a sense of humour. Instructors must be qualified in sailing, canoeing and climbing or hillwalking.
Wages depend on qualifications and experience. Full time work, with one day off per week. Free board and lodging provided; accommodation in tents. Period of work from May to September. For details, send 6" x 9" s.a.e. to The Administrator, Camp Windermere, at the above address.

MOUNTAIN VENTURES LTD: 120 Allerton Road, Liverpool L18 2DG (tel 0151-734 2477; fax 0151-734 2997).
SUMMER ASSISTANTS to work for a mountain activity holiday centre from June.
ASSISTANT INSTRUCTORS (4) also usually needed April-May.
Pocket money of £10 per week plus food, accommodation in a cottage, tent or caravan and some outdoor training opportunities. To work 40 hours per

week. No special qualifications are essential, but qualified people are also needed. Applications to Ms Jean Kewley, Director, at the above address.

NORTH YORK MOORS ADVENTURE CENTRE: Park House, Ingleby Cross, near Osmotherley, Northallerton, North Yorkshire DL6 3PE (tel 01609-882571). Private outdoor centre, established for 20 years, set in a National Park, catering for small groups of up to 24 people.
INSTRUCTORS (2) to instruct in rock climbing, canoeing, caving, orienteering and mountain biking. Also to help with day-to-day running of the activity centre, e.g. equipment repairs and building work. Min. age 21. Driving licence essential.
COOK'S ASSISTANT (1) to help with catering for visitors (guests do their own washing up). Possibility of helping with instruction or joining in with outdoor pursuits. Min. age 18.
  Wages and hours by arrangement. Free B & L. Period of work March to end of September, min. period 3 months. English-speaking overseas applicants welcome. All candidates must be able to attend an interview. Applications with s.a.e. from 1 February to Mr Ewen Bennett, North York Moors Adventure Centre.

NORTHUMBRIA HORSE HOLIDAYS: East Castle, Annfield Plain, Stanley, Co. Durham DH9 8PH (tel 01207-230555/235354). A horse-riding centre that offers fully catered holidays for riders of all abilities.
POST TRAIL LEADERS (2). From £80 a week. Outgoing, pleasant personality needed plus good horse-riding skills and knowledge.
RIDING INSTRUCTORS (2). From £140 a week. Must have British Horse Society Instructors Certificate, or equivalent foreign qualifications.
HOTEL STAFF (2) to cook, clean, and do waiting and bar work. Wages from £110 a week. Must be able to work to a high standard.
  Free B & L available. Period of work Easter to end of October. Min. work period 2 months. Overseas applicants with necessary qualifications, documentation and experience will be considered. Applications a.s.a.p. to the above address.

THE OUTDOOR TRUST: Windy Gyle, Belford, Northumberland NE70 7QE (tel/fax 01668-213289). Registered charity 1052677. Runs outdoor adventure courses for all ages and abilities from individuals to groups of management trainees.
LEAD INSTRUCTORS (10). Remuneration to be negotiated. BCU, RYA, MLTB, SPA, windsurf and first aid qualifications all relevant.
VOLUNTARY TRAINEE INSTRUCTORS (15). Receive full board and training. First aid qualification an advantage.
  To work long hours, 6 days a week. Work is demanding but varied and a lot of fun. Training given. Free accommodation available. Possibility of discount on equipment purchases. Min. period of work 3 months, all year round. Overseas applicants considered. Applications to Mr Colin Jeffery at the above address.

RIPON OUTDOOR SKILLS CENTRE: 12 Littlethorpe Park, Ripon HG4 1UQ (tel/fax 01765-604071). Runs day courses and adventure holidays. Activities include abseiling, canoeing, rock climbing, mountain walking, caving, windsurfing and mountain biking.
INSTRUCTORS (2), CHIEF INSTRUCTOR (1). £250 per week. Hours

specified on application. Must have relevant qualifications, including BCU, MIC, MLC, LRC, LCL, RYA, SPSA, First Aid and Life Saving. Accommodation is not provided. All applicants must be available for interview. Applications to Mr J. M. Bull at the above address.

THE VENTURE CENTRE: Lewaigue Farm, Maughold, Isle of Man IM7 1AW (tel 01624-814240). Adventure training centre giving introductory instruction in outdoor activities to children aged 9-15.
INSTRUCTORS (3). Wage according to experience. Hours dependent on groups under instruction: 7-day week at times. Free B & L. Min. age 21 years. Essential training given to suitable candidates. At least one NGB Award required. Min. period of work 5 months between March and August. Applications before March to Mr D. Read, Director, The Venture Centre.

Language Schools

YORKSHIRE INTERNATIONAL SCHOOL: 21 St Helens Gardens, Leeds LS16 8BT (tel 0113-261 1603; fax 0113-261 3794; e-mail gordonmills@po-box.com; website HTTP://WWW.YORKSHIRENET.CO.UK/MILLS). English language and activity holiday summer school for foreign students set in beautiful parklands north of Leeds.
ENGLISH TEACHERS (2). £400 for 3 weeks between July 1 and August 25. Applicants must have a degree and at least two years of English teaching experience. No accommodation available. Apply from April 1 to Gordon Mills at the above address. Note interview is required.

Vacation Traineeships

Accountancy and Insurance

COULSONS: P.O. Box 17, 2 Belgrave Crescent, Scarborough, North Yorkshire YO11 1UD (tel 01723-364141; fax 01723-376010).
Coulsons, a firm of chartered accountants, takes on trainees to work in its Scarborough office, mainly during the summer vacation. Candidates would normally be UK undergraduates intending to pursue chartered accountancy as a career. Vacation work would be offered only to students giving an undertaking to take up a training contract with Coulsons on the completion of their academic studies.

For further details contact Mr P. B. Hodgson, Student Training Officer in April, at the above address.

LISHMAN SIDWELL CAMPBELL & PRICE: Administration Office, Eva Lett House, 1 South Crescent, Ripon HG4 1SN (tel 01765-690890; fax 01765-690296). A firm of Chartered Accountants established in 1938 with 14 offices stretching from Sheffield to Middlesborough. Specialists in dealing with the self-employed, and small business units.

Lishman Sidwell Campbell & Price offers vacation traineeships to students throughout the year, although the majority of placements are held over the summer vacation. The positions may be in any of the firm's offices.

Students at any stage in their education will be considered, as long as they are seriously contemplating accountancy as a career. Suitably qualified applicants from abroad will also be considered. The salary is fixed according to their age.

Applications should be made as early as possible to the Vacation Training Officer at the above address.

Business

THE BOOTS COMPANY: Graduate Recruitment Department, D31 Building, Nottingham NG2 3AA (tel 0115-959 2167). An international organisation operating in retail, manufacturing and the marketing of leading consumer brands.

The Boots Company offers undergraduate students opportunities available in a variety of areas including marketing, logistics, retail management, finance, personnel, engineering, telecommunications, manafacturing and technical, and information systems. Placements last for 8 weeks over the summer vacation and take place at the Head Office in Nottingham. Accommodation is provided.

Applications to the above address by 19th February 1999.

Law

ADDLESHAW BOOTH AND CO: Sovereign House, Sovereign Street, Leeds LS1 1HQ (tel 0113-209 2000; fax 0113-209 2060; e-mail jru@addleshaw-booth.co.uk).

Addleshaw Booth and Co. run a Summer Vacation Scheme which offers 24 students the opportunity to spend 2 weeks undertaking work usually given to trainee solicitors, and gives them the chance to know what to expect if offered a training contract. The scheme is open to second year university Law students and third year university non-Law students upwards. Salary of approx. £125 per week.

Placements are located in the company's Leeds and Manchester offices. The Graduate Recruitment Officer can act as a clearing house for summer students who can offer or require accommodation. Overseas applicants are considered, but only if they are interested in applying for a training contract.

Application forms can be obtained from Joanna Rue, Graduate Recruitment Officer.

Science, Construction and Engineering

DAVID BROWN MOBILE EQUIPMENT DRIVES GROUP: Park Works, Lockwood, Huddersfield, West Yorkshire HD4 5DD (tel 01484-465500; fax 01484-435292).

David Brown Mobile Equipment Drives Group is a manufacturing company, operating worldwide in the production of high quality gears and gear units. It has occasional summer vacancies for students, who will be employed in such areas as Manufacturing Engineering, Production Control, Manufacturing and General Site Services.

Applicants should be studying Mechanical Engineering and have an interest in engineering manufacturing processes and/or gearing. Suitably qualified overseas applicants will be considered.

The salary is about £150 per week and no assistance with accommodation is given. Applications should be made to Central Personnel Training Services, at the above address.

FILTRONIC COMPONENTS LTD: Airedale House, Royal London Industrial Estate, Acorn Park, Charlestown, Shipley, West Yorks BD17 7SW (tel 01274-531602; fax 01274-531539).
Filtronic Components Ltd is an expanding company dealing in the research, development and manufacture of RF and microwave filters and sub-systems. It offers occasional summer vacation placements in manufacturing and administration, preference being given to local students. Those interested should contact Jacky Haines, Personnel Manager, at the above address.

RELIANCE GEAR COMPANY LTD: Rowley Mills, Penistone Road, Lepton, Huddersfield HD8 OLE (tel 01484-601000; fax 01484-601001).
Reliance Gear is a design and manufacturing company which specialises in the production of precision gears and general assemblies for use in servo-mechanisms and control applications. The company serves clients in the defence, aerospace, robotic and medical engineering industries.

The company usually offers work experience over the summer to two or three students who are about to enter their final year of study. Candidates should be motivated and keen to explore the engineering sector as a potential career field. Training is offered through general experience gained in a number of the company's departments, including business sales, marketing, engineering, design, production control and quality control.

Wages are commensurate with the candidate's age, experience, qualifications and the job offered. Overseas applicants will be considered.

Applications, in early January and February, to J.D. Selka, Managing Director, at the above address.

Scotland

The hotel industry in Scotland remained buoyant even during the recession, particularly in the Highlands, Perthshire and the Islands, and has received huge boosts during the hot spells of recent summers. Since many hotels are in isolated areas, a considerable number of staff have to be recruited from outside. However, you will almost certainly be expected to work for the entire season, and should have the temperament to suit living in a remote place. The Jobcentre in Fort William is a good source for this type of work, as is the Jobcentre in Perth. The majority of hotels in rural Perthshire offer live-in accommodation, and frequently employ students over the summer. The Jobcentre in Inverness advertises vacancies as far afield as Ullapool, Gairloch and Lochcarron on the West coast and Aviemore, Kingussie and Grantown-on-Spey to the South as well as in the town itself. Due to the high level of local unemployment in less remote parts the only vacancies that remain are usually for skilled or experienced staff. While in many areas employers routinely offer accommodation, Inverness is however an exception and few live-in jobs are available there.

Fruit picking jobs are particularly abundant in Perth and Tayside. The season usually lasts from the end of June until mid-September. In addition to the vacancies listed in this chapter, jobs are also advertised in the Jobcentre in Blairgowrie, but not in the Jobcentre in Perth.

Edinburgh attracts a considerable number of tourists each year, particularly during the Festival in late August. As a result there is a wide range of jobs available particularly in hotels. With the introduction of a Scottish Parliament the need for hotel and catering staff in Edinburgh will increase further. If you speak a foreign language you could land yourself a job as a guide, and the District Council engages extra assistant or experienced gardeners to maintain the city gardens and flowers. There are usually plenty of vacancies displayed in the Edinburgh Jobcentre. Note that accommodation is rarely provided with a job in Edinburgh, and can be difficult to find.

In the winter season, those seeking employment could try the skiing resorts of Aviemore and Aonach Mor.

Business and Industry

KILLYMADDY TOURIST INFORMATION CENTRE: 190 Balleygawley Road, Dungannon BT10 1TF (tel 01868-767259; fax 01868-767911). Run by Dungannon District Council, the centre provides a comprehensive tourist information service.
TRAVEL ADVISOR (1). To work a 35 hour week with the possibility of overtime. Must be over 18 and hold 5 GCSEs or the equivalent (including English and Maths). Knowledge of a foreign language preferred. Must have experience of working in a customer service environment. Keyboard skills an advantage. No accommodation available.

Min. period of work 6 months from April to September. Overseas applicants who can communicate effectively in English considered. Interview necessary.

Applications to Libby McLean or Julie Francis from January.

THE STEWARTRY MUSEUM: St Mary Street, Kirkudbright DG6 4AQ (tel/fax 01557-331643; e-mail DavidD@dumgal.gov.uk). Run by the Department for Community Resources of Dumfries and Galloway Council.
MUSEUM ATTENDANTS (2) to assist permanent staff in the high season, working predominantly in the cafeteria at the Tolbooth Art Centre in Kircudbright. Wages £3.997 per hour. To work 15-18 hours per week. No accommodation is available. Min period of work 13 weeks between mid June and mid September.

Applicants should be over 18 and experience would be useful. Interview necessary. Applications by May 1st to Dr David F. Devereux.

Children

EAC ACTIVITY CAMPS: First Floor, 46 Bavelaw Road, Balerno, Edinburgh EH14 7AE (tel 0131-449-7036; fax 0131-538-7407). Multi activity day and residential camps in Edinburgh and Glasgow. For children aged 5-16.
QUALIFIED INSTRUCTORS required for canoeing, wall climbing/abseiling, archery and swimming. £100 per week. Relevant qualifications essential: BCU Instructor, MLTB/SPSA, GNAS, or Bronze Medallion/PLG.
GROUP CAPTAINS (8). £90-£120 per week. GROUP MONITORS (16) £80-£100 per week. Accommodation and food provided. Must have all round sporting ability and be enthusiastic. Sporting qualifications and coaching awards preferred.

All staff to work 40 hours per week. Min. period of work 7 weeks between June and September. The work is hard but good fun. Overseas applicants welcome. All applicants must be available for interview. Applications from January to Andrew Fisher, EAC Activity Camps.

PGL TRAVEL: Alton Court, Penyard lane (874), Ross-on-Wye, Herefordshire HR9 5NR (tel 01989-767833). Over 50 staff needed to assist in the running of children's activity centres in Perthshire. Europe's largest provider of adventure holidays for children has offered outstanding training and work opportunities to seasonal staff for over 40 years.

QUALIFIED INSTRUCTORS in canoeing, sailing, windsurfing, pony trekking, hill walking, fencing, archery, judo, rifle shooting, fishing, motorsports, English language and many other activities. Min. age 18.

GROUP LEADERS to take responsibility for small groups of children and ensure that they get the most out of their holiday. Previous experience of working with children necessary. Min. age 20.

Pocket money £36-£70 per week plus free B & L. Vacancies available for short or long periods between February and October. Overseas applicants eligible to work in the UK welcome. Requests for application forms to the Personnel Department at the above address.

Holiday Centres and Amusements

ARDMAIR POINT CARAVAN SITE/BOAT CENTRE: Ardmair Point, Ullapool, Ross-shire (tel 01854-612054; fax 01854-612757). Situated in a scenic area 3 miles north of the fishing village of Ullapool on a beach headland facing the Summer Isles

CARAVAN SITE ASSISTANTS (2). Duties include reception/shop work, cleaning and grass-cutting. A large proportion of the work is out of doors and involves some tractor driving.

BOAT CENTRE ASSISTANT (1) for boat handling. Duties include renting out small boats and equipment, assisting with repair of fibreglass boats, and the servicing and repair of outboard engines.

COFFEE SHOP ASSISTANTS (3) for general counter duties in cafe.

CATERING ASSISTANT (1) to assist chef in coffee shop.

EASTER WORK. Two people required for general pre-season work.

Wage £4.00 per hour. To work 45 hours/5½ days per week, with shifts covering 8am-8pm. Accommodation available. Min. age 18 years. All jobs best suited to people interested in water sports and/or outdoor pursuits. Overseas applicants with fluent English welcome. For further details and application form send s.a.e. to the above address.

WILLIAM GRANT & SONS: The Glenfiddich Distillery, Dufftown, Banffshire, Scotland AB55 4DH (tel 01340-820373; fax 01340-820805).

TOUR GUIDES (20+) to conduct members of the public on tours of the distillery. £155 for 32½ hours per five-day week. No accommodation available but local B & B costs approx. £60-£70 per week including evening meal. Self catering accommodation can usually be found at £50-£60 per week. Min. age 18 years. Min. period of work all of July and August. Must be fluent in at least one foreign European language.

Experience with the general public desirable but not essential. Job requires a bright, cheery and very outgoing personality. Only applicants with fluent English considered. All applicants must be able to attend an interview at the distillery. Interviews are held during the Easter Vacation period. Applications between January and March to Mr D. C. Mair at the above address.

KINDROGAN FIELD CENTRE: Enochdhu, Blairgowrie, Perthshire PH10 7PG (tel 01250-881286).
GENERAL ASSISTANTS. £85 (approx) a week including B & L. To work approx. 35 hours per week, mainly split shifts. Work available March to the end of October, min. period 12 weeks. Duties include working in kitchen/ pantry area or main house. Ideal for students of environmental studies interested in using the library or laboratory facilities; and there will be opportunities to join in some field courses. Min. age 18. Please apply early to the House Manager, Kindrogan Field Centre.

LADY MACPHERSON: 27 Archery Close, London W2 2BE (tel 0171-262 8487).
HOLIDAY HELPERS required in holidays for a Scottish Highland home with children and animals. House is 1000 ft high and near the river Spey. Surrounding villages hold many relatives. New tennis court would appreciate an enthusiast. Some indoor work and painting, driving and dyke building. B & L provided, wages negotiable. Ample time for touring eg. Loch Ness, weather rarely very warm. Two character references required. Applications to the above address.

RICKSHAWS SCOTLAND: 37 Roseburn Street, Edinburgh EH12 6AW (tel 0131-476-7180; e-mail rickshaw@direct.com).
RICKSHAW RUNNERS (100) to give guided tours to tourists in Edinburgh. To work 8 hour shifts between one and seven days per week. Wages £5-£10 per hour plus tips. Help can be given in finding accommodation. Applicants must be over 16. Period of work by arrangement.

Rickshaws Scotland is also helping to find rickshaw runners for connected companies in Dublin, Galway, Limerick and Cork, and it is possible that personnel may be needed for similar schemes which may be starting in London and Glasgow this summer.

Applications to The Operations Officer at the above address.

TUMMEL VALLEY HOLIDAY PARK: Tummel Bridge, By Pitlochry, Perthshire PH16 5SA (tel 01882-634311; fax 01882-634302).
GENERAL ASSISTANTS (2). £3.30 per hour plus tips. Accommodation provided, for which £13.05 per week is deducted from wages. To work 6 days per week, variable hours as required. Period of work March to October; minimum 10-12 weeks. Min. age 18. No experience needed. Overseas applicants with fluent spoken English considered. Applications to the General Manager, Tummel Valley Holiday Park.

Hotels and Catering

ABERNETHY TRUST: Ardeonaig, by Killin, Perthshire FK21 8SY (tel 01567-820523; fax 01567-820955). A residential outdoor centre.
HOUSEKEEPING STAFF (2), CATERING STAFF (2), GENERAL ESTATE WORKERS (2) to work 5½ days a week as part of a residential Christian staff team. Wages £20 per week plus board and lodging. Staff required from June to September; minimum period of work 4 weeks. Minimum age 18. Christian commitment essential.

Applications from January to Philip Simpson, Centre Director, at the above address.

ABINGTON HOTEL: Abington, By Biggar, Lanarkshire ML12 6SD (tel 01864-502467; fax 01864-502223). The MacBride family own and run this friendly hotel open all year round in a rural setting, which is quiet but reasonably close to major centres, and an hour's bus journey to Edinburgh.
GENERAL ASSISTANTS (2) to participate in all aspects of hotel work, including serving in the bar and restaurant and servicing rooms. £100 per week plus free board and accommodation (and share of tips). To work 50-55 hours per week, split shifts over 5 days. Min. period of work 3 months. Must be over 18, a non-smoker, and have some hotel work experience. Overseas applicants with good English welcome. Applications, including recent photograph, references and s.a.e. should be sent to Mr Duncan MacBride at the above address.

ARISAIG HOUSE: Beasdale, Arisaig, Inverness-shire PH39 4NR (tel 01687-450622; fax 01687-450626; e-mail ArisaiGHse@aol.com.uk). A secluded family run hotel which has beautiful gardens and breathtaking views, and provides croquet, billiards and fine dining.Fairly remote and in a beautiful, West Highland coastal situation; location would not suit an urban dweller needing city amenities.
KITCHEN ASSISTANT (1). £125 per week plus gratuities. Some experience required. Minimum age 18.
COMMIS CHEF(1). £115 per week plus gratuities. Basic kitchen training required. Minimum age 17.
CHEF DE PARTIE (1). £200 per week plus gratuities. Must have solid base of experience and college exposure. Minimum age 22.
All the above positions to work a 6 day week. Also required:
HOUSEMAIDS (2). £115 per week plus gratuities. Previous experience preferred.
RESTAURANT STAFF (2). £120 per week plus gratuities. Must have good appearance and manners, and a willingness to work.
Housemaids and restaurant staff work a 5 day week and must be aged at least 18.
All staff are needed from 1 April to end of October; minimum period of work June until the end of September. Accommodation, staff meals and uniform provided at no extra charge. Overseas applicants with spoken English at level of a native welcome.
Applications from 1 January to David J. Wilkinson at the address above must be accompanied by an s.a.e. or postal coupons for a reply.

AVIEMORE HIGHLANDS HOTEL: Aviemore Mountain Resort, Inverness-shire PH22 1PF (tel 01479-810771; fax 01479-811473; e-mail sales-@aviehighlands.demon.co.uk). A modern 3 star 103 bedroom hotel in the middle of a small mountain resort, which caters for coach parties, private guests and families. The area is good for walking and sightseeing. The bus and train station is 800m away.
WAITING STAFF (4). Wages £2.75-£3.15 per hour, live-in. To work 39 hours over 5 days a week plus overtime.
CHAMBER PERSONS (4). Wages £2.75-£3.15 per hour, live-in. To work 30 hours over 5 days with the possibility of overtime.

TABLE SERVICE DRINK STAFF (2). Wages £2.75-£3.15 per hour, live-in. To work 39 hours a week over 5 days, with the possibility of overtime. COMMIS CHEF (1). Wages £3.15 per hour, live-in. To work 39 hours a week over 5 days with the possibility of overtime. Some kitchen/cooking experience is required.

Accommodation is available, at a cost of £17.50 per week which is already deducted from wages quoted above. Min. period of work 3 months between March and November.

Applicants should be smart, willing, and speak good English. All applicants must be over 18. Overseas applicants with good English are considered. A telephone interview may suffice. Applications from January to the Personnel Manager.

AVIEMORE MOUNTAIN RESORT LTD.: Aviemore, Inverness-shire PH22 1PN (tel 01479-810624; fax 01479-810862). There are a number of vacancies within A.M.R. Ltd. including:
GROUND CREW to work within Santa Claus Land Theme Park. Straight shifts.
SILVER SERVICE WAITING STAFF. Split shifts.
BAR STAFF, KITCHEN PORTERS. Occasionally split shifts.
ROOM ASSISTANTS, CHALET CLEANERS. Straight shifts.

Staff paid £3.30 per hour, for approx. 39 hours work per week. To work any 5 days out of 7. B & L provided. Period of employment May to October; min. period 3 months. Min. age 18, experience preferred but not essential. Applicants are usually required to attend an interview. Overseas applicants will be considered. Applications in writing to Denise Mackintosh, Personnel Department, at the above address.

BALCARY BAY HOTEL: Auchencairn, nr Castle Douglas, Dumfries and Galloway DG7 1QZ (tel 01556-640217; fax 01556-640272). Country house hotel noted for its warm welcome and excellent service.
WAITING STAFF and KITCHEN STAFF. £3.75 per hour for 37 hours per week. Must have relevant previous experience. Min. age 20. To work from April to October; the minimum period of work is four months. Accommodation available at no extra charge. The hotel is located in a rural area and is not particularly well suited to students wishing to explore Scotland in its entirety on their days off. Overseas applicants fluent in English welcome. An interview is not always necessary. Apply from February to Clare Lamb at the above address.

BALMACARA HOTEL: Kyle of Lochalsh, Ross-shire, Scotland IV40 8DH (tel 01599-566283; fax 01599-566329).
RECEPTION STAFF (2), BAR STAFF (2). Must be aged over 19.
HOUSE STAFF (2), WAITING STAFF (2). Must be aged over 17.

Wages £90-£100 per week plus tips live-in, with own room and meals provided. To work 5-6 days per week, hours by arrangement. Period of work May to September. Overseas applicants considered. Applications to the Manager at the above address.

BALMORAL HOTEL: 1 Princes Street, Edinburgh EH2 2EQ (tel 0131-622 8802; fax 0131-558 1766). A 5 star hotel in the centre of Edinburgh owned by Rocco Forte hotels.

WAITING STAFF (6), with waiting experience, smart presentation and customer service skills.
ROOM ATTENDANTS (6). Must be available until the end of November.
CONCIERGE PORTERS (2). Must have clean driving licence and smart presentation.
KITCHEN PORTERS (2).
Wages for all positions £3.60 per hour for a 39 hour week. No accommodation is available. Min. period of work 4 months between May and October/ November.
All applicants must be over 18. Overseas applicants with good English considered. Interview necessary. Applications from February to Susan Forrest, Personnel Officer.

BRAEMAR LODGE HOTEL: Glenshee Road, Braemar, Aberdeenshire AB35 5YQ (tel 013397-41627).
GENERAL ASSISTANTS (2) to assist the owners in the day-to-day running of the hotel. £100 per week plus tips, food, accommodation and laundry. Varied jobs include work in bedrooms, the laundry and bar, restaurant, kitchen, etc. To work 39 hours per 6-day week (9.30am-1.00pm and 7-10pm) with afternoons free. Period of work April to October.
No qualifications necessary as training will be given. Applicants must be self-motivated, adaptable and outgoing, with a sense of humour. The hotel is situated in an isolated village at the foot of the Cairgorms, hence ideal for those interested in outdoor pursuits such as hill climbing and mountain biking. Suitably qualified overseas applicants considered. Applications to the above address.

BURTS HOTEL: Market Square, Melrose, Scottish Borders, Scotland TD6 9PN (tel 01896-82 2285; fax 01896-82 2870; e-mail burtshotel@aol.com).
WAITING STAFF (4), BAR PERSON (1). Applicants over 18 preferred. Experience essential.
Applications from 1 February to Nicholas Henderson at the above address.

CALEDONIAN THISTLE HOTEL: 10-14 Union Terrace, Aberdeen, Scotland AB10 1WE (tel 01224-640233; fax 01224-641627). Part of the Thistle Hotel chain, the 80 bedroom Caledonian is situated in the heart of Aberdeen city centre.
FOOD SERVICE STAFF (2) for the cafe/bar or dining room. Wage £3.38 per hour (board and lodging included). To work split shifts for a 39 hour week. Min. period of work 3 months from April to October.
Staff should be at least 18 years old, and experience is preferred. Suitably qualified overseas applicants are welcome. Applications to James Wichary from January onwards.

THE CEILIDH PLACE: West Argyll Street, Ullapool, Ross & Cromarty, Scotland IV26 2TY (tel 01854-612103). A complex of buildings including a small hotel with 13 rooms, a bunk house, bar, coffee room, restaurant, bookshop, gallery and venue for music and drama.
COOKS (3) with natural skill and enthusiasm.
HOUSESTAFF (2). Must be fit and fussy.
WAITERS/WAITRESSES to serve breakfast and dinner.

RECEPTIONISTS (2). Computer skills essential as is the ability to work to a tight schedule.
COFFEE SHOP ASSISTANTS (6). Serving food and drink and clearing tables.
BAR STAFF (2). Serving/stocking drinks and assisting with food service.

Wages paid monthly; basic wage £624 per calendar month (less board and lodging allowance) for workers over 18. Work available between February and December, min. period 3 months: no shorter period considered. Overseas applicants eligible to work in the UK and with necessary documentation welcome. For further information and an application form write to Jean Urquhart at the above address.

CLACHAIG INN: Glencoe, Argyll PA39 4HX (tel 01855-811252; fax 018552-811679; web site www.glencoe-scotland.co.uk). A busy, vibrant country inn set in the heart of Glencoe, popular year-round with hillwalkers and mountain bikers.
GENERAL ASSISTANTS (15) required throughout the year to help in all aspects of the business; bar work (serving both drinks and food), waiting on tables and helping out in the kitchen, housekeeping, renting and maintaining mountain bikes, and various odd jobs.

Previous experience is helpful, but a friendly outgoing personality and enthusiasm are more important. You must be clean and presentable, able to communicate well, and be able to work well as part of a team. Accommodation and all meals are provided. The minimum period of work is at least 3 months. Positions are available year round; those able to work over the New Year and Easter have priority when it comes to the summer months. Applications (with a covering letter and detailed c.v.) should be sent to Guy Daynes at the above address approximately one month before you are available for work.

CLIFTON HOUSE HOTEL: Nairn, Nairnshire (tel 01667-453119).
WAITER/ WAITRESS, HOUSE and KITCHEN ASSISTANTS (6-7). Wages and hours by arrangement. B & L provided, charge to be discussed. Experience preferable but not necessary. Min. work period 4 weeks between March and October. Overseas applicants who speak French or English welcome. Applications in writing to Mr J. Gordon Macintyre, Proprietor, Clifton House.

CRAIGARD HOUSE HOTEL: Boat of Garten, Inverness-shire (tel 01479-831 206). Deluxe country house hotel.
CHAMBER STAFF (2), WAITING STAFF (2), BAR TENDER (1). Wages on application. Experience an advantage but not essential as training will be given. Min. age 18 years. B & L provided for the right applicants. Overseas applicants with excellent English welcome. 5½ days per week. Anyone with a good personality, willing to work hard and enjoy life in the Highlands please contact Mrs Cunningham at the above address.

CRAW'S NEST HOTEL: Bankwell Road, Anstruther, Fife KY10 3DA (tel 01333-310691; fax 01333-312216).
KITCHEN HANDS (2). £175 per week plus end of season bonus. No experience necessary.
WAITING STAFF (3). £175 per week. Some silver service experience would be useful, though is not essential.

All staff to work 5 days per week. Accommodation available and meals provided on duty. Min. period of work 3-4 months between May and September. Applications with photograph and s.a.e. to Mr I. Birrell at the above address.

CRINAN HOTEL: Crinan, nr Lochgilphead, Argyll PA31 8SR (tel 01546-830261; fax 01546-830292). Fishing village and sailing centre in a beautiful location.
WAITING STAFF (8). Split shifts for meal times.
BAR STAFF (6). Split shifts.
COFFEE SHOP STAFF (4).
ROOM ATTENDANTS (10). Hours 7am-3pm.
RECEPTIONISTS (3).
Wages £105 per week plus accommodation. Minimum age 21 years. Experience helpful but not essential. Applications from January to N.A.Ryan, Managing Director, at the above address, enclosing a recent full length photograph.

THE CROWNE PLAZA HOTEL, EDINBURGH: 80 High Street, The Royal Mile, Edinburgh EH1 1TH (tel 0131-557 9797; fax 0131-557 9798). A busy city centre hotel aiming to provide first class service for an international clientele.
WAITING STAFF (5), waiting experience preferred. Applicants must be over 18.
CHAMBERMAIDS (5), no experience necessary. Applicants must be over 16.
Wages for all positions £3.75 per hour. All staff to work 20-40 hours a week on a rota system. No accommodation is available. Min. period of work 15th June to 4th October. Interview necessary (but could be conducted by telephone). Overseas applicants with valid work permits considered.
Applications from March to Sarah Allanson.

DALMUNZIE HOUSE HOTEL: Glenshee, Perthshire PH10 7QG (tel 01250-885 224). Country house hotel on 6,000-acre estate in a remote mountain situation.
GENERAL HOTEL STAFF (6). Wages and hours by arrangement according to type of job. To work 5 days a week. B & L provided. Min. age 18 years. Period of work January to late October. Overseas applicants with good

English welcome. Only applications enclosing s.a.e. will receive a reply. Applications to Simon and Alexandra Winton, Proprietors, Dalmunzie House Hotel.

DUISDALE HOTEL: Isle Ornsay, Sleat, Isle of Skye IV43 8QW (tel 01471-833202).
KITCHEN ASSISTANT (1). Some cooking experience necessary.
GENERAL ASSISTANTS (2). Mainly chambermaiding and waiting; some barwork and reception work.
 Wages by arrangement. Free B & L provided. Min. age 20. Previous experience preferred. Min. period of work 3 months between April and October. Overseas applicants with fluent English accepted. Applications to Mrs Campbell, Duisdale Hotel.

DUNDONNELL HOTEL: Little Loch Broom, Near Ullapool, Ross-shire (tel 01854 633234; fax 01854-633366: Web http://wwwsol.co.uk/d/dundonnellhotel; e-mail selbie@dundonnel.hotel.co.uk). Busy family run 30-bedroom hotel just south of Ullapool in an area of outstanding mountain scenery. Location is remote but beautiful, and has no discos or shops. The following staff are needed to work in the 3 star quality establishment.
ASSISTANT CHEF/COOK (with experience), COMMIS CHEF/COOK, DINING ROOM STAFF (3), one to take charge, GENERAL ASSISTANTS (3) for kitchen and stillroom, BAR STAFF (2), CHAMBER STAFF (2), PETROL STATION ATTENDANT.
 From £130 per 5½-day week, with higher rates for skilled and senior personnel. Free B & L in excellent accommodation (own room). Uniform provided. Min. period of work 12 weeks but longer period preferred. Most posts from Easter to October, with some from mid-May to end of September. Applications with s.a.e. and photograph, including details of any previous work experience and dates of availability, to Mr and Mrs S.W. Florence, Dundonnell Hotel.

FERNHILL HOTEL: Portpatrick, nr Stranraer, Wigtownshire (tel 01776-810220). A 20 bedroom 4 Star family run hotel with a restaurant, which caters to a mixture of business and holiday customers, most of whom return again.
WAITER/WAITRESSES (2), BAR STAFF (1), CHAMBER STAFF (1). £120 per week plus tips and free B & L. To work 40 hours per week, 5 days on, 2 days off. Overtime available at £4.50 per hour. Experience is not essential but must be willing workers and interested in the job. Min. period of work 2/3 months: 1 April to end of June, or mid-August to the end of October. Applications after 1 March to Mrs Anne Harvie, Fernhill Hotel.

FORTE POSTHOUSE GLASGOW CITY: Bothwell Street, Glasgow G2 7EN (tel 0141-248 2656; fax 0141-221 8986).
HOUSEKEEPING ROOM MAIDS (5). To work full time and part time at market rate wages. Min.age 17. Accommodation limited. Min. period of work 10 weeks between June and October. Overseas applicants welcome. All applicants must be available for interview. Apply anytime to the Personnel Manager, at the above address.

FREEDOM OF THE GLEN HOTELS: Creag Dhu House, Near Fort William, Scotland PH33 6RY (tel 01855-821582; fax 01855-821463). A family business in the Scottish Highlands which operates 3 small distinctive hotels and an innovative visitor attraction.
RESTAURANT STAFF (4) for silver service work; 5 day, 45 hour week. Wage £100 per week plus accommodation. Should be aged 22 or over.
KITCHEN PORTERS (2) to work 45 hours per 5 day week on split shifts. Wages £90 per week plus accommodation. Should be aged 18 or over.
RESTAURANT STAFF (3) to work in an informal bistro serving up to 100 covers. To work 45 hours per week on a mixture of split and straight shifts. Wage £90 per week plus accommodation and a retainer. Should be aged 22 or over; full training will be given.
   Staff for the above positions are needed to begin work as soon as possible.
RECEPTIONIST to work from mid May to mid September. Duties include welcoming customers, provide information etc and work in the shop. To work from approx. 9.30am-6pm, 5 days per week. Wages £3.50 per hour; to live out. Jobs would suit a local student.
CAFE ASSISTANT to serve behind the food servery, at the till etc. To work from 12 noon-5pm 5 days per week, from mid May to mid September. To live out; wage £3.50 per week. Job would suit a local student.
   Applications for the above positions to Margaret Holyoake, Training and Development Co-ordinator, at the above address.

GRAND ISLAND HOTEL: Bride Road, Ramsey, Isle of Man IM8 3UN (tel 01624-812455; fax 01624-815291).
BREAKFAST CHEF to work 36 hours per week.
SOUS CHEF, CHEF DE PARTIE, MAITRE DE WAITERS, WAITING STAFF (4+), BAR STAFF (3), HOUSEKEEPING STAFF (4), DAY/ NIGHT PORTERS (2) to work 40 hours per week.
   Details of wages, accommodation etc. on application. To work from June onwards. All applicants must be college trained. Applications should be sent to Ms Leigh Corrin, Asistant Manager, at the above address.

THE GROG AND GRUEL: Traditional Alehouse and Restaurant, 66 High Street, Fort William PH33 6DY (tel 01397-705078). A traditional Alehouse situated in the town centre serving a selection of real ales and malt whiskies, with a family restaurant on the upper level, offering home-cooked dishes.
GENERAL ASSISTANTS (5) to help in bar and restaurant, and possibly in the kitchen. To work a 5 day week (occasionally 6 days) of typically 40 hours. Min. period of work 3 months.
   Accommodation cannot be provided, but is available locally. Staff should be at least 18 years old, but enthusiasm and a friendly, outgoing personality are more important than experience.
   For further details, or an application form, contact the General Manager at the above address.

INVEREWE GARDEN: Poolewe, Ross-shire IV22 2LG (tel 01445-781200; fax 01445-781497). A National Trust property incorporating a modern 200 seater self-service restaurant.
RESTAURANT GENERAL ASSISTANTS (2-6). To perform general duties including food production/ servery/ till work. To work 39 hours over a 5 day week. Min. age 18; wages £3.70 per hour. Min. period of work 20 weeks from

May to September. Furnished accommodation available at £3 per week. Overseas students with good English will be considered. Applicants must be able to work as part of a team and be self motivated. Note that applicants must be able to attend an interview. Apply from mid March to The Administrator at the above address.

INVERSNAID PHOTOGRAPHY CENTRE: Inversnaid Lodge, by Aberfoyle, Stirling FK8 3TU (tel 01877-386254). A residential photography workshop centre which hosts tutors of international repute in areas such as landscape, wildlife, and documentary. Situated on the shores of Loch Lomond, in an area of outstanding natural beauty 1½ hours from Glasgow.
DOMESTIC HELPER (1) for general cleaning duties and helping in the centre. Wages £125 per week with free B & L provided. To work 40 hours a week. Min. age 20. Cleaning and waiting experience preferable. Overseas applicants with good English will be considered. Min. period of work 6 months between April and October. Note that applicants must be able to attend an interview. Applications from February to Ms Linda Middleton at the above address.

KYLESKU WEST HIGHLAND HOTEL: Kylesku, By Lochinver, Sutherland, Scotland IV27 4FX (tel 01971-502231; fax 01971-502313).
BAR ASSISTANTS (2) to be responsible for running a busy small bar; duties include ordering, stock-taking, cleaning etc. To work two straight shifts, 8am-4pm and 4-11pm. Minimum age 18. No qualifications required; full training given. To work over the summer period until the end of October if possible.
ODD JOB PERSON to help in all areas; variable working hours according to duties so must be flexible. Must be practically-minded and able to paint, wash up, clean windows etc. To work over the summer period until the end of October if possible.
WAITING/ROOM STAFF to wait on tables, in the bar and restaurant and assist in bedrooms. To work over the summer period.
COOKS (2) to work various shifts 8am-9.30pm, so must be very flexible. All levels of cooking experience considered; must be hard working with an easy going personality. To work over the summer period.
Wages of £130 per week plus accommodation, food and good tips. Applications should be sent to Andre Klein, Manager, at the above address.

LEDGOWAN LODGE HOTEL: Achnasheen, Wester Ross IV22 2EJ, Highlands of Scotland (tel 01445-720252).
COCKTAIL BAR, HOUSE, PANTRY, KITCHEN and WAITING STAFF. Average gross wage £180 per working 6-day week, depending on age and experience. To work approx. 55 hours a week with 1 day off. Accommodation available in own room. Min. period of work 12 weeks between Easter and October. Overseas applicants with fluent English considered. Send applications a.s.a.p., enclosing photograph, age and references if possible, to Mr G.T. Millard, Ledgowan Lodge Hotel.

LOCH IALL BREWERS FAYRE: An Aird, Fort William, Scotland PH33 6AN (tel 01397-703707).
BAR STAFF (3). To work hours as required, 7 days a week.
WAITING STAFF (3). Flexible hours over 7 days a week.
CHAMBER STAFF (3). To work 9.00am-4.00pm, 7 days a week.
Wages £3.66 per hour (1998 rates). Applicants must be over 16. Experience

is not necessary as the right candidates will be trained. Accommodation is not available. Period of work March to October.

Overseas applicants considered. Interview necessary. Applications from January to the Manager.

M. F. WELLS (HOTELS) LTD.: Inversnaid, by Aberfoyle, Stirlingshire FK8 3TU (tel 01877-386301; fax 01877-386305). A family run hotel and tour group with 5 hotels and its own fleet of coaches.
KITCHEN ASSISTANT, DINING ROOM STAFF, HOUSEKEEPING STAFF & BAR STAFF to work 40 hours a week. Wages £400 per month plus board and accommodation. Minimum period of work 6 weeks at any time of year; dates of work negotiable.

Applications at any time to Mrs E. Nicols at the above address.

MACNAUGHTONS: 73 High Street, Ardersier, Inverness IV1 2RP (tel 01667-462477; fax 01667-462034). Tea room and antiques and crafts shop in Ardersier. Fort George is operated on behalf of Historic Scotland, Aviemore for a visitors' centre, and Forres contains an Art Gallery.
COUNTER/WAITING STAFF, KITCHEN HELP needed to work in businesses in Ardersier, Forres, Aviemore and Fort George. Wages of £4 per hour: dates of work by arrangement. To work 40 hours per week on rotas between 10am and 6pm. Applicants should have happy personalities and ready smiles, good general common sense and a strong awareness of hygiene.
Applications to Ms Maura Macnaughton, Owner, at the above address.

McTAVISH'S KITCHENS (OBAN) LTD: Restaurants in the West Highland resort towns of Oban and Fort William.
WAITING STAFF, SELF-SERVICE ASSISTANTS, KITCHEN ASSIS-TANTS, COOKS, BAR STAFF and CLEANERS. There are a number of vacancies, particularly for students, between April and October. Meals and accommodation provided without charge. Possibility of overtime. Late availability (mid-August to end of September). Written applications only, enclosing photograph and s.a.e., to McTavish's Kitchens, 8 Argyll Square, Oban PA34 4BA or McTavish's Kitchen, High Street, Fort William PH33 6AD.

MONESS HOUSE HOTEL AND COUNTRY CLUB: Crieff Road, Aberfeldy, Perthshire PH15 2DY (tel 01887-820446; fax 01887-820062). A private company offering holiday accommodation in a 12 bedroom hotel and 75 self catering cottages situated in 35 acres of grounds overlooking the picturesque town of Aberfeldy in the heart of Scotland.
PLAY LEADER (1). Wages £3.50 per hour live-out. Must be over 18 and be experienced in working with children.
BISTRO STAFF (2), RESTAURANT STAFF (2). Wages £3.20 per hour live-in. Must be over 18 and have food service experience. Bistro staff must have wine service experience.

All staff to work 39 hours a week. Min. period of work 10 weeks between July and October. Overseas applicants with good working English considered. Interview not necessary. Applications from May to the General Manager.

NEWTON LODGE: Kylesku, Sutherland IV27 4HW. A small hotel in the remote North West Highlands.
GENERAL ASSISTANT required for duties as required including dining

room, kitchen help, bedroom work and general cleaning. Wage £120 per 6 day week, including own room with shower. Period of work mid May to mid September.

Must have previous hotel experience. As the area is remote, a driving licence would be an advantage. Non-smoker only. Applications with photo and reference to Mrs Brauer.

THE OLD INN: Gairloch, Ross-Shire IV21 2BD (tel 01445-712006; fax 01445-712445).
WAITING STAFF (2/3) to work 40 hours per week.
BAR STAFF (2/3) to work 40-50 hours per week.

To live-in with meals provided: wages £3.25 per hour. Period of work from May to September. Applicants should be aged 18-30. Applications to D. Carruthers at the above address.

PRIORY HOTELS LTD: The Square, Beauly, Inverness-shire IV4 7BX (tel 01463-782309; fax 01463-782531). Small company operating hotels and restaurants in Inverness-shire.
KITCHEN ASSISTANTS (4), FRONT OF HOUSE STAFF/GENERAL ASSISTANTS (6) required to work in busy hotels in Beauly and Dalwhinnie. Hours: 40 per week. From £120, plus free B & L. Smart appearance, good interpersonal skills and bags of common sense essential. Min. period of work 3 months but six month contract preferred. Good fun with a bustling team of people. Overseas applicants welcome. Applications any time to Mr S.A. Hutton, Director, at the above address.

QUALITY CENTRAL HOTEL: 99 Gordon Street, Glasgow G1 3SF (tel 0141-221 9680; fax 0141-221 7959). A 221-bedroom Victorian railway hotel.
WAITING STAFF (1) to work in hotel restaurant. Hours: 7am-10.30am, 11am-2.30pm and 5.30pm-10.30pm.
HOUSEKEEPER/ROOM ATTENDANT (1). Working hours 8am-3pm and 5-8pm.

All staff receive £115 per week, live out. Period of work June to December. Applications to Paul Catford, Regional Personnel Manager, at the above address.

RAASAY OUTDOOR CENTRE: Isle of Raasay, By Kyle, Ross-shire, Scotland IV40 8PB (tel 01478-660266; fax 01478-660200; e-mail raasay.house-@virgin.net). An outdoor centre located on a remote and peaceful Hebridean Island.
KITCHEN MANAGER (1). Must have at least 6 years cooking and organisational experience. Wages £125 per week.
PREPARATION COOKS (2). Must have general cooking experience. Wage £65 per week.
KITCHEN ASSISTANTS (2). To perform kitchen preparation and washing up duties. Must be motivated. Wage £55 per week.
CAFE/BAR/SHOP ASSISTANTS (3). Must have experience and be organised and motivated. Wage £55-£75 per week.
HOUSEKEEPER (1). Must have organisational and cleaning experience. Wage £55-£75 per week.

All positions are for 44 hours work per week between March and October. Min. period of work 1 month. Board and accommodation provided at no extra charge.

Overseas applicants must speak good English. Interview is necessary. Apply from March to Freya Rowe at the above address.

ROSEDALE HOTEL: Portree, Isle of Skye IV51 9DB (tel 01478-613131; fax 01478-612531). A family-run hotel located on the harbourside in Portree, the administrative and commercial capital of the island and the adjoining mainland.

RECEPTIONIST/DUTY MANAGER (1). Min. age 24. Must be educated to at least A level standard and be well presented, articulate and mature. Hotel background and training essential.

SECOND CHEF (1). City and Guilds 706/1 and 706/2 required, plus two years' post-qualification experience. To assist AA rosette chef and be able to take charge in his absence preparing quality food with imagination and style.

GENERAL ASSISTANTS (6). To work a mixed rota in many departments but mainly restaurant and bar, with some housekeeping. Aged 21 + . Should be well presented, articulate and interested in working with people. Hotel experience an advantage.

Wages specified on application. Free B & L provided. All staff work approx. 40-45 hours per week. Min. period of work early May to mid October. Priority given to those able to work the full or greater part of the season. An end of season share of gratuities is made upon completion of contract period. Non-smoking applicants only. Write for an application form from mid-February to Keith White, Manager, at the above address.

THE ROYAL HOUSEHOLD: Buckingham Palace, London SW1A 1AA (tel 0171-930 4832; 0171-839 5950).

ASSISTANTS for general cleaning/laundry duties of staff accommodation/ bedding, and the occasional cleaning of more islolated buildings used for barbeques, at Balmoral Castle. Must be able to work between mid July and mid October inclusive. Not suitable for students returning to college in September. Wages on application; accommodation is provided, as are meals during court visits. To work 35 hours per week on a rota. Applicants should be aged between 20 and 50; no previous experience is necessary as training is given. All staff to be security screened before employment-this can take up to 2 months if candidates are from overseas.

Applications, by April 1999 at the latest, to Miss Heather Colebrook, Chief Housekeeper, at the above address.

ROYAL ZOOLOGICAL SOCIETY OF SCOTLAND: Edinburgh Zoo, 134 Corstorphine Road, Edinburgh EH12 6TS (tel 0131-334 5001; fax 0131-334 7462). Edinburgh Zoo is Scotland's second most popular tourist attraction, with over half a million visitors a year viewing the world-famous animal collection.

GENERAL CATERING ASSISTANTS (40) for work involving cash handling, customer service and general duties in a busy bistro style restaurant within the zoo. Wages £115.25 per week.

WAITING ASSISTANTS (3) to work in the highly rated members' restaurant and lounge. Wages of £125.50 per week plus tips; these wages may change depending on the timescale for implementation of minimum wage legislation. To work around 4-8 hours overtime a week is available at $1\frac{1}{2}$ times the usual rate. Experience of previous similar work preferred but not essential as full training is provided.

To work from 10am-6pm, 5 days a week. Period of work from May to October. Applications to Stuart Douglas, Personnel Manager, at the above address.

RUFFLETS COUNTRY HOUSE HOTEL: Strathkinness Low Road, St. Andrews KY16 9TX (tel 01334-472594; fax 01334-478703; e-mail rufflets@standrews.co.uk).A privately owned 25 bedroom hotel which holds two AA rosettes for food quality.
HOUSEKEEPING ASSISTANT (1), RESTAURANT ASSISTANT (1), LOUNGE SERVICE ASSISTANT (1). Wages range from £3.50 to £3.90 per hour. All staff to work hours as required, 5 days out of 7. Accommodation is available at £3.50 per day. Min. period of work 6 months between 1st April and 30th November.
Experience is not essential, but all applicants must be over 18 years old. European and Australian applicants fluent in English considered. Interview not always necessary.
Applications from January to John W. Angus.

SCOTLAND'S HOTEL: Bonnethill Road, Pitlochry, Perthshire, Scotland PH16 5BT (tel 01796-472292; fax 01796-473284). A luxury 75 bedroom hotel with conference facilities, a leisure club, and an Italian restaurant, situated in an excellent location, just two hours away from Edinburgh, Glasgow, Aberdeen and Inverness.
BAR ASSISTANT. £120 per week. Min. age 18 years. Split and straight shifts.
WAITING STAFF (2). £120 per week. Silver service training or experience preferred. Split shifts.
HOUSE STAFF (2). £120 per week. Cleaning or housekeeping experience preferred. Split and straight shifts.
All staff to work 8 hours per day, 5 days per week with no overtime. Single bedroom accommodation available. Free meals on and off duty. Health and Leisure club restricted membership for all staff. Uniform provided and training will be given. Min. period of work 2 months between April and October. Overseas applicants with a good knowledge of English welcome. Where possible it is preferred that applicants are available for interview. Applications from March to the Personnel Manager at the above address.

STAKIS EDINBURGH AIRPORT HOTEL: Edinburgh International Airport, Edinburgh EH28 8LL (tel 0131-519 4400; fax 0131-519 4422). Recently built 134 bedroom hotel within the boundaries of Edinburgh airport, popular with both tourists and business travellers.
ROOM ASSISTANTS (5), BISTRO HOSTS (8). Wage for both positions £3.58 per hour. All staff to work 5 days out of 7. No accommodation is available. Min period of work 3 months between March and December.
Experience is preferred, although training can be given. Applicants must be over 18. Overseas applicants with a working knowledge of English considered. Interview necessary.
Applications any time to the Personnel Department.

STAKIS EDINBURGH GROSVENOR HOTEL: Grosvenor Street, Edinburgh EH12 5EF (tel 0131-226 6001; fax 0131-220 2387).
ROOM ASSISTANTS (10) to work 8:30-4:30 for 39 hours a week.
BREAKFAST SERVERS (6) to work 6-11:30am for 5 days a week.

BANQUETING HOSTS (15-20) to work approx.15 hours a week.
　Wage for all positions £3.58 per hour.Training will be given. Applications to the above address.

STAKIS HOTELS: Stakis PLC, Stakis Coylumbridge Hotel, Coylumbridge, Aviemore, Inverness-shire PH22 1QN (tel 01479-813076; fax 01479-813067). Stakis Aviemore operates 3 hotels and a family entertainment facility in the heart of the Scottish Highlands, whose attractions include golf,watersports and horse riding.
KITCHEN, RESTAURANT WAITING, BAR, & HOUSEKEEPING STAFF required. To work 39 hours over a 5-day week. Salary £3.47 per hour (less 15p per hour for first 8 weeks training rate). Min. age 18. Experience preferred. Overseas applicants with basic English (communication level) welcome. Staff required from June to October. Min. period of work 12 weeks. Accommodation paid for out of wages at a rate of 62p per hour for 39 hours work.
Applications from April/May to the Personnel Department at the above address.

STONEFIELD CASTLE GROUP: Bowfield, Howwood, Renfrewshire PA9 1DB (tel 0150-570 5225; fax 0150-570 5230). Owns four sites in West/Central Scotland.
BAR STAFF (5), WAITING STAFF (5), RECEPTION/OFFICE STAFF (2), GENERAL ASSISTANTS (4), KITCHEN STAFF (4), GARDENS/ GROUNDS STAFF (2). £3-£4 per hour live-in depending on age and experience. To generally work 40 hours per week over 5 days. Min. age 18 years. Catering experience an advantage but not essential. Full training given. Min. period of work 6 months between April/May and September/October. Anglophone overseas applicants welcome. Apply from February to Alistair Campbell, Managing Director, at the above address.

SUMMER ISLES HOTEL: Achiltibuie by Ullapool, Ross-shire IV26 2YG (tel 01854-622282). A remote but renowned hotel offering excellent food and service in a relaxed informal setting. Located on the west coast of Scotland and set in magnificent scenery.
KITCHEN ASSISTANT (1). To assist head chef in a Michelin starred restaurant. Experience essential. Excellent opportunity for keen cook.
GENERAL ASSISTANTS for dining room, bar and reception work, room cleaning, laundry and dishwashing.
　Wages min. £152 for 50 hours/6 days per week. Free B & L provided. Experience preferred but training given. Applicants should be available for whole season, starting April/May. The jobs are suited to professional motivated people prepared to work hard and make the most of their free time by enjoying outdoor activities. Applications, with s.a.e. and photograph, to Mr Mark Irvine, Summer Isles Hotel.

THAINSTONE HOUSE HOTEL: Inverurie, Aberdeenshire AB51 5NT (tel 01467-621643; fax 01467-625084). A four star country house hotel and leisure club, committed to training employees to a high level.
WAITERS/WAITRESSES (4), BARTENDERS (2), HOUSEMAIDS (2). Wages by arrangement. All positions to work a 39 hour week. Min. period of work 3 months Between May and the end of September.
　Board and accommodation is available for a 10p deduction from the hourly

wage. There are no deductions for meal breaks, and staff may use the hotel leisure facilities. Experience is preferable, but training will be given. References are required.
Applications from April onwards to the Personnel Manager.

WOODLEA HOTEL: Moniaive, Dumfries-shire DG3 4EN (tel 01848-200209).
GENERAL ASSISTANTS (2). £3.60 per hour live-out, for employees over 21 years. Tips in addition. To work variable hours. B & L available for females only. Expected to help in all aspects of hotel including serving in the bar, toilet cleaning and kitchen and dining room work. Staff free to use swimming pool and other sports facilities when not in use by guests. Work available from Easter to end of October. Min. work period 3 months, preferably to the end of September. Applications enclosing s.a.e., 2 references, personal details, a recent photograph and dates of availability, to Mr M.R. McIver at the above address.

Outdoor

BALMORAL ESTATES: Estates Office, Balmoral, Ballater, Aberdeenshire AB35 5TB (tel 013397-42334; fax 013397-42271)
GROUSE BEATERS (6) to work from mid August to the end of September. Beaters receive £17.50 per day plus accommodation, dinner, bed, breakfast and packed lunch in exchange for working 8am-5pm. Applicants must be healthy and fit enough for a day's walking in the Scottish hills.
Applications to P.J. Ord, Factor at the above address.

MR S. CAMPBELL: Cairntradlin, Kinellar, Aberdeenshire AB21 0SA (tel 01224-790056; fax 01224-791581). A farm growing strawberries and raspberries for Safeways, Marks and Spencers and a local pick-your-own, situated 7 miles from Aberdeen.
STRAWBERRY/RASPBERRY PICKERS (15). Piece work rates paid daily. Picking as and when required, weather and crop conditions permitting; days off as arranged. Social evenings, eg barbeques and Scottish nights, arranged for student workers. Self-catering accommodation (£7) provided in portacabins, with male and female dormitories, kitchen, toilets and showers. Camping area also available for those with equipment. Applicants must bring eating utensils, warm sleeping bags and warm clothing. Period of work 5 July until the end of August. Overseas applicants welcome. Applications to Mr S. Campbell at the above address.

D. & B. GRANT: Wester Essendy, Blairgowrie, Perthshire PH10 6RA (tel 01250-884389).
FRUIT PICKERS (50) to pick strawberries and raspberries. Help also required to process fruit for freezing. To work 6 days a week. Rates and shifts to be negotiated. Caravan accommodation provided free of charge. Period of work from July 10 to August 31. Applications to Colin M. Grant at the above address.

W. HENDERSON: Seggat, Auchterless, Turriff, Aberdeenshire AB53 8DL (tel 01888-511223; fax 01888-511434). Situated in the heart of the castle and distillery county of Aberdeenshire.
STRAWBERRY PICKERS/PACKERS. Piece work rates: around £20 per day

but dependent on size of crop and weather. To work 7 hours per day, 6 days per week, but must be prepared to work variable hours. Self-catering accommodation available, for which there is a charge of £10 per week, but must bring own sleeping bag and eating utensils. Situated 1 mile from main road, with regular bus service between Aberdeen and Inverness. Period of work early July to mid August, min. 4 weeks. Applications from 30 January onwards to Mr W. Henderson, at the above address.

MESSRS. DAVID McINTYRE: Cruachan, Wester Essendy, Blairgowrie, Tayside PH10 6RA (tel 01250-884212).
FRUIT PICKERS (15) to pick strawberries and raspberries for supermarkets to a high standard of quality and hygiene. Payment at piece work rates; average of £24 per day. Days off by arrangement and when unripe fruit or wet weather dictate. Accommodation provided free, with 4 people sharing a 6 berth caravan. Pickers required in July and August. Should be fit and able to adapt to outdoor work; a willingness to help the East European students also on the site with their English would be an advantage. Applications to Euan McIntyre, Partner at the above address.

NEWTON OF LEWESK: Old Rayne Insch, Aberdeenshire AB52 6SW (tel/fax 01464-851 250).
STRAWBERRY PICKERS to work from 10 July to 10 August. Pay according to piece work rates (£3-£4 per hour possible). Accommodation but not meals provided. To work 6-8 hours a day, 6/7 days a week, weather permitting. Min. period of work 3 weeks. Overseas applicants with work permits welcome. Applications (only those with s.a.e. will receive a reply) from January to Messrs G. & B. Walker at the above address.

J.G. PORTER: East Scryne, Carnoustie, Angus, Scotland DD7 6LL (office tel (9-12.00am) 01241-852895, mobile 04111-148757).
STRAWBERRY PICKERS. Pay at piece work rates and/or hourly rate depending on job. Hours can vary with the weather conditions, but average out at 8 hours a day. Youth hostel and camp site facilities available. Applicants must be fit as the work is hard, but is rewarded well.
  Applications to James Porter, Partner, at the above address.

L. M. PORTER: East Seaton, Arbroath, Angus, Scotland DD11 5SD (tel 01241-879989; fax 01241-871220). East Seaton is situated on the clifftops by Arbroath where conditions are ideal for growing fruit for Marks and Spencer, Tescos and Sainsburys.
STRAWBERRY/RASPBERRY PACK HOUSE STAFF/PICKERS (20) for soft fruit picking, packing and quality control in July and August. Piece rate and/or hourly rate (depending on job). Hours can vary with the weather conditions but otherwise average 8 hours a day. Youth hostel and camp site facilities available. Applicants must be fit as work is hard but well rewarded. Applications to Deborah Porter, Partner, at the above address.

THOMAS THOMSON (BLAIRGOWRIE) LTD: Bramblebank Works, Blairgowrie, Perthshire PH10 7HY (tel 01250-872266; fax 01250-875090). The family owned farms are 1km from Blairgowrie in beautiful Perthshire. Produces quality fruit (some with rain protection) for supermarkets. Discos and Scottish dances arranged after work.
STRAWBERRY/RASPBERRY PICKERS (100). Piecework rates, approx.

£20-£40 per day. To work 6/7 days a week. No experience required. Min. period of work 6 weeks between 20 June and 31 August. Must work 15 July to 10 August. Accommodation available in caravans for £10 per week. Overseas applicants welcome. Applications should be made from 1 January to Mrs Melanie Thomson at the above address.

Sport

AVALON TREKKING SCOTLAND: Bowerswell Lane, Kinnoull, Perth PH2 7DL (tel/fax 01738-624194).
WALKING GUIDES/DRIVERS (2). Wages £80-£100 per week plus free board and accommodation. To work a 6 day week. Staff required from April to November; minimum period of work 1 week. Applicants must be over 25 years old with experience of walking/guiding, and able to drive a minibus.
Applications from February to Tom Sandiford at the above address.

CALEDONIAN DISCOVERY LTD.: The Slipway, Corpach, Fort William PH33 7NN (tel 01397-772167; fax 01397-772765). Organises activity holidays based on a barge touring the Great Glen. The 12 guests take part in various outdoor activities at numerous stops along the way. Activities include sailing, canoeing, windsurfing, walking, and biking, with other specialist weeks available. The work is hard, but varied and great fun.
MATE/INSTRUCTOR (1). £140 per week. Experience and preferably qualifications in open canoeing and mountain walking required (windsurfing and sailing an advantage).
BOSUN (1). £50 per week. Main duties: maintenance of boat, driving of safety boat, helping on deck. Training provided. Personal experience of outdoor sports an advantage. Must be keen to learn, with practical nature.
COOK (1) to prepare food for 18 people. £140 per week. Must have experience in good cooking.
ASSISTANT COOK (1 each week) to assist cook. To work their passage: no wage paid.
All staff to work 6½ days a week and live on board the barge. To work from mid April to mid October. Staff must be available for the whole season with the exception of the assistant cook whose minimum period is one week. A two day recruitment event will be held in February or March.
Applications from December to Martin Balcombe at the above address.

GALLOWAY SAILING CENTRE: Shirmers Bridge, Loch Ken, Castle Douglas DG7 3NQ, South West Scotland (tel 01644-420626). A family owned centre in a glorious setting, which aims to give its visitors an enjoyable yet educational time in a safe and friendly atmosphere.
SAILING INSTRUCTORS: DINGHY (10), WINDSURFERS (5), CANOES (5). Courses start at 10am and finish 5pm. Must be RYA qualified or have a similar level of competence. Overseas applicants with equivalent qualifications welcome.
COOK/GENERAL HELP (2). No special qualifications needed but experience an advantage.
CHALET GIRL (1). Must enjoy working with children.
Wages negotiable, hours variable. Applicants should be versatile, good with people and prepared to accept responsibility. Knowledge of DIY an advantage. Free B & L provided. Period of work from May to September, or

peak season only. Applications to Mr R. Hermon, Principal, at the above address.

GLENCOE OUTDOOR CENTRE: Glencoe, Argyll PA39 4HS (tel 01855-811350). A residential holiday and outdoor activity training centre situated in the north west Highlands amongst the spectacular scenery of Glencoe.
DOMESTIC/SPORTS ASSISTANTS (4). £20 per week including free B & L. To work 8 hours per day, 5 days per week: 3 out of 4 weeks domestic work (split shifts, afternoons free) and 1 out of 4 weeks assisting the team of instructors. Plenty of opportunity to take part in activities during free time. Min. period of work 2 months between January and end of July. Min. age 18. Applicants should be committed Christians willing to work hard as part of a Christian team. Applications a.s.a.p. to Debbie Williams, Director, at the above address.

GREAT GLEN SCHOOL OF ADVENTURE: South Laggan, by Spean Bridge, Inverness-shire PH34 4EA (tel 01809-501 381 ext. Leisure; fax 01809-501 218). A multi-activity centre catering for both family and group activities, situated at the highest point of the Caledonian, on the shores of Loch Oich.
INSTRUCTORS (5) to carry out various tasks including instruction in archery, windsurfing, sailing, rafting; duties also include equipment maintenance, client reception and staff training. Wages £120 per week. Hours of work vary. Accommodation provided at a cost of £15 per week. Minimum period of work May to August. Applicants must have a first aid certificate, driving licence and a qualification relevant to the sport that they are teaching, e.g. Power Boat II or III, or Raft Guide Level 2 or 3.
Applications at any time prior to February to D. McCartney, Leisure Manager, at the above address.

LATHERON PONY CENTRE: Upper Latheron Farm, Latheron, Caithness KW5 6DT (tel 015934-224).
STAFF to work with show ponies and youngstock. £30-50 a week depending upon experience. Free B & L. Work available from April to September, no min. period. Some experience required. Applications to Mrs Camilla Sinclair, Owner, Latheron Pony Centre.

LOCH INSH WATERSPORTS & SKIING CENTRE: Insh Hall, Kincraig, Inverness-shire PH21 1NU (tel 01540-651272; fax 01540-651208). A 14 acre outdoor centre 6 miles from Aviemore offering accommodation and activity holidays. Watersports take place between May and October, and skiing between December and April.
WATERSPORTS INSTRUCTORS. RYA and BCU qualified, or trainee instructor standard. To work 6 days a week.
SKIING INSTRUCTORS. BASI-qualified, or trainee instructor standard. To work 6 days a week.
RESTAURANT STAFF. To work a 5 or 6 day week. Experience preferred.
Wages variable. B & L provided either free or at a charge of up to £40 a week. Free watersports and skiing for staff. Min. period of work 3 months, with work available all year round. Free watersports and winter skiing for all staff. Non-smokers only. Overseas applicants with good spoken English welcome. Applications to Mr Clive Freshwater, at the above address.

RAASAY OUTDOOR CENTRE: Isle of Raasay, By Kyle, Ross-shire, IV40 8PB (tel 01478-660266; fax 01478-660200; e-mail raasay.house@virgin.net). An outdoor centre located on a remote and peaceful Hebridean Island.
OUTDOOR ACTIVITY INSTRUCTORS (10). To work 44 hours per week between March and October. Min. period of work 1 month. Must have first aid qualifications plus one of the following: Windsurfing RYA, Sailing RYA, Kayak BCU, Absail and Climb Walking S.P.S.A. Salary £50-£100 per week; board and accommodation provided at no extra cost.
  All applicants must speak good English. An interview is required. Apply to David Croy from March at the above address.

STAKIS PLC: Stakis Coylumbridge Hotel, Coylumbridge, Aviemore, Inverness-shire PH22 1QN (tel 01479-813076; fax 01479-813067)
LEISURE STAFF. Must have Lifeguard certificate and First Aid. Possible split shifts over a 5-day week. Min. age 18. Staff required from June to October. Min. period of work 12 weeks. Overseas applicants with basic English (communication level) welcome. Shared accommodation in staff hostel with basic facilities available for 62p per hour for up to 39 hours a week.
Applications from April/May to the Personnel Department at the above address.

TIGHNABRUAICH SAILING SCHOOL: Tighnabruaich, Argyllshire. Large sailing school in the West Highlands.
SAILING INSTRUCTORS (10), BOARDSAILING INSTRUCTORS (2). £64.00 per week with free B & L. Hours: 9.30am-5.30pm, 6 days per week. Possession of RYA Instructors' Certificate preferred, but good sailors who can train for certificate also considered. Overseas applicants with good English welcome. Min. period of work 3 weeks (longer period preferred) between April and the end of September. Applications from January onwards to the Sailing Master, Tighnabruaich Sailing School.

Language Schools

EDINBURGH SCHOOL OF ENGLISH: 271 Canongate, The Royal Mile, Edinburgh EH8 8BQ (tel 0131-557 9200; fax 0131-557 9192; e-mail: mail@e-dinschl.co.uk). Founded in 1969, ESE is a year round school. Courses are directed by permanent staff, and have the back up of a permanent organisation. Arranges English language summer courses for school children (9-17 years) in Aberdeen, Edinburgh, Dundee and Strathallan.
ACTIVITY LEADERS to be responsible for the smooth running of the afternoon, evening and weekend leisure programme. The job involves taking students on various cultural visits and organising and supervising sports. One leader is employed for every 10 students. Some leaders are required to live and supervise in halls of residence in addition to the above. Hours by arrangement. B & L available for a few applicants only. Courses are run between mid-June and early September, and also during April. Min. period of work 3 weeks.
  Applicants should be aged over 21, with a sound knowledge of one of the above locations. They should be enthusiastic and energetic, have good organisational abilities, get on well with teenagers and be interested in sports and cultural visits. Fluent English speakers only. Applications to The Principal at the above address.

Vacation Traineeships

Science, Construction and Engineering

GEC MARINE YARROW: South Street, Scotstoun, Glasgow G14 0XN (tel 0141-957 4257; 0141-957 4114).
Offers opportunities to approx. 10 students to undertake various projects within the Operations, Technical, Projects and Service departments. Applicants should be university students studying Electronic Engineering, Mechanical Engineering, Naval Architecture, Engineering with Management or Business, Manufacturing and Risk Management. Salary depends on year of study.

Placements occur in June-September at the Head Office in Glasgow. No accommodation is provided. Overseas applicants are considered, but security clearance may be a problem.

Applications by March/April to Sandra McConnell.

HONEYWELL CONTROL SYSTEMS LTD.: Newhouse Industrial Estate, Motherwell, Lanarkshire ML1 5SB.
Honeywell's design and manufacturing complex in central Scotland is involved in the development of a wide range of instrumentation and control products. The company's vacation training positions are mainly within their Research and Development and Industrial Engineering areas, and are open to students studying Electrical, Electronic and Mechanical Engineering, or Computer Science. Some vacancies also occur within their Data processing, Production and Central Services departments. Qualifications for openings in the Central Services would include subjects such as Business Studies and Marketing.

Applicants should be students at undergraduate or HND level who have usually completed two years of their course. Honeywell generally takes students from local Scottish universities, but students from other tertiary educational establishments will also be considered. Impressive students are often brought back for second or third vacation spells.

Placements are for the summer vacation period only. Wages will vary in accordance with the student's year of study.

Applications should be made by mid-February to the Human Resources Department at the above address.

Wales and Northern Ireland

Wales. Most of the seasonal jobs in Wales are to be found in hotels, restaurants and holiday centres. The towns offering the largest number of vacancies are Aberystwyth, Brecon, Cardiff, Llangollen, Llandudno, Newport, Porthcawl, Rhyl, Rogerstone, Swansea and Tenby. If you have some knowledge of riding, or are a good group leader, there are numerous riding schools and trekking centres in more remote locations; for those not local to Wales the advantage with this work is that accommodation will normally be provided. In the resort towns rented accommodation is limited and expensive.

Most Jobcentres, including those in Llandudno and Llangollen, advise jobhunters to contact them early. Local job ads appear in the *Brecon and Radnor Express*. The best paper for jobs around Llandudno is the *North Wales Weekly News* or the *Liverpool Daily Post*. Llandudno Jobcentre usually has a high number of vacancies for staff between April and September. In and around Llangollen, try the *Evening Leader* or the *Shropshire Star*. It is worth noting that there is very little chance of finding work with accommodation provided in the Llandudno area. In Tenby *The Tenby Observer* and *The Western Telegraph* are worth looking at while Swansea Jobcentre recommends the Workpost Job Feature which appears in Wednesday editions of *The South Wales Evening Post*.

Aberystwyth can offer a comparatively good supply of jobs — not only in pubs, hotels and restaurants, but at nearby holiday parks and caravan sites too. Rented accommodation in the town is limited since students from the local university take up most vacancies. The local *Cambrian News* carries job advertisements.

In South Wales, Newport Leisure Services usually advertises vacancies for its playscheme in March or April each year. While Newport may not have the appeal of Llangollen or Brecon, it is one of the few towns in Wales to have plenty of rentable accommodation.

Large manufacturing firms which may require temporary staff include Tetra Pak (who make cardboard milk and juice cartons) in Wrexham, the Driver and Vehicle Licensing Agency in Morriston, and R.F. Brookes in Rogerstone. Apply early to these firms and contact the necessary job centre to establish whether or not application forms will be available.

The Royal Welsh Show in Builth Wells in late July provides a number of jobs for a few weeks.

Northern Ireland. Unemployment has been particularly high in Northern Ireland for many years, and Irish students have often had to come to England and Wales to find summer work.

In and around Belfast most vacancies are in the retail, hotel and restaurant trade. Further afield hotel work is more plentiful in the lakeland areas of Co. Fermanagh and in seaside towns such as Portrush and Newcastle.

Students may register for seasonal work with private employment agencies or Training and Employment Agency offices which are located throughout Northern Ireland. Holiday job vacancies for specific areas are usually advertised in local newspapers, jobclubs and libraries.

Children

ACORN VENTURE LTD.: Acorn House, Worcester Road, Hagley, Stourbridge DY8 1AN. Established in 1932, the company runs multi-activity centres in North Wales and the Lake District which provide outdoor activity courses for schools and youth groups.
INSTRUCTORS. Must hold at least Instructor status with e.g. BCU or RYA, or have passed SPSA or MLTB assessment. Other nationally recognised coaching awards may be considered.
ASSISTANT INSTRUCTORS. Must be registered as training for the above award(s).
SUPPORT STAFF. Maintenance and/or catering. No experience necessary.
FULLY QUALIFIED NURSE.
Please note that all staff must be available from April/May to September: full period only. Application for further details with full c.v. only to the Personnel Department at the above address from 1 October onwards.

Holiday Centres and Amusements

ANGLESEY MUSEUMS SERVICE: c/o Anglesey Heritage Gallery, Rhosmeirch. Llangefni LL77 7TW (tel 01248-724444).
SEASONAL MUSEUMS ATTENDANTS to work in the museum shop, in ticketing and admissions, cleaning, security, guiding, customer care and stock control. Wages £4 per hour. To work from either Easter until the end of September or Whitsun until the end of September. All applicants must be available for the entire season. Min. age 18. Must speak Welsh fluently, and be a good communicator, organised and with an interest in museums and heritage.
Applications to the Heritage Education Officer at the above address before the end of February.

FIELD STUDIES COUNCIL: Dale Fort Field Centre, Dale, near Haverfordwest, Dyfed SA62 3RD (tel 01646-636205; fax 01646-636554). Provides environmental education for schools, universities and adult groups of all ages in the heart of the Pembrokeshire coast National Park.
DOMESTIC ASSISTANTS (4). £74 per week plus free B & L. To work 7am-12.30pm and 5-7.30pm, 5 days per week. Will have opportunity to be involved in the Centre's courses. Min. age 18. Should be interested in field studies and the environment. Required from February to November. Min. work period 3 months. Overseas applicants with a good level of English welcome. Applications a.s.a.p. to the Bursar, Dale Fort Field Centre.

GREENHILL YMCA NATIONAL CENTRE: Donard Park, Newcastle, Co Down, Northern Ireland BT33 0GR (tel 013967-23172; fax 013957-26009).
INSTRUCTORS (20). To work up to 3 sessions per day. Experience or qualifications in one of the following is required: mountaineering, canoeing, orienteering, archery, environmental studies or working with young people on day camps. Min. age 18 but persons over age 20 preferred. Staff will be responsible for children and young people, so vetting references as to suitability in this area will be required.
DRIVERS. Must be over 25 years old, reliable, safe and experienced in driving minibuses and towing trailers. An up to date clean driving licence will be required.
DOMESTIC HOSTS (5). Must be hard-working, sociable and responsible.
COOKS (3). Basic cooking and catering qualifications necessary.
All staff are given expenses of £18 a week plus free B & L. Hours variable, 5 days a week in most cases. Min. period of work 6 weeks. Instructors and day camp staff must attend a staff training programme from 25 June to 1 July. The summer camp period is from 3 July to 28 August. Greenhill is a Christian Centre; applicants should therefore be supportive of its Christian ethos and promotion of the same. Applicants must speak fluent English and supply photocopies of relevant qualifications. One year Instructor posts are also available for mature people who are active in the Christian faith. (September to August.)
Applications should be sent a.s.a.p. to the Volunteer Co-ordinator at the above address.

THE SMALLEST HOUSE IN GREAT BRITAIN: The Quay, Conway, North Wales LL32 8DE (tel 01492-593484; fax 01492-593484). One of Wales's main tourist attractions. Visitors come from all over the world, so staff are handpicked.
STAFF (4) to greet visitors and sell souvenirs. Wages £3 per hour. To work 2 hour shifts. No accommodation is available. Period of work between 31st March and 31st October. Applicants must be over 18, have attractive personality, the ability to speak at least one foreign language, and have knowledge of the local area. Staff must wear Welsh costume (which is provided).
Interview necessary. Applications from January 1st to Margaret Williams.

TRANS-WALES-TRAILS: Pengenfford, Talgarth, Brecon, Powys LD3 0EU (tel 01874-711398; fax 01874-711122; web site http://www.transwales.demon.co.uk). Based at a remote farm guesthouse in the black mountains of S.E. Wales: specialists in horse riding holidays for international adult visitors.
GENERAL DOMESTIC ASSISTANTS (2). £100 per week. To work approx.

40 hours a week, with 1 day off which may be carried forward. Free horse riding, and free B & L suitable for females only. Age: 18-25 years. Duties include helping in kitchen, bedmaking and cleaning. Assistants must be smart, responsible, of high moral standard and prepared to speak English clearly to foreign guests. Min. period of work 3 months between 1 April and 30 September. Overseas applicants with college-level English welcome. Applications during February and March to Mr and Mrs Michael Turner, Trans-Wales-Trails. Note: Only affirmative responses will be made.

Hotels and Catering

AMBASSADOR HOTEL: Grand Promenade, Llandudno, North Wales LL30 2NR (tel 01492-876886). A family run seafront hotel in the largest resort in Wales. Known for its unspoilt Victorian image, the hotel is close to Snowdonia National Park.
WAITERS/WAITRESSES (2). Wages by arrangement. Good conditions and hours. Free B & L. Must be over 17 years of age. Min. work period 2 months at any time of year. Applications to Mr D.T. Williams, Proprietor, Ambassador Hotel.

BLACK LION HOTEL: New Quay, Dyfed SA45 9PT (tel 01545-560209). GENERAL ASSISTANTS (4). Live-in. Flexible hours and adequate free time. Must be energetic and adaptable. Min. age 18. Min. period of work the summer vacation. Overseas applicants with good working knowledge of English welcome. Also vacancies at the Feathers Royal Hotel, Aberaeron. Applications (with photograph) to Mrs K. Hunter, Black Lion Hotel.

CHRISTIAN MOUNTAIN CENTRE — PENSARN HARBOUR: Pensarn Harbour,Llanbedr, Gwynedd LL45 2HS (tel/fax 01341-241646; e-mail CMCPensarn@aol.com).
HOUSE STAFF (4). £25-£75 per week plus full board and lodging. No qualifications necessary. To work 40 hours per week: min. period of work 3 weeks between March 1 and October 30. Applicants must speak English to the standard of that of a native speaker. The CMC is a Christian Centre and requires applicants who have a sympathy towards the faith. Note candidates must be available for interview. Apply from November onwards to Mr R. Mayhew at the above address.

COBDENS HOTEL: Capel Curig, Snowdonia National Park, North Wales LL24 0EE (tel 01690-720 243; fax 01690-720 354). Situated in the heart of Snowdonia, Cobdens is family owned and popular with climbers and walkers.
HOUSEKEEPING/BAR/WAITING STAFF (3). Good rate per hour plus free food and accommodation. To work 40 hours over five days per week. Experience preferred but personality more important.
KITCHEN STAFF. Must have a real interest in food.
Min. period of work 6 months. Staff required all year round. Work is hard and to a high standard, but good fun. Overseas applicants with a reasonable standard of English welcome. Applications any time to the General Manager at the above address.

COURT HOTEL: Lamphey, Pembroke, Pembrokeshire SA71 5NT (tel 01646-672273; fax 01646-672480).

GENERAL ASSISTANTS (2) £90-£140 a week.
BREAKFAST COOK (1). £90-£150 a week.
GARDENER (1). £90-£140 a week.
All staff work 5 days a week. B & L is available at £30 a week. Hotel experience helpful. Min. work period 4 weeks, between Easter and the end of September. Some full-time positions are also available. Overseas applicants welcome. Applications from February onwards to Mr or Mrs Lain, at The Court Hotel.

DUNADRY INN: 2 Islandreagh Drive, Dunadry, Co. Antrim, Northern Ireland (tel 018494-32474). Grade A country hotel set within 10 acres of beautiful grounds. Ideal for weddings, it is located 15 minutes drive from Belfast, close to the Internatiornal Airport.
WAITING STAFF (2). £120 per week including accommodation. To work split shifts (10am-2pm and 7-11.30pm) any 5 days per week. Work available from March/October. Some experience in silver service work required. Overseas applicants considered. Applications to Ms Deirdre McDermott at the above address.

GRANGE TREKKING CENTRE: The Grange, Capel-y-ffin, Abergavenny, Gwent NP7 7NP (tel 01873-890215). A small, informal family run centre.
ACCOMMODATION WORKER/ASSISTANT to perform cleaning, waiting, cooking, gardening and customer care duties. Wages and hours negotiable, with free accommodation in a caravan with shower block. Min. period of work 1 month between Easter and October. Overseas applicants with good English welcome; note that all candidates must be available for interview. Contact Jessica Griffiths from February onwards at the above address.

LION HOTEL: Y Maes, Criccieth, Gwynned LL52 0AA (tel 01766-522460; fax 01766-523075). A friendly, family-run hotel in seaside town.
RESTAURANT/BAR STAFF (2), BEDROOM ASSISTANTS (1). £3.20 per hour. To work 39 hours a week over 6 days. Qualifications and experience not necessary. Clean accommodation is available, at a price to be negotiated. Min. period of work 3 months between April/ May and end September/October. Work also available at Christmas and New Year. Applications from 1 March to Mrs S.A. Burnett, Manageress, at the above address.

MARINER'S INN: Nolton Haven, Haverfordwest, Pembrokeshire, Dyfed SA62 3NH (tel 01437-710469). A friendly residential inn, set beside the sea.
BAR STAFF (2), WAITING STAFF (3), GENERAL ASSISTANT (1). To work 10am-2pm and 4.30-11pm, split shifts.
CHAMBER STAFF (1). To work 10am-2pm, split shifts.
Wages from £3.00 per hour. Overtime is available. Min. age 18. Min. period of work 3 months from June to September. B & L is sometimes available. Overseas applicants welcome. Applications from Easter to Mr C. Quinlan at the Mariner's Inn.

METROPOLE HOTEL: Temple Street, LLandrindod Wells, Powys LD1 5DY (tel 01597-823700; fax 01579-824828). Family owned and a member of the Best Western group, The Metropole is a three star hotel with 121 bedrooms and extensive conference and banqueting facilities.
WAITING STAFF (6). £3.20 per hour (if over 18).
COMMIS CHEF (4). £3.20 per hour (if over 18).

All staff to work 5 days per week plus overtime if necessary. Accommodation available at a cost of £25.00 per week. Min. age 16 years. Min. period of work 6 months; staff required all year round. Overseas applicants welcome. All applicants must be available for interview. Applications any time to Miss Gayle Jackson, Assistant Manager, at the above address.

MIN-Y-DON HOTEL: North Parade, Llandudno LL30 2LP (tel 01492-876511; fax 01492-878169). Located on the north shore seafront, opposite the famous Victorian pier.
ROOM ASSISTANTS (2), HOTEL ASSISTANTS (2), DINING ROOM ASSISTANTS (2) to work from June to October. Wages and hours by arrangement. Accommodation is available. Applicants should be under 21. Overseas applicants welcome. Applications to the Manager at the above address.

THE OYSTERCATCHER: Terra Nova Way, Penarth, South Glamorgan CF64 1SB (tel 01222-709836; fax 01222-708615).
BAR STAFF (2), WAITING STAFF (2), GENERAL ASSISTANTS (2) and KITCHEN STAFF (2). £140 per week plus board and lodging. To work 40 hours per week between April and September. Min. period of work 3 months. Overseas applicants with valid working permits welcome. No qualifications necessary. Apply from March 1 to Rob Waldram at the above address.

PORTH TOCYN HOTEL: Abersoch, Gwynedd LL53 7BU (tel 01758-713303). A country house hotel by the sea filled with antiques. The house has been in the family for 50 years, and has been in the Good Food Guide for over 40 years.
GENERAL ASSISTANTS (10), ASSISTANT COOKS (4). Wages in accordance with the new minimum wage, or better. To work a 4½-day week in split shifts. Free B & L and use of tennis court and swimming pool. Intelligence and sense of humour required. Cooking experience useful but not essential. Min. period of work 6 weeks between Easter and November. Applications with s.a.e. to Mrs Fletcher-Brewer, Porth Tocyn Hotel.

ROYAL GATE HOUSE HOTEL: North Beach, Tenby, Pembrokeshire SA70 7ET (tel 01834-842255; fax 01834-842441). Family run hotel with superb views of Tenby harbour and Carmarthen.
WAITING STAFF (3). To work 6 days a week. Shifts 7.30-10.30am and 6-10pm, plus some lunchtimes (noon-2pm). Min. age 18. Silver service experience preferred, but not essential.
CHAMBER STAFF (4). To work 8am-1pm, 6 days a week. Min. age 18. Experience preferred.
BAR PERSON (1). To work shifts of 10.30am-3pm, and 6-11pm, 6 days a week. Also shifts of 11am-7pm and 7pm until closing in the residents' bar. Min. age 18. Experience essential.
Wages by arrangement. Some accommodation is available. Period of work May/June onwards. Applications to Mr G.T.R. Fry at the above address.

ST BRIDES HOTEL: St Brides Hill, Saundersfoot, Pembrokeshire SA69 9NH (tel 01834-812304; fax 01834-813303). A privately owned three star hotel set on a clifftop overlooking a harbour and beaches. Located in National park, ideal for visiting castles, sports and recreation facilities. 3 miles from Tenby, and 4 miles from Pembroke.

WAITING STAFF (2) to serve in hotel restaurant. £400 per month. Some previous experience essential.
ROOM MAID (1) to service and clean bedrooms, and assist in kitchen cleaning. £400 per month. No experience necessary.
All staff to work 38 hours over 6 days a week. Min. period of work 3 months from April to September. Free B & L available. Applications from 1 March to M.J. Whitehead, Manager, at the above address.

TYN-Y-COED HOTEL: Capel Curig, Betws-y-Coed, Gwynedd (tel 01690-720331). A small friendly hotel in the centre of Snowdonia, which caters mainly for mountain users and tourists.
GENERAL ASSISTANTS (4). £3.60 per hour for approx. 40 hours a week. To work 5 days per week on split shifts. Full board accomodation available at £50 per week. Min. age 18. Applications to G.F. Wainwright, Tyn-y-Coed Hotel.

Outdoor

JOHN BROWNLEE: Knockmakagan, Newtownbutler, Co. Fermanagh, Northern Ireland (tel 01365-738277/01365-738275(home)).
FRUIT PICKERS (4-6). Wages at piece work rates. Free accommodation at farm. Period of work September and October. Overseas applicants welcome. Applications to Mr John Brownlee at the above address.

DAVISON CANNERS LTD: Ardress, Portadown, Co.Armagh, Northern Ireland (tel 01762-851661; fax 01762-852288; web site info@davisonfreshfood-.demon.co.uk). Harvests and processes fruit for retail, catering and bakery markets, mainly in the UK and Ireland.
FRUIT PICKERS. Wages at piece work rates. To work five to six days a week for approximately six weeks from September until the end of October.
FACTORY WORKERS. To can fruit. Positions are available year round.
Accommodation is available. Applications to Mr Ronnie Davison at the above address.

Sport

ARTHOG OUTDOOR EDUCATION CENTRE: Arthog, Gwynned LL39 1BX (tel 01341-250455). A Local Education Authority run centre situated below mountains, about 1km from the sea. Fully staffed by 7 professional instructors, it takes up to 90 clients.
OUTDOOR INSTRUCTORS. Activities include mountaineering, canoeing, sailing, walking etc. Wages according to qualifications. RYA, ML, or BCU qualifications useful, teaching certificate a bonus. Interested applicants without qualifications may be taken on, but on a voluntary basis. Work equivalent to 5 days a week, but long hours. Free B & L provided. Overseas applicants considered. Applications to the above address.

CANTREF TREKKING CENTRE: Brecon, Powys LD3 8LR (tel 01874-665223).
PONY TREKKING GUIDES (2). Wages on application. B & L available. Hours according to length of treks, with possibility of overtime. To work 6 days a week. Min. age 18. Pony Club B or BHS Stage 1, also Riding & Road Safety qualifications essential. Must be experienced rider and able to get along well

with people. Period of work 1 June or 1 July to 1 September. Applicants must be prepared to work the specified length of time. Interview essential. Applications, enclosing s.a.e., from March to M. Evans, Cantref Pony Trekking Centre.

CHRISTIAN MOUNTAIN CENTRE: Rensarn Harbour, Llanbedr, Gwynedd LL45 2HS (tel/fax 01766 512616).
INSTRUCTORS (2). £25-£70 per week plus full board and accommodation. Must have the following qualifications: SPSA, ML, BCU level 2 coach and a full driving licence. To work 40 hours per week: min. period of work 3 months between March 1 and October 30. Overseas students with a high standard of English welcome. The CMC is a Christian Centre and requires applicants who have a sympathy towards the faith. Note that an interview is necessary. Apply from November onwards to Mr R. Mayhew at the above address.

CLYNE FARM CENTRE: Westport Avenue, Mayals, Swansea SA3 5AR (tel 01792-403333; fax 01792-403339).
ACTIVITY AND HORSE RIDING INSTRUCTORS. Wages negotiable. To work 40 hours a week. Min. age 18. Min. period of work 4 weeks from June to September. Accommodation may be available, charge to be negotiated. Overseas applicants with good spoken English and eligible to work in the UK welcome. All applicants must be available for interview. Applications from January to the Manager at the above address.

COPLEY STABLES: Bishopston, Swansea SA3 3JA (tel 01792-234428).
STABLE ASSISTANTS/GROOM (2). Wages negotiable, but includes training opportunities. To work 5 days a week. Experience is essential. Period of work May to September, min. period the month of August. Accommodation is not available. You may be required to attend an interview. Applications from April to Wendy Hemns-Tucker at the above address.

EAST TARR FARM AND RIDING STABLES: St Florence, Tenby, Pembrokeshire SA70 8ND (tel 01834-871274). Modern mixed farm incorporating riding and trekking centre, located 2½ miles from the seaside resort of Tenby.
GROOMS (2). To work 6 hours a day, with Saturdays free. Must be able to ride to a reasonable standard and have enough experience to take charge of rides and treks. B & L provided.
Min. age 17 years. Must be cheerful and willing to work hard. Overseas applicants welcome. Min. period of work 2 or 3 months between April and October. Applications with references should be sent to Mrs H.E. Williams, East Tarr Farm.

GRANGE TREKKING CENTRE: The Grange, Capel-y-ffin, Abergavenny, Gwent NP7 7NP (tel 01873-890215). A small, informal family run centre.
TREK LEADER and ASSISTANT LEADER for a variety of work including mucking out, trek leading, tack cleaning, maintenance and dealing with customers. Some training available. Salary and hours negotiable. Free accommodation in caravan with shower block. Must be over 18 years old with first aid qualifications.
Min. period of work 1 month between Easter and October. Overseas applicants with good English welcome. Note that all candidates must be

available for interview. Apply from February onwards to Jessica Griffiths at the above address.

HIGH TREK SNOWDONIA: Tal y Waen, Deiniolen, Caernarvon, Gwynedd LL55 3NA (tel/fax 01286-871232). A small company which offers guided walking holidays in Snowdonia.
TREK ASSISTANT (1). £60 a week with free B & L. To work 5 days a week including some evenings. Duties include help with driving, group leading, domestic chores, etc. Applicants should be over 21, have a full driving licence, mountain leadership training and First Aid certificate. Must be very fit and have a strong interest in the outdoors and countryside. Should also have a flexible nature and be able to do anything from paper work to portering loads. Overseas applicants who fulfil these criteria will be considered.
    Min. period of work 6 weeks between Easter and October. Priority is given to those able to work the whole season. Applicants must be available for interview. Applications should be sent as early as possible to Mrs Mandy Whitehead, at the above address.

LAKELAND CANOE CENTRE: Castle Island, Enniskillin, Northern Ireland BT74 5HH (tel 01365-324250; fax 01365-323319). An outdoor activity centre with activities including canoeing, sailing and mountain biking.
ASSISTANT INSTRUCTOR (2), KITCHEN HELPER (1). Minimum period of work 1 week from March to October. Board and accommodation provided free of charge. Minimum age 18. Applicants must be interested in young people. Applications from February, enclosing a photo, to Gary Mitten, Director, at the above address.

MOUNTAIN VENTURES LTD: Bryn Du, Ty Du Road, Llanberis, Gwynedd LL55 4HD (tel 01286-870454). Outdoor pursuits centre and water sports and activity centre. Provides residential packages for groups, including kayak and canoe paddling, rock climbing, abseiling and mountain walking from centres in the Snowdonia National Park.
Mountain Ventures offers work opportunities for instructors to people who have appropriate qualifications and experience. There are also opportunities for assistant staff to take on work of a general nature, helping instructors and domestic staff in exchange for accommodation, food, some payment and the opportunity for some training in Snowdonia National Park during June and July, together with a group of other young people. Applications to the above address.

PGL TRAVEL: Alton Court, Penyard Lane (874), Ross-on-Wye, Herefordshire HR9 5NR (tel 01989-767833). Over 300 staff needed to assist in the running of children's activity centres in the Brecon beacons and Black Mountains. Europe's largest provider of adventure holidays for children has offered outstanding training and work opportunities to seasonal staff for over 40 years.
QUALIFIED INSTRUCTORS in canoeing, sailing, windsurfing, pony trekking, hill walking, fencing, archery, judo, rifle shooting, fishing, motorsports, arts and crafts, drama, English language and many other activities. Min. age 18.
GROUP LEADERS to take responsibility for small groups of children and ensure that they get the most out of their holiday. Min. age 20. Previous experience of working with children necessary.

Pocket money from £36-70 per week plus full B & L. Vacancies available for short or long periods between February and October. Overseas applicants eligible to work in the UK welcome. Requests for application forms to the Personnel Department at the above address.

RHIWIAU RIDING CENTRE: Llanfairfechan, North Wales LL33 OEH (tel 01248-680094; fax 01248-681143).
INSTRUCTOR/RIDE LEADER to work from 7.30am-5.30pm, 5½ days per week. Wages of £60 per week with full board provided. Must be aged over 18 and have either a BHS Preliminary Teaching or BET qualification.
ASSISTANTS to give general help in the house and organise evening activities. Wages £50 per week plus full board. To work from 8.15-10.15am, 12.30-1.30pm and 6-9.30pm, 6 days per week.
Period of work from June to September. Applications to Ruth Hill, Proprietor at the above address.

SHARE HOLIDAY VILLAGE: Smiths Strand, Lisnaskea, Co. Fermanagh, BT92 OEQ (tel 013657-22122; fax 013657-21893; e-mail share@dnet.co.uk). The largest activity centre in Northern Ireland. A charity dedicated to providing opportunities for able bodied and disabled people to take part in a wide range of activities together. A team of 25-30 paid staff and volunteers works with families, individuals and groups of all ages.
OUTDOOR ACTIVITY INSTRUCTORS (6) to work 5 days plus one night a week. Applicants must be aged over 18 and have one of the following qualifications; RYA dinghy sailing; BCV canoe or kayak instructor plus current first aid certificate; or RYA rowboat handling level II.
SOCIAL PROGRAMME ACTIVITY LEADERS (2) to plan and run a programme of social activities including arts, drama, singing, storytelling, folk dancing etc. To work 5 days a week. Must love working with people and have plenty of different skills in arts, drama and dance.
Wages £50-£100 per week depending on qualifications plus meals and accommodation. To work from early May to the end of September/early October.
Applications to Dawn Latimer, Director at the above address.

TAL Y FOEL RIDING CENTRE: Dwyran, Anglesey LL61 6LQ (tel 01248-430977).A friendly BHS approved centre on the shores of the Menai Straits. Facilities include outdoor menage, cross country training course, four miles of grass tracks, liveries, lessons and treks. Best Small Tourism Business in Wales 1998.
YARD STAFF/RIDE LEADERS (4). £50 per week plus free accommodation in a caravan. To work 6 days a week from June to August; min. period of work 8 weeks. Must be qualified in riding and stable management. Overseas applicants who are available to attend an interview welcome. Apply from Jan to Dr Judy Hutchings or Miss Kayte Lloyd Hughes at the above address.

TYN-MORFA RIDING CENTRE: Rhosneigr, Anglesey LL64 5QX (tel 01407-810279). Rhosneigr is on the west coast of Anglesey, enabling rides to occur on the beaches.
TREK LEADERS or ASSISTANTS (2) to escort rides on the beach. Wages negotiable, according to age and experience. Hours: 8am-5pm, 6 days per week. Free B & L in caravan. Applicants should be aged 18 + , be able to ride well and be responsible enough to take charge of rides. Season begins mid-

May. Applications from 1 May to Mr A.J. Carnall, Tyn-Morfa Riding Centre.

Language Schools

ENGLISH STUDY CENTRE: 19-21 Uplands Crescent, Swansea, West Glamorgan SA2 0NX (tel 01792-464103; fax 01792-472303).
EFL TEACHERS (3-4) to teach adults or junior groups. £11-£12.50 per hour. 15 to 30 hours per week. No accommodation provided. Must be graduates with TEFL qualifications and/or experience. Min. period of work three weeks between the beginning of June and the end of August. Where possible it is preferred that applicants are available for interview. Applications from March to Esther Richards, Principal, at the above address.

UNIVERSITY OF WALES ABERYSTWYTH: Language and Learning Centre, Llandinam Building, Penglais Campus, Aberystwyth SY23 3DB (tel 01970-622545; fax 01970-622546; e-mail: language+learning@aber.ac.uk). Attractive working environment in a peaceful seaside location between the coast of Cardigan Bay and the Cambrian Mountains. The centre offers courses to language learners and language teachers in a warm and welcoming academic environment.
LANGUAGE TUTORS (6-10). £300+ per week. 19 hours teaching per week, plus 16 hours social duties per month and 12 hours administration per month. Min. period of work one month between mid July and early September. B & L available at approx. £8 per day. Applicants must speak English to the standard of someone whose first language it is. First degree, TEFL qualifications and 3 years experience required. Interview necessary. Applications from January 1 to Rex Berridge, Director, at the above address.

Vacation Traineeships

Science, Construction and Engineering

DAVIES, MIDDLETON & DAVIES LTD: Phoenix Estate, Caerphilly Road, Cardiff CF4 4XH (tel 01222-623317; fax 01222-617575).
Davies, Middleton & Davies is a firm of civil engineering and building contractors. The company is offering one or two traineeships in the Easter and summer vacations. Students will act as assistants to site engineers setting out construction projects in South Wales and the South West.

Applicants should be studying, or preparing to study, for an Engineering degree. Suitably qualified students from abroad are welcome to apply. Efforts will be made to locate trainees near their homes, but where this is not possible assistance will be given in finding accommodation. Wages are negotiable.

Interested students should write to Mr C.H. Morris, Chief Engineer, at any time of the year at the above address.

VOLUNTARY WORK

Archaeology

ARBEIA ROMAN FORT: Tyne & Wear Museums Service, Baring Street, South Shields, Tyne & Wear NE33 2BB (tel 0191-454 4093; fax 0191-427 6862; e-mail liz.elliott@tyne-wear-museums.org.uk). South Shields has good parks and beaches and is an ideal base from which to visit nearby cities or countryside.
VOLUNTEERS (10 per week) to excavate the site, record and process finds, draw the site and take photographs. To work from 8.45am-4.45pm, Monday-Friday. Volunteers are responsible for their own travel, board and other costs. Needed from January to December 23. Min age 16; disabled people may find access to the site difficult. Applications to Elizabeth Elliott, Office Manager, at the above address.

COUNCIL FOR BRITISH ARCHAEOLOGY: Bowes Morrell House, 111 Walmgate, York YO1 9WA (tel 01904-671417; fax 01904-671384). The CBA works to promote the study and safeguarding of Britain's historic environment, to provide a forum for archaeological opinion, and to improve public interest in, and knowledge of, Britain's past.
Details of excavations and other fieldwork projects are given in the Council's publication *CBA Briefing*, a supplement to the magazine *British Archaeology*. The magazine appears ten times a year and is accompanied by *Briefing* every other issue (in March, May, July, September and November). An annual subscription costs £19; however, it also forms part of an individual membership package which is available for £20 per year and brings extra benefits. Having studied *Briefing,* you should apply to the director of the projects which interest you. The min. age for many projects is usually 16.

SEDGEFORD HISTORICAL AND ARCHAEOLOGICAL RESEARCH PROJECT: Hill Farm, Church Lane, Sedgeford, Hunstanton, Norfolk PE36 5NA. A long-term investigation into the origins of the English village which dates from Middle-Saxon times.
ARCHAEOLOGICAL & HISTORICAL FIELDWORKERS (75) wanted from mid July to late August. Subsistence charge of approx. £80 per week. Hours 8.30am-5pm, 6 days a week with Saturdays off. It is recommended that students come for a minimum of two weeks. No professional qualifications needed. Applications to Pauline Thinkettle at Orchard House, Ringstead Road, Sedgeford, Norfolk PE36 5NQ.

Children

BIRMINGHAM PHAB CAMPS: c/o Tony Gray, 52 Green Lanes, Sutton Coldfield, West Midlands B73 5JW (tel 0121 382 7218). Established in 1967, PHAB camps is a charity run by volunteers, so administrative costs consume less than 1% of funds. 200 children take part each summer.
VOLUNTEERS (16+) to take groups of disabled children, or mixed groups of disabled and able-bodied children, aged 6-17 for one-week holidays between end of July and end of August. No pocket money, but board and lodging provided; volunteers will need to get to Birmingham to meet the coach. Must be able to work, play with, care for, and entertain the children; many children need feeding and changing, but the holidays are fun. Volunteers who are qualified nurses or able to drive mini-buses especially welcome. Applications to Tony Gray, Volunteer Organiser, at the above address.

BRIXTON VISITORS CHILDRENS PLAY AREA: H.M.P. Brixton, P.O. Box 369, Jebb Avenue, London SW2 5XF.
VOLUNTEER CRECHE WORKERS required from Monday-Saturday, 2pm-4pm; each volunteer must work at least two sessions per month. No wages are paid but £3.40 travelling expenses per session are provided. Childcare qualifications such as: PPA, NNEB, BTec, etc. desirable but more important is experience of working with children informally. Minimum age 21. Help is needed around the year. All applicants will be subject to security clearance which is the normal procedure for those working with children or within the Home Office.
    Written applications only, as soon as possible to Annetta Bennett, Volunteer Co-ordinator, at the above address.

B.Y.V.ASSOCIATION LTD: 4th Floor, Smithfield House, Digbeth, Birmingham B5 6BS (tel 0121-622-2888). Volunteers act as key-workers with 2 or 3 children during the week. Children are from disadvantaged backgrounds and greatly benefit from the positive contact.
VOLUNTEERS (120) needed to accompany children on week long summer breaks, either residential or camping, in Wales and the Midlands. No qualifications are necessary as training is available, but an interest and experience of work with children and young people is advantageous. All volunteers are police-checked. No wages are given, but all expenses on the camp are met. Camps take place in the school summer holidays; approx. July 20 to September 5. Commitment is required 24 hours a day for the length of the camp.
    Birmingham and Midlands based volunteers are particularly encouraged to apply. Apply from January to the BYV Co-ordinator at the above address.

CHILDREN'S COUNTRY HOLIDAYS FUND (CCHF): 42/43 Lower Marsh, London SE1 7RG (tel 0171-928 6522; fax 0171-401 3961).
CCHF is a registered Charity which has been providing holidays for children from disadvantaged London homes since 1884. One of the aspects of CCHF's work is to run residential summer camps. These camps provide a variety and balance of activities designed to meet the needs of all the children on them. Volunteers needed during the school summer holidays to work as Camp Supervisors, looking after small groups of children (aged 8-12) under the guidance of an experienced Camp Leader.
    Ages 18 upwards. Relevant experience desirable although full training will

be given. Supervisors are responsible for the care and welfare of children in their group for the duration of the camp. A camp lasts for 9 days, on a variety of dates in July and August and are held in residential centres in the south of England. Accommodation, board, insurance, travel and pocket money are provided.To ensure the safety of the children, applicants must have been residents of England or Wales for five years to enable Home Office checks to be made of them. Apply by May at latest.

THE CHILDREN'S TRUST: Tadworth Court, Tadworth, Surrey KT20 5RU (tel 01737-357171; fax 01737-373848). Offers care, treatment, and education to approx. 80 children with exceptional needs and profound disabilities, and gives support to their families.

The Trust requires volunteers to work on residential summer scheme for profoundly disabled and exceptional needs children, who normally live at home. The services are provided in a children's hospital and at a residential school. The work involves acting as a friend to the children, carrying out basic personal care, organising games, encouraging them to take an active part in daily activities, escorting them on outings and organising evening activities.

Previous experience with children or handicapped children is preferable, but not essential. Only those wishing to go into the caring profession should apply. Creative skills, handicraft or musical ability welcomed. The work is very rewarding but is also physically and emotionally tiring. 15 volunteers are appointed each year. Minimum age 18. To work a $37\frac{1}{2}$ hour week with 2 days off per week. Mid July to first week in September. Students are expected to stay for the duration of the scheme. Accommodation is provided free of charge and an allowance of £49 per week is paid. Travel expenses from mainland England will be paid. Apply before 31 March to Rachel Turner at the above address.

The Residential School also requires volunteers for 6 to 12 months to assist with the daily routine of physical care and education of the children in both the residential home and school. Under the guidance of teachers, therapists and senior care staff, work as part of an interdisciplinary team on the individual planned programmes for the children. Minimum age 18, to work a $37\frac{1}{2}$ hour week, 2 days off per week. Lodging and meal allowance of £51 per week. Travel expenses within England can be reimbursed. Apply to Rachel Turner, Voluntary Services Organiser.

CLAN: 3 Hiplands Road, Halesowen, West Midlands B62 0BH.

CLAN provides short holidays for children aged 7-13 who would not normally benefit from a change in their daily environment. Five outdoor activity day holidays are held during July and August at centres in the Midlands.

Volunteers interested in assisting on a holiday should apply from January to the above address enclosing a long s.a.e. Experience of working with children an advantage, but enthusiasm and reliability are more important. Minimum age 16. UK residents only. Travelling expenses paid.

COTSWOLD COMMUNITY: Ashton Keynes, nr Swindon, Wiltshire SN6 6QU (tel 01285-861239). A rural, therapeutic community providing long-term care, treatment and education for severely emotionally disturbed and abused boys, aged 9-18. The community consists of four separate households (10 boys each), a school, and a farm which, together with staff accommodation, creates a therapeutic village.   Volunteers are needed throughout the year for periods of 6 months. Free B & L provided plus £23.50 a week. Volunteers must work

5 very full days a week. Min. age 20. Some previous childcare experience helpful. Excellent training and support for staff. EEA applicants welcome. For further information contact Mr John Whitwell, Principal, Cotswold Community.

MANSFIELD OUTDOOR CENTRE: Manor Road, Lambourne End, Essex RM4 1ND (tel 0181-500 3047; fax 0181-559 8481).
Mansfield Outdoor Centre is situated in 60 acres of open country. As well as organising leisure activities, it aims to encourage social interaction amongst the young, disabled and disadvantaged within a Christian framework.
Helpers are needed to work 37½ hours/5 days per week, including some weekends. Experience of outdoor activities, such as climbing, canoeing, archery, farmwork, etc. required, as well as experience of working with young people. Travel and expenses to be discussed, and free B & L is sometimes available. Activity and youth work training will be given. Volunteers required for new 'Summer Work Camp' during June, July and August. Applicants must be available for interview. Applications a.s.a.p. to Peter Newton, at the above address.

NATIONAL ASTHMA CAMPAIGN/NATIONAL ECZEMA SOCIETY: Providence House, Providence Place, London N1 ONT (tel 0171-226 2260, ext. 316; fax 0171-704 0740; e-mailmfantom@aol.com). Runs PEAK (Project for Eczema and Asthma Kids)
VOLUNTEER HELPERS, DOCTORS and NURSES to work with children and young people with asthma and eczema on five one-week adventure and activity holidays in July and August. The young people are aged aged 6-9, 10-13, 14-17 and 18-30 and the camps take place in Edinburgh, the Lake District, Buckinghamshire, Nottinghamshire and Northamptonshire.
Board and accommodation are provided; those accepted must take part in a training weekend, with travel and board paid. Applicants must be aged at least 18 and are expected to stay for the duration of a camp; relevant medical or sporting and childcare experience are essential. Volunteers will also be needed for a camp next Easter.
Applications should be sent to Michael Fantom at the above address.

ONLY CONNECT: Cambridge House, 131 Camberwell Road, London SE5 7JZ (tel 0171-701 0769; fax 0171-703 2903). A charity which runs services for people with learning disabilities in the London borough of Southwark.
VOLUNTEER SUPPORT/PLAY WORKERS (40) needed to work from 7.45am to 3.45pm. No experience is necessary but volunteers must be over 16. The work is unpaid but travel expenses in London will be met. Work is available from July 28th to August 30th; minimum period of work three weeks. Accommodation is not available.
Applications from June 5th to the Play and Respite Care Manager at the above address. All applicants must be available for an interview. For details of further opportunities with Only Connect see the entry in the London and Home Counties chapter.

SCRIPTURE UNION: 207-209 Queensway, Bletchley, Milton Keynes, Bucks MK2 2EB (tel 01908-856000; fax 01908-856111; e-mail holidays@scripture-union. org.uk; web site http://www.scripture.org.uk).
VOLUNTEERS to help as team members on Scripture Union residential holidays around the UK lasting 7-10 days for young people aged from 8-18 + .

Volunteers are expected to be on site 24 hours a day to help organise activities during the holiday as part of a team; training is given before the beginning of the holiday.

Volunteers pay for their own accommodation and meals, but a Volunteer Grant Fund may assist with some of the costs. Minimum period of work one week. Applicants must be committed Christians in sympathy with the aims of the Scripture Union and aged over 18; there are particular needs for people with qualifications in catering, first aid, life-saving, sports, mountaineering and working with disabled people. Applications should be sent to the Holidays Administrator at the above address.

STANLEY YOUTH CENTRE SUMMER PLAYSCHEME AND WORK CAMP: Stanley, Co. Durham.
VOLUNTEERS (30) needed to help at a summer activity centre for 130 children aged 5-12 years. Activities include arts and crafts, music and dance, drama, sports, games and environmental activities.

Volunteers must be able to work as a member of a team looking after a group of up to 30 children. Workers must be able to provide a daily programme within the advice/guidelines provided by staff at the centre. Volunteers must wish to work with children; musical, artistic and sporting abilities are welcome, but not essential. Full time staff are qualified to provide deaf and disability support.

Workcamp takes place from July 17-August 2/3. Min. age 18; accommodation provided free of charge. Applications to the Co-ordinator, Youth Action for Peace, Methold House, North Street, Worthing, BN11 1DU (tel/fax 01903-528619).

Conservation and the Environment

BTCV (BRITISH TRUST FOR CONSERVATION VOLUNTEERS): 36 St. Mary's Street, Wallingford, Oxfordshire OX10 0EU (tel 01491-839766; brochure line 01491-824602).
Volunteers aged 16 upwards are wanted to take part in over 500 conservation working holidays in the UK and overseas. These usually last one week or a weekend and take place all year round. Projects include: helping to uncover an 18th century water cascade in Gloucestershire, creating a new habitat for the natterjack toad on the sand dunes of the Sefton Coast and reviving the ancient craft of willow wattling in Herefordshire.

No previous experience in conservation work is needed. Prices start at £17 for a weekend and £35 for a week to cover food, accommodation and training in conservation skills. On a typical day, volunteers work from 9am-5pm with evenings free and a day off during the week. Accommodation ranges from village halls to volunteer centres, cottages etc.

For further information contact the above address.

BRITISH TRUST FOR ORNITHOLOGY (BTO): The National Centre for Ornithology, The Nunnery, Thetford, Norfolk IP24 2PU (tel 01842-750050; fax 01842-750030).
The BTO promotes and encourage the wider understanding, appreciation and conservation of birds through scientific studies using the combined skills and enthusiasm of its members, other birdwatchers and staff. In pusuit of these aims, the Trust seeks to maintain high scientific and professional activities in all

its activities; co-operate with others engaged in relevant research; work constructively with those whose activities impinge upon the conservation of birds and their environment; ensure that its projects widen participants' experience, knowledge and understanding of birds and their environment.

BTO itself does not normally offer paid vacation work but does sometimes take on a limited number of volunteers for work at Thetford. For further details contact the Director of Services at the above address.

CATHEDRAL CAMPS: 16 Glebe Avenue, Flitwick, Bedfordshire MK45 1HS (tel 01525-716237). Registered Charity No. 286248.

VOLUNTEERS required to work in groups of 15-25 people undertaking maintenance, conservation and restoration of cathedrals and their surroundings all over the country. Hours normally 8.30am-5.30pm, 4½ days a week. The one-week camps take place from July to September. A contribution of approx. £45 is asked to go towards the cost of the camp and board and lodging. Min. age 16, most are aged 17-25. For further details and an application form contact Shelley Bent at the above address.

CONSERVATION VOLUNTEERS NORTHERN IRELAND: 159 Ravenhill Road, Belfast, Northern Ireland BT6 0BP (tel 01232-645169; fax 01232-644409; e-mail: CVNI@BTCV.org.uk).

VOLUNTEERS to participate in practical conservation work throughout Northern Ireland. This includes tree planting, dry stone walling, path creation, river clearance etc. A number of week-long working holidays and weekend breaks are organised throughout the year or for those who wish to become Volunteer Officers, a commitment of at least six months is requested; types of positions available are: weekday officer, education officer, publicity officer, local groups officer, and tree nursery officer.

To work 6 hours a day. No experience is necessary. Minimum age 18. Board and accommodation provided for working holiday volunteers at a cost of £42-£82 a week; limited amount of free accommodation for volunteer officers. Applications for working holidays to Maddy Kelly, and for volunteers and Volunteer Officers to Billy Belshaw, at the above address, at any time of the year.

CORAL CAY CONSERVATION LTD: 154 Clapham Park Road, London SW4 7DE (tel 0171-498 6248; fax 0171-498 8447; www.coralcay.org). Recruits paying volunteers to help alleviate poverty through research, education, training and alternative livelihood programmmes worldwide.

ASSISTANT SCIENCE CO-ORDINATORS are required to assist with management, analysis and synthesis of scientific data collected from coral reef and tropical forest conservation expeditions to the Caribbean and Southeast Asia.

FUND-RAISERS are required to assist with fund-raising campaigns on behalf of the Coral Cay Conservation Trust, a UK-registered charity which supports conservation education and training projects in developing countries.

ADMINISTRATION ASSISTANTS are required to help manage Volunteer recruitment campaigns.

The above are needed to work for Coral Cay Conservation (CCC), a non-profit organisation established in 1986 to provide support for the conservation and sustainable use of coastal and marine resources. CCC maintains full-time expedition projects in Belize, the Philippines and Indonesia.

To work 8 hours a day, 5 days a week at CCC's London offices. Work is available all year round. Board and lodging is not provided, but travel and subsistence costs are included. The jobs are essentially voluntary but in some cases a basic wage can be negotiated. Volunteers are provided with full training- no previous experience is required. Applications at any time to Peter Raines at the above address.

THE CRAFT CENTRE: St George's Island, Looe, Cornwall PL13 2AB (tel 0836-522919).
The privately-owned St George's Island, located one mile off the South Cornish coast, is open to visitors as a non-profitmaking project. Only 1 boat is allowed to bring visitors to the island at half hourly intervals, so that all visitors are met by the owner. Six to eight volunteers are required for conservation work and to attend to day visitors to the island, i.e. meeting the boats, helping in the craft shop, etc. Working hours vary according to the weather and tides. Self-catering accommodation is available at a cost of £15 a week. Min. period of work one week between Easter and the end of September/early October. Send applications as soon as possible (please note — s.a.e. or IRC essential for a reply) to R.A. Atkins at the above address.

EAST MIDLANDS NATIONAL TRUST: Stableyard, Clumber Park, Worksop, Nottinghamshire S80 3BE (tel 01909-486411; fax 01909-486377). Founded in 1895, the National Trust is the largest conservation charity in Europe, caring for historic houses, industrial monument, coastlines and open countryside, in order to enable public access.
Opportunities exist for volunteers to perform a variety of indoor and outdoor jobs. Hours of work vary, depending on the project available. Min. period of work 4 weeks. Min. age 18 years. No remuneration or accommodation is provided but volunteers receive travel expenses and other benefits, such as free entry to National Trust properties.

LONDON AND WEST MIDDLESEX NATIONAL TRUST VOLUN-TEERS: c/o Hughenden Manor, High Wycombe, Buckinghanshire HP14 4LA (web site http://members.tripod.com/-lwmntvl/). The largest regional volunteer group of the National Trust, with over 250 members from all over the UK. Members carry out practical conservation all over the country.
VOLUNTEERS to repair paths, build bridges, clear scrub, repair dry stone walls and carry out other general land management and access work. Volunteers participate in weekend programmes, staying in Basecamps, converted outbuildings on estates, usually dormitory style accommodation with basic facilities. Volunteers work all day Saturday, until lunchtime on Sunday.
Basecamps are supervised by National Trust wardens who provide safety equipment and tools. The group is open to anyone over 16. Volunteers need enthusiasm and old clothes. The weekends have leaders who organise catering and travel. Membership of the group costs £6 per year. A typical weekend will cost around £10 for food, accommodation and travel.
Contact the above address for an information pack.

THE MONKEY SANCTUARY: Looe, Cornwall PL13 1NZ (tel 01503-262532).
VOLUNTEERS are required to work 40 hours per week in the sanctuary which is home to a colony of Amazonian grey woolly monkeys. Volunteers are essential in allowing the team of keepers to care for the colony. Help is needed

in the shop and with cleaning while the sanctuary is open to the public between April and September; during the closed season (October to March) volunteers assist with general maintenance work and cleaning. No qualifications are necessary but workers must have an interest in animal welfare and conservation.

Food and accommodation are provided. Min. age 18. Overseas applicants with a good standard of English welcome. Applications, four or five months in advance, should be made to Lucy Molleson at the above address, enclosing stamped s.a.e. or Iinternational Reply Coupon.

THE NATIONAL TRUST: Working Holidays, PO Box 84, Cirencester, Glos., GL7 1RQ. A charity dependent on volunteers which cares for 240,000 hectares of outstanding countryside, almost 600 miles of unspoilt coastline, and over 300 historic houses.

The National Trust organises working holidays in outdoor conservation work, biological surveying, archaeology, construction and various other interests. These take place on National Trust properties in England, Wales and Northern Ireland throughout the year. Each project books 12-20 volunteers and lasts for 1 week to 10 days. There are also some weekend projects.

Volunteers pay from £45 per week to help cover the cost of board and lodging, and are responsible for their own travel expenses. Accommodation varies from purpose-built hostels to converted barns; volunteers supply bedding or sleeping bags. Min. age 17. Overseas applicants welcome but must be over 18 and have good conversational English. For a brochure, please telephone the Brochureline on 0891 517751. (Calls cost 50p per minute). Alternatively send two 1st class stamps to the above address.

OTHONA COMMUNITY: Burton Bradstock, Dorset.
VOLUNTEERS (8) needed for conservation and maintenance work work in a Christian based community which aims to strengthen international relationships and facilitate communication among people speaking different languages and also to form new ways of communication through art, music etc. There will be many opportunities for outings, discussions, intercultural learning and fun. Volunteers should be willing to participate fully in the daily life of the community. Othona asks for a voluntary donation of £50 towards the cost of food (payable on arrival).

Volunteers needed in July. Apply to the Co-Ordinator, Youth Action for Peace, Methold House, North Street, Worthing BN11 1DU (tel/fax 01903-528619).

ROYAL SOCIETY FOR THE PROTECTION OF BIRDS: The Lodge, Sandy, Bedfordshire SG19 2DL (tel 01767-680551; fax 01767 692365; e-mail volunteers@RSPB.ORG.UK).
Voluntary help needed for many tasks (especially in the winter and spring months) including practical management work, bird counts or helping visitors to find their way around. Accommodation is provided for volunteers who stay for at least a week, maximum stay a month (Saturday to Saturday only). Minimum age 18, and applicants should be interested in Conservation. Overseas applicants with good spoken English welcome. For further details, please write to the Voluntary Wardening Scheme, Youth and Volunteers Department (VWP), at the above address. Enclose a self-addressed label with two first class stamps or an international reply coupon.

THISTLE CAMPS: The National Trust for Scotland, 5 Charlotte Square, Edinburgh EH2 4DU (tel 0131-243 9470; fax 0131-243 9444).

Thistle Camps are voluntary work projects organised by The National Trust for Scotland to help in the care and practical management of its countryside properties. Each year there are approx. 40 camps, running from March to October and lasting from one to three weeks. They are always of a practical nature, undertaking such tasks as mountain footpath improvement, habitat management, archaeology or working with crofting communities on Fair Isle (Britain's most remote inhabited island) and Canna. Volunteers must be aged over 16.

Camps are usually accommodated in a Trust basecamp or in similar hostel-type lodgings. All food is provided but volunteers are expected to help with the preparation of meals as well as general domestic tasks during the week. Participation in a camp costs from £40 (£25 unwaged), and volunteers must pay their own travel expenses to a central pick-up point near the camp location. All volunteers must bring good waterproofs and sturdy footwear.

The 1999 programme is available from January from the above address. Overseas applicants must apply by February to ensure a place.

THE WILDLIFE TRUST WEST WALES: 7 Market Street, Haverfordwest, Dyfed, Wales SA61 1NF (tel 01437 765462).

Voluntary assistant wardens are required for Skomer Island, a National Nature Reserve off the Welsh coast. Work involves meeting day visitors, census work, general maintenance and recording, etc. To work 7 days a week for a minimum of 1 week between Easter and 31 October. Self-catering accommodation is available free of charge. Min. age 16, and volunteers should have an interest in natural history. Overseas applicants welcome.

Applications should be sent to Mrs J. Glennerster, Islands Booking Officer, at the above address. It is advisable to contact Mrs Glennerster from September onwards to book for the following year as places go very quickly.

WWOOF (Willing Workers on Organic Farms): PO Box 2675, Lewes, Sussex BN7 1RB. (tel/fax 01273-476286).

Volunteers are needed to spend time working on organic farms, gardens and smallholdings around the UK: organic farming avoids the use of artificial fertilisers and pest killers, and can be labour intensive. Simple accommodation and food are provided. Once participants have spent two weekends working, it is possible to arrange longer stays. Applicants must have a genuine interest in furthering the organic movement. Applications welcomed from students/individuals of any nationality all year round. For further information send a s.a.e. to the above address. £10 membership fee.

Festivals and Special Events

BIRMINGHAM INTERNATIONAL FILM AND TELEVISION FESTIVAL: 9 Margaret Street, Birmingham B3 3BS (tel 0121-212 0777; fax 0121-212 0666). The Birmingham International Film and Television Festival is the UK's only festival of its kind. It screens the best of international cinema and has developed a specialism in South Asian cinema.

VOLUNTEER FESTIVAL ASSISTANT, TECHNICAL ASSISTANT, PRESS AND MARKETING ASSISTANT and RUNNER (3/4). All positions are unpaid although reasonable travel expenses will be met. To work initially 3-5 days per week, then 6-7 days per week during the festival buildup, and the festival itself. No accommodation available.

Applicants should be studying or have studied a media orientated degree, or have some experience in film and TV. The posts involve long hours, so applicants should be enthusiastic and not afraid of working hard. However, the work is very rewarding, provides the opportunity to work and learn at the same time and gain good contacts for the future. Min. period of work 2 months between July and September. An interview is necessary.

Applications from May/June to Yen Yan, Festival Administrator.

BROADSTAIRS FOLK WEEK: Pierremont Hall, Broadstairs, Kent CT10 1JH (tel 01843-604080; fax 01843-866048). The Broadstairs Folk Week Trust, a registered charity, organises events throughout the year and an annual festival. 1999 will be the festival's 34th year. The whole town and its promenade, jetty, bandstand, taverns, halls, churches and streets becomes the venue for international music, song and dance.

VOLUNTEERS (over 100) are needed as door stewards, information and shop staff, PA and sound technicians, drivers, campsite stewards and collectors. Volunteers are also needed to handle publicity and liaise with international personnel. Posts are unpaid, but staff receive a season ticket for access to all events. Free camping is available. Volunteers work 4 hours a day. Min. period of work 3 days between 6th and 13th August. Overseas applicants with good English are considered. Interview not necessary. Applications from March to Ian Harker.

GATESHEAD METROPOLITAN BOROUGH COUNCIL: Department of Leisure Services, Civic Centre, Regent Street, Gateshead NE8 1HH (tel 0191-477 1011 ext.3822; fax 0191-478 2345). Gateshead hosts the 13th World Veterans Athletics Championships in 1999: 10,000 competitors are expected from around the world. 1,500 volunteers are required for the event. The Council also offers paid and unpaid opportunities on playschemes and sports camps.

DRIVERS (20) to drive competitors/VIPs between competition venues. Expenses and meals paid. To work 8am-3pm or 3pm-9pm from 20th July to 12th August. Must be over 21 and have a clean driving licence and an interest in sport/athletics.

TRANSLATORS (12) to work at the information desk translating into French, German and Spanish, and compiling information packs. Accommodation, meals and expenses paid. To work from 1st April to 12th August. Must speak French/German or Spanish. Can be any age.

CATERING SUPPORT STAFF (20) to distribute packed lunches, prepare food and move catering equipment, and set up and take down equipment at functions. Some bar work is involved. Expenses and meals paid. To work 9am-3pm/3pm-midnight from 20th July-10th August. Must have an interest/experience in catering. Can be any age.

EVENTS STEWARDS (50) for all aspect of the Championships; the marathon, walking, cross-country and stadium events. Expenses and meals paid. To work flexible hours from 20th July to 12th August. Must have an interest/experience in sports events.

Application to the above address.

Heritage

THE ALICE TRUST: Waddesdon Manor, Aylesbury, Bucks HP18 0JH (tel 01296-651282; fax 01296-651293). Waddesdon Manor is a magnificent French Renaissance-style chateau. The gardens contain a parterre, large parklands with many mature trees, splendid walks and a rococo-style aviary.
VOLUNTEER GARDENERS (2) required to be involved in a diverse range of maintenance tasks, working alongside a team of eleven other professional gardeners. 8 hour days, Monday to Friday. Min. period of work one month if residential. Some travel expenses may be met; rent free accommodation with heat and light may be available. Age 17-60. No experience necessary but commitment and reasonable fitness are required. Overseas applicants who are fit and able to make basic communication with English speakers welcome.
Volunteer gardeners also required to join Sunday Task Groups, spending one Sunday a month undertaking a range of project and maintenance work. Applications with c.v. and references a.s.a.p to Michael Walker, at the above address.

BERRINGTON HALL: Near Leominster, Herefordshire HR6 0DW (tel 01568 615721). A National Trust Property. Provides the opportunity to mix with people from all weeks of life with a common interest in conservation.
VOLUNTEER ROOM STEWARDS (11) required every day from April to October.
CAR PARK ATTENDANT (1). To work Bank Holidays.
GARDEN HELP.
Min. age 18 years. No accommodation is available but travel costs are provided (up to 40 miles round trip). Volunteers who offer 50 hours of work receive a volunteer card entitling them to free entry to National Trust Properties in the UK and 10% discount in the shops. Overseas applicants welcome. All applicants must be available for interview. Apply a.s.a.p. to the House Steward at the above address.

CYFARTHFA CASTLE MUSEUM AND ART GALLERY: Brecon Road, Merthyr Tydfil, South Wales CF41 8RE (tel/fax 01685-723112).A registered museum set in a regency gothic castle in 160 acres of parkland. The museum displays range from fine art to the industrail revolution.
VOLUNTEERS (2) needed around the year to assist with museum functions including documentation, cataloguing, producing text for leaflets and guides, work with schools and exhibitions. Work is normally unpaid, but it may be possible to provide accommodation. Should be aged to at least A level standard; would suit students wishing to pursue a career in museum, gallery or heritage work.
Applications to Mrs C. Dovey-Evans, Museums Officer at the above address.

DIDCOT RAILWAY CENTRE: Didcot, Oxon OX11 7NJ (tel 01235-817200). Operated by the Great Western Society, whose volunteer members restore the trains and are developing the centre as a living museum of the Great Western Railway.
VOLUNTARY CLERICAL ASSISTANTS (2) to assist with mail-outs, answering the telephone and general administration. Needed May to end of September.

VOLUNTEERS to assist with the general maintenance and restoration of steam locomotives. Required all year round.

VOLUNTEER GARDENERS to help maintain gardens and lawns. Needed at any time.

VOLUNTEER STEWARDS to see people on and off the trains on steam days. Required mainly at weekends and on Wednesdays in August.

WORK WEEK VOLUNTEERS reuires from 31st July to 7th August to restore trains, and perform various civil engineering activities. Evening social activities organised. Overseas applicants welcome. Applications to the Manager at the above address.

FESTINIOG RAILWAY COMPANY: Harbour Station, Porthmadog, Gwynedd, North Wales LL49 9NF (tel 01766-512340; fax 01766-514576; web site www.festrail.co.uk). The world's oldest passenger carrying narrow railway. 13½ mile long route through Snowdonia National Park.

Volunteers are required to help in the maintenance and running of the 150-year-old narrow gauge railway. It is a good opportunity to meet new people and learn new skills. A wide variety of work is available in the Traffic and Commercial Department, Locomotive Operating Department, Mechanical Department, and the Civil Engineering Department. The Active Buildings, Parks and Gardens Department needs skilled and unskilled assistance with improving the appearance of the station surrounds and picnic areas. Qualified and experienced electricians and builders also needed. Training is given where necessary. Min. age 16. All volunteers must be fit. Overseas applicants must speak English to the standard of that of a native.

Limited self-catering hostel accommodation is provided for regular volunteers, for which a small charge is made; food is extra. Camping space and a list of local accommodation also available. Applications to the Volunteer Officer at the above address.

GREAT CENTRAL RAILWAY PLC.: Great Central Road, Loughborough, Leics LE11 1RW (tel 01509-230726; fax 01509-239791). Britain's only mainline steam railway. Over 180,000 people visit the 8 mile long steam railway every year.

RETAIL ASSISTANT (1). Should be able to use a till.

CATERING ASSISTANTS (2). Need to be polite. Varied duties including assistant chef, waiter, etc.

TICKET COLLECTOR (1). Training given.

CARRIAGE CLEANER (1). Involves relatively light duties.

All posts are voluntary from May to September. Pay by arrangement. To work a 5 day week, 37½ hours. Minimum age 18. Applications to M. Ashworth at the above address.

IRONBRIDGE GORGE MUSEUM TRUST: The Wharfage, Ironbridge, Telford, Shrophire TF8 7AW (tel 01952-583003; fax 01952-588016). A World Heritage site.

VOLUNTEERS required for demonstrations of exhibits, site maintenance, street animation and wardrobe. Min. age 18. Must have good communication skills, be reliable and self motivated, and have excellent spoken English. Volunteers required from April to October; the Trust is open Monday-Sunday 9.45am-5.15pm. Min. period of work 2 weeks.

Some historical background is a plus although training, costume, equipment and supervision are provided. Workers are given a luncheon voucher for a full days volunteering, plus free entry to other I.G.M.T. sites. Museum insurance covers all volunteers. No accommodation available. Overseas applicants welcome providing their English is of a good standard. An interview is not essential although it would help both parties to visit prior to placement. Other opportunities to volunteer are available at the Museum's other sites in the valley. Applications year round to Lisa Wood, Blists Hill Victorian Town, at the above address.

KENTWELL HALL: Long Melford, Sudbury, Suffolk CO10 9BA (tel 01787-310207; fax 01787-379318). A redbrick Tudor mansion offering re-creations of Tudor domestic life.
VOLUNTEER TUTORS (700) needed for historical re-creations for the summer. Duties consist of demonstrating 16th century life and activities to visiting schoolchildren and the public. The re-creations run for 7 days a week for 3 weeks; most volunteers stay one or two weeks during June/July. Take 16th century skills or learn them there. All ages and Nationalities welcome.
RETAIL AND CATERING STAFF (10) to serve in a temporary shop/restaurant in a marquee during 16th century re-creations; duties also include marshalling school parties. Applicants will need stamina.
    All meals, evening entertainment and space on campsite provided. Applicants can be of any age; and interest in the 16th century would be helpful. For these positions applications must be made in January or February. Applications should be sent to Mary Fitzgerald at the above address.

LAKE DISTRICT ART GALLERY AND MUSEUM TRUST: Abbot Hall Art Gallery, Kendal, Cumbria LA9 5AL (tel 01539-722464; fax 01539-722494). An independent charity which runs a prizewinning art gallery and museums of social history, archaeology, and natural history.
Volunteer curatorial assistants, reception staff, events helpers and coffee shop staff are required to work in Kendal Museum, Abbot Hall Art Gallery and the Museum of Lakeland Life and Industry. To work during July, August and September. The work would suit both undergraduates and postgraduates hoping to gain museum experience.
    The gallery also requires graduate or post graduate students for unpaid museum and gallery work experience. To work 9.30am-5.30pm if using free lodging, part-time hours if living out. Free accomodation only available for 2 staff, but staff must pay for gas, electricity and personal phone calls. Interview if possible. Overseas students welcome, but working English is required. Applications at any time to Cherrie Trelogan at the above address.

LEIGHTON HOUSE MUSEUM: 12 Holland Park Road, London W14 8LZ (tel 0171-602 3316). The house was built between 1864-79 to designs by George Aitchison. It is the expression of Leighton's vision of a private palace devoted to art.
VOLUNTEERS to work at the home of Frederic, Lord Leighton (1830-1896), the great classical painter and president of the Royal Academy. Duties include office work and helping mount exhibitions. Hours are flexible. Applicants must be interested in museums and be graduates or currently studying. No accommodation is available.
    Min period of work 1 month at any time of year. Overseas applicants with good communications skills are considered. Interview necessary. Applications at any time to Reena Suleman.

LOSANG DRAGPA BUDDHIST CENTRE: Dobroyd Castle, Pexwood Road, Todmorden, West Yorks OL14 7JJ (tel 01706-812247; fax 01706-818901).
Losang Dragpa Centre is a Buddhist college and retreat centre based at Dobroyd Castle in the heart of the Pennines. Volunteers (up to 7) are required to help restore the building to its former beauty. Working holidays for a period of at least one week are offered throughout the year, free food, accommodation and teachings are provided in exchange for 35 hours work a week. Volunteers are able to experience life in a Buddhist community, attend teachings and meditations and enjoy beautiful surroundings. Those with specialised skills (plumbers, electricians, decorators, joiners, gardeners, plasterers etc.) welcome but not essential as work can be found for any willing hands. Minimum age 18. Applicants of all nationalities welcome. Contact the receptionist by telephone between 2-4pm daily for more details.

THE MUSEUM OF OXFORD: St Aldates, Oxford OX1 1DZ (tel 01865-815559; fax 01865-202447). A museum in the centre of Oxford that tells the story of the city and the university. In the summer the museum is open Tuesday to Sunday.
VOLUNTEER MUSEUM ASSISTANTS (3) to assist museum visitors and work at the front of house. Foreign applicants would be encouraged to translate for visitors. Needed to work 6 hours a day, 1-5 days a week. Min. period of work 1 month between the beginning of July and the end of September. No accommodation is available. Must be over 18. Experience useful.
Overseas applicants who can converse in English considered. Interview not necessary. Applications from May to the Manager.

STRATHSPEY RAILWAY CO. LTD.: Aviemore Station, Dalfaber Road, Aviemore PH22 1PY (tel 01479-810725; fax 01479-812220). Highlands steam railway which runs for 5 miles between Aviemore and Boat of Garten. Work is being done to extend the line.
VOLUNTEER GUARDS, TICKET INSPECTORS and BOOKING CLERKS. Volunteers are also needed to help maintain the railway and its rolling stock and locomotives. Free but very basic accommodation in sleeping car at Boat of Garten station. Hostel for members who work at Aviemore £2.50 per night. Minimum age 16. Fitness needed for some jobs. Vacancies all year. Applications to the above address.

WATERWAY RECOVERY GROUP LTD: 114 Regents Park Road, London NW1 8UQ (tel 0171-586 2556; fax 0171-722 7213; e-mail wrg@waterway.demon.co.uk).
VOLUNTEERS (400) needed to restore Britain's derelict canals: work may involve restoring industrial archeology, demolishing old brickwork, driving a dumper truck, clearing mud and vegetation and helping at a National Waterways festival. To work either on weekends or week long canal camps. Work is available year round; minimum period of work 1 day. No experience or qualifications are necessary but applicants should be at least 17 years old.
Accommodation and food are available in a village hall for £35 per week and £10 per weekend. Overseas applicants welcome. Apply to Neil Edwards at the above address.

WELSHPOOL AND LLANFAIR RAILWAY: The Station, Pool Road, Llanfair, Caereinon, Welshpool, Powys SY21 OSF (tel 01938-810441; fax 01938-810861). Volunteer operated steam railway in mid-Wales.
VOLUNTEER MAINTENANCE STAFF (up to 10 at any time) for varied duties including the clearing of vegetation at any time of year. No pocket money paid, but accommodation available at cheap rates. Should be over 16, fit, healthy and enthusiastic. Applications to Andy Carey, at the above address.

WORDSWORTH TRUST: Town End, Grasmere, Cumbria LA22 9SH (tel 015394-35544; fax 015394-35748; e-mail ww@dovecott.demon.co.uk). A registered charity (no. 1066184) in the heart of the Lake District. An internationally renowned literary centre with a unique collection, which offers accredited museum training.
VOLUNTEER MUSEUM ASSISTANTS (10) needed around the year to guide visitors around Dove Cottage, the home of William Wordsworth, help in the shop and assist in the museum with tasks including providing reception and information services, cataloguing the collection and security. To work a 37½ hour, 5 day week on a 7 day rota; accommodation is available. Applicants must be aged 18 and over and registered as unemployed: New Deal placements are available for those who are eligible.
   Applications to Ann Lambert, Personnel Officer at the above address.

YORKSHIRE CARRIAGE MUSEUM: Aysgarth Falls, Wensleydale, North Yorks DL8 3SR (tel 01969-663399; fax 01969-663699). Situated in the heart of the Yorkshire dales. Aysgarth falls is famous for its 3 grades of waterfalls on the river Ure.
The museum is a three storey, Grade II listed building, housing a Victorian Carriage Collection. Restoration on the Mill Building is an ongoing project performed by a Charitable Trust and requires voluntary landscape gardeners, carriage cleaners, stone cleaners, plaster removers, stonewallers, general workers, brickworkers/stoneworkers and re-pointers. Experience is only required by prospective stonewallers and brickworkers/stoneworkers. Help is needed around the year, period of work by arrangement. No accommodation is provided. Contact Ann Kiely, Administrator, at any time, at the above address.

Physically/Mentally Disabled

AFASIC - OVERCOMING SPEECH IMPAIRMENTS: 347 Central Markets, Smithfield, London EC1A 9NH (tel 0171-236 6487; fax 0171-236 8115). Represents young people and children with speech/language impairments. Disabilities range in severity from an inability to articulate speech, to a failure to understand the basic elements of language.
VOLUNTEERS (50-70) to act as constant companions to children and/or young people aged 18-25 with speech and language impairments on one week activity holidays. The work involves participation in outdoor pursuits such as canoeing, abseiling, walking and beach activities. Free accommodation and meals provided. Applicants should be aged at least 18 with good spoken English. Applications to the above address.

BEANNACHAR: Banchory-Devenick, Aberdeen AB1 5YL. (tel 01224-869138).

Beannachar is a training community for teenagers and young adults with learning disabilities. Volunteers are needed for household, workshop, garden and farm duties during the summer, and also long-term volunteers at any time of year. Free B & L plus pocket money provided. To work long hours, 6 days a week. Min. age 19. Must have lots of enthusiasm and a positive attitude. Overseas applicants must speak fluent English. Min. work period 2 months between June and September, 1 year for long-term volunteers. Applications anytime to Ms E.A. Phethean at the above address.

BREAK: 7a Church Street, Sheringham, Norfolk, NR26 8QR (tel 01263-822161). Registered Charity no. 286650.
Volunteers required at two centres on the Norfolk coast providing holidays and respite care for children and adults with learning disabilities. Volunteers are required to help with all the needs of guests' care and recreational programme and with essential domestic tasks.
Approx. £25 a week pocket money provided, plus free B & L and travel expenses within the UK. To work 40 hours a week on a rota basis. It is demanding work requiring well-adjusted and stable staff. Min. period of work 6 weeks. Longer periods of up to 12 months also possible. Centres open all year round. Overseas applicants welcome but must be able to understand and speak English to a reasonable standard. Applications to Mrs G. Gray at the above address.

THE CAMPHILL VILLAGE TRUST: Delrow House, Hilfield Lane, Aldenham, Watford, Herts WD2 8DJ (tel 01923-856006).
The Association of Camphill Communities runs working communities for mentally handicapped adults and children throughout Britain. They are based on anthroposophy, as founded by Rudolf Steiner. Voluntary helpers are required for the household, workshop or on the land. There is a limited number of summer jobs available, otherwise the min. period of work is 12 months. Free B & L is provided and a small personal allowance. Min. age 20. Overseas applicants welcome.
For a list of the addresses of Camphill Village Trust centres, write to the Secretary at Delrow House.

FAMILY INVESTMENT LTD.: 51 Old Dover Road, Canterbury, Kent CT1 3DE (tel/fax 01227-456963).
CARE/SUPPORT WORKERS (3) required throughout the summer months to support family groups of learning disabled adults living with staff in their daily life. Duties include escorting on outings, taking part on instructional basis in their work placements. Hours: between 7.30am and 10.30pm. Accommodation provided within family groups of staff and learning disabled adults. All meals and out of pocket expenses when undertaking duties provided. Minimum age 18. Mature applicants with a sense of humour and a realistic attitude to life desirable. Applications to Mrs L. Stapley, Resident Householder, at the above address.

FOCUS: Komtech House, 255/257 London Road, Headington, Oxford OX3 9EH (tel 01865-308488; fax 01865-742235). Focus has four branches around the country which will organise 14 camps in 1999.
VOLUNTEERS (35 or more per camp). To work on Easter and summer residential projects or camps, based either in Leicester, Oxford, Cambridge or Nottingham. FOCUS camps are for teenagers with limited opportunities and

adults with either a physical or a learning disability. On camp everyone joins a team, run by an experienced team leader and takes part in a range of art, sport and drama based activities. To work nine days per camp. Experience with disabled adults or teenagers is an advantage athough all necessary training will be given. Minimum age 18. Accommodation is available at a negotiable price of £25 per camp. Overseas applicants who can speak English welcome.

Apply by February for the Easter camps and by May for the summer camps, to Charlotte Dix at the above address. Note that all applicants must be available for an interview or have recent references. For further information on other staff required see the nationwide chapter.

HERTFORDSHIRE ASSOCIATION FOR THE DISABLED: The Woodside Centre, The Commons, Welwyn Garden City, Herts AL8 7HG (tel 01707-324581; fax 01707-371297).
Volunteers (6 per fortnight) are required to assist with holidays for people with disabilities at Hertford House Hotel, Clacton. Helpers work on a rota basis, aiding the mobility of guests, to give companionship and assist them in dressing, transferring from wheelchair to bed/bathroom/toilet, pushing guests in wheelchairs to shops, church, the seafront etc. and escorting them on outings in hotel minibus.

Free return transport to hotel from Welwyn Garden City provided. Period of work all year round. Volunteers usually work for a two-week period. Min. age 20. Experience of working with disabled people would be helpful. Write a.s.a.p. for an application form, enclosing two character references, to the Manager at the Hertford House Hotel, 11 Parkway, Clacton-on-Sea, essex CO15 1BJ (tel 01255-475994)

INDEPENDENT LIVING ALTERNATIVES: Trafalgar House, Grenville Place, London NW7 3SA (tel 0180-906 9265).
Volunteers required to provide support for people with disabilities, to enable them to live independently in their own homes. The work involves helping them get dressed, go to the toilet, drive, do the housework, etc. Volunteers receive £63.50 a week plus free accommodation, usually in the London area. ILA offers a chance to learn about disability issues and see London at the same time. No qualifications required, except good English. Vacancies arise all year round. Applications should be sent to Tracey Jannaway at the above address.

INDEPENDENT LIVING SCHEMES: Lewisham Social Services, Louise House, Dartmouth Road, London SE23 3HZ (tel 0181-314 7239 (24 hours); fax 0181-314 3014; e-mail ken.smith@lewisham.gov.uk).
VOLUNTEERS (15) to help disabled people by acting as their arms and legs. Duties include dealing with the personal care and assisting with the leisure and social activities of independent people with severe disabilities. Allowances of £60 per week and an additional £15 per month are paid, plus free shared accommodation with all bills covered. To work on a rota basis with other volunteers; usually 24 hours on (sleeping in) followed by 48 hours off.

Volunteers (2) are needed around the year; those who can make a six month commitment are preferred. Applicants should be aged between 18 and 50 and should have a commitment to civil rights for disabled people. Applications to Kenneth Smith, Project Worker, at the above address.

KITH & KIDS: c/o Haringey Irish Centre, Pretoria Road, London N17 8DX (tel 0181-801 7432). A family support group meeting the needs of people with learning, physical and/or sensory disabilities.
VOLUNTEERS (50-60) to work with disabled students (two volunteers to one student) on a non-residential social training project lasting two weeks. No pocket money provided, but travel expenses within the Greater London area will be reimbursed. Period of work from the end of July or early August.
VOLUNTEERS (50 or more) to work on a similar scheme held on a summer camp in the Guildford area from late August. Accommodation will be provided. Min. age 16. Training given.
Overseas applicants will be considered. Applications to Kith & Kids at the above address.

LEONARD CHESHIRE: Central Office, 30 Millbank, London SW1P 4QD (tel 0171-802 8200).
Leonard Cheshire runs Homes for adults with physical and learning disabilities throughout the UK. Voluntary workers are required in some Homes to assist with the physical care of residents and their social activities.
Period of work from 3 to 12 months. Pocket money of £30 a week and free B & L provided. Travel expenses cannot be reimbursed. Overseas applicants with good spoken English welcome. Application form available from the National Information Officer at the above address.

LIFESTYLES INDEPENDENT LIVING PARTNERSHIP: Worcestershire Lifestyles: Woodside Lodge, Lark Hill Road, Worcester WR5 2EF (tel 01905-350686; fax 01905-350684). An independent charity established in 1991 to enable disabled people to exercise freedom of choice, extend their horizons, and make decisions about the lifestyle they wish to pursue.
VOLUNTEER WORKERS are needed to enable people with a disability to lead as normal a life as possible in their own home. Duties can include intimate personal care, cooking, housework, shopping and sharing leisure interests. Full-time work in shifts can include weekends and sleeping over. Volunteers receive free accommodation in the counties of Herefordshire and Worcestershire, plus an allowance of £53.95 per week. Accommodation is shared with other volunteers, and all heating and lighting bills are paid by the social services.
Volunteer workers are required at all times of year. The normal minimum commitment expected is four months, but it may be possible to arrange placements during college vacations. Volunteers should be aged at least 18 and be honest, trustworthy, reliable and caring. Applications should be sent to the Volunteer Recruiter at the above address.

QUEEN ELIZABETH'S FOUNDATION FOR THE DISABLED: Lulworth Court, 25 Chalkwell Esplanade, Westcliffe-on-Sea, Essex SS0 8JQ (tel 01702-431725; fax 01702 433165). A registered charity and a friendly, hardworking organisation. Lulworth court is a seaside holiday/respite centre for people with physical disabilities. Nearby Southend on Sea has bars, cafes, shops and a cinema.
Volunteers are required for 1-2 weeks to help provide lively informal holidays for our guests. No experience necessary. Training provided. Work involves assisting nursing staff to look after guests, many of whom are confined to wheelchairs and need complete help with all aspects of personal care.

Volunteers also escort the guests on visits to theatres, pubs, shops, seafront walks and day excursions. The work is fun but demanding. A sense of humour certainly helps. Min. age 18.

Volunteers are needed late January-mid December. Free B & L provided and volunteers are given £15 a week towards travelling and other expenses. Overseas applicants are welcome providing they have a working knowledge of spoken English.

To find out more, phone for an informal chat, or write to the above address for information.

RADAR (Royal Association for Disability and Rehabilitation): 12 City Forum, 250 City Road, London EC1V 8AF (tel 0171-250 3222; fax 0171 250 0212; minicom 0171 250 4119). A national organisation run by and working with disabled people to remove architectural, economic and attitudinal barriers. Areas include civil rights, holidays, mobility, employment and social services.

Each year RADAR draws up a list, *Voluntary and Paid Opportunities* giving details of organisations and various clubs which run holidays for people with disabilities. Volunteers are needed to help on these holidays (which last for at least one week), providing personal assistance to the holidaymakers. Free B & L is generally provided. Min. age usually 18. For further details write to the Information Department at the above address.

SHAD (HARINGEY): Winkfield Resource Centre, 33 Winkfield Road, London N22 5RP (tel 0181-365 8528)

SHAD (Support and Housing Assistance for people with Disabilities) enables tenants with physical disabilities to live in their own homes. Volunteers are needed to act as the tenants' arms and legs under their instructions.

Volunteers receive £55 a week, free accommodation and expenses. Work is on a rota basis: volunteers can expect a minimum of 4 days off a fortnight and regular long weekends.

No experience is necessary and support is guaranteed. This is an excellent opportunity to gain excellent work experience in a friendly and supportive environment. Full lifting training and induction is provided. The work takes place around the year and a commitment of at least 3 months is required. All nationalities are welcome but a good standard of English is essential. Applications to Sue Denney at the above address.

SHARE HOLIDAY VILLAGE: Smith's Strand, Linaskea, Co. Fermanagh, Ireland BT9 0EQ (tel 013657-22122; fax 013657-21893; e-mail share@dnet.co.uk).

Share Holiday Village is looking for volunteers to work as carer companions to elderly and disabled guests who come on respite care holidays in the summer months. There are also limited places for volunteer outdoor pursuit instuctors with relevant recognised qualifications e.g. RYA, BCU and First Aid Instructor Level.

Approximately 200 volunteers are required for a minimum stay of 7 days from May until September. Shared accommodation and all meals are provided as are necessary travel expenses within Northern Ireland. Min. age 18. Applications to the Volunteer Coordinator at the above address.

SPEYSIDE TRUST: Badaguish Outdoor Centre, Aviemore, Inverness-shire PH22 1QU (tel 01479-861285; fax 01479-861258; e-mail badaguish@cali.co.uk).

The Centre specialises in outdoor recreation holidays for children and adults with learning or multople disabilities. Clients enjoy various adventure activities and 24 hour respite care in a spectacular setting.
VOLUNTEER CARE ASSISTANTS to work with people with Special Needs for 1/2 weeks from April to October. Volunteers are expected to work 10 hours a day with 2 days off a week. £30 pocket money per week plus B&L.
SEASONAL CARE ASSISTANT/ INSTRUCTOR. Paid post from April-October. Accommodation available at the Centre; residential work experience essential. 2 references required. For more information write to the above address.

SUE RYDER FOUNDATION: Headquarters and Sue Ryder Home, Cavendish, Sudbury, Suffolk CO10 8AY (tel 01787-280252). A christian based charity.
This international Foundation runs more than 20 Homes in Britain, providing care for the sick, disabled and physically handicapped. Volunteers are needed throughout the year to do essential duties at the Headquarters or at the retreat house at Walsingham, Norfolk, or at certain Sue Ryder Homes: this may include helping with patients, doing domestic, office or a variety of other jobs.
Minimum period of work is normally 8 weeks. Simple accommodation, meals and pocket money are provided free of charge. Min. age 16. Send applications (enclosing s.a.e./IRC) to the above address.

THE 3H FUND: 147a Camden Road, Tunbridge Wells, Kent TN1 2RA (tel 01892-547474; fax 01892 524703).
CARERS (around 100) required to assist with one-to-one care for physically disabled people on holiday. In 1999 3H Fund is holding six holidays in Jersey, Spain and the UK, including an adventure holiday and a trip on the Lord Nelson Sailing Ship. Holidays are usually for one week to 10 days and take place between May and September.
B & L are provided, but a contribution of £60 is requested for the overseas holidays: advice can be given on raising this by sponsorship. Applicants should have a sense of humour, a strong back, great patience and a sense of responsibility. Experience is an advantage but not essential. Volunteers can enjoy a working holiday with much fun and laughter whilst enabling the people with disabilities also to enjoy a holiday. Applicants should be aged between 18 and 60.
Applications to Peggie King, Holiday Organiser, from November at the above address.

UK ACTION GROUP: Edinburgh, Scotland.
VOLUNTEERS (10) needed to provide services to the community for people with learning difficulties and their carers. A positive and enabling attitude towards working with people with learning disabilities is essential. Training for all volunteers is organised and runs over a four day period. Min. age 20. Accommodation provided free of charge.
Needed from 19 July-17 August. Applications to the Co-Ordinator, Youth Action for Peace, Methold House, North Street, Worthing BN11 1DU (tel/fax 01903-528619). Note: two letters of reference and *YAP Children's Act Declaration for the Protection of Children and Others* form are required.

WINGED FELLOWSHIP TRUST: Angel House, 20-32 Pentonville Road, London N1 9XD (tel 0171-833 2594; fax 0171-278 0370).
WFT provides respite care and holidays for severely disabled people and their carers. Volunteers are needed for one or two weeks at a time, to help trained staff enhance the holiday atmosphere for the guests. Holidays are available at purpose-built centres in Essex, Nottingham, Surrey, Merseyside and South-ampton, where guests can enjoy a break with or without their regular carer.
Volunteers are provided with free accommodation and meals in exchange for their time. Overseas applicants with good English welcome. For an application form please contact Elizabeth at the above address.

WOODLARKS CAMP SITE TRUST: Tilford Road, Lower Bourne, Farn-ham, Surrey GU10 3RN (tel 01252-716279).
The Trust provides camping facilities for organisations interested in running summer camps for physically handicapped people, particularly children. Teams of voluntary helpers are organised by the camp leader to assist campers. Camps last one week and a small fee is usually paid by helpers to the leader to cover the cost of food. All camping equipment is provided including blankets. Anyone interested should write, enclosing s.a.e., to the Honorary Secretary, Kathleen Marshall House, at the above address.

YOUNG DISABLED ON HOLIDAY: Flat 4, 62 Stuart Park, Edinburgh EH12 8YE (tel 0131-339 8866).
VOLUNTARY WORKERS (as many as possible) required for holidays for disabled people in the U.K. and abroad for one week throughout the summer. Each volunteer needs to help a disabled person on a one-to-one basis. Workers are expected to make a minimum contribution towards accommodation, food and trips. Preferred age group 18-35, though anyone up to the age of 40 will be considered. No previous experience required, just patience. Overseas appli-cants welcome. Applications to Alison Walker at the above address.

Social and Community Schemes

L'ARCHE: 10 Briggate Silsden, Keighly, West Yorkshire BD20 9JT (tel 01535-656186; fax 01535-656426). Seeks to reveal the particular gifts of people with learning disabilities who belong at the very heart of their communities, and who call others to share their lives.
VOLUNTEER ASSISTANTS (20) required to share life and work with people with learning disabilities in an ecumenical Christian-based community. Volunteers receive upwards of £25 per week and free B & L. Staff required all year round for a minimum of three months. After completing the application form candidates are invited to visit the community and interviews are held. Overseas applicants in possession of the necessary work visas are welcome. Applications by Easter to L'Arche, 10 Briggate Silsden.

THE BAPTIST UNION OF GREAT BRITAIN: Baptist House, PO Box 44, 129 Broadway, Didcot, Oxon OX11 8RT (tel 01235-517700; fax 01235-517715). A union of over 200 Baptist churches, colleges and associations with its National Offices situated in Didcot. The Task Force programme is part of the youth work offered by the Department for Research and Training in Mission.
VOLUNTEERS are required as members of Task Force teams for a whole

range of community projects from working with children and young people to the elderly on social action projects. The programme is designed to give those still studying, and those in full time employment the opportunity to experience missionary life in the UK.

Applicants should be Christians, and 16-25 years old. The programme lasts 3 weeks from 27th July to 14th August. Accommodation is available. The cost of participating in the scheme is £75. Overseas applicants are welcome. Interview not necessary. Applications at any time to the Task Force Administrator.

CSV (COMMUNITY SERVICE VOLUNTEERS): 237 Pentonville Road, London N1 9NJ (freephone 0800-374991; fax 0171-837 9318).

Arranges projects for young volunteers to work in close contact with people in need — including children, young people, homeless people, adults with learning or physical disabilities, and the elderly — in homes, hospitals, hostels, in community centres or wherever their help is needed.

Volunteers must work full-time 4-12 months at any time of the year and be aged 16 to 35. They are placed in the UK and work alongside professionals. No one is rejected. Free food, accomodation, bills, and a weekly allowance of £24 are provided. CSV also places volunteers from overseas who are aged 18-35, have good English and are able to meet British visa requirements. Overseas volunteers work on the same projects as UK ones, and receive the same benefits, pocket money, etc. There is a £499 placement fee for foreign visitors from outside the EC. EC Nationals under 25 may be exempt from this fee.

Further details from the above address or from freephone 0800-374991. Applications are welcome at any time but preferably submitted at least 2 months prior to starting date.

COTTAGE & RURAL ENTERPRISES LTD.: 9 Weir Road, Kibworth, Leicester LE8 OLQ (tel 0116-2793225; fax 0116-2796384). CARE is concerned with giving support to people with a learning disability, through the provision of residential accomodation and work facilities which offers each person the opportunity to live a full and purposeful life.

VOLUNTEERS to provide an additional reserve to supplement the work of staff in assisting people with learning disabilities in CARE's communities around England. Around 40 hours work a week; volunteers receive an allowance and board and lodging.

A minimum commitment of 4 weeks is expected at any time of year. Min. age 18; must have good communication skills. Applications to Mr Stuart Hines, Regional Director (Central), at the above address.

EDINBURGH CYRENIANS: 107A Ferry Road, Edinburgh EH6 4ET (tel 0131-555 3707). Works with homeless young people and encourages creative ways to overcome homelessness.

The Cyrenian Trust runs two community houses (one in the city centre and another on an organic farm in West Lothian) that are primarily for young adults who are otherwise homeless, and who have experienced a variety of difficulties which they are seeking to overcome. Residential volunteers, of a similar age to residents, live alongside residents sharing the life and work of the community. Support and regular training is provided by non-residential staff. Some experience preferrred.

Volunteers receive full B & L, weekly pocket money of £28, holiday, leaving grants, and access to a time-off flat. Minimum commitment 6 months. Vacancies all year round. Overseas applicants with good working use of the English language welcome. For further information and application form contact Isla Robertson or Gordon Annand at the above address.

THE GRAIL CENTRE: 125 Waxwell Lane, Pinner, Middlesex HA5 3ER (tel 0181-866 0505; e-mail WAXWELL@compuserve.com; fax 0181-866 1408).
The Grail is both a conference centre and the home to a community of Christian women. The Elizabethan house has modern extensions and is set in 10 acres of wooded garden.

5-6 volunteers are needed throughout the year to live alongside the resident community and help to maintain the house and garden and assist in running the centre. Much of the work is household/manual. Duties are arranged on a flexible basis and volunteers are required to be available for 6½ hours daily. There is one full day off a week and often a half day on Sunday. Those who need a well defined timetable/ fixed hours would find this pattern unhelpful.

Volunteers are offered board, their own room and pocket money, currently £18.50 per week. Min. age 20; no upper limit. No special skills are required, but goodwill and sense of humour essential. Overseas applicants pay their own fares and arrange the correct immigration clearance but an invitation letter is provided on request. European community applicants should be familiar with the medical cover between their country and the UK. Others should be insured or prepared to pay the cost of any treatment they may require. Applicants must have enough spoken and written English to function in this very busy household. In-house lessons can be arranged for those interested. Religious observance is not a requirement.

Send a letter (to the Volunteer Co-ordinator), c.v. and a recent photograph, 5/6 months ahead of the time you wish to start, to the above address. All applications must include a s.a.e. or an IRC.

GREAT GEORGES COMMUNITY CULTURAL PROJECT: The Blackie, Great George Street, Liverpool L1 5EW (tel 0151-709 5109; minicom/fax 0151-709 4822).
Opportunities for anyone over 18 to try alternative education and the arts together with some sport, recreation and welfare in an inner-city context: including youth work, crafts and games; regular workshops with local youngsters; staging exhibitions and events; and projects from cookery to contemporary and African dance, from photography to fashion. Share cooking, cleaning, administration and some rebuilding work. Endless opportunities to learn and unlearn, to teach and to create. Wonderfully long hours. Stamina, a sense of humour and a sleeping bag required. Accommodation provided. Volunteers are expected to stay for at least 4 weeks and to contribute towards food costs. Volunteers are welcome throughout the year and particularly over the summer, winter and spring holiday periods. The Blackie has recently passed its 30th anniversary. For further information write to the Duty Office at the above address.

HEALTHPROM: Star House, 104-108 Grafton Road, London NW5 4BD (tel 0181-284 1620; e-mail healthprom@compuserve.com; fax 0171-284 1881).
VOLUNTARY ADMINISTRATIVE ASSISTANT to perform general office administration and desktop publishing.Must be able to type and use computers, preferably Microsoft Word for Windows.

TRANSLATER/INTERPRETER fluent in Russian.

The above are needed to assist a charity which works to enhance healthcare in the former Soviet Union through partnership project work, postgraduate education and advocacy. No pocket money paid but local travel expenses will be refunded.

Applications to the Administrator at the above address.

HACKNEY INDEPENDENT LIVING TEAM: Richmond House, 1a Westgate Street, London E8 3RL (tel 0181-985 5511 volunteer hotline ext. 227; fax 0181-533 2029; web site http://easyweb.easynet.co.uk/~hiltdirector/). Supports adults with a learning difficulty in Hackney to live in the community as independently as possible, and to continue to develop their independence and personal identity.
INDEPENDENT LIVING SUPPORT VOLUNTEERS (12). Volunteers may be involved in all projects and activites of HILT. Some of the ways in which volunteers have supported service users include sports, leisure and social activities, arranging and accompanying on holidays sand assessing education and training opportunities. Volunteers support service users in achieving goals, and support in personal development. Wages £53.50 per week, plus weekly zones 1-2 Travelcard. To work 35 hours a week.

Applicants must be over 18 and must be committed to enabling people with learning difficulties to have as much control over their lives as possible. They should also help provide a service which reflects the cultural, racial and religious needs of service users, and promote anti-discriminatory practice. They should have a willingness to understand service users' emotional needs, and attend regular supervision and communicate ideas and suggestions.

Min. period of work 4 months at any time of year. All volunteers have their own furnished room, including all bills apart from telephone. Food allowance is incorporated into weekly allowance. Overseas applicants must have a good level of conversational English, and the right to enter the UK. Interview necessary.

Applications as far in advance of intended start date as possible to the Volunteer Co-ordinator.

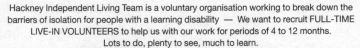

HOTHORPE HALL CHRISTIAN CONFERENCE CENTRE: Theddingworth, Leicestershire LE17 6QX (tel 01858-880257). 18th Century manor

house surrounded by beautiful countryside. Caters for up to 150 residents. 40 staff. English lessons given. Possibility to take Cambridge exams.
Volunteers are needed throughout the year at this Christian conference centre. Duties include serving meals and drinks to guests, washing up, servicing bedrooms and meeting rooms and maintenance.

Full B & L provided plus £42 a week pocket money. To work approx. 40 hours/6 days a week. Min. age 18. Overseas applicants from EU countries or with valid working visas, who can speak and understand English well welcome. All applicants should be committed Christians. Min. period of work 4 weeks. Application form and further information available from Mrs Sheila Dunning, Director, Hothorpe Hall.

IONA COMMUNITY: The Abbey, Isle of Iona, Argyll PA76 6SN (tel 01681 700 404).
An ecumenical Christian Community sharing work, worship, meals and recreation with guests visiting the Macleod and Abbey centres on Iona, and Camas, the more basic outdoors centre on nearby Mull.

On Iona volunteers work in the kitchen, coffee house, shop and office, help with driving, gardening, maintenance, housekeeping and with the children's and craft work activities programme.

At Camas, jobs include working with groups of young people, instructing in outdoor skills (e.g. canoeing and rafting) and cooking.

Volunteers are needed for between 7 and 18 weeks between March and October. They receive full B & L, travelling expenses within the U.K. and pocket money. Volunteers should be in sympathy with the Christian faith and the ideals of the Iona Community. Volunteers of 18+ are required, and the Community likes to have a number of people aged over 30. Overseas applicants with reasonable English welcome.

Recruitment begins in October/November. For details write to the Staff Coordinator, Iona Abbey, enclosing a stamped addressed envelope or International Reply Coupon.

MADDHYAMAKA BUDDHIST CENTRE: Kilnwick Percy Hall, Kilnwick Percy, York YO42 1UF (tel 01759-304832; fax 01759-305962; e-mail info-@madhyamaka.org.uk). A large residential Buddhist college situated in a beautiful 40 acre historic estate. The centre offers a range of meditation classes and retreats suitable for all.
VOLUNTEERS (usually no more than 5 at any one time) for a variety of jobs including gardening, cleaning, cooking, painting, building and making repairs. Three vegetarian meals a day and dormitory accommodation are provided in return for work; free access is granted to a range of Buddhist meditation classes for those who are interested.

Volunteers may stay for periods of up to one week every three months; they are expected to work for 35 hours a week, or 5 hours per day if staying for a shorter period. No particular qualifications or experience are required but applicants aged over 18 are preferred.

Applications should be sent to Kate Charles, Deputy Director at the above address.

MANJUSHRI MAHAYANA BUDDHIST CENTRE: Conishead Priory, Ulverston, Cumbria LA12 9QQ (tel 01229-584029; fax 01229-580080; e-mail

manjushri@tcp.co.uk). A residential Buddhist community with over 100 residents, founded in 1977 to provide a peaceful and inspiring environment where people can learn about the Buddhist way of life and practice meditation.
Volunteers needed for various duties including building, kitchen/garden help, and general household work/cleaning. Must have a good sense of humour and a willingness to work. Free board and accommodation are provided in return for work. Volunteers are also welcome to join in with centre activities such as meditation classes and courses.

Volunteers required to work 35 hours per week, Monday to Friday. Staff are needed from May to August, with a min. 1 week work period. Min. age 18. Overseas applicants with a reasonable standard of English welcome. There is no smoking or drinking alcohol on the site. Apply year round to Fiona Hind at the above address.

OTHONA COMMUNITY: Bradwell-on-Sea, Essex.
VOLUNTEERS (8-10) needed to help with maintenance and decorating. Volunteers should be physically fit for duties including track maintenance, digging and trailer loading. Various themes to be explored including Celtic spirituality and meditation. Othona asks for a voluntary donation of £50 towards the cost of food (payable on arrival).

Dates from July 5-July 26, although volunteers can stay longer if they wish. Apply to the Co-Ordinator, Youth Action for Peace, Methold House, North Street, Worthing, BN11 1DU (tel/fax 01903-528619).

THE PRINCES TRUST-VOLUNTEERS: 18 Park Square East, London NW1 4LH (tel 0171-543 1234; fax 0171-543 1367).
A personal development programme open to all 16-25 year olds, whether employed or unemployed. Certificates in skills, including team-working and communication are awarded on completion. The majority of unemployed people who take part go on to jobs or education after finishing. The programme lasts 60 days including a week of outdoor activities as well as various tasks in the community. It takes place at approximately 150 centres throughout the UK. Each year there are places for about 6,000 participants. No qualifications or experience are necessary and anyone claiming benefit can still do so while taking part. To find out where the nearest Prince's Trust Volunteers programme is call 0800-842 842 (in the UK).

SIMON COMMUNITY: PO Box 1187, London NW5 4HW (tel 0171-485 6639).
The Simon Community is a community of volunteers and homeless people living and working with those of London's homeless for whom no other provision exists. Volunteers are expected to help run its night shelter or one of three residential homes, as well as participate in group meetings, regular outreach work, campaigning and fund raising. The community also has a farm near Canterbury, and does tea runs round London, and other outreach work.

B & L is provided plus £26 per week pocket money. Volunteers are required throughout the year for a minimum of 3 months. All applicants should be aged 19 or over, have a mature and responsible attitude and a good command of the English language. Initial enquiries to the above address.

SOUTHWARK HABITAT FOR HUMANITY: PO Box 14284, London SE22 82H (tel 0181-693 3090; fax 0181-299 1754; e-mail Tim-Idle@GEO2.poptel.org.uk).
VOLUNTEER CONSTRUCTION WORKERS to work with an innovative community self-help group on its first project building four houses to provide affordable housing for people with low incomes. Southwark HFH is part of HFH Great Britain, an ecumenical Christian housing ministry working to provide high quality affordable housing to those on low incomes and in need of housing.

The construction programme is continuous throughout the year so help is needed on weekdays and at weekends; volunteers can help for as little as one day. Volunteers must pay for their own transport and provide their own lunch. Applicants should be aged over 18; no building skills or experience are needed as skilled supervisors direct the work.

Applications should be sent to Sarah Clark at the above address.

SPEAR: 24 Kew Road, Richmond, Surrey TW9 2NA (tel 0181-948 5564; fax 0181-332 7382; e-mail SPEAR@hostels.org). A 12 bed night shelter where 12 residents can stay for up to 28 days, during which time staff conduct resettlement work to move people on to more appropriate long term accommodation. SPEAR also holds drop-ins providing food and advice for rough-sleepers 4 times a week.
VOLUNTEERS are needed for drop-ins, which take 2/3 hours, 4 times a week. Volunteers are also needed for decorating, maintenance, cooking, cleaning and providing services such as reflexology and hairdressing etc. for drop-ins. Hours are negotiable, but should be over 2 hours a week. Min. period of volunteering 2 months between June and September/October. No accommodation is available.

Overseas applicants considered. Interview necessary. A understanding of homelessness and the issues faced by homeless individuals is vital. Applications to Michele Kemp or Helen Standen from March.

SURVIVAL INTERNATIONAL: 11-15 Emerald Street, London WC1N 3QL (tel 0171-242 1441; fax 0171-242 1771; e-mail survival@gn.apc.org). A worldwide organisation which supports tribal peoples. It represents their right to decide their own future and helps them protect their lands, lives and human rights.

A few volunteers are required all year round to work for at least 3 months. Work is in the Membership Department at Head Office, and involves routine clerical and office work. The posts are open to all who care to apply, as all applicants are assessed according to an application form and interview. Clerical skills are an advantage. No accommodation is provided. Overseas applicants with reasonable English are considered.

Write to Survival International at the above address for an application form.

TOC H: 1 Forest Close, Wendover, Aylesbury, Buckinghamshire HP22 6BT (tel 01296-623911; fax 01296-696137).
Toc H runs short-term residential projects throughout the year in Britain and Belgium, lasting usually from a weekend up to three weeks. Project work undertaken can include: work with people with different disabilities; work with children in need; playschemes and camps; conservation and manual work;

study and/or discussion sessions. These projects provide those who take part with opportunities to learn more about themselves and the world we live in.

Minimum age 16, but there is no upper age limit. The Toc H events programme is published yearly. There is no closing date for applications, but you are advised to apply early. Annual recruitment is over 500.

Workcamps

ATD FOURTH WORLD: 48 Addington Square, London SE5 7LB.

ATD Fourth World is an international voluntary organisation which adopts a human rights approach to overcome extreme poverty. It supports the effort of very disadvantaged and excluded families in fighting poverty and taking an active role in the community. Founded in a shanty town on the outskirts of Paris in 1957, it now works in 27 countires on 5 continents.

ATD Fourth world organises workcamps, street workshops and Family Stays in London, Surrey and Scotland. The workcamps are a combination of manual work in and around ATD's buildings, conversation and reflection on the lives and hopes of families living in extreme poverty and on the aims and objectives of the organisation.

The street workshops bring a festival atmosphere to underprivileged areas. Voluntary artists, craftsmen etc share their skills with the children and their parents. These street workshops for painting, crafts, computing and books etc. take place in the streets of deprived areas and make it possible to break down barriers allowing freedom of expression and building confidence.

The family stays allow families split up by poverty, perhaps with children in care, to come together for a break. The volunteers assist ATD Fourth World workers to give the families a holiday to grow together and learn new skills. The camps, Street Workshops and Family stays take place from June to September. Most last two weeks. Participants pay their own travel costs plus a contribution to the cost of food and accommodation. ATD is willing to take on foreign applicants.

For further information volunteers should contact ATD Fourth World at the above address enclosing a s.a.e.

INTERNATIONAL VOLUNTARY SERVICE: IVS-GB South, Old Hall, East Bergholt, Colchester CO7 6TQ (tel 01206-298215; fax 01206-299043); IVS-GB North, Castlehill House, 21 Otley Road, Leeds LS6 3AA (tel 0113-2304 600); IVS-Scotland, 7 Upper Bow, Edinburgh EH1 2JN (tel 0131-226 6722).

International Voluntary Service (IVS) is the British branch of Service Civil International (SCI). It organises about 40 workcamps in Britain each year as well as sending volunteers to workcamps in over 35 countries overseas. Volunteers work for two to four weeks in an international team of 10-20 people, sharing domestic and social life as well as the work. The projects include work with children, work with people with physical or mental disabilities and manual work, often connected with ecology or conservation. The projects are not holidays: the work can be hard and demands commitment.

Most workcamps are between June and September. Volunteers pay membership plus a registration fee (£35-£115) and their own travel costs, and must be 16 or over (or 18 for workcamps overseas). Free B & L is provided on the project. IVS is working toward equal opportunities and welcomes applications from women, Black people, people with disabilities, people from ethnic minorities, gay men and lesbians. Applicants from overseas should apply for IVS Schemes through partner voluntary organisations in their own country. Americans should contact SCI, Innisfree Village, Route 2, Box 506, Crozet, Virginia 22932, USA.

Write for more information to one of the regional addresses above, enclosing £4 for the listing of summer workcamps (available from April). Enquiries from January will be put on a mailing list to receive the listing when it is ready.

PILGRIM ADVENTURE: 120 Bromley Heath Road, Downend, Bristol BS16 6JJ (tel 0117-957 3997). An ecumenical Christian partnership founded in 1987.

VOLUNTEER TEAM MEMBERS (3) to help lead small groups taking part in Pilgrim Adventure's annual programme of Pilgrim Journeys within the UK, Spain and Ireland staying in hostels, monasteries and small hotels. Duties include assisting with worship and chores. Volunteers receive full board, accommodation and travel. Period of work early May to mid-October, although shorter periods will be considered. Each Pilgrim Journey lasts for between 5 and 15 days, with usually 2 or 3 days off between trips.

Applicants must be aged at least 18, with an interest in outdoor activities. Applications to Mr David Gleed at the above address.

QUAKER INTERNATIONAL SOCIAL PROJECTS (QISP): Friends House, 173/177 Euston Road, London NW1 2BJ (tel 0171-663 1043; fax 0171-663 1045)

QISP runs short-term (2-3 weeks) volunteer projects in Britain and Northern Ireland each year which mainly take place in the summer. The topics include manual projects, work with adults or children who have mental or physical disabilities, playschemes, youth work or community art events. All projects meet a particular need in a local community which could not be met without the help of QISP volunteers.

Food and accommodation (usually basic) is provided free of charge. Volunteers pay for their own travel to the project and their own pocket money, and a small registration fee is also charged.

Special experience is not required. Volunteers with disabilities are welcome to apply. Min. age is 18. Half the volunteers come from abroad, but overseas applicants must apply through an organisation in their own country. QISP can only deal with applications from UK residents. There are opportunities to go on projects in other countries (Western and Eastern Europe, USA and Japan). Min. age 18.

The new Summer Programme is available in April; to obtain a copy please send a large stamped s.a.e. to the above address.

UNITED NATIONS ASSOCIATION (WALES): International Youth Service, Welsh Centre for International Affairs, Temple of Peace, Cathays Park, Cardiff, South Glamorgan CF1 3AP (tel 01222-223088).

Volunteers required for international voluntary projects in Wales for social, manual, playscheme and environment projects. Usually 6-8 hours work per day, 5 days per week. Must pay own travel costs but free B & L provided. Min. age 18, no qualifications required. Period of work varies according to project but usually 2-4 weeks. Camps arranged all year round. Registration fee from £50. The UNA workcamps are primarily for overseas volunteers, though there are a few places for UK workers on some camps. Volunteers resident outside the UK must apply through the workcamp organisation in their own country. (British volunteers are also sent to projects overseas: registration fee from £80.)

Project leaders are also required. They are trained over one weekend in April, pay no fee and have travel expenses reimbursed.

Au Pair
Home Help
and Paying Guest

Finding a job as a mother's help or au pair in Britain is comparatively easy and is ideally suited to overseas visitors eager to improve their English. Families taking home helps are most common in London and the South-East, but mothers returning to work have brought a steady increase in demand nationwide. The majority prefer a commitment of six months to a year, but others require help for just two or three months over the summer.

The work may involve little more than light housework, playing with the children and some simple cooking. The pay, hours and training of au pairs are not supervised by any regulatory body at present, and so while a few work long hours and are treated like a skivvy, others are given great freedom, the use of the car and *Cordon Bleu* meals. It is not yet clear how the new National Minimum Wage will affect this type of work. Most enjoy something between the two and find working with a family to be a positive experience.

Hours vary according to the position: au pairs work 25-30 hours per week, *demi pairs* should expect to work less than that and *au pair plus* more. Mother's helps tend to work longer hours still, and are therefore usually UK nationals (see below). While the earning potential of qualified nannies has seen a dramatic rise recently, with the weekly salary of some as high as £350, au pairs should still except to receive pocket money of £25-£45 per week. Mother's helps and au pairs plus can expect in the region of £40-£60. Free board and lodging is included. Qualifications are rarely required (except for nannies), but babysitting experience is always useful.

Changes to the law six years ago now permit the employment of males in what has been a traditionally female trade. Undeniably, au pairs remain predominately female, however the growing number of progressive agencies taking male au pairs find that increasingly more and more families are willing to try one and are in general pleased with their decision. Kingston College in Surrey recently accepted two male students on their National Nursery Examination Board nanny training course for the first time ever.

Many agencies specialise in the recruitment of home helps, and it is important to contact several in order to compare terms. Some may charge for their services, so check beforehand. You will be asked to fill out a questionnaire and should then receive a contract laying down working conditions, hours, pay, etc. Insist on being given more choice if you are not satisfied with the family allotted to you.

Immigration: nationals of the EU and of European Economic Area Countries are free to take employment in the United Kingdom including taking up 'au pair' placements.

Nationals of any of the following countries are also permitted to work as au pairs in the UK: Andorra, Bosnia-Herzegovinia, Croatia, Cyprus, Czech republic, The Faroes, Greenland, Hungary, Macedonia, Malta, Monaco, San Marino, Slovak Republic, Slovenia, Switzerland and Turkey. Nationals of Bosnia-Herzegovina, Macedonia, the Slovak Republic and Turkey must obtain a visa from their designated British Embassy or Consulate before travelling to the United Kingdom. Some au pair agencies only deal with EEA nationals.

The Home Office lays down certain regulations regarding au pairs; they must be single and without dependants; aged 17-27; should help in the home for a maximum of 5 hours per day, with 2 free days per week; receive full board, a reasonable allowance (normally up to £35 per week) and sufficient time to attend language classes.

The au pair should produce, on arrival, a valid passport and a letter of invitation from the host family giving full details of the family and household, the duties they will be expected to undertake, the allowance they will receive and the amount of free time they will have for study and recreation.

ACADEMY AU PAIR AGENCY: 42 Cedarhurst Drive, Eltham, London SE9 5LP (tel 0181-294 1191; fax 0181-850 8932). An established London based company which is a member of FRES. Staff are friendly, knowledgable, and always available to assist in enquiries.
AU PAIRS. £40 for 25 hours work per week. Must be aged between 18 and 27 with some babysitting experience. Non smokers and drivers preferred.
AU PAIRS PLUS. £50-£60 for a min. of 30 hours work per week. Conditions as above.
MOTHERS HELPS. Starting at £120 per week for a 40/45 hour week, must be experienced in sole charge childcare. Must be able to produce a current c.v. and references.
NANNIES. Min. of £180 for 40/45 hours work per week. Qualifications required, such as BTECH, NNEB, NAMCW. CVs and references required.

Placements are throughout the UK from Edinburgh to the south coast of England. Work is available from mid June/early July to the beginning/mid September; min. period of work 2 months. Accommodation available at no extra charge. Overseas applicants welcome. An interview is not necessary for the au-pair positions, but may be necessary for those wishing to work as nannies. Applicants should apply enclosing an International Reply Coupon-before the 1st of March to Mrs Sheehan or Mrs Scrivoletto at the above address.

ANGLO CONTINENTAL NANNY & AU PAIRS PLACEMENT AGENCY: 21 Amesbury Crescent, Hove, East Sussex BN3 5RD (tel/fax 01273-705959; e-mail anglocont@applied-tech.com). Est. 10 years.
AU PAIRS recruited from Finland, France, Holland, Iceland, Spain, Sweden, Croatia, Turkey, Italy, Norway, Germany, Switzerland, Austria, Czech Republic, Slovakia and Hungary. Pocket money £35-£55 per week, plus board and lodgings in your own room, for approx. five hours' work per day. Length of stay from 2-3 months (summer only) to 2 years. Also summer stays and long term stays for UK applicants can be arranged abroad. Also wanted MOTHER'S HELPS from Australia, New Zealand South Africa.

All applications to Mrs Sharon Wolfe at the above address.
Also HOTEL WORK possible for applicants from EEC, Australia, New
Zealand and South Africa, previous work experience is essential. Applications
as above.

AU PAIR CONNECTIONS: 39 Tamarisk Road, Hedge End, Hampshire
SO30 4TN (tel/fax 01489-780438).
AU PAIRS/MOTHERS HELPS (300). £45 per week for au pairs and a
minimum of £60 for au pairs plus. To work 25 hours per week or more. Must
have a minimum of two years childcare experience and be at least 18.
Accommodation available free of charge. To work from mid June-mid
September; min. period of work six weeks.
   Apply from January to mid June to Denise Blighe at the above address.
Note that all applicants must enclose either an IRC or a s.a.e.

AU PAIR INTERNATIONAL EMPLOYMENT AGENCY: 7 Thornley
Crescent, Bredbury, Stockport, Cheshire SK6 1AX (tel/fax 0161-612 2676).
Offers professional and friendly service on a national and international
basis.
DEMI PAIRS (200) to work a maximum of 2-3 hours daily plus normally 2-3
evenings babysitting per week. Two days completely free per week. £15.00
pocket money. Own room and meals provided. Opportunity to attend English
classes. Requirements: must be aged 17-27, with some babysitting experience,
and speak at least basic English; should enjoy working with children and be
prepared to do some light housework.
AU PAIRS (200) to work a maximum of 5 hours daily plus normally 2-3
evenings babysitting per week. Two days completely free per week. £35.00
pocket money per week. Own room and meals provided. Opportunity to
attend English classes. Requirements: should be aged 17-27, with some
babysitting experience, and speak at least basic English; should enjoy working
with children and be prepared to do some light housework.
AU PAIR PLUS (200) to work a maximum of 8 hours daily plus normally 2-3
evenings babysitting per week. Two days completely free per week. £50.00
pocket money per week. Own room and meals provided. Opportunity to
attend English classes. Requirements: must be aged 17-27, with some
babysitting experience, and speak at least basic English; must enjoy working
with children and be prepared to do some light housework.
MOTHERS HELP (200) to work a maximum of 8 hours daily plus normally
2-3 evenings babysitting per week. 1-2 days free per week. £70.00 pocket
money per week. Own room and meals provided to residential positions, we
also place daily Mothers Helps. Requirements: must be aged at least 17, with
previous childcare experience, current driving licence an advantage, light
housework and cooking may be required.
NANNIES (200) to work 8-9 hours per day plus normally 2-3 evenings
babysitting per week for residential positions. Minimum age 18. NNEB or
similar qualification preferred. Must be responsible and willing to take sole
charge of children. Salary £120-150 net per week.
PAYING GUESTS: arranged with one of the many families welcome paying
guests into their homes and offering bed, breakfast, packed lunch and evening
meal at a rate of £9.50 per person per day.

A back-up service is offered to all Au Pairs. The agency puts Au Pairs in touch with others locally, sends welcome packs and can assist with translating. Male and Female applicants are considered, on a short or long term basis.

Period of work 2 months. Applications to work in the UK are welcome from citizens of EU countries and Andorra, Bosnia — Herzegovina, Croatia, Czech Republic, the Faeroes, Greenland, Lichenstein, Macedonia, Malia, Monaco, San Marino, Slovenia, Switzerland and Turkey. Language courses also arranged: write for details. Apply at least 4 weeks before earliest available starting date to Helen Morrison or David Wilkinson at the UK office. Please enclose s.a.e. and IRC if possible.

AVALON AU PAIRS: 7 Highway, Edgcumbe Park, Crowthorne, Berks. RG45 6HE (tel/fax 01344-778246) Established 42 years ago and workingwith approved families in Southern England. Their services are free to Au Pairs, and they provide support and assistance during stays. F.R.E.S and I.A.P.A. member.

AU PAIR placements with approved families in southern England available throughout the year. Age 18-27 years. Minimum stay 6 months (10 weeks in summer). Applications to above address.

BELAF STUDY HOLIDAYS: Banner Lodge, Cherhill, Calne, Wiltshire SN11 8XR (tel 01249-812551; fax 01249-821533). Since 1975 BELAF has been organising holiday placements for European students in carefully selected families in Southern England, London and the surrounding regions, Wiltshire, Dorset, Hampshire, Gloucestershire and Somerset.

AU PAIRS (200). £40-£60 per week plus accommodation. To work 25 hours per week from mid June to late August. Min. period of work 6 weeks. Min. age 18; all applicants must speak reasonably good English. Overseas applicants welcome. Apply from January-May to Carole Browne at the above address.

BUNTERS AU PAIR AND NANNY AGENCY: The Old Malt House, 6 Church Street, Pattishall, Towcester, Northants NN12 8NB (tel 01327-831144; fax 01327-831155; e-mail caroline@aupair-bunters.demon.co.uk).

AU PAIRS (50 or more). Min. £35 for 25 hours and 2 evenings work over 5 days per week. Board and lodging included. Applicants should have some childcare experience such as babysitting. Must be aged between 18-27. Staff required from May to September, min. period of work 8 weeks. Overseas applicants with good English and valid working visas welcome. Apply before May to Mrs Caroline Jones at the above address.

CHELTENHAM NANNIES: Wharf Office, The Wharf, Coombe Hill, Near Cheltenham, Gloucestershire GL19 4BB (tel/fax 01242-680999; e-mail nanniesc@aol.com). By matching applicants to clients carefully the agency tries its best to bring about win-win situations. They also offer pre and post placement advice and guidance.

NANNIES, PROXY PARENTS, MATERNITY NURSES, MOTHERS' HELPS, NANNY HOUSEKEEPERS, DAY NURSERY STAFF OF ALL LEVELS (around 200 per year in all) placed in the UK and overseas. Wages, dates etc. depend on the employer. Relevant experience and checkable references are essential; qualifications can be an advantage. Minimum age 18; a driving licence can be an advantage.

Applications to Lynne Shrubb, Proprietor, at the above address.

NICOLA J. CUFFE: 1 Paxton Gardens, Woodham, Surrey GU21 5TR (tel 01932-341704; fax 01932-341764).
SUMMER AU PAIRS from June to September. £35-£40 per week depending on family and duties. Approx. 5 hour day, 5 day week, but must be flexible. Childcare experience desirable. Age limits 18-27. Must have references. Applications to the above address.

CURA DOMI-CARE AT HOME: 8 North Street, Guildford, Surrey GU1 4AF (tel 01483-302275; fax 01483-304302).
CARERS required to care for elderly and disabled people in their own homes. Positions are either residential (nationwide) or non-residential (local to Guildford, Surrey). Wages vary according to the position being offered but are typically £225-255 a week, plus accommodation and travel expenses, as relevant. Period of work by arrangement. Applicants are given an interview and training session. Overseas applicants with fluent English and the necessary documents to work in the UK welcome. Applications to the above address.

EDGWARE AU PAIR AGENCY: 1565 Stratford Road, Hall Green, Birmingham B28 9JA (tel 0121-745 6777; fax 0121-243 4200; e-mail edgware@100s-aupairs.co.uk).
AU PAIRS placed in London and the Home Counties. They live as family members, have their own bedrooms and receive weekly pocket money. Families available all year round. Age required 18-27. Some basic childcare experience is required. Must be able to provide a Dear family letter, references (both character and child-care), a medical certificate and photographs. Some families require drivers in which case it is necessary to have an International Driving licence.
Applications to the above address.

ELITE AU PAIRS AND NANNIES: (tel 01903-693718; e-mail elite@lineone-.net). An agency based in Worthing/West Sussex which provides childcare services for families throughout the UK and abroad. Friendly and helpful service. Positions always available.
AU PAIRS for placements abroad: to earn £60-£100 net per week with free board and lodging in exchange for 25 hours of childcare and light housework per week, with 2 days per week off. Applicants must be aged 18-27. Summer positions available.
NANNIES for childcare placements in the UK and abroad. Wages for full time live-in or live-out positions are £150-£200 net per week in the UK or £200-£350 net per weekabroad. Full and part-time positions available; 2 days off a week for the full time posts. Applicants must have either a childcare qualification or experience in childcare and be aged at least 19.
   Period of work by arrangement at any time of year. For more information call Robert Bannon on the above phone number.

EUROYOUTH LTD: 301 Westborough Road, Westcliff, Southend-on-Sea, Essex SS0 9PT (tel 01702-341434; fax 01702-330104). Established in 1961, Euroyouth places Au Pairs, Paying Guests and School Groups, with or without language and sports courses. Au Pairs are placed throughout Britain, other positions are only for the Southend area.
AU PAIR positions arranged throughout the year. Min. length of stay 6

months throughout the year. For placement during the summer the latest starting date is 1st June for no less than 3 months. Min. age 18.

Euroyouth arranges Paying Guest Home Stays in Southend on Sea for groups, with or without English courses, plus optional golf/tennis/riding instruction and activities, thorughout the year. Paying Guest Stays are available for individuals but courses in summer only. All participants are accomodated in selected families.

Write enclosing IRC/s.a.e. for details to Euroyouth, at the above address.

HOME FROM HOME AU PAIR AGENCY: Gobles Court, 7 Market Square, Bicester, Oxon OX6 7AA.
SUMMER AU PAIRS (30). £35 a week plus full board. To work minimum 25 hours a week. Duties include childcare, household duties, cooking and general everyday work in the home. Applicants should have common sense and some knowledge of childcare. Non-smokers preferred, and the ability to swim and drive in the UK is helpful. Period of work June to end-September. Min. period of preferably 3 months. Applications should be sent to Jill Barnes, at the above address.

JOLAINE AU PAIR & DOMESTIC AGENCY: 18 Escot Way, Barnet, Hertfordshire EN5 3AN (tel 0181-449 1334; fax 0181-449 9183; e-mail aupair@jolaine.prestel.co.uk).
Arranges au pair/plus and mother's help positions in the UK throughout the year. Min. stay 3 months, max. 2 years. Payment is from £90 per week for a mother's help and £40-£60 for an au pair/plus. Also arranges Paying Guest family stays in the London suburbs throughout the year, from £80 per week. Accommodation available for individuals or groups of any size. Visits, excursions, activities and classes arranged on request. For further information and application forms write anytime enclosing s.a.e. or IRC to the above address.

LIVING LANGUAGES: 7 New Pond Parade, West End Road, Ruislip Gardens, Middlesex HA4 6LR (tel 01895-623777; fax 01895-623331; e-mail livlang@dircon.co.uk).
An agency providing work experience placements for European trainees and students wishing to improve their language knowledge and acquire first hand knowledge of international commerce. Placements are for a min. period of 3 months and up to 1 year. Au Pairs wishing to stay for a min. period of 6 months are also required. Min. age 19. For more information contact the above address.

MRS A. MALLINSON: 28 Albion Street, London W2 2AX (tel 0171-262 1717; fax 0171-706 2266).
SUMMER HOLIDAY HELPER required for seaside holiday home to help occupy nine grandchildren under the age of 9 years. This may include occasional cooking and reading bed-time stories; also rambling, swimming, bicycling and visiting places of interest. Ability to play a musical instrument or sing and help with acting and making simple fancy dress clothes would be an advantage. Period of work: up to six weeks. Two references essential. Applications to Mrs T S Mallinson, 28 Albion Street, London W2 2AX, by 30th April.

MRS J. MARBER: 27 Ham Farm Road, Ham Common, Richmond, Surrey TW10 5NA (tel 0181-546 9457).
AU PAIR required for an adult family. Duties to include light housework, ironing, washing up and walking the dog. Own bedroom and bathroom provided. Period of work April to October. Minimum stay 3 months. To work 5 hours a day/6 days a week. Position most suitable for a female student: aged 17-25, non-smoker and with a good knowledge of English. Public transport is available in the area. Applications, including a recent photograph and s.a.e. or IRC, to Mrs J. Marber at the above address.

MONDIAL AGENCY: 32 Links Road, West Wickham, Kent BR4 0QW (tel 0181-777 0510; fax 0181-777 6765).
Arranges placement of au pairs, who must be able to stay for at least 6 months. Min. age 18. Also arranges paying guest positions. Applications enclosing s.a.e. to Mrs J.K. Talbot, Mondial Agency.

NORFOLK CARE SEARCH AGENCY: 19 London Road, Downham Market, Norfolk PE38 9BJ (tel 01366-384448; fax 01366-385226). Most work is based in the East Anglia region, and offers competitive salaries and good conditions for live-in staff.
DOMESTIC NANNIES and MOTHERS' HELPS. £100-£150 a week plus full B & L. To work an 8-10 hour day. Min. age 18. Positions available all year. Staff must be based in the UK.
AU PAIRS. £40-50 per week, plus board and lodging. Language courses available. Min. period of work 4 months. All applications welcomed.
   Enquiries enclosing s.a.e. to Mrs V.A. Parker, Proprietor, Norfolk Care Search Agency.

OPTIONS TRUST STAFF RECRUITMENT: 4 Plantation Way, Whitehill, Bordon, Hampshire GU35 9HD (tel 01420-474261).
A non-profit making organisation, set up and run by a number of disabled people who employ staff to enable them to live in homes of their own in the community.
PERSONAL ASSISTANTS (4-10). £90-£200 a week plus free B & L. The work involves personal care, domestic duties and driving. Min. period of work 6 months at any time of year. Min. age 18. Driving licence required but no previous experience is necessary. Applications to Mrs V. Mason at the above address.

RICHMOND & TWICKENHAM AU PAIRS: The Old Parsonage, Main Street, Barton Under Needwood, Staffordshire DE13 8AA (tel 01283-716611; fax 01283-712299). An established agency running since 1992, run by Vicki and Linda who have both been Nannies/Au Pairs. The agency places mainly French, Spanish and Danish girls, and all girls are given a second chance.
AU PAIRS (500 per year). Must have childcare experience, and be happy and confident with a good command of the English language. Duties involve childcare, ironing, washing up and 2 nights babysitting a week. £35 per week plus accommodation. To work at least 25 hours per week all year round; min. period of work 2 months in the summer.
   Applicants must be aged between 17-27. Overseas applicants welcome;

interview is not necessary. Most au pairs are placed in south west London. Apply as early as possible to Vicki Whitwell at the above address.

SOLIHULL AU PAIR AND NANNY AGENCY: 1565 Stratford Road, Hall Green, Birmingham B28 9JA (tel 0121-733 6444; fax 0121-733 6555).
AU PAIRS placed all over the UK, including England, Ireland, Wales and Scotland. Live in as part of the family, own bedroom, weekly pocket money and free time to study. Positions for six months or longer. Basic/fair knowledge of English required. Applicants must complete and return an application form along with references (both childcare and character), photographs, a 'Dear Family' letter and a medical certificate. Must be flexible with regard to choice of area. Families available all year round.
QUALIFIED NANNIES placed in top jobs in many areas including London and the West Midlands. Drivers and non smokers always in demand.
MOTHERS HELP positions available for young and less experienced girls.
For further details contact the Solihull Au Pair and Nanny Agency at the above address.

SOUTH-EASTERN AU PAIR BUREAU: 39 Rutland Avenue, Thorpe Bay, Essex SS1 2XJ (tel 01702-601911; fax 01702-462857).
AU PAIRS. To work 5 hours per day, plus 2 evenings babysitting per week. Two days off per week. To live as part of the family, assisting with housework and child care.
AU PAIRS PLUS: To work increased hours for more pocket money. Duties as above. EEA applicants welcome.
DEMI-PAIRS, MOTHERS' HELPS and NANNIES in the UK and abroad also needed.
Vacancies arise throughout the year, with jobs available all over the UK. Wages £140-£500 per month, dependent on position, with considerably more for qualified nannies. Basic childcare experience is always an advantage. Period of work 6 months to 2 years, although summer placements are available. Min. period of work 6 weeks. B & L almost always available. Applications at any time, enclosing IRC (or s.a.e. if in the UK), to the above address. For applicants coming into the UK this is a completely free service.

MRS M.E. THOMSON: Thomas Thomson (Blairgowrie), Bramblebank, Rattray, Blairgowrie PH10 7HY (tel 01250-872062; fax 01250-872266.
MOTHERS' HELP to look after children and a house, cooking etc., on a fruit farm from mid May-late August. Wages of £115 per week plus board, lodging and the use of a car; to work from 7.15am-5pm 6 days per week. Should be aged at least 22, a non-smoker and with a driving licence and references; the job could suit a couple as other farm work might be available for the partner. See entry under *Outdoor* section. Applications to Mrs Melanie Thomson at the above address.

UNIVERSAL AUNTS LTD: PO Box 304, London SW4 0NN (tel 0171-738 8937).
HOUSE KEEPERS, NANNIES, MOTHERS HELPS, etc. required, in both residential and non-residential positions. Must be available to sign on with the agency for min. of 2 months. Please note the agency does not place au pairs. Applications any time to Universal Aunts Ltd.

UNIVERSAL CARE: 9 Windsor End, Beaconsfield, Bucks HP9 2JJ (tel 01494-678811; fax 01494-671259).
AU PAIRS for any period of 6 months or more, or a minimum of 3 months in the summer. Board and lodging and approx. £35 weekly pocket money. 25 hours a week of looking after children and some light housework; 2 days a week free. Should be aged 17-27 and single with some childcare experience. Applicants must be authorised to work in the UK. Applications to C. Marvell at the above address.

USEFUL PUBLICATIONS

CENTRAL BUREAU FOR EDUCATIONAL VISITS AND EXCHANGES: 10 Spring Gardens, London SW1A 2BN (tel 0171-389 4880).

The Central Bureau publishes *Working Holidays*, an annual guide to short-term paid and voluntary work opportunities available throughout the year in Britain and 70 countries worldwide. Price £9.99.

The Bureau also publishes *Volunteer Work*, a guide to medium and long-term voluntary work (3 months to 3 years), with information on over 140 recruiting organisations active in Britain or abroad. Price £8.99.

A Year Between gives details of voluntary projects, work placements, study and adventure opportunities in Britain and abroad for those taking a year out of education, particularly school-leavers and graduates. Price £9.99.

Workplace offers practical advice and information for those seeking work experience and work placements; also covers workshadowing and work observation, and details finding placements, preparation, funding and progression. Price £9.99.

Teach Abroad covers a wide range of opportunities throughout the world including TEFL jobs, short and long-term posts for qualified teachers of most subjects, exchange possibilities and placements with voluntary organisations. Practical advice covers country profiles, courses, recognised qualifications, work and residence permits, travel and further resources. Price £9.99.

Home from Home gives details of agencies which can arrange homestays, exchanges, farm stays and term stays throughout the world, plus practical advice on organising activities. Price £9.99 (publishing date Dec.1998).

The *Ten Ways* series includes four A3 posters giving ideas for work, study and travel opportunities: *Ten Ways to Work and Travel; Ten Ways to discover the World; Ten Ways to fill the Gap; Ten Ways to discover France.* Available free of charge.

The above guides are available from bookshops or direct from the Central Bureau, £3 charge for postage and packing for overseas orders.

ISCO PUBLICATIONS: 12a Princess Way, Camberley, Surrey GU15 3SP (tel 01276-21188; fax 01276-691833).

ISCO publishes the booklet *Opportunities in the 'Gap' Year* which is aimed at school leavers taking a year off before going into higher education. It gives details of paid and voluntary work, inside and outside the UK, as well as study opportunities. It also includes sections on the armed forces, expeditions and outdoor work. The booklet is available from ISCO for £3.95 (including postage).

JOB MAGAZINE (Job Opportunities Bulletin): ULCS, 50 Gordon Square, London WC1H 0PQ (e-mail job.subs@careers.lon.ac.uk).
London based weekly vacancies magazine advertising summer, temporary and part-time positions and a range of permanent opportunities for graduates and students. Every edition carries a work related feature article, and there are regular updates on the employer milkroud for graduate job hunters. Subscriptions available at £16 for twelve copies of JOB, plus complimentary copies of Prospects Today included. Call 0171-554-4552 for further information, or subscribe by sending your contact details and a cheque made payable to the University of London to the above address.

LENNARD PUBLISHING: Windmill Cottage, Mackerye End, Harpenden, Herts. AL5 5DR (tel 01582-715866; fax 01582-715121).
Publish *The Book from The Side*, formerly *Go for It!—Martyn Lewis' Essential Guide to Opportunities for Young People*, which covers possibilites for short term and voluntary work as well as careers and further education. The 1999 edition was published in October 1998 and is available from the above address for £8.99 (post free).

LIFETIME CAREERS PUBLISHING: 7 Ascot Court, White Horse Business Park, Trowbridge, Wiltshire BA14 0XA (tel 01225-716023).
Publishes *A Year Off. . . A Year On?*. This is a guide to employment, voluntary work and working holidays for gap year students and anyone considering taking a break during their education or career. It provides information, addresses, and ideas. Price £8.99.

THE PROSPECTS SERIES PUBLICATIONS: CSU, PROSPECTS House, Booth Street East, Manchester M13 9EP (tel 0161-277 5270).
Produced by the officail publisher for the UK Higher Education Careers Service, the PROSPECTS Series publishes job advertisements for graduates and final year students. If you have graduated you can subscribe to PROSPECTS TODAY, which gives details of graduate jobs for immediate applications. PROSPECTS Directory and PROSPECTS Finalist provide information on over 1,200 graduate employers, along with details of how to apply for their vacancies.
   Further details are available from Anne Kelly at the above address, or from a Higher Education Careers Service.

VACATION WORK PUBLICATIONS: 9 Park End Street, Oxford OX1 1HJ publishes or distributes the following titles in the UK.
1999 May Supplement to Summer Jobs(£6.00). Requirements for summer staff from employers in Britain and Abroad which arrive too late for inclusion in *Summer jobs in Britain* or *Summer Jobs Abroad* are published in this booklet.
Working in Tourism-The UK, Europe & Beyond (£10.99). A comprehensive guide to short and long-term work in the tourist industry.
Working in Ski Resorts-Europe and North America (£10.99). Includes details on how to get a job with a British based ski operator and how to get a job after arriving in a ski resort.
Work Your Way Around The World (£12.95). Contains invaluable information

on ways to find temporary work worldwide, both in advance and when abroad.

Teaching English Abroad (£10.99). Covers both short and long term opportunities for teaching English in Britain and abroad for both qualified and untrained teachers.

Working with the Environment (£9.99). A guide to the enormous range of possibilities for short and long term work with the environment, both in Britain and around the world.

The International Directory of Voluntary Work (£9.99). A comprehensive guide to worldwide residential and non-residential voluntary work.

ANY COMMENTS?

We have made every effort to make this book as useful and accurate as possible for you. We would appreciate any comments that you may have concerning the employers listed.

Name:

Address:

Name of employer:

Entry on page:

Comments:

Have you come across any other employers who might merit inclusion in the book? (A free copy of a Vacation Work title of your choice will be sent to anyone who sends in the name and address of an employer subsequently included in the Directory.)

Please send this sheet to:
David Woodworth, Vacation Work,
9 Park End Street, Oxford OX1 1HJ, U.K.